Jacob's Gift

Jacob's Gift

A Journey into the Heart of Belonging

JONATHAN FREEDLAND

HAMISH HAMILTON
an imprint of
PENGUIN BOOKS

HAMISH HAMILTON

Published by the Penguin Group
Penguin Books Ltd, 80 Strand, Lc
Penguin Group (USA) Inc., 375 H
Penguin Group (Canada), 10 Alcc
(a division of Pearson Penguin C
Penguin Ireland, 25 St Stephen's
(a division of Penguin Books Ltd
Penguin Group (Australia), 250 (
Camberwell, Victoria 3124, Aust
Penguin Books India Pvt Ltd, 11
Panchsheel Park, New Delhi – 1
Penguin Group (NZ), cnr Airbc
Auckland 1310, New Zealand (a
Penguin Books (South Africa) (1
Rosebank 2196, South Africa

Penguin Books Ltd, Registered

www.penguin.com

First published 2005
1

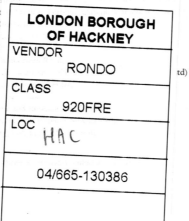

Copyright © Jonathan Freedla

The moral right of the author has been asserted

Set in 12/14.75 pt Monotype Dante
Typeset by Rowland Phototypesetting Ltd, Bury St Edmunds, Suffolk
Printed in Great Britain by Clays Ltd, St Ives plc

A CIP catalogue record for this book is available from the British Library

ISBN 0–241–14243–1

For Sarah, who gave Jacob and Sam the gift of life – and me the gift of love

'The family is the country of the heart'
    – Giuseppe Mazzini, 1858

Contents

Contents

Part Three: Reckonings

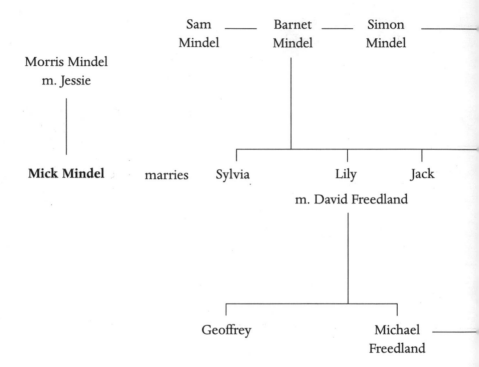

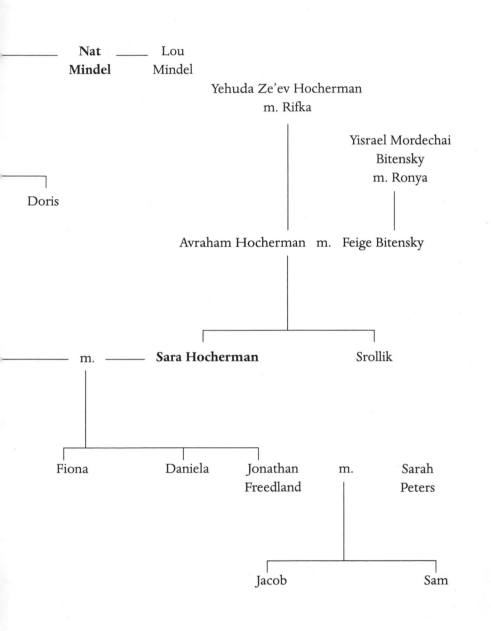

Nat **Mindel** — Lou Mindel

Yehuda Ze'ev Hocherman
m. Rifka

Yisrael Mordechai
Bitensky
m. Ronya

Doris

Avraham Hocherman   m.   Feige Bitensky

m. — **Sara Hocherman**   Srollik

Fiona   Daniela   Jonathan   m.   Sarah
                          Freedland   Peters

Jacob   Sam

Acknowledgements

My first debt is to Alan Rusbridger, the editor of the *Guardian*, who, during one warm spring evening in Jerusalem, not only encouraged but urged me to write this book, and then patiently allowed me the time and space to do it.

So began an extraordinary professional experience, involving many agreeable hours spent talking with my own relatives. For Nat's story, I am especially indebted to his grandson, Gali, an accomplished genealogist whose collection of documents, assiduously acquired over many years, became a great resource. Nat's surviving children, Yehuda and Aviva, and his son-in-law, Eli Zamir, were exemplary interviewees, generous with their time and memories. So was the late Julius Mindel, Nat's redoubtable nephew. I am also grateful to Sybil Gottlieb, whose father, Sam Epstein, was such a good friend of Nat's: the correspondence between them, stretching over nearly three decades, proved invaluable. The Israeli historian Tom Segev became my lead guide to the Mandate period, chiefly through his definitive book, *One Palestine Complete*, but also in the course of a couple of very helpful conversations. Norman Carp-Gordon painted a picture of life in Nat's home town of Dunilovich, while Haim Sharett and David Jacobs both shed light on the milieu he inhabited in Palestine – a world he shared with their fathers, Moshe and Julius. John Arnott provided some choice pictures of Nat and his colleagues in the Department of Migration, while staff at the following opened up essential papers: the archives of the Joint Distribution Committee and Central Zionist Archives in Jerusalem; the Haganah archive in Tel Aviv; and the Public Records Office in London. Mark Lobel laid some vital groundwork, ferreting through the records and interviewing some key witnesses.

For Mick's story, my search began with those who loved him:

wife, Sylvia, daughter, Ruth, and his surviving brother Jack. Sylvia deserves special mention as the woman who, in recent years, has served as matriarch to the Mindel family and who has always been a kind of fairy godmother to me. Few people are loved as widely and deeply as she is. For the tale of Mick and Sara Wesker, I am indebted to her nephew Arnold and niece Della, both of whom uncorked some sharp reminiscences of that great romance. Professor Chimen Abramsky was a font both of stories about Mick, a one-time comrade, and insights into the Jewish relationship with communism. The Sharma family testified to Mick's later work as a trade unionist. Further help came from the fact that, in retirement, Mick became a veritable human archive, regularly interviewed by a series of scholars. Tapes and transcripts of their conversations, especially those generously supplied by Henry Srebrnik and Andrew Whitehead, proved indispensable. I know that Mick came to regard Andrew as a friend and I am indebted to him. Jon Calver gave his own time to rescue hours of ancient tape from oblivion, allowing me to hear crackly recordings of Mick as a speechmaker. Dr Anne Kershen was another interviewer-turned-friend of Mick, as well as being the lead authority on the tailoring trade unions that dominated his life. Her book on the subject was a constant companion and she was kind enough to review the relevant chapters of this one, ensuring they fitted the historical record. Perhaps she learned that generosity from her mentor, Professor William J. Fishman, who allowed me to dip into his vast pool of knowledge of East End politics more than once. I am grateful too to Leon Silver, a true gentleman, whose walking tour of the Jewish East End brought that vanished world to life. Documents from Julia Bard and Juliet Duff were of great value, as was Silvia Grieser's research and translation of German newspapers held at the British Library's newspaper archive at Colindale. The Yiddish that appears comes courtesy of the incomparable Anna Tzelniker.

There are almost no documents to illuminate my mother's life. Luckily I was aided by her brother, Yisrolic, her aunt Rochel and her late and much-missed aunt Yiddi. Extensive conversations with all three helped fill countless gaps. But the chief source was my mother herself. She submitted herself to hours of interviews with me, often having to recall some very painful memories. I hope the debt of love I owe both to her and to my father is clear from the pages that follow.

Research into the book's wider themes has probably been under way all my life, but specific help came from Devorah Baum, David Hare, Ronnie Landau, Jeremy Leigh, Matthew Taylor and Rabbi Jonathan Wittenberg. Professor Steve Jones guided me on questions of genes and identity, while Clive Lawton was an inspiring source on the biblical Jacob. Laura Blumenfeld, Jonathan Kestenbaum, Seumas Milne, Matthew Reisz and Katharine Viner all read early drafts, offering welcome encouragement and wise advice. Robbie Gringras was a formidably perceptive reader, greatly improving what he saw – and putting in more hours than it was reasonable to demand.

Simon Prosser lived up to his reputation as one of London's shrewdest and most nurturing publishers, assisted by the patient and perceptive Juliette Mitchell. The text was copy-edited by Lesley Levene, showing a degree of care that I now realize is the hallmark of the team at Hamish Hamilton.

There are some people without whom this book could not have been written. Jonathan Cummings is not just an outstanding researcher, apparently able to reach any information in any language in any country. He is also a man who wrestles deeply with the themes set out here; he began as a researcher and became a trusted comrade.

Officially, Jonny Geller is my agent. In truth, he is one of my oldest and best friends. He believed in this book when it was no more than an itch nagging at me. From then on he proved to be a rock of encouragement, good humour and wise counsel. No writer can have a better ally.

My wife, Sarah, lived this book as much as I did. She was a constant source of both moral support and sage advice, reading the manuscript with perception but also with love. If this book is about family, I am glad every day that I am making mine with her.

Acknowledgements

Finally, I want to say a word to my beloved son Sam, born a few weeks after this book was completed. Be in no doubt, the stories told here belong to you as well; they are your inheritance. In every possible sense, this book is Sam's gift too.

Author's Note

This book tells the stories of three people. It imagines their lives, their conversations, even their thoughts. But it is not fiction. Every scene, line of dialogue or episode recounted here is rooted in fact, whether backed by public records, letters or interviews with those who were there. A full note detailing those sources appears at the end.

PART ONE

Beginnings

1 *Entering the Covenant*

Jacob was, if anything, too eager to see the world. In his rush to gaze upon all that life promised, he looked upward, his face aimed at the stars.

At least, that's how I like to think of it. The doctors called it 'presenting the brow': instead of tucking his chin on his chest, curling himself into the right shape for a smooth journey out, Jacob was trying to lead with his forehead. I picture him like an eager toddler, standing on tiptoes, trying to peek through a letter box when he was meant to be eyes-down, baring only his neck. He pushed and pushed like that for twenty-four hours, his brow bashing up against his intended escape hatch. Eventually the doctors ruled that our baby would have to leave by a more direct route.

So Jacob was born in an operating theatre, pulled from the tummy of his sleepy, elated mother like a rabbit from a conjuror's hat. In a gesture that seemed to belong to the oldest civilizations, our African doctor grabbed him under the arms and held him up high – as if introducing him to the gods.

I gasped at the sight. Jacob's skin was clay grey, as if he had just been moulded, straight from the potter's wheel. Grey all over, but for one splash of colour. His mouth was plump, daubed in the freshest, brightest red.

'We have a beautiful little boy!' I breathed, as much to convey the news to Sarah as to exhale the joy I was feeling: the joy of relief. Flat out, all she could see was the screen installed to block her view of the operation. She needed to know, because, though we had had our suspicions, we had never had medical confirmation of our baby's sex. We guessed, but we did not know. And the 'beautiful' was my way of telling Sarah that, at first glance, everything was OK. As my mother would say, 'ten fingers, ten toes'.

With Sarah still prone and sedated, the nurses handed Jacob to me. After nearly seventy-two hours in the hospital, with next to no sleep and several midnight medical scares along the way, I was a wreck, emotionally fit to burst. I held this beloved stranger, this unknown intimate, with the gentle nervousness of new fathers everywhere – all elbows and shoulders.

But somehow I held him and my eyes, welling with full, exhausted tears, gazed into a face I had never seen and yet recognized as my own. I looked into his eyes, and was sure – no matter what the experts say about a baby needing weeks before he can focus, let alone see – that Jacob was looking back at me. It was a look of bewilderment, a little fear and, above all, a request: look after me.

And then I heard a string of words I had not expected. They sounded strange in this antiseptic, stainless-steel place where everyone, including me, was clad only in surgeon-green scrubs. But here they were.

Baruch ata adonai, eloheinu melech ha'olam, she'hechiyanu v'kiymanu v'higianu, lazman hazeh. Blessed are you, Lord our God, King of the Universe, who has given us life, sustained us, and brought us to this time.

It was the prayer Jews utter in thanks for something new and wonderful, and the voice saying it was my own.

Just over a week later and Jacob was home. We had stumbled through those first few days in the fog of euphoria and sleeplessness that descends on all new parents. The procession of visitors, the deluge of cards, the sudden panics – Why's he that colour? Careful, his neck! – but until now we had held something back about our baby. No one but us knew his name.

We were following the tradition which demands that a baby boy be named at his circumcision, the traditional eight days after his birth. It was part superstition, part a sense of theatre: we enjoyed keeping the family in suspense. So our son's name had been our little secret.

I know there are many couples who go through great anxiety

about the prospect of circumcision. There is a substantial movement against it, insisting that to cut the foreskin off an infant is an act of mutilation, even child abuse, inflicting real pain and leaving psychological scars which endure for a lifetime. They say circumcision involves immediate health risks and that in later life it can reduce both sexual pleasure and sex drive. There is even a movement among adult 'survivors' of circumcision to undo the damage and have a foreskin grafted back on to their penis.

We were not one of these couples. We were not exactly looking forward to the moment, but nor did we consider avoiding it. This was a tradition which every Jewish male had obeyed for thousands of years. Even the Jewish man with the slackest link to his heritage was marked by it. It was inconceivable that Jacob would be different. We agreed: when he looked at his father, he should see himself. (I thought, less proudly, when I look at him, I do not want to see the shape of a stranger.)

So now – early in the morning, as tradition demands – Sarah and I, our parents and siblings, were crammed into our London living room while Alan, a doctor during office hours and a *mohel*, a circumciser, in his spare time, arranged the furniture for what would be part religious ceremony, part medical procedure.

He gave an introductory talk, promising that he would do all he could to reduce the baby's pain; that if our son cried, we should be relieved rather than distressed, because tears are a baby's way of releasing adrenalin; and that he had done this a thousand times before. He explained the origin of the ritual and said that, for today, and since everyone there was so close to Jonathan and Sarah, we would all play the traditional roles of *kvatter* and *kvatterin*, the godfather and godmother who watch over the baby until the key moment arrives.

So Jacob was carried in, like a priceless vase, and then passed from person to person, prompting an ooooh, an ahhhh or an overwhelmed gulp from each until he was finally placed in my arms. *Baruch haba b'shem adonai*, we said in chorus: Blessed be he who comes in the name of the Lord.

Now I was to speak. Cradling my little boy, I declared, first in Hebrew and then in English, 'I am ready to fulfil the commandment to circumcise my son, as the creator, blessed be He, has commanded us. For it is written in the Torah, "And God said to Abraham, You shall keep My covenant, you and your children after you throughout their generations. This is My covenant which you shall keep, between Me and you and your children after you; every male among you shall be circumcised."'

I handed Alan my baby, formally delegating to him the duty that was officially mine. He gently lowered Jacob on to a cushion placed on the knees of my father, who was to serve as *sandak*, the man honoured with holding the child on his lap during the circumcision. Sarah's father was at his side, appointed by us as a kind of co-*sandak*, and now the three of them did what had to be done. Men's business, with both fathers vying to seem less perturbed than the other by what they were about to witness. They were being men, determinedly unsqueamish, the way dads are when they kill a bug for a terrified child: it's nothing. But the bandages and the blades and Alan's stream of reassuring patter had the combined effect of making both men pale by the time it was over.

Jacob cried for only a few seconds, a bleat that quickly sank beneath the waves of exhausted sleep. Perhaps he was pacified by the ritual drop of wine he had tasted on my father's finger, a kind of post-op reward. Whatever calmed him, he was snugly wrapped up, a breathing parcel, in time for the next stage of the morning ceremony.

I was to speak again. 'Blessed are you, Lord our God, King of the Universe, who . . . commands us to enter our sons into the covenant of our father, Abraham.'

Following the printed sheets each one of us clutched, my sisters, my mother, my in-laws, my family responded together, 'Just as he has entered into the covenant, so may he also enter into the blessings of Torah, of marriage and of good deeds.'

First in Hebrew and then in English, Alan declared, 'Our God and God of our fathers, support this child and may his name be called in Israel Jacob Aaron David, son of Jonathan Saul. May his father and mother rejoice in him. With love and wisdom may they teach him the meaning of the covenant which he has entered today, so that he may practise righteousness, seeking truth and walking in the ways of peace. May this young child grow into manhood as a blessing to his family, the family of Israel and the family of mankind. Just as he has entered into the covenant, so may he also enter into the blessings of Torah, of marriage and of good deeds.'

Those who missed it first time, got it in translation and the name was repeated in whispers throughout the room. Jacob! *Jacob.* Alan called on me to explain our choice. I said that we chose Jacob simply because we liked the name: it suggested bravery and strength, I said, and our boy, in his first few days, had shown he had both. Aaron was for Sarah's grandfather, to whom she had been very close, and David – David was for my grandfather, whom I had loved very much.

And that was almost that. There was food – bagels, smoked salmon and cream cheese, just the way tradition likes it – but not many stayed for that. My young nieces produced pieces of paper to prove they had guessed the baby's name in advance; others dashed off to work. We drank a lot of tea and Jacob slept soundly through it all.

I, though, kept coming back to the events of that bright June morning. I did not regret what we had done; I was not about to log on to jewsagainstcircumcision.com. But I found myself contemplating the drama, the scale, even the oddness, of the ritual we had performed long after we had so automatically decided to do it.

It was not so much the circumcision itself: like I said, anything else would have seemed even stranger. It was not the deed done so much as the words spoken which returned to me.

'Blessed are you, Lord our God, King of the Universe, who . . . commands us to enter our sons into the covenant of our father, Abraham.' That's what I had said. Put aside the invocation of a supreme deity – a King of the Universe – and all the trouble proudly rational, secularly educated people like me have with such a notion.

I regarded those words as an incantation uttered less for its precise meaning and more as a combination of Hebrew sounds that have become part of tradition.

No, it was the latter part of the sentence that preyed on me. *Enter our sons into the covenant of our father, Abraham.* For the ceremony that had just taken place was a *brit milah*, where *brit* means covenant and *milah* means circumcision. It is the sign, the mark, of the covenant that binds the Jews and the Almighty. I had made Jacob – little eight-day-old Jacob – a signatory in blood to this compact. I had entered him into the House of Israel, even naming him after its founder, Jacob.

But what did that mean? What exactly had I done to this child who had stared at me with such trust minutes after he was born? *Look after me.* What burden was I placing on his young, new head? How many thousands of years of history, of divine obligation, of cosmic meaning was I lowering on to his weak, helpless shoulders?

Perhaps all new parents asked themselves this question: what exactly am I going to pass on to my child? We might give them our looks; perhaps a personality trait or two. We certainly give them a name. If we teach them a certain way, we might endow them with a set of values. Even if we do not plan it, our behaviour and actions will certainly affect them for life.

But this was about an influence greater even than the shaping of a personality. That morning with Jacob I had seen it: I was bequeathing him an identity. And all parents do it, consciously or unconsciously. The very moment a child is born, he is enrolled in several groups whether he likes it or not. His family is one; his place of birth dictates another. Born in Britain or France or America, a key part of his identity for life is already decided: he will be British or French or American.

I had heard other new fathers talk about this. After years spent in the arrogant assumption that they stood at the end of their chain of ancestors, the culmination of their family's history, they were suddenly jolted by a new realization. The moment a child arrived, they understood the chain did not end with them after all; they were simply another link, extending their son or daughter into the future. It would be up to these new parents to make sense of that legacy, to work out what inheritance they were passing on. One day they would have to explain, telling their child where they belonged – and what it meant to belong.

If this was a universal task, my own case had a particular edge. For I had formally inducted Jacob into the Jewish people, one of the two or three oldest civilizations in the world. It is a tiny nation – just 13 million scattered across the planet, a speck in a global population of 6 billion and counting.

What did it mean to make my son a part of a minnow people that had somehow produced some of the defining figures of human history, from Moses to Jesus, Marx to Einstein and Freud? Jewish teaching brands us a holy nation, a kingdom of priests whose mission is to serve as a light to the nations. We tell ourselves we are God's chosen people – but chosen for what exactly?

For Jacob was also being given a mark that had brought suffering and pain upon all who carried it. Jews had been singled out for hatred and oppression from the very beginning. Our central myth tells of the Children of Israel's bondage in Egypt: we were slaves. We were expelled from our homeland not once but twice, embarking on a 2,000-year exile that included horrors without end. Hounded as God's murderers, blamed for the death of the Lord's son, Jews were excluded, humiliated and slaughtered wherever they wandered. Jacob would one day be able to flick open his schoolboy atlas almost anywhere, jab a random finger and find a place where Jews had been massacred. Even the map of his own country was pockmarked with the sites of medieval Jewish torment: Lincoln, Norwich, York.

What kind of inheritance was this to give a child? To make him one of the despised, a victim-in-waiting for what one historian calls 'the longest hatred'? He would be forced to read some of the darkest chapters in the human story and see himself on the page. He would learn of the Spanish Inquisition, and not be able to feel the comforting distance of academic study: he would know it was people like him who were sent packing from a land they had made their home. He would learn of the Crusades, and know that then, too, Jews like him were an infidel target. Above all, and there was no escaping it, he would live a life in the shadow of the event which throws darkness over every Jewish heart. For him the Nazi Holocaust would not be just the subject of endless TV documentaries, a 'module' in school history classes, the textbook case study deployed by any teacher, politician or philosopher anxious to illustrate the extreme possibilities of human behaviour. For him this gravest event in history would be a personal affair: he would always know that the Nazi whirlwind would have engulfed him.

Nor was this burden solely a matter of the past. By entering Jacob into this covenant, by making him part of the House of Israel, I was enlisting him into a current conflict – one of the world's bitterest. Strictly speaking, the battle between Israel and its neighbours should have nothing to do with Jacob – born in London, like his parents; a British citizen, like his parents.

But that's not how it has worked out. Jews the world over have been sucked in. Perhaps they are moved and inspired by Israel, forming a connection with that country they cannot shake, visiting often, even moving there eventually. Or they feel the duty, from a distance, to defend the Jewish state from its critics, detecting in every attack on Israel an attack on a version of themselves. Or, on the contrary, they feel a sense of shame at what this faraway country is doing in their name. Either way, Jews cannot run from Israel; they are tied to its destiny, moored to its fate.

So when Osama Bin Laden sought to stir support among the world's 1.2 billion Muslims, he named the Jews as his enemy. Not Israelis or Zionists, but Jews. The less the Palestinian–Israeli dispute becomes a quarrel over real estate, the more it becomes a theological, existential war between Jew and Arab, the less people like Jacob will be able to stand outside it. It is expanding and enveloping us, and him.

Of course, these were not entirely new questions; I had grappled with some of them for much of my adult life. But now they had a focus, one that was immediate and anything but abstract. It was no longer just about me, but the fate of another person: my son. What a heavy burden I was giving him! And yet I had not hesitated. I had opted for a *brit milah* with barely a second thought, and during those excited nine months of pregnant anticipation, when we debated names, Sarah and I instinctively rejected any that sounded insufficiently Jewish. He was never going to be William or Harry, let alone Matthew or Luke. Too English. We had been drawn to names sturdy and robust in their enduring Jewishness; Bible names, names that had been ours for ever.

Obviously I did not believe I was passing on a curse to Jacob, like some defective gene. I must have felt I was giving him something worth preserving, something Jews had cherished despite all their travails down the centuries. Could I say what it was? Did I even know?

2 *Looking for the Promised Land*

I was born on a Friday night in February 1967. It was winter in an outer suburb of London and I was the third child to arrive in less than three and half years. My parents lived in a tiny, newlywed home and owned nothing else. She was a secretary from the dirt-poor streets of the Jewish East End of London who had given up work to raise her children. He was a journalist who, like her, had left school at sixteen, becoming a copy boy on the local paper – dictating stories to the hot-metal printers in the basement composing room – in his provincial, Bedfordshire home town of Luton before finally making it to Fleet Street at the start of the 1960s. He would go on to meet prime ministers and interview movie stars, but back then he took what felt like the gamble of his life, setting up as a freelance – selling stories on everything from the plight of the traditional corner shop to the fate of a marriage riven by the husband's decision to keep a pet lion in his back garden to anyone who would buy them. It is no lie to say that among my earliest memories is the voice of my father, whose study adjoined my bedroom, filing 'copy' to newspapers down the telephone. 'Freedland, Kenton,' he would begin: it was his call sign, locating him in that humdrum suburb even years after he had left. My idea of a lullaby was the sound of typewriter keys clacking away into the night, as my father worked and worked.

And Jewishness was never separate from that. In 1971 he launched a radio programme for the BBC's London station called *You Don't Have to be Jewish*. He hit on the slogan during a visit to New York – the city that made other diaspora Jews marvel at the warm bear hug it gave to all things Jewish – where Levy's rye bread was promoted in a poster campaign across town. Big smiling pictures of nuns and black kids and Italian construction workers, all munching

Levy's rye above that single sell-line: You don't have to be Jewish. For the programme, the *Radio Times* ran a secondary line of explanation: 'The world through Jewish eyes – but not necessarily for Jewish ears'.

I grew up with that show as a kind of soundtrack. I was no more than five or six when my favourite day out became a Thursday with Dad at the radio station. So many buttons to press, so many machines with big knobs and bright dials! I kept coming back, meeting the procession of rabbis, authors, musicians, community busybodies and would-be politicians who formed the roster of regular guests. I got to know them, and somehow, through the ether, absorbed their debates, their preoccupations. I might have been wearing a pair of giant, 1970s headphones, speaking into a microphone and flicking the 'echo' switch to make myself sound like a Dalek, or perhaps I was seeing what would happen if I put one of my toy Matchbox cars on a turntable spinning at 78rpm, but somehow the words got through. I was getting an education in Jews.

When Israel mounted its audacious raid on Entebbe in 1976, rescuing a group of Israeli hostages from a hijacked plane in the depths of East Africa, I was with my father as he hastily brought the news to London's Jews. I met the Yiddish-speaking old-timers, the Holocaust survivors with the bruise-blue tattoos marking their forearms, the loud, confident Americans – and the young Israeli artists and musicians who looked so different from all of them. I would bring them vending-machine coffee and tea, guide them to the toilets and, very occasionally, fire up the tape recorder when no one else was around to do it.

A good number of the books that came into the house were Jewish – whether a new tome on the fate of Yiddish socialism or a memoir by some now-forgotten Israeli politician. So was the air I breathed. My nursery school was housed in the local synagogue. I was a founder pupil and, as the only boy in my class, a natural for the role of Judah Maccabee in the Chanukah play. Kitted out with my cardboard shield and my foil-covered sword, I was to make a heroic debut speech: 'I am Judah Maccabee. I am brave as brave can be!' Except I never got as far as that second 'brave'. Toddler tears and stage fright overwhelmed me.

I did not go to a Jewish school but the atmosphere endured. I took off weekdays for the 'high holydays' of Rosh Hashanah and Yom Kippur, the Jewish New Year and the Day of Atonement, which follows it ten days later. But that was not all. I stayed away from school at other times too, dressing in my best suit and heading to the synagogue, while my classmates were fiddling with protractors or playing rugby, during the festivals of Sukkot and Shavuot. Teachers and curious pupils would sometimes ask me what it was all about. I would manage something about harvests and a test of our faith – with God requiring that Jews live in a semi-outdoor structure, the *sukkah*, for eight days – or I'd mutter about a celebration of the day in Sinai when the Jews received the tablets of stone that contained the Law. But I was winging it. Mainly I knew that we were Jewish and this was what Jews did. Or were meant to do.

For a while that feeling of difference lived on. I could not eat school dinners because they were not kosher, so I sat with the other 'packed-lunch' boys on what might as well have been called the Jew table. Once there was a family tree project. Each of us had to trace our ancestors back as far as we could. Boys with names like Lowe, Sutherland and Blyth returned with hefty, parchment-style scrolls – unfurling forebears whose lives were etched on church records stored since medieval times in villages in Suffolk or Corn-wall. One boy had gone all the way back to 1066; his scroll touched the floor. I held a single sheet of A4 paper bearing the names of my great-grandparents and the – estimated – date of 1880. That was as far back as I could go; for the oldest generation the place names, surnames and dates were all guesses.

By the time I was a teenager, things had changed. The school was in Hampstead, in north London, and perhaps 50 per cent of the kids there were Jewish. Before long, we were debating the same questions I had once heard come through the studio glass. Was Israel right or wrong to have invaded Lebanon in 1982? Was it anti-Semitic to condemn Menachem Begin or to brand his Defence Minister, Ariel Sharon, a war criminal? We were precocious kids, raised in the kind of London public school which encourages its charges to believe they are the heirs to the world, that there is no one cleverer or more talented. In the dining room – the refectory, we called it – straight after a double lesson in Latin or the history of Tudor England, we would engage in that most Jewish of sports, argument, our battle lines drawn in parallel with those slicing up the wider Jewish world. There were religious Jews, some of them pushing an aggressive brand of right-wing Zionism; secular ones, some of them devout lefties; and a probable majority of determined assimilationists, anxious to get on in life, with no ethnic tie holding them back.

And, just down the road, there was the girls' school. Plenty there were like us, bright, bespectacled Jewish young women, their talk full of ideas, their hair full of dark curls. But there were also the others, the Kates, Katherines and Sophies who were unmistakably *other*.

Their very ordinariness, the straightness of their hair, the button brevity of their noses, made them irresistibly exotic. They were so *English*. They sang choral music. They played viola. Their living rooms did not have big TV sets, like ours, but music stands. No thick carpets, but hard wooden floors. Their mothers did not boast shades of hair colour unknown in nature – reds, auburns and ash blondes that somehow defied the years – but wore their hair as the ageing process intended: straight and iron grey. Their houses did not ring out with the sound of parental shouting – in ours the basic mode of even good-natured communication, by no means reserved for confrontation – but of Radio 3.

After a school play I struck up a romance with one of these delicious others. To me even her last name was erotically foreign: Aitchison. I called her at home once, but her mother answered first. Seconds later, in a voice of cut-glass, debutante confidence, my teenage belle came on: 'My mother says you sound very Jewish and brisk.' I had said perhaps ten words, but apparently it had been enough. For some reason, our romance never took off.

I made that phone call upstairs in our house, in private. I did not want my parents to know anything about Miss Aitchison. I knew that in the business of love, and especially marriage, You Most Certainly Did Have to be Jewish.

And through it all, I had another life. From the age of twelve I had been a member of a youth movement, meeting every Sunday afternoon and for 'camp' in winter and summer. It sounded lame to anyone outside, but for those on the inside it was a place of pure, uncomplicated delight.

It was called Habonim, Hebrew for the Builders, and amounted to the youth wing, among the Jewish diaspora, of Israel's kibbutz movement. The kibbutzim funded it to persuade young Jews in Britain, America, France, South Africa, Latin America and Australia to leave their homes, abandon their bourgeois parents and move to Israel – as we always put it, 'not just to work in a bank in Tel Aviv' but to become pioneers, tilling the land of Israel in the collective settlements that claimed to be the closest realization yet of the communist ideal.

That was the big picture. What pulled kids like me in was the delicious combination of meeting girls, sitting around in torn jeans, strumming guitars and sounding off. For a mouthy teenager it was a natural habitat: in draughty old halls and over terrible food, we'd be debating the rights and wrongs of nuclear arms one minute, devising a sketch show to be performed an hour later the next. (Little wonder that several Habonim kids went on to make a splash in British improvisation and comedy: Ali G's alter ego, Sacha Baron-Cohen, stand-up David Baddiel and film director Mike Leigh among them.) And all through a thick, sweet cloud of adolescent hormones.

I loved it, returning for a week every winter and a fortnight each summer as well as Sunday after Sunday. There were no adults around, just the older teenagers and college students who served as 'leaders'. We had our own way of speaking – full of pidgin Hebrew – our own way of dressing – scruffy – and, truth be told, our own little world. The most committed stayed involved for years, running things by the end, until our university studies caught up with us: I was twenty-one when I finally said goodbye. But the friends I made there are the friends I have to this day. Sometimes, in my sleep, I find myself back there, singing the old songs, hoarse with talk of the future. I dream of it still.

They were such formative years and they left their mark: the loves, the obsessions, you forge in youth become your companions for life. And I suppose that's how it was for Israel and me.

I had always felt a connection with the country. How could I not? My mother was born there, back when it was British-ruled Palestine; I had family all over; we had visited on holiday perhaps three times before I had turned thirteen, the age of bar mitzvah. But I had not fallen in love. That would have to wait till I was sixteen, ready for what was then a rite of passage across the Jewish diaspora: after my O-levels, I went with Habonim for a six-week summer tour of Israel.

Looking back now, I can see what a shameless exercise in Zionist indoctrination it was. We stayed on a kibbutz, up before dawn to pick tomatoes. We saw the sights of Jerusalem, 'worked' with the poor in Ashkelon, danced all night in Tel Aviv. We hiked through the Negev and Judaean deserts, following sandalled guides, their skin weathered by the sun, watching in awe as they magicked an edible fruit from a rocky outcrop, or scratched a few dry twigs into fire, ready to make nettle tea from the leaves we had just brushed past. Jewish kids who knew nothing of the countryside back home were suddenly wading through wadis, ducking under waterfalls and sleeping under the stars.

Of course, all this was mere backdrop. The main action was each other: teenage fumbling in sleeping bags, the drunken discovery of the highly potent Middle Eastern brew arak, the intimacy of friends talking in the dark about love. And we told ourselves this was Israel.

By the time I got back to London I was infatuated. I felt I had seen my future home. I put up an Israeli flag, directly above my bed, as if to guard my sleep. I began to read anything I could about the country, gobbling up the novels of Amos Oz and A. B. Yehoshua.

I used a kibbutz-style satchel for school. I listened to the music of Yehudit Ravitz, Israel's Joni Mitchell, on my mono record player – playing one song over and over, a tune that seemed to fill the room with the scent of orange groves and the melancholy beauty of Israel.

All my life I had had a potential Hebrew teacher, ready and willing for duty, living under my roof. But I had never asked my mother to instruct me in her language, for reasons I understood then only dimly. Now, though, Habonim had Ruti, a 22-year-old emissary from the kibbutz movement, who had come to inspire us to make *aliyah*, to 'ascend' to Israel. Her hair was the sun-baked blonde the movies associate with California, her body full and shapely – a socialist realist's vision of a daughter of the soil. Her eyes were faraway, her manner the gentle unworldliness of a latecoming hippie. My crush was instant.

So when she sent out elementary, teach-yourself-Hebrew work-sheets, I completed them dutifully – an infant again, mastering the spelling for dog and cat, hot and cold. I did not mind. I was gearing myself up for the next stage in my Habonim career: a year in Israel, in the gap between school and university, which we activists referred to, in the language of the old Zionist pioneers, as a 'year of preparation'. Preparation for *aliyah*, for emigration.

Those twelve months worked the same magic as my aged-sixteen summer trip, only more intensely. Now the Zionist propaganda did not rely merely on sensory, and sensual, experience. For half the year, we were enrolled in a programme for diaspora youth leaders, funded by the Jewish Agency – then, and now, the quasi-governmental Zionist organization that straddles Israel and the Jewish world. Our teachers told us how long Jews had maintained an unbroken presence in Palestine; how the years in exile had been marred by constant persecution; how the Jews had nevertheless kept their eyes fixed on Jerusalem, facing towards the city in their synagogues lest they forget the site of their long-lost temple. Our field trips took us into the Israeli heartland, south towards the border with Egypt and north towards Lebanon, with regular stops at archaeological sites revealed as the buried location of an ancient synagogue or house of learning – places that would, once again, confirm just how long Jews had been here. We went to the West Bank, visiting what was then the new village of Ariel. In fairness to our teachers, they showed us the place with no enthusiasm, using it as the trigger for yet another set-piece political argument. Today Ariel is no village, but one of the biggest settlements in the Occupied Territories.

We learned of Zionism's founding fathers, the ragtag bunch of crazed Russian and Polish intellectuals who had mixed socialism with a rich dose of nineteenth-century romantic nationalism to come up with the movement for Jewish return to the Promised Land. We sat through lectures on the successive waves of immigration to Palestine, including those in the 1930s that came in defiance of the wicked British colonial rulers of the land. We heard of their motives: some inspired by the vision of a socialist Jewish Utopia, a workers' paradise where at last Jews would end their estrangement from the soil, others answering the divine call to settle Eretz Yisrael, the blessed land of Israel. We also learned of those who stayed away, including the communists intoxicated with the Jewish zeal for revolution, determined like so many Jews before them, and since, to change the world. And we visited Yad Vashem, Israel's state-sponsored Holocaust museum, to see with our own eyes the fate of all those unlucky enough to be left outside the homeland's saving embrace.

By the time I returned to England, to take up a place at Oxford, my hair was down to my shoulders and my head was bursting with it all. I was consumed with doctrines and ideals that had raged nearly a hundred years earlier; I had joined an argument a century too late. While my college contemporaries were lobbying for a university boycott of Times Newspapers – in protest at Rupert Murdoch's move to Wapping – my mind raced with the men and women who had left their families in Riga or Vilna for a new life in the Galilee.

It made for an uncomfortable fit. Admittedly it did not help that Wadham College had decided to pair me with a room-mate who announced, on our very first day, his great pride in his two grand-fathers: one a Spaniard who had served as a close aide to General Franco, the other an American who had risen to the rank of Imperial Wizard in the Virginia chapter of the Ku Klux Klan. His fascist pedigree was double-barrelled. In search of a friendlier face, I discovered the Bradford lad downstairs unpacking his books – including a pristine, hardback collection of the works of David Irving, the notorious Holocaust denier and anti-Semite. Somehow this did not feel like the right place for a would-be kibbutznik.

The trouble is, I had drunk the spirit of Habonim too neat. I had allowed its lessons to flow too directly into my bloodstream. I accepted the key Zionist contention that the diaspora could never be a secure home – that a Jew like me would always feel an outsider in a place like Britain. Oxford's thousand-year-old stones and Nor-man chapels seemed to confirm the thesis, so far away from the hot tempers and Levantine passions I had lived among the previous year. People in England were polite and reserved, elegantly batting back and forth matters that whetted their intellectual appetite; they did not debate ferocious questions of life and death like the ones that burned up Israel.

So I became an outsider of my own making. I still listened to that Yehudit Ravitz tune, 'Song with No Name', but now it sounded like a melody of consolation. Not that I withdrew from college life completely. I had been ambitious enough to apply to Oxford in the first place and, despite the hair, not all of that had faded in the scorching Israeli sun. The Jewish impulse to get on, the parental pressure to gain a better education than they had, still throbbed. Eventually, I cut my hair and threw myself into Oxford life.

And so the two worlds learned to exist side by side. Inside college, I could chat with the Camillas and Kims; outside, I still pined for those Galilee nights. During the week I was editing *Cherwell*, the university newspaper; Sundays, you would find me away from the student haunts or the union bar, in the Jewish community centre, leading a group of local kids in a Habonim singsong. I managed the juggle; trouble only came when the two worlds collided. When a group of sharply dressed, in-crowd Wadhamites saw me, Pied Piper-like, with a clutch of gawky thirteen-year-olds marching back from Oxford bus station, following some Habonim outing – that was not a good day.

Oxford led to a job on a newspaper, which led to another one at the BBC and eventually a four-year posting in Washington, DC. For most of those years, in the early 1990s, I kept the *aliyah* flame burning – still imagining I would, eventually, move to Israel, perhaps, who knows, as a foreign correspondent for a British paper. But time changes you and, one day, when you are not really looking, you realize that a childhood dream has vanished. Maybe I had exorcized the wanderlust with my American adventure. Perhaps I had come to appreciate my own family and no longer wanted to live a long flight away from them. Maybe I had come to see that my love affair had been with an experience – the freedom of youth, constant friendship and permanent sunshine – rather than a country. I used to joke that, if Habonim had pumped us full of visionary talk about – I don't know – Belize, and sent us to Belize for a year and called it a 'year of preparation' for emigration, maybe I would have slept under that country's flag and be listening even now to the Belizean equivalent of Joni Mitchell.

That fire began to burn out, but the Jewish one never did. Instead it raged in new directions. I faced the dilemma so many Jews grapple with in their twenties and thirties, wondering if I could ever take the ultimate step away from tradition – by marrying a woman who was not Jewish. Why was such a move prohibited, especially to those who, like me, did not believe Judaism's obligations and diktats were handed down from an all-watching Father in the sky? Was this not just a racist preference for one set of genes over another? What kind of tradition could regard two people finding each other as an offence to be banned, and why would I want to make such a costly sacrifice to preserve it? Did all this really boil down to a child's desire to stay loyal to the ways of his parents? Or did this matter to me too, in a way I could barely begin to explain?

3   Two Tribes

One of my most precious possessions is a palm-sized *siddur*, the basic Jewish prayer book, given to me by my grandparents when I was just a few months old. What fascinated me as a child was its hard, metal cover: I then believed it was made of the finest silver, though I now reckon stainless steel is more likely. There are whirl patterns in the metal which, three decades later, captivate Jacob too. There is only one symbol and one word on the cover of this book. The symbol is the Star of David and the word, contained inside it, is Israel, in Hebrew characters. My grandparents bought that for me on their first trip to the country, a matter of weeks before the Six Day War.

For all my life Israel, Judaism and Jewishness had been fused together. It was taken as read that an attack on one was an attack on the other; to defame Israel was to defame all Jews. Now a father rather than a grandson, I was wondering how sound this logic was. How much was Jewishness bound up with Israel? Did one ineluctably entail attachment to the other? And if so, why?

By the time Jacob was born, my relationship with Israel had become that of the diaspora Jew: simultaneously tied and torn. I could feel proud of its achievements, defensive of its people and shamed by its conduct – all at the same time. Among Jewish friends or family, I would slam the latest folly of the Israeli government. To outsiders, I would feel obliged to explain why Israel behaved the way it did. I turned both ways at once.

I would meet some Jews who were not so conflicted. 'People who attack Israel are not really objecting to this policy or that military action,' they would say. 'The truth is, they loathe the very idea of a Jewish country. They prefer Jews when we are victims, weak and powerless: that's when they love us. For dead Jews, they'll roll out the red carpet: Holocaust memorial days, poignant documentaries about the lost world of the *shtetl*, a warm radio feature on the near-extinct language of Yiddish. Those kinds of Jews the world likes! With their hands in the air, like the little Warsaw ghetto boy in the black-and-white photograph – the picture of defencelessness, always about to die. But the moment Jews refuse to play dead, the second they demand a place of their own, the moment they play the game like everyone else in the neighbourhood, fighting for what's ours, the moment, in short, the Jews choose life – well, then the *goyim* don't like it, do they? Suddenly it is Israel the Forever Wrong, the wickedest regime in the world – never mind all those crazy Arab states where Muslims have fewer rights than they do in Israel, never mind all those African tyrannies and kleptocracies. No! It's little Israel, smaller than Wales, smaller than New Jersey, Israel the great offender! Nearly 3 million people can die in four years in the Congo and it gets on the front page, when? Never! But Israel? Three thousand dead after three years, and it's page one every time a Palestinian gets a nosebleed. What's that about? It's about a world that just will not accept Jews as equal, that's what. It used to be the individual Jew who was the shunned outsider. Now it is Jews in our national home who are shunned. Israel, the untouchable, leper state. But it's the same idea: you cannot live among us. Today the world lives in nation states, therefore Jews cannot have one. Like that writer says, the one all the lefties like so much, what's his name? Kibbutznik, peacenik, you know the guy. Amos Oz! Even he says it: Israel is the only country in the world that is on probation, whose existence is conditional on good behaviour. Like he says, "If you behave in such-and-such a way, you have the right to exist. If not, you don't have the right to exist and the whole thing was one big mistake." Russia kills all those Chechens, flattening their cities from the air, and do you hear anyone say a word? Does anyone say, OK, this is proof that Russia has no right to exist? Of course they don't. So why do they say it about Israel? Because it is a Jewish state, and that makes it different. We Jews are always different. So different rules apply. Israel has no right to exist? I tell you why they say that. Because, for them, Jews have no right to exist.'

I would encounter versions of that wherever I travelled. In America that kind of talk was particularly popular, to say nothing of Israel itself. European Jews were not immune to its appeal either. But others had a different response to the news coming nightly from the Middle East. 'You know what, I can't even bear to read the papers now,' they would say. 'I scan the front page, dreading that there'll be a story on Israel. It's not so much those pictures of wailing Palestinian mothers, beating their chests or their heads because they have lost a baby daughter or a son, though they're hard enough. No, it's the response from the Israeli government that I just cannot stomach. Those spokesmen, always so cocksure, with their quasi-American accents saying, "Look, this is a tough neighbourhood." Or, "This was a precise, military operation," on the day that a car full of Palestinian schoolchildren has been blown up. Each time they tell us it was a "targeted assassination" of "a top Hamas leader" – but somehow a dozen people end up dead and we are not meant to notice. What, were they all Hamas leaders? Even the nine-year-olds? I am Jewish and I am proud to be Jewish – but I want nothing to do with this. Not any more; not in my name.'

In truth, these two camps did not always exist behind clear, separate lines. Instead they often pitched themselves within individual Jewish hearts, waging a mighty battle inside. There would be two voices inside the same head: the stout defender and the harsh critic. Some were angered by Israel's behaviour but would never say so in public, lest that give succour to the country's enemies. They could not join a public chorus that, they felt, if circumstances were different, would be loudly jeering not at Israel or Zionism but at Jews. At the turn of the twenty-first century, Jews were divided against each other but, above all, they were divided against themselves – heart against conscience, both wrestling for the soul.

The same battle raged within me. Like many reporters, I had

been moved by Palestinian testimonies of houses demolished, of sons beaten, of roads blocked, of livelihoods denied, of a society dispossessed. Like many Jews, I paled at the dread pictures from Tel Aviv or Jerusalem following a suicide bombing: the flashing emergency lights, the harried rescue workers, the screaming survivors, their faces syruped in blood, the ultra-orthodox volunteers in Day-Glo aprons, scouring the scene for human remains – a finger, a toe, a clump of scalp – obeying the Jewish teaching that the body is sacred and must be buried intact.

All this had an added, professional dimension. By now I worked as a columnist for the *Guardian*, which prided itself on its unflinching reporting of the Middle East conflict. That had not endeared the paper to many Jewish readers, in Britain or around the world. Some had come to regard the *Guardian* as implacably hostile to Israel and, therefore, to them. This same group saw me as a traitor simply for working there. When I was introduced as a guest speaker at one Jewish event, the audience hissed at the very mention of my employer.

To make things harder, I found myself in a curious, double role. Outside the *Guardian*, I would defend the paper I worked for and whose values I believed in. But inside the *Guardian* I sometimes felt compelled to adopt a different voice, relaying the concerns of those who felt our Middle East coverage had got things badly wrong. I began to feel odd. I was explaining Jews to the *Guardian* by day, and the *Guardian* to the Jews by night. Occasionally a representative of one 'side' would put his arm around me as if to say, 'I don't know how you can stand those people: they must drive you crazy!' I belonged to two worlds, both of which were often misunderstanding each other.

I wrote regularly about the Israel–Palestine conflict, especially as the second intifada ignited in 2000. I sought to be fair-minded, but when I believed Israeli policy was leading the country to disaster, I said so. My motive was that of the candid friend, offering anguished advice not to hurt but to help. The result, though, was the support of Israel's enemies and condemnation from my fellow

Jews. I was branded a court Jew, a ghetto Jew, a self-hating Jew. At least three rabbis denounced me from their pulpits.

Things came to a head in August 2002 when I interviewed Britain's Chief Rabbi, Dr Jonathan Sacks. He was about to publish a book, *The Dignity of Difference*, an essay on the necessity of diversity, in human life as much as in ecology. 'The key narrative is the Tower of Babel,' Sacks would explain. 'God splits up humanity into a multiplicity of cultures and a diversity of languages.' God's message to Abraham was, 'Be different, so as to teach humanity the dignity of difference.' Variety was not a problem to be solved but was built into God's plan for the world.

It was a beautiful idea and an inspiring book. The Chief Rabbi is an eloquent communicator and had a powerful message to preach. I asked him how his ideas applied to the Middle East, especially given the core injunction 'Treat well the stranger, for you were once a stranger in a strange land.'

'You cannot ignore a command that is repeated thirty-six times in the Mosaic books,' he replied. '"You were exiled in order to know what it feels like to be an exile." I regard that as one of the core projects of a state that is true to Judaic principle. And therefore I regard the current situation as nothing less than tragic, because it is forcing Israel into postures that are incompatible in the long run with our deepest ideals.'

I asked how he had reacted when he read reports of Israeli soldiers posing for a photograph with the corpse of a slain Palestinian.

'There are things that happen on a daily basis which make me feel very uncomfortable as a Jew,' he said.

Sacks's remarks became the 'splash' on the *Guardian*'s front page, triggering a response that was immediate and worldwide. Israeli radio led its morning bulletins with the story. The *Jerusalem Post* ran an editorial, 'Resign, Rabbi Sacks'. His remarks were 'morally inexplicable and astonishingly naïve', the paper said. 'Diaspora Jewish leaders are not required or expected to blindly support the Jewish state, or even to refrain from criticizing Israel. But they are required not to endorse the gross double standards and false morality applied by Israel's most bitter opponents' – which included, the *Post* implied, the *Guardian* newspaper.

A procession of Anglo-Jewish worthies besieged the Chief Rabbi's office, demanding that he explain himself. Israeli government ministers and American clerics weighed in. I was bombarded with emails. Those that did not denounce Sacks for his remarks denounced me for reporting them. One casually branded me a *Sonderkommando* – blithely using the term the Nazis coined for those Jews who staffed the gas chambers, helped herd Jews to their deaths or dragged them to the crematoria when the gassing was done. Another prayed for me and my family to be struck with a bereavement so hideous I hesitate to set it down here, lest I make it more real.

I seemed to have nowhere to stand. Ranged on one side were the Israelis and Jews who defended and perpetuated the 1967 occupation. I regarded them the way I might view friends careening at breakneck speed over a cliff: I was begging them to stop. When I did, they called me a betrayer. I counted myself among them, yet every time I raised my voice they seemed determined to push me away. And on the other, a world of haters only too ready to pounce on any Jewish misdemeanour to confirm their most lurid fantasies. Or, more frequently, well-meaning liberals whose sympathy for the Palestinians was earnest and sincere, but who somehow seemed to have no room in their hearts for my people, the Jews. They wanted Israel to be the diabolical villain, the Palestinians to be the saintly victim, and for Israel to do the right thing and exit the stage. Sometimes these people saw me as their ally when I wanted to be no such thing. I did not belong on either side.

Days after the Sacks story broke, Jews around the world gathered to see in the New Year. I was relieved for the break. As always, I had cleared the time of work and planned to spend the two successive mornings of Rosh Hashanah at synagogue – taking up my usual seat next to my father, now with the added pleasure of having Jacob on my lap.

British Jewry is a small community and I spotted a familiar face. He came close and beckoned me forward, bending to whisper in my ear, 'I'm amazed you dare show your face here.' I stiffened. It was only one person and only one comment, but I had just felt the breath of excommunication.

I realized I needed to learn anew what it was I believed and where I belonged.

4   The People of the Story

I suspected I was not the only one. Plenty of Jews needed to understand this thing called Jewishness, what obligations it carried, what blessings it conferred. For the Jews themselves were suffering an identity crisis. The clearest proof of it was the slippery inconstancy of the words they used to describe themselves. Jew, Zionist, Israeli, Hebrew – where did one begin and the other end? And what category did Jews most naturally occupy? Were they a religion, with synagogues, fast days and dietary laws? Or a nation, with a language, history and a right to a homeland? Were they a race, where membership was conferred through the blood tie of the mother, a simple yes-or-no matter of DNA? Or were they all of the above, all at the same time?

This was more than a lively topic for the seminar room. Each answer would carry different, real-world consequences. If Jews were merely a religion, they could hardly be entitled to the national right of self-determination: Episcopalians do not have their own state, so why should Jews? Moreover, if Jewishness were a narrow matter of faith, non-believers would be excluded and would be both free of its bonds and denied its blessings. On the other hand, if they were a nation, how could Jews simultaneously be members of other nations, British, French or American? The Jews needed resolution, for their own sake.

There was deep confusion. Friends who had moved away from the religion wondered what else should tie them to their heritage. Was it just guilt, duty to what the Jewish philosopher Emil Fackenheim had called 'the eleventh commandment': Thou shalt not hand Hitler a posthumous victory? Was this the reason to be Jewish, to spite those who had tried to erase Judaism from the face of the earth? Or, in a slight variation, was it our obligation to keep a tradition alive for the simple reason that it had somehow eluded extinction thus far? Was this the Jewish duty: to survive because we had survived?

Again, this was not an abstract business. Jews who had had next to no Jewish upbringing and now found themselves poised to marry a non-Jewish partner would be confronted by distraught parents and grandparents – including those who had themselves long grown distant from their roots – demanding to know: how could you break the line? How could you end the tradition that has defined our family for so long? These young Jews – and I live among them and could so easily have become one of them – were only waiting to hear a persuasive answer to a simple question. They wanted to know what was so special about their inheritance that it was worth a mighty sacrifice – the surrender of love. All they wanted was for someone to answer this: why be Jewish?

Any answer could not be confined to Jewishness alone; it would have to grapple with the very idea of identity. Perhaps a return to what the philosophers call first principles was in order. As they might put it, setting an undergraduate test, 'What does the identity of a person consist in?' The deepest thinkers had worried away at that since ancient times. We imagine we know what makes a person, but it is a harder question than it looks. What, for example, makes me the same person as that little boy in the Judah Maccabee costume? I cannot claim to be physically 'continuous' with him; every single cell that made up his flesh and blood has since died and been replaced by new ones in the 'me' that lives today. Identity must be a more psychological entity than that. Perhaps it resides in that inner voice, the one that tells you who you are, from the inside. Is that you?

Unfortunately, under the harsh light of philosophical inquiry, even this individual consciousness can be made to look unreliable. Philosopher Bernard Williams noted that it was at least theoretically possible to have somebody else's memories pumped into your brain. Would we still be 'us', or would we become 'them'? And what would represent the borderline, the moment when 'we' died and became that other person? Fellow scholar Derek Parfit concluded that there could be no sharp borderline, neither physical nor psychological, and that personal identity was simply not the cut-and-dried business we imagine it to be. Instead it inhabited a grey area. To ask whether x was really x was an 'empty' question, Parfit explained, because the answer could only ever be 'indeterminate'. The result was clear: philosophically speaking, personal identity does not matter.

But that is not how it works down here, in the real world. Emotionally, identity matters a lot: wars are fought over it, lives are shaped by it. After 11 September 2001 it seemed to matter more than ever. The question became insistent: in the great clash of civilizations, whose side are you on?

Maybe a different kind of science could help. If our essence as people could not be tracked down to a simple matter of flesh and blood, or of consciousness, perhaps it was located in the tiny parcels that seem to hold so many of humanity's secrets. Maybe our identity is in our genes.

After all, Sarah and I had certainly given Jacob a genetic inheritance – he might get her lips and my eyes, or my hair and her nose, or, with any luck, all his looks from her – but what of his wider clan? Was there a genetic legacy from the Jews too? Had Jacob received a Jewish gene and, if he had, what might be in it?

Biology certainly has something to say about belonging and our need for it. As social primates, we have this much in common with our ancestor the gorilla: we need company. (That is why solitary confinement is the worst punishment for any human being: keep someone alone long enough and he will go mad.) But that is hardly a matter of ethnic genes. Human beings are so needy, we will cling to almost any group, not just our ethnic 'kin'. Researchers cite the experiments that arbitrarily assign people colours. Within minutes blues are huddling together; soon they hate reds; before too long, the blues have hit out and the reds are plotting their revenge.

As for Jewish genes, plenty of people have come unstuck looking for those. Geneticist Steve Jones discovered that almost every race on the planet has, at some time or other, believed itself to be Jacob's lost heirs. Pathans, Afghans and Burmese still cling to the idea, along with the Japanese who claim to be the descendants of the tribe of Zebulon. Meanwhile, the Lemba people remain convinced they are the real lost tribe of Israel. Scattered across the border lands of Zimbabwe and South Africa, they do not eat pork, they give their children biblical names and they retain a mysterious dialect: Hiberu. And they circumcise their sons.

Jews might imagine they stand on firmer ground, able to trace a genetic past that makes them the direct descendants of Abraham, Isaac and Jacob, albeit 200 generations down the line. The genetic picture does lend that notion some weight. Today's European Jews, for example, show enough genetic similarity to suggest a shared ancestry. According to Jones, 'Genes link most of them together into a diffuse family.'

But it is blurry. The genetic record shows that Jews have always mixed with their neighbours, through intermarriage and mating, wherever they have lived. The Jewish gene pool has not remained clear, unchanged since the days of the patriarchs; plenty of 'foreign' DNA has poured in. The Y chromosomes of Jewish men from the Balkans differ markedly from those of other European Jews. Yemenite Jewry, meanwhile, is biologically distinct from every other Jewish community in the world. The genetic make-up of Ethiopian Jews puts them closer to other Africans than to any birthplace in the Middle East. To complicate matters further, Judaism has absorbed whole groups of genetic outsiders. Jews may be famously wary of converts now, but in an earlier age Judaism was a missionary faith, eager to win new recruits. Its greatest scalp was the eighth-century king of the Khazars, who became a Jew, taking his entire people along with him – prompting the theory that today's European Jews are all, in fact, the descendants of converts. The strongest proof is the modern state of Israel. That country is a veritable genetic fruit salad, a DNA mix. What Israeli genetic pattern there is looks uncannily close to that of the Palestinian Arabs.

In other words, even if Jacob's humanness would make him yearn to be part of something larger, his Jewish inheritance would not work so neatly. A person is a Jew if he or she has a Jewish mother, making Judaism, in Jones's words, 'the most genetic of all religions', but genes could not tell the whole story. That should be a relief for Jews, who ought to be wary of any attempt to explain human behaviour by blood; we know where such thinking leads. So Jacob did not carry a gene marked J that, once decoded, would explain Jewishness the way scientists now understand cystic fibrosis or blue eyes. I was going to have to look elsewhere if I wanted to understand Jacob's inheritance.

In the last few decades, a body of scholars started paying attention to the way children construct the world around them. They do it through story. Even the smallest experience is processed through a narrative: a beginning, middle and end, with one event causing another, then another, culminating in a resolution. But it was not just children. These same scholars soon realized this was a fundamental human trait. In the words of a leader in the field, Alastair MacIntyre, 'Man . . . is essentially a storytelling animal.'

Narrative is the way we organize the world around us, how we give meaning to our daily experience, including the behaviour of other people. Why is that man digging in a garden? We answer with a story or at least fragments of a story. Because he is tired of supermarket food and wants to grow his own. Because he killed his wife and is about to bury her body. Because he is keeping up with the Joneses and wants a garden as pretty as theirs. We need a sequence of cause and effect to give meaning to even the most basic human conduct. Indeed, it is a sign of madness when we can no longer explain our own actions. When others are similarly stumped, when they can tell no story about a person that makes sense, they say, 'His behaviour is inexplicable,' and it is a shorthand for insanity.

According to this view, man is *Homo narrans*. Indeed, not only is the weaving of narrative what distinguishes us from the animals, it also lies at the heart of personal identity. My body is not the same as it was; my opinions change. So how do I know who I am? Through the story I tell, knitting together all my experiences and binding them with meaning. I may tell different tales at different times, but I have an overall narrative that is coherent and communicable – and it is here that my identity resides. In the words of the Nigerian novelist Chinua Achebe, storytelling is 'the basis of our existence – who we are, what we think we are, what people say we are, what other people think we are'.

This narrative approach to identity – we are the sum of the stories we tell – does not apply to individuals alone. We slot our personal stories into wider stories, those of our families or, wider still, our tribes. These groups, in turn, consist not of the people who form them; that changes with the passing of the generations. They are defined instead simply by their collective stories. Their outer trappings, their location, their personnel may change, but their core narrative endures.

If I were to honour the vow I had made that day, agreeing to teach my son 'the meaning of the covenant which he has entered', I would have to start with a story. It seemed a Jewish way to proceed. After all, how does the Torah, the Bible, begin except with a story? It opens with Genesis, packed with one yarn after another, only later moving to the rulebook of Leviticus. Judaism understands in its marrow that stories precede laws: that without stories, there is no context for laws.

In the autumn of 2002 I had visited Jonathan Wittenberg, a leading London rabbi, in search of counsel, asking what Jewishness meant to him. His answer had stayed with me: 'This is your family, this is your story, this is your place to grow.' I remembered the *brit milah* ceremony: besides the *mohel*, the key participants had been Jacob's grandfathers, his grandmothers, aunts, uncles and cousins. The final prayer had asked that Jacob grow up to be a 'blessing to his family, the family of Israel and the family of mankind'. The same word, three times. When I picture the definitive Jewish moment of the week, I see the dinner on Friday night. As a child, that meant my sisters and parents around a table with *shabbes* candles at the centre, trading news and gossip from the week. Soon, I hoped, Jacob, Sarah and I would do the same thing. And where had I received my fundamental education in Jewishness but at home?

If events mean nothing without context, without story, then the context for Jacob's birth was us, his family. He would need to know about his parents and their parents and their parents: the layers of narrative that make up a family. If I were ever to understand what I was giving Jacob – whether it was a blessing or a curse – I would have to look deep into the immediate, intimate clan he had joined that day. He was part of the Jewish people because he was part of a Jewish family. The two could not be separated. For me to understand what I was passing on to my son, I needed to know what I had received from my own forebears. It would mean looking for the individuals whose lives shed the brightest light on the inheritance I had been given – and was about to give. I needed to know their story.

As a child, I never did manage that family tree. It was time to try. And, as the rabbi had said to me, so I would say to Jacob: this is your family, this is your story.

PART TWO

Wanderings

5   *Stranger in a Strange Land*

The backdrop is brown, and so are their suits, their ties, their eyes, their hair. The sepia of the photograph makes everything look that way – everything, that is, but their pallid Russian skin and the starch stiffness of their collars. Those are white even now, a century later.

There are five of them in this photograph, handed to me by a favourite aunt perhaps ten years ago. In our family these men are known simply as the Five Brothers, a phrase I like: it gives them the status of the Founding Fathers. That picture, mounted on a plain brown card, is my own Mount Rushmore.

There are several things I always point out. A party trick is to ask guests to look closely at the man seated on the far right. Look hard, I say. Look at his arm. There is the faintest glow, a radioactive halo, just above his elbow. It is the only sign that this brother, Sam, did not sit for the portrait in pre- 1914 London along with the others, but was pasted in afterwards. Not by some digital wizard, but by scissors and glue at the turn of the twentieth century. Sure enough, once you know, Sam does look different from his brothers. The lines of his suit are sharper, as if in higher resolution. And it might be just your imagination, but his eyes seem to be far away.

There was no other way to get Sam in the picture. The eldest brother and always the trailblazer, he had left London, taking the ship to New York, seeking his fortune. It sounds too good to be true, but there it is: Uncle Sam went to America. (Legend has it he was murdered there by his wife, who saw to it that he 'fell' down the stairs.)

Next to him is the man who was always the oldest person I knew. Uncle Lou, born Levi, lived till he was 103, still leaping on to London buses deep into his nineties. No one was ever completely sure how he earned a living, but he had once been a commercial

salesman, lugging a suitcase full of samples from shop to shop. One of his specialities was barbers' supplies: razor blades, shaving brushes – and condoms. In the 1980s, when he heard of the rise of Aids and the new pressure for safe sex, the nonagenarian Lou spotted an opportunity. His wife found him rummaging in a spare-room cupboard, turfing out long-forgotten hatboxes and old shoes. He was looking for those samples. If condoms were back in vogue, he was damned if he was going to miss out. It's not easy to know what the hairdressers' salons of London's West End made of an old man in a raincoat, thirty years past retirement age, sidling up to the tradesman's entrance, anxious to show off rubber supplies with a sell-by date from the Attlee era.

In this picture, though, Lou is just a boy. A teenager, his face is the one that comes closest to a smile – as if poised to break into giggles at the sobriety of the whole occasion. He is in a suit and waistcoat, but the memory of short trousers seems fresh. He is leaning against the chair at the centre.

The man sitting there seems to be playing patriarch. Old enough to be losing his hair, he has a clear, even distinguished face, set off by a thick moustache, its tips waxed into straight lines. He is wearing a wing collar, while a watch-chain arches across his waistcoat. He is my great-grandfather, father of my father's mother, and his name is Barnet, though he was born Berel. I have only an infant's memory of him; in fact, all I have is a remembered sensation: the scratchiness of his old-man stubble as I gave him a child's peck on the cheek. I know that he was a tailor and that he went from nothing, an immigrant who slept under the table in a sweatshop, to owning his own store. It had one of those mosaic floors by the entrance: B. Mindel & Co. I know; I have seen the photograph.

But my eye does not usually linger on my great-grandfather, or on the man seated next to him, Uncle Simon. Instead I look at the brother standing between them. (I notice that other people pick him out too.) Perhaps it is the old-fashioned armless spectacles, apparently attached, like a P. G. Wodehouse monocle, to a chain. Perhaps it is the elegance of his Brylcreemed centre parting, the neatness of his wing collar and tie. Perhaps it is that he is the tallest, that his jacket is the only one not to betray a crease or that, thanks to those glasses, he seems the cleverest. It might be the hint of arrogance, even hauteur, in his lips, slightly pursed, that makes him look every bit the Edwardian English gentleman. Whatever it is, I find myself staring at Uncle Nat.

His face is so young in the picture, the skin of his one visible hand so smooth, that it reveals next to nothing of what was to come. I think that's what I like about this photograph: these five brothers, who had crossed all of Europe to reach this moment, and still their lives had barely begun. So full of promise! It is a new century and they are poised to write a new chapter.

I never knew Nat – he was dead before I was born – but I knew some of his family; I stayed with them a few times, on teenage visits to Jerusalem. And I knew that Nat had served a British king and that he had been decorated for his trouble: he ended his life as an Officer of the Most Excellent Order of the British Empire, Nathan Isidore Mindel, OBE.

I never knew much more than that. I did not know that he lived his life racked by a terrible dilemma, by a choice he never quite made. I did not know that his heart was torn so wide and so long, it eventually broke. I did not know of his lifelong search to find the place where he belonged. I did not know that his own life had been dominated by the great upheavals of the twentieth century, including the end of an empire and the birth of a nation. I never knew him.

The date, the place of birth and even the name of Nathan Isidore Mindel stand on shaky ground. The record says he came into the world on 3 August 1891, but his family would later hear that the real date was a year earlier. Apparently Nat's father was behind the switch, anxious to make his son appear twelve months younger. It took the family a long while to discover why.

His birthplace is also only half clear. It was the tiny village of Dunilovich, near the place the Jews called Vilna. On the numerous identity forms that Nat would complete throughout his life, he placed Dunilovich variously in Lithuania, Poland, Russia and Byelorussia. It was that kind of place, constantly changing hands: you went to bed in Poland and woke up in Russia. For the Mindels, like many hundreds of thousands of Jews, lived in the disputed territories of Eastern Europe, the border lands the great powers had fought over, sliced up, labelled, relabelled and traded for centuries. He was not born in no man's land so much as every man's land.

It changed flags, but his home town did not move. It stayed stuck where it was, a tiny speck on a cold, grey map of what is now the Belarus interior. A village of fewer than 1,000, more than half of them Jewish, it would have come close to the *shtetl* of folk tales and buried memory: a *Fiddler on the Roof* hamlet of rabbis and paupers, matchmakers and merchants, where everyone knew everyone else's business.

As for his name, Nat was not yet Nat. He, along with his six brothers and sisters, was known then by his Hebrew name. His was Menachem Yitzhak. All the Jewish children in the *shtetl* had names

like that, one of the countless things that separated them from the
Lithuanians, Poles and Russians all around. The Jewish children
played among themselves. In the summer they would swim in the
River Sarzanska, which ran through the town. In the winter it
overflowed, flooding the street the Jews called Kaiser Strasse, where
all the Christians lived. Their parents were not farmers – none of
the Jews were – but this was the countryside and so Menachem's
was a rural boyhood. He grew up among animals, and the memories
stayed with him for life. He once saw the penis of a pig aroused to
full attention: he never forgot that. Or the boys might fish in nearby
Lake Blada, scarpering the second they were spotted by one of
Yashinsky's retainers. Yashinsky was the local lord of the manor,
owner of houses and fields, even the lake and the forest, for all the
kids knew. He was as rich as could be, but he was a gentleman and
he never raised a hand to the Jews under his wing.

In Dunilovich the Jews had their own lives. Vilna Road was the
high street, and every one of its shops and traders was Jewish. If
you wanted to find a Gentile store, you would have to take a side
street. This was a little Jewish republic, with its own theatre troupe,
its own choir, its own high schools – one for the religious, one for
the secular – even a Jewish Scout movement. You could read all
the Dunilovich news in Yiddish in *Hayint*, or join one of the Jewish
political parties organized in the *shtetl*. And there was ample choice.
A population of 500-odd Jews needed at least a few rival parties:
Zionists, anarchists, socialists, they were all there.

So the Jews had what they needed to see them through the cycle
of life. There was a *mikve*, or ritual bath: one for men, in which a
groom would immerse himself on the eve of his wedding and where
every man would bathe before the Sabbath and high holydays, and
one for women, for use following the end of the menstrual period.
There was a cemetery, right next to the Christian one. And there
were synagogues – plenty of them.

For the old joke – two Jews, three opinions – did not come from
nowhere. There were three synagogues in Dunilovich. The *klayna*,
or little, *shul* was where the majority of poor, pious Jews prayed.

The well-to-do – the ironmongers, the glaziers, the local village pharmacist – prayed at a second synagogue. But the oldest and largest was the *misnagdishe shul*, which even had its own rabbi. The congregants of that synagogue were Mitnagdim – literally Opponents – of the breakaway Hassidic movement, which in the early eighteenth century had challenged the stuffy, scholastic formalities of ultra-orthodoxy. In *shtetls* throughout Eastern Europe the pattern was repeated: the two camps immovably apart, their synagogues dug in at opposite ends of the village. Intermarriage between them was inconceivable.

Not that the Jews lived entirely apart. They had to deal with the outside world, which was no small feat. In later life, Nat/Menachem would joke that living in Dunilovich required the skills of an international diplomat: the Jews spoke Yiddish among themselves, but had to speak Russian with officials, Lithuanian to the peasants around and Polish to the landowners. The most regular contact with non-Jews, though, came on market days, three times a week. The Jews and their neighbours traded with each other, but things often degenerated. As one villager would remember nearly a hundred years later, 'The market provided an outlet for the *goyim* to overdo it. They all seemed to get drunk. By the day's end, they had lost whatever they had set out to sell.'

A handful of the Jews of Dunilovich had money, but most were dirt poor. A weekend treat was a *shabbes* stroll to the big mountain. If anyone ever needed to get out of town, which was rare, they would either ride in a wagon or walk the almost six-mile stretch to Varpaiva, the nearest train station.

So no one had it easy in Dunilovich, including Menachem's father, Iddle. He was a tailor, pious enough to keep his head covered and grow a beard that would, a century later, look positively rabbinic. But he had reason to doubt the Almighty's kindness. His great pride was his oldest son, Zalman Moshe, who had shown some early promise as a scholar. Zalman had been sent to Vilna, the historic centre of Jewish learning once hailed as the new Jerusalem, to study at one of the city's many *yeshivot*, or talmudic

Iddle Mindel, the tailor.

academies. But Zalman was a *yeshiva bocher*, a Talmud student, with passion. One day, arguing some point a tad too fiercely, he enraged a fellow student who, quite literally, threw the book at him – scoring a direct hit on his head. Maybe Zalman was a sickly lad of unsteady constitution, but that textual missile dealt a dreadful blow. Nat/Menachem would always remember how his father rushed to Vilna to take care of his injured son – only to return, in silence, to the family waiting back home. Iddle said nothing. He simply came in and kicked off his shoes, the first act of sitting *shiva*: the period of ritual mourning had begun. Zalman Moshe Mindel had become the first Jew since Bible times to be struck down by the word of God.

There are almost no memories of the family's other loss. They had one daughter, Leah, who died before Levi was born – he was named after her. But her death came attached to no story that might pass into family mythology: her siblings are now long gone, she left no children of her own; she died in a place and time – the *shtetl* of the late nineteenth century – where records were scarcely kept at all. And so, Leah Mindel is forgotten. And, because of that, her existence is becoming ever fainter, as if she never lived.

Perhaps it was the death of these children that made the Mindels dream of a new life; or maybe it was the widespread fear many Jews had of conscription into the tsar's army – legend has it that, once press-ganged, a Jew could be tied to his uniform for twenty-five years, separated from his family and his people for the best years of his life.

The story later generations of Mindels told themselves, however, was more specific. Iddle was one of Dunilovich's best tailors and had won the custom of the local nobleman (perhaps Yashinsky himself). This nobleman grew to like Mindel and so, in the autumn of 1902, when word spread that a pogrom was coming, he called for his trusted tailor. In a whisper he told him that he should take his family and get out. The Mindels wasted no time; they gathered up their few possessions and hurried to Varpaiva station. What little they had, they sold for the train fare and headed west. The money was tight, so only Iddle and wife, Gesha Reva, along with the older boys Berel and Shimsel had tickets; Menachem and Levi had to hide under the seats.

That's the story, anyway. Maybe it does sound uncannily similar to the turning point of *Fiddler on the Roof*, when the Russian police chief slows his horse to warn Tevye that the Cossacks are coming, prompting the philosophical milkman to round up his infuriating daughters and leave Anatevka once and for all. And it certainly does not explain why Shmuel or Sam, the eldest surviving son, had already left for England. But there is no one left to ask, so that remains the story.

It is plausible enough. The turn of the twentieth century brought a surge in anti-Jewish persecution. Take the Jews of Kishinev, for example, sandwiched between Romania and the Ukraine in what is the capital of today's Moldova. Less than six months after the Mindels made their journey, those Jews experienced a pogrom whose notoriety endures. On 6 April 1903, anti-Semitic hoodlums looted synagogues, desecrated the sacred Torah scrolls within and killed fifty Jews for standing in their way. Maybe that would never have happened in Dunilovich; maybe the Mindels were chiefly economic migrants. But the fear of persecution was real enough.

They arrived in November 1902, straight into the pea-soup murk of Edwardian London. For the youngest children, it was a huge adventure. They may have been in the shabby end of Hackney, but this was an enchanted landscape: the first city they had ever seen.

And soon it began to work its big-city magic, casting a spell on the Dunilovich family – the same spell cities have cast on immigrants throughout time. London began to pull the new arrivals, especially the younger ones, towards its bosom, whispering in their ear like a seductress: become like me.

They never consciously decided to surrender, but it happened almost immediately: they started changing to fit in. Menachem had only to turn up for his first day at the Christian Street Board School to get the message. The old religious costume of his father would have to go. He and his brothers would no longer cover their heads, not if they wanted to get by in English playgrounds or on English streets. As every five-year-old child knows, the basic law of juvenile anthropology is 'don't be different'. To stand out is to be cast out. Like Charles Darwin's tortoises and turtles, the Mindel boys would have to adapt to survive, and that meant mastering the new language.

Menachem had not spoken his first word until he was three years old, but he was always bright. Back in Dunilovich, if the kids were stumped at *cheder*, they would say to the Hebrew school teacher, 'Ask Menachem, he'll tell you.' Now a twelve-year-old Eastern European immigrant boy, smuggled into London by train and with Yiddish his only real tongue, he would have to summon all his brainpower if he was not to be marked for ever as a foreigner.

He was determined and, while his parents struggled with the strange sounds and unfamiliar alphabet, Menachem hurled himself into English, swimming in the letters, diving into the words, until, within a few months, he was speaking, thinking and dreaming in the language of his new land. The word he used for himself changed too. Menachem Yitzhak sounded alien; too many people struggled with the 'ch' that was best sounded by pretending to hoick phlegm from the back of the throat. His parents gave him an alternative they thought would be easier on the English mouth and ear: Nathan Isidore. And, as if to give away even fewer clues, that soon became Nat. His brothers did the same: Berel to Barnet, Shimsel to Simon, Levi to Louis.

Nat did well, passing enough tests to win a scholarship to the Grocers' Company's School, a kind of faux public school aimed at the improvement of bright working-class boys from the East End of London. Unfortunately, and to his parents' great dismay, he was technically too old to qualify. Luckily, and in one of the few cases where an immigrant background was to prove an advantage, there was no birth certificate. Which is how Nathan Mindel came to lose a year of his life. Born in 1890, he would thereafter declare the year of his birth to be 1891.

Three years earlier he had been living among Polish peasantry, his afternoons spent catching glimpses of porcine genitalia. Now he was learning the rules of football and cricket. And though he was newer in the country than most, he was not alone. Among the Hacketts, Powells and Walmsleys on the school register, there was also a Horwitz, Finerman and Rudmanski. The headmaster was kindly and tolerant towards his alien charges and word spread: the Grocers' became the school of choice for Jewish boys of ambition.

Nat was an eager pupil. He looked around at his immigrant contemporaries, almost all out of school by the time they were fourteen, if not younger. They would be earning pennies doing piecework in one of the hundreds of clothing sweatshops crammed into the East End. A boy of his age might have been a presser, wielding a heavy steam iron, or a machiner, seeing his fingers grow calluses from the repetition of thousands of stitches an hour. Nat did not fancy that, and not only because the work was backbreaking. He also understood that it offered no way out. Tailors and pressers all stayed in the East End, behind those unseen ghetto walls. An education would be his escape route.

He knew there were obstacles. Britain's Parliament had passed the Aliens Act of 1905, designed expressly to keep people like him out. Quotas limiting the number of Jews allowed at the best schools, universities and gentlemen's clubs, if not outright bans, were commonplace. But none of that was going to hold Nat back. Staying on at school past the age of sixteen was unusual, eighteen a rarity, but he was determined to pass those milestones and go further. In 1910 he won another scholarship, training to be a history teacher – with courses at University College, London. Less than a decade out of the *shtetl* and Nat Mindel was at London University.

He was ready to take what would surely be the final step in his moulding into a proper, educated English gentleman. He could hardly wait. Not yet twenty-one and still underage, he was eager to commit himself. He applied for naturalization as a British subject, citing as his motive his desire to become a member of the University College branch of the Officers' Training Corps. It was as if he could not contain his impatience to serve his new king and country.

The naturalization process would require Nat to prove he had made the immigrant's journey from strange outsider to regular Brit. The Metropolitan Police officer who investigated his application noted that Nat Mindel 'speaks, reads and writes the English language well', a happy contrast with Nat's 'father, with whom he resides, [who] would be unable to obtain a Certificate of Naturalization, owing to his insufficient knowledge of English'. The sergeant assigned to Nat's case, one Charles Frost, recorded too the applicant's promise to teach at an 'English school' (rather than a Jewish one). Finally Sergeant Frost recorded, 'Because [Nathan Mindel] has resided in the United Kingdom for five years, because his sympathies are English having been educated in England, he therefore seeks to become a citizen of the United Kingdom.' So, duly completed, the form was signed, sworn and sent off for formal approval by the Home Secretary of the day – the Rt. Hon. Winston Spencer Churchill. By 12 November 1912, exactly ten years after he climbed out from under the seats of that trans-European train, the boy from Dunilovich placed his hand on the Old Testament and said out loud, as it was written before him, 'I Nathan Isidore Mindel swear by Almighty God that I will be faithful and bear true allegiance to His Majesty King George the Fifth, His Heirs and Successors, according to law. So help me GOD.'

Invoking the Almighty did not feel overblown, just as Nat's form had him 'humbly praying for a Certificate of Naturalization'. Such holy language seemed about right. For what gift from the heavens was it to be a subject of the British Empire in the early years of the twentieth century! How rescued from oblivion a man of ambition like Nat must have felt. No longer confined to a Russian backwater, but given all the privileges of the greatest kingdom on earth, to be granted equal status with the imperial masters of the universe!

For his final year, Nat would have walked through University College with his head tilted towards the sky. He was an alien no longer. And Nat loved being a student. He socialized day and night, diverting so much time from his work that he graduated with only a third-class degree. He started taking out a girl, one more off limits than a Hassid to a Mitnaged, more forbidden than one orthodox faction to another, back in the old country. She was not a Jew at all. That is how far Nat had come.

Nat honoured his promise to Winston Churchill and became a teacher in an English school. But he did not like it. Maybe it was too small a place to contain his ambitions; maybe he was just not that good a teacher. Either way, he could not hide his irritation. The pupils saw how quickly his temper could flash: they called him Sparks.

Soon he was rescued by an opportunity to prove his devotion to his new homeland beyond all doubt. He would have volunteered as soon as war broke out in 1914, but he had damaged his foot during exercises with the Officers' Training Corps. It turned out to be a lucky injury. The rest of the boys in the corps joined up and were sent to the front; few came back. Nat missed those first months, finally enlisting on 16 August 1915.

Despite his officer's training, Nat's entry rank was that of a humble private. To make matters worse, he was assigned to a body rather short on martial glory: the 2nd London Sanitary Company, Royal Army Medical Corps. Their work was much as the name suggested and Nat was trained in the business of military hygiene, digging latrines and learning how to keep a camp free of flies.

His brother Barnet had an equally unglamorous perch in the military. His war would be fought with needle and thread rather than bayonet and gun, serving as a military tailor, also in the Royal Army Medical Corps, repairing and stitching the blue uniforms worn by sick and wounded soldiers.

Sometimes, it seems, fortune has a foul stench. Nat's posting with the London Sanitary Company had kept him from the killing fields of the eastern and western fronts, the trenches of the Somme and Verdun. In the autumn of 1915, he received orders to transfer to a rather different theatre of war. He was bound for Egypt.

Once there, Nat rapidly found himself part of a fighting force assembled for what promised to be one of the boldest strikes of British military history. The destination was the Turkish peninsula of Gallipoli. The Allied aim was to inflict a sufficiently humiliating defeat on the Turks that the Constantinople government would collapse, leaving Germany and Austria-Hungary exposed on their eastern flank. With the Black Sea opened up, Russia could be re-supplied and storm westward to take Berlin. All the Allied ships had to do was blast their way through the narrow stretch of water at Gallipoli.

Nat watched as troops from Britain, France, India, Australia and New Zealand assembled in Alexandria, along with comrades from assorted corners of the British Empire. Among them was the Zion Mule Corps. Formed in Egypt, it claimed to be the first Jewish unit to go into combat since the Roman capture of Jerusalem in AD 70.

The Allies' first move was to establish a naval base on the Greek island of Lemnos, at Mudros Harbour. Nat and the rest of the Medical Corps would stay there, seeing off the combat troops as they were ferried to battle at Gallipoli. Now, when the commanders originally dreamed up their plan, doubtless explaining it with salt and pepper pots at the officers' dining table, it probably sounded like a capital idea. But they had underestimated the Turks. Their grand strategy ended up as just another one of those First World War fantasies that stole so many young lives. From April 1915 to January 1916, half a million men were landed at Gallipoli; 300,000 of them ended up dead.

Along with the corpses, the injured were taken to Mudros, to be treated by the company that included Nat Mindel. He did not bind their wounds himself; instead he carted their shit, by the bucketload. The sight of so much suffering never left him. He would not say that he was traumatized – people did not speak like that back then. But his family always believed that Mudros scarred Nat deeply. It also left another mark. Now he had more than a piece of paper signed by the Home Office to bind him to Britain. He had mopped his countrymen's blood, shit and tears. He was one of them.

The Egyptian Expeditionary Force returned to Alexandria, Nat along with it. After Mudros, he was itching to do more than dig cesspits. He yearned for the life his college training had prepared him for: he wanted to be an officer. Once again, he set about filling in forms, pleading for the authorities to think well of him. In 1916 he was interviewed and on 5 February 1917 it was sealed: Nat Mindel was awarded a commission as a 2nd lieutenant in the Army Service Corps. It was not an elite unit, but he could scarcely imagine a greater honour.

Nat and his brother Barnet would later book themselves in at a photographer's studio to capture for posterity their arrival at the heart of British life. This time it was Barnet's turn to stand, in deference to his brother's superior rank. On Nat's shoulder are his lieutenant's pips, on his right sleeve three stripes for the three years since he joined up. They are both in pith helmets, the kind worn by jungle explorers in a Victorian picture book. They look as if they are about to shoot an elephant. Barnet's moustache is a plainer, more abrupt affair now: the wax tips have been lopped off, discarded

perhaps as a frivolity of peacetime. He is in shorts, with socks up
to his knees. Nat sits as relaxed as a viceroy, privileged to wear the
long trousers denied his brother. A shirt and tie are visible beneath
the khaki jacket, along with the Sam Browne across his chest. The
spectacles of the earlier sitting have gone, their place as guards of
the eyes taken now by the lush eyebrows that will accompany him
for the rest of his life. His face is as fine-boned as before; it has an
almost feminine beauty. And there is a smile of satisfaction. Behold,
he seems to say, here sits an officer and an English gentleman.

Nat Mindel was still the tailor's son from Dunilovich. For all the
nights spent mastering the English of Shakespeare and Jane Austen
or learning the history of Agincourt and Trafalgar, for all the sworn
oaths of loyalty to the crown, for all the stripes on his arm and pips
on his shoulder, he always had been. Even as a child, days that
began early with Latin lessons at the Grocers' had ended late with

after-school *cheder*. In becoming Nat, he had never been allowed to abandon Menachem.

Nor had this *cheder* been the conventional, synagogue-based Hebrew classes. Nat was a pupil at Redmans Road Talmud Torah, whose revolutionary method was Ivrit Be-Ivrit, the teaching of Hebrew *in* Hebrew. Scorning the traditional, line-by-line transla- tions of dusty biblical texts, Ivrit Be-Ivrit held to the more progress- ive view that the only words heard or spoken in the classroom should be Hebrew ones. That meant treating Hebrew as a modern, living language – which made Ivrit Be-Ivrit highly controversial, a movement as much as a method. For most Jews, Hebrew was a sacred tongue, reserved solely for worship; Yiddish was the lan- guage of every day. (Not until the late nineteenth century and the lexicographer Eliezer Ben-Yehuda, whose belief in the revival of the Jewish people through language bordered on fanaticism, did Hebrew have words for commonplace items like ice cream, hand- kerchief and bicycle.) To insist that Jews needed a single common language, rather than a clutch of dialects like the German hybrid Yiddish or the Spanish-based Ladino, was to argue that the Jews were a nation. That was heresy. That was Zionism.

At that time, mainstream religious Judaism believed a return to Eretz Yisrael, the land of Israel, was both inevitable and desirable – but it would be the work of God himself, in the age of the Messiah. For Jews to attempt to hasten that outcome, to speed up the holy clock by returning from exile at their own whim, was a terrible usurpation of divine authority. Ivrit Be-Ivrit, by attempting in its own small way to make history rather than wait for it, was complicit in this heresy. Which is why, in time-honoured Jewish fashion, it led to a split, with a non-Zionist faction breaking away from Redmans Road to form their own, traditional *cheder*.

Nat stayed with it, though, learning Hebrew as a language to be spoken by the living, in the here and now. It mattered to him the way mastering the Bible stories mattered. He may have left fastidi- ous religious observance behind in Dunilovich, but in his heart he had never stopped being a Jew.

That remained true even when he was striking out on his own in the world, as a student at University College. He could shatter every one of his parents' taboos by having a Gentile girlfriend. But when she invited him to take tea with her mother and father, he dropped her immediately: that would be to suggest something might come of this flirtation and, in his gut, he knew nothing ever could.

So it was perhaps only natural that he would, in 1917, soon after his elevation into the officer class, acquire a new ambition. He wanted to fight in the British Army not solely as an Englishman but also as a Jew. Perhaps it was the sight of the Zion Mule Corps on the road to Gallipoli that did it, but the notion of Jews fighting as Jews appealed to Nat. For all the fervour he had demonstrated in his naturalization papers just five years earlier – 'his sympathies are English' – he now sought to be recognized as something other than an ordinary Englishman. He applied for a transfer to the 38th (Jewish) Battalion of the Royal Fusiliers, one of three created and known collectively as the Jewish Legion.

The wider Zionist movement shared Nat's enthusiasm. It had campaigned for a Jewish Legion, hoping that such a body would prompt Britain's governing circles to see the Jews as a distinct, national group. Besides, if Jewish units were involved in the defeat of the Turks and the conquest of Palestine, then perhaps the Jews – in the form of the Zionist movement – might get a slice of the prize. Britain's diplomats and military brass thought the idea ridiculous and a logistical nightmare. But the Zionists had an unlikely champion in the Prime Minister, David Lloyd George. A devout Christian, he had a sentimental sympathy for the notion of a Jewish return to the Holy Land. (He once remarked that his Methodist upbringing had left him more familiar with Jewish history than with that of his own country: 'I could tell you all the kings of Israel. But I doubt whether I could have named half a dozen of the kings of England and not more of the kings of Wales.') And, like so many others before and after him, he wildly overestimated Jewish influence. He imagined Jews pulled the strings of governments from Moscow to Washington, controlling much of international finance to boot. In the closing years of the First World War, he feared the Jews were agitating for an end to hostilities. The prospect of a Jewish-aided capture of Palestine might persuade them the war was worth continuing.

'I want to do my bit,' Nat would tell friends. 'As a student of history I think it would be rather special to make some history, don't you? Jews taking up arms! I'd be a modern Maccabee.'

'They're not exactly short of officers,' his pals would reply. 'What do they need with a novice like you, holding down a soft job in the Army Service Corps?'

It was true. His new posting hardly made him a latter-day Jewish warrior and he was duly rejected. Not that he missed out on much glory: militarily, the Jewish Legion was insignificant. The British conquest of Palestine went ahead in the autumn of 1917 without it. General Allenby marched on Jerusalem before the Jewish Legion had even reached the country.

But the idea of a Jews' militia had stirred something in Nat all the same. It meant holding your head up high, which was what Ivrit Be-Ivrit had been about too. To him, both movements seemed to be saying the same thing: it was time to put aside the meekness of the Jewish past and strive for a prouder Jewish future. Jews did not have to accept history's assigned role for them as defenceless victims, just as they did not have to accept that their language had died and would never breathe again. They should look instead to the land where they had once lived like every other people, with an army, a vibrant language and all the other trappings of nationhood.

Such thinking was hardly mainstream. When Nat discussed it with friends, he would hear a dozen different objections. Not many were pious enough to present the religious view that it was a cheek for man to do God's work. More common was the Jewish brand of socialism known as Bundism, which had originally flowered in Russia and which took a similarly negative view of Zionism, though for different reasons. The Bundists believed that the Jews' place was in the great international struggle for workers' freedom. Come the revolution, Jews might well want cultural autonomy – the right to run their own communities, read their own newspapers, stage their own plays and speak their own, Yiddish, language – but full-blown nationalism was an affront to socialist internationalism.

Even Jews who deferred to neither the synagogue nor the Yiddish leftism of the Bund, the mass Jewish socialist movement, had little sympathy for Zionism. In its most extreme form, this view held that Jews had only made trouble for themselves by standing apart from the societies in which they had lived. Such separateness may have been defensible when it was imposed by law, but now that the ghetto walls were down why would Jews want to make new fences of their own, shutting themselves off from the rest of humanity? Gentiles had always punished Jews for their distinctiveness, their desire to huddle together, so surely the solution was to erase those distinctions and dissolve into the rest of society. No longer would Jews feel torn between their ancient kin and the country they lived in.

For these Jews, assimilation was not just a social trend but a Jewish ideal: Jews who shed their tribal, superstitious outer skins were evolving to a higher stage. They were emerging from the medieval shadows into the sunlight of modernity. The country where this kind of assimilationist thinking was most advanced was, of course, Germany.

Most of the time, however, assimilation was not an ideology or a theory but a tacit, even unconscious process. Immigrants found themselves modifying their clothes, trimming their beards and eventually changing their names out of what they imagined was convenience. It was a burden always to stand out, to have to say no to certain foods or to stay home on Friday nights. So gradually there would be some nibbling away at the edges of the dietary laws. A slight change in the accent would follow and, before they knew it, these one-time outsiders were on the path towards assimilation.

Such people were not interested in a movement that aimed first to stop that process and then to throw it into reverse, making strangers of Jews all over again. Nat would hear a version of this argument from his own brothers, eager to get on with their new lives in their new countries. 'If I was Sam, I'd want to be an American,' Simon or Barnet might say. 'But since I'm here, I'm happy to be an Englishman. What's that phrase: an Englishman of the Mosaic persuasion? That would suit me all right. After all I've done here and all I've worked for, I don't want people calling me some Hebrew foreigner. Or even thinking of me that way.'

Jewish families all around the world were having arguments like that, never more explicitly, more cogently or for higher stakes than around – of all places – the British Cabinet table. For several years, the Zionist movement and its leader, Chaim Weizmann, had petitioned London to back its quest for a Jewish homeland. That effort had intensified with the onset of war, as Zionists predicted the collapse of the Ottoman Empire and the arrival of a new master with Palestine in its gift. Weizmann had gained access to both Lloyd George and his Foreign Secretary, Arthur Balfour, and repeatedly took the Zionist case directly to them.

Weizmann's voice was not the only one to be heard in Downing Street. Lloyd George was also pushed and pulled by two Jewish colleagues, cousins, who became the Jacob and Esau of Zionism, between them putting the Jewish case for and the Jewish case against a state for their people.

In one corner was Herbert Samuel, the first Jew to serve in a British Cabinet who had not first been baptized a Christian. He had had no connection with the Zionist movement; nor did his job have any bearing on foreign or colonial matters – he was Postmaster-General. Nevertheless, in conversations with the Prime Minister, Samuel raised the idea of a British-sanctioned Jewish state in Palestine – and he did so as early as November 1914, long before London was in charge of the Holy Land. Within months, Samuel had circulated two memos, painstakingly setting out the case for Zionism as a British interest. Breaking from the formal aridities of most such Cabinet memoranda, he came on like a prophet of Zion. 'Let us not presume that there is no genius among the countrymen of Isaiah or no heroism among the descendants of the Maccabees,' the Postmaster-General wrote, quoting the historian Thomas Macaulay. The Jews had pined for the land of Israel since the beginning of time, but for centuries they had been denied their inheritance. A people without a land was like a soul without a body, wrote Samuel. Joined once again with the land of Israel, the Jewish soul would return to the world at last – and make it a better place.

But Lloyd George had an alternative paper waiting for him in his prime-ministerial red box. This too was written with the authority of a Jew. Samuel's cousin Edwin Montagu was also in the Cabinet, as Minister of Munitions; he was later to serve as India Secretary. He attacked Zionism's core idea: that the Jews were a nation. For him, Jewishness was more akin to a denominational affiliation, like being a Baptist or a Methodist. His being Jewish did not make him a member of a separate people. If it did, then how could he be an Englishman? How could a French Jew demand to be an equal citizen of France? This was more than an objection on grounds of logic. Montagu feared a Jewish state would complicate and trouble the lives of Jews outside it. A British declaration of support for a Jewish national home in Palestine would, for example, be a declaration that all Jews outside Palestine were foreigners. 'The country for which I have worked since I left the University – England – the country for which my family fought,' wrote Montagu, 'tells me that my national home, if I desire to go there . . . is Palestine.' He considered Zionism 'a mischievous political creed, untenable by any patriotic citizen of the United Kingdom. If a Jewish Englishman sets his eyes on the Mount of Olives and longs for the day when he will shake British soil from his shoes and go back to agricultural pursuits in Palestine, he has always seemed to me to have acknowledged aims inconsistent with British citizenship and to have admitted that he is unfit for a share in public life in Great Britain, or to be treated as an Englishman.' Anti-Semites would legitimately ask why a foreigner was allowed to serve in the British Cabinet. They would ask what right he had to stay in the country at all; they would demand instead that the Jews be expelled to their new national home. Montagu wanted to be an Englishman.

A Jewish Englishman, perhaps – but an Englishman, not a Hebrew. After all, as he put it, he had striven his whole life to 'escape from the ghetto'.

Every Jewish family or kitchen table had its Samuel and its Montagu, thrashing out this fundamental question of the age. Nat was a committed Samuelite, persuaded that the Jews' problem of perennial wandering, of permanent guest status in the lands of others, would only be solved by a national home of their own. He had accepted the idea at Ivrit Be-Ivrit and refined it in late-night arguments with student friends at college.

But Zionism had always been a theoretical matter for Nat, an ideological position. In 1917 that changed. Nathan Mindel fell in love.

The Egyptian Expeditionary Force's patch extended north to cover Palestine, a backwater province of the Ottoman Empire when Nat had arrived but now the latest possession of the British crown. He may not have been in Palestine's conquering army, but he could make forays into the country. He went back again and again. Nat was bewitched.

Never mind that 18,000 British lives had been lost in the taking of Palestine, along with 25,000 Turkish ones, or that nearly 1,700 Britons had been killed in the battle for Jerusalem. Never mind the dire state of Britain's newest colonial capital. At the end of 1917, more than a third of the city's people had emptied out, reducing the population to a rump of 50,000. Hunger and disease competed for control of the country: refugees were on the move, malaria and trachoma following them, while medicine was scarce. Some 3,000 Jewish children were homeless; Arab orphans slept on the streets; underage prostitution was rife. Yet Nat was not deterred. He confessed to Sam Epstein, a pal from their days at the Grocers' school who would remain a friend for life, 'The Orient has captured me.'

Back in Ivrit Be-Ivrit, he had been filled with ideas of Zion – the abstract belief in a Jewish homeland. He had been enough of a Jewish nationalist to want to serve in an all-Jewish legion of the

British Army. But this was different. Nat was smitten with the actual, physical place: the dazzling sunlight, the cypress trees, the scorched hills. Palestine was no longer an idea to debate but a country to live in. 'As for our dear Holy Land – I have now seen some of it and have enjoyed real Jewish surroundings,' he would write home from his new perch in the Camel Transport Corps. (Assembled in Egypt, the corps deployed – as the name suggests – the local Egyptian animal of choice as a military vehicle. When General Allenby made his first attack against the Turks, he was backed by a forty-mile column consisting of 30,000 camels marching two abreast.) 'People ask me how do I like it? It always strikes me as a rather crude question. One might almost as well ask how I like my mother.' This, Nat told his friends and family back home, was what he had been 'dreaming of for a life-time'.

They would try to point out the drawbacks. 'But, Nat, it's a desert, isn't it? Do you even have running water?'

'It's not the ideal holiday resort, I grant you,' he would say, attempting the dry wit of his commanding officers, 'and if you are looking for an ordinary civilized place, one that offers all the usual comforts of home, then you will be disappointed. But none of that is going to stop us. I tell you, one day this country will be the Belle of the Orient.'

Soon after Allenby had taken the city, Nat spent his first Pesach, Passover, in what he liked to call 'redeemed Jerusalem'. Like every Jew, in every land and in every era, he had sat around the *seder* table each spring, sharing a family meal and retelling the story of the Children of Israel's exodus from Egypt: 'Once we were slaves, now we are free men.' Each year, whether as a child in Dunilovich or a teenager in Hackney, he would have sung the same song, '*L'shanah haba'ah b'Yerushalayim*': 'Next year in Jerusalem'. But in 1918, Nat Mindel lived the *seder* story for real. He left his base in Egypt, travelled through the Promised Land and celebrated the season of Jewish freedom in Jerusalem.

He was intoxicated. 'In Jerusalem I always dream,' he wrote to Sam back home. 'The place throws a spell over me. While I am there I want to forget there is a world outside.' Nat knew what people back in London were saying: that this was a mere holiday romance, that his passion would soon fade and he would be back in London. But he knew different.

He loved everything about this new land: the light, the language, the women. There were heaps of girls in Palestine, he told his envious chums back in Hackney, some of them extremely pretty. The trouble was, electricity was in such short supply that the evenings tended to be short: even people his age were tucked up in bed by nine. And they all worked so hard! This pioneering business was not all rhetoric; the young 'Palestinians', as the local Jews were then known, were forbiddingly serious. Nat was frustrated. If only he had the chance to meet girls of the Yishuv – the term used to describe the Jewish community in Palestine – he reckoned the rare combination of his officer's rank and fluency in Hebrew would have them swooning. In the meantime, he wrote to the boys back home, he would have to be content 'to feast my eyes on their appearance and outward character'.

There was another problem too. Before the war, he had all but committed himself to a girl, Ethel Offstein, back in London. He felt obliged to stay faithful to her, but it was not easy. There was the temptation of the local women, but also his ever-growing feeling that it was in Palestine he belonged. He had been putting off the inevitable confrontation for months, but the War Office soon ended his procrastination. After the armistice of 1918 he was demobbed, a beneficiary of the rule which released students and teachers first. Nat Mindel's war was over.

Back in London, he could not have been unhappier. He found work selling umbrellas, doubtless falling under the influence of his kid brother Lou, but he was no salesman and he hated it. The coming winter confirmed that the sceptics had been wrong after all: Nat's love for the Orient was no holiday romance. If it were, it would have faded once he had come back to reality. But now it was London that seemed unreal.

He arranged to see Ethel. They hugged, kissed chastely and then sat together in the living room of her parents' house, side by side on a couch. He had gifts for her, woodcarvings bought from the Arab market in Jerusalem, souvenirs that he hoped would convey some of the magic of Palestine. He explained them and she listened attentively, even enthusiastically. But she was too polite; she did not seem to know what to do with her arms. It was all too awkward and Nat could stand it no longer.

'Ethel, I have to speak to you truthfully. This place, Palestine, makes me feel completely different. I feel alive there, the way I've never felt before.'

'I know. It's been a wonderful experience for you.'

'No, that's not what I mean. I don't see it as an "experience".' He was sounding like Sparks the schoolteacher. 'I am not ready to put this behind me. Ethel, you have to see it to know what I mean. You would love it. The heat, the aroma of orange blossom, the Old City of Jerusalem – the new city of Tel Aviv! Imagine that, a new city arising out of the desert! You can walk on the beach by the Mediterranean before you start work. Compare that to this dark, cold place.' He gestured out of the window, where it was indeed dark at four o'clock in the afternoon. 'What's more, Ethel, Tel Aviv is a Jewish city. Palestine will one day be a Jewish country. Don't you want to be part of that?'

But he could tell it was not going to work. She had not seen what he had seen; she had not been cooled by the night breezes of Jaffa; she had not touched the ancient stones of Jerusalem or felt the warm dust of Judaea. She was not in love the way he was. Why would she drop everything, come with him and start a new life?

'Anyway,' he said, moving to change the subject. He did not need to say any more. His ultimatum was now hanging in the air: love me, love my new country. And Ethel's silence had been eloquent. She needed time to think.

Nat, though, had made up his mind. Like so many returning soldiers, he found he could not settle back home; unlike most of them, however, he yearned to revisit the land where he had fought his war. He marched straight back to the War Office to re-enlist in the army. It was not that Nathan Mindel loved being a soldier; his career in uniform had been as much frustration as fulfilment. But the military offered him what he wanted most: a route back to Palestine.

The army was delighted to see an officer coming back for more. In the Britain of 1919 such men were in short supply; so many hundreds of thousands had been lost. They warned him there were no guarantees where he would be sent – Nat feared he might be dispatched to Russia, as Britain took sides in the post-revolution civil war – but he was prepared to take his chances. The prospect of Palestine was worth it.

His gamble paid off and he was ordered back to the Middle East, with Egypt his first stop. He had promised the Orient his heart and he had honoured his pledge. Now all he had to do was cross the border into Palestine itself. And so Nat took to leaving his post at the supply depot at Kantara in Egypt whenever he could, to go knocking on doors in Jerusalem.

The city was full of ambitious young men like him, eager to forge a career in the Jewish homeland-to-be. But Nat was different in one crucial respect. When these others arrived, they would rapidly sever their ties to the countries they had left behind. They would no longer be Polish, Russian or German; from now on they would be Palestinian. Lest there be any doubt, many Hebraicized their names: Gruens became Ben-Gurions, eventually Shertoks became Sharetts, Myersons became Meirs.

Not Nat Mindel. He was an unwavering Zionist, but he also wanted to remain an Englishman. He had never seen a contradiction when he was at the Grocers' school by day and Ivrit Be-Ivrit by night and he saw no contradiction now. On the contrary, he believed his desires to serve the British Empire and build a Jewish national home were perfectly compatible. He would hear British leaders spell out their vision for Palestine and it struck him as not so far from his own dreams.

While Nat was imagining a future Belle of the Orient, Herbert Samuel was planting similar images in the mind of Lloyd George.

If Britain would let them, the Jews would bring modernity to a squalid backwater, the Postmaster-General promised. The Jews would play their part in what was, after all, the mission of the British Empire: to spread civilization to the primitive corners of the earth. The Jews would turn the Holy Land from a desert into a garden; the result would add prestige to the crown and lustre to the empire.

Nat's fellow Zionists and his fellow Englishmen even shared the same prejudices. Palestine's new rulers often took a dim view of the native Arab population. 'The *fellah* was a shivering bundle of rags,' wrote Sir Ronald Storrs, the first British Governor of Jerusalem. 'Beggars swarmed, and the eye, the ear and the nose were violently assaulted at every corner.' His successor in the post, Edward Keith-Roach, also gazed down at the natives from on high. 'Arabs are pleasant people to live among and their long loose garments cover a multitude of sins. They inherit good manners and, although when aroused they go absolutely mad with passion and will commit murderous assaults with indifference, once the mood has passed, they will regret that Allah had taken away their senses.' Their children were like 'wild beasts', their customs 'mediaeval'.

Nat too regarded the Arabs as primitives. He wrote to Sam Epstein, 'Problems abound here. Not the least is the question of relations with Arabs and Armenians. We have to be very politic and tactful and show friendship to these races. But my God, it's a horrible prospect to be put on a level with them. One might as well form an alliance between Letchworth and Wapping or the Poplar Chinese quarter. The comparison is a poor one. You have to know Arabs and Armenians to realize the humility of the situation. And to compare them to us – we who are the stiff-necked race and proud – it's terrible. It's only one of the problems we have to face.'

Attitudes like that had occasionally landed Nat in trouble. Back in London he had got into a fierce row with an old university friend. 'How dare you suggest a Jewish national home in Palestine when there are people already there: to wit, a large number of Arabs who

65

are on the land and in the majority?' this chap had fumed. Nat realized this was, indeed, a powerful objection. But the solution was simple. Jews had to increase their numbers, so that they, not the Arabs, formed the majority.

Anything less, including the do-gooding dreams of the binationalist crowd, who imagined Jews and Arabs could govern the country together, fifty-fifty, was doomed to fail. How he had laughed, albeit blackly, at a letter in the *Jewish Chronicle* in which some self-described Jewish nationalists suggested the solution might lie in a change of name, from Palestine to Israel: 'A change of name to bring about peace between us and the Arabs! To weld together the primitive Arab with the hyper-civilized Jew!!' As if.

Nat had few doubts as to the justness of the Zionist cause. He was fully aware that another people lived in Palestine but, like most of his Zionist contemporaries, that gave him few moral qualms. For Nat Mindel, like so many men of his time, the problem was not that Zionism, in order to right the wrong of Jewish exile, would have to wrong another people. Rather it was that the Arabs were too inferior to combine with the Jews in forging a new nation. And these attitudes did not put him far out of step with his fellow Brits, those who regarded the Arabs as pleasant enough but stuck in the Middle Ages.

And so the British Empire and the Zionist dream seemed to Nat like the two rails on a single track, both heading in the same direction. Nat reckoned he could ride them both comfortably, and that they would take him where he wanted to go: forward, forward, forward.

He first sought a position with the new power in the land, the Occupied Enemy Territory Administration (OETA). But he hit a roadblock: very few Jews were getting hired. Much of the Yishuv had assumed the Balfour Declaration of 1917 – the document which stated that Britain viewed 'with favour the establishment in Palestine of a national home for the Jewish people'– would trigger the instant creation of a Jewish quasi-government. They were badly disappointed when the British military governors, far from handing over the keys to a new Zionist administration, seemed anxious to shut Jews out altogether. 'Palestinians' were deemed unfit for government service. The 25,000 or so 'pre-Zionist' Jews, those who had lived in Palestine for centuries, long before the first waves of immigration started in 1882, spoke Arabic but the newer arrivals did not. Not many spoke English either and plenty were citizens of foreign powers, the enemy states of Germany and Austria among them. The British occupying army concluded they would be better off running Palestine without them.

Nat could have comforted himself that this slight was nothing personal; among the British military, this policy extended to the highest level. When the generals in Jerusalem heard that Herbert Samuel, a Jew, was Lloyd George's choice to head the civil administration for Palestine, they made the cable lines to London crackle with indignation. General Louis Bols drafted a memo: 'By British government, the people of the country understand a non-Jewish government, because they know that a British Jew is a Jew first and a Britisher afterwards . . . I fear that British Christian officers will not be found to take service under a Jewish governor.' The Director of Military Intelligence, General Thwaites, concurred: 'Class of man required is good Christian Colonial Governor . . .'

If a Cabinet minister like Samuel was encountering such resistance, it was hardly a surprise if Nat was struggling. He would make light of it to friends: something would come along, he shrugged. And to those who thought he might lose heart and come back to London, he was firm enough to put his resolve in writing: 'I have already said, the definite thing about me is that the Orient has captured me and here I remain.'

As for his other love, Ethel Offstein finally gave her answer: yes to Nat but no to Palestine. She knew the consequences of that decision; months earlier Nat had told her that a 'condition of our union will have to be the settling down here in the East'. He kept his word and broke off their engagement, announcing the decision in a telegram. It was a scandal that would hover over his name for years to come. The Offsteins found it hard to forgive both Nat

Mindel's breach of promise and his means of delivering it. As for Ethel, she did not heal easily. There were those who believed she still pined for Nat, even after she married someone else.

It was a low point for Nat. Alone and with dim job prospects, he wondered if he was making a terrible mistake. He wanted the advice of those who had succeeded in serving both Britain and Zionism with distinction. He called on Max Nurock, an Irish-born Zionist official dispatched to Palestine by Weizmann who would go on to become private secretary to High Commissioner Samuel, and on one of Weizmann's top lieutenants, David Eder, a socialist adventurer who had dined with cannibals in the Andes, fought riot police in London and studied psychoanalysis with Sigmund Freud in Vienna. (Later Freud wrote that he had recognized something of himself in Eder: 'We were both Jews and knew of each other that we both carried in us that miraculous thing in common which – inaccessible to any analysis so far – makes the Jew.') He got no promises but he was encouraged. He saw those men, each carrying some status in Jerusalem, and thought, it can be done.

Finally, in 1920, Nat's persistence paid off. He had risen to become the British officer in charge of supplies in Jerusalem when, according to family legend, the breakthrough came. It was on a train: Nat suddenly found himself sharing a compartment with Chaim Weizmann himself. The story is that Nat was already an acquaintance of Chaim's brother, Moshe, and that gave him the excuse to start a conversation. Apparently, Nat asked Weizmann to explain the great scientific idea of the age: Einstein's theory of relativity. By the end of their chat, the leader of world Zionism had promised to use his influence to secure a position for this young British officer with a Jewish heart.

Evidence of such an encounter is elusive and it does shade rather closely towards an oft-told anecdote about Weizmann and Einstein himself. (The two are said to have shared a long boat journey, during which the professor patiently explained his theory; at the end of the voyage Weizmann quipped that Einstein at least understood it very well.) So perhaps this is an example of the apocrypha of family. Nevertheless, Nat would certainly have appealed to the Zionist movement: they were stretching every sinew to place their people in the government of Palestine. As Britain was handed the mandate to run the country, agreed by the League of Nations at Versailles in 1919, the Zionists calculated that they needed officials within the British administration who shared the Balfour Declaration's support for the creation of a Jewish national home. Weizmann would use his influence to ensure that Nat became one of those. At last he would be able to aid the Jews, while doing his duty as a British subject. He would have a chance to serve his nation – both of them.

His personal life was brightening too. All contact with Ethel had broken off and he was the 'free man' he had yearned to be. Now he could do more than feast his eyes on the 'heaps of girls' in Palestine. And, as he had predicted, opportunities for a man like him – someone with both status in the country's new order and the ability to speak to local women in their own tongue – were plentiful. Before long, he would tip his hat at one of the new Jewish maidens of Palestine.

Miriam Weinberg was the closest the old Yishuv got to aristocracy. She was born in Jerusalem and could trace her family's presence in the city back eight generations – a rarity in a community of immigrants where twelve months' residence qualified you as a veteran. Both her parents were the fruit of rabbinic dynasties, scholars stretching back generations. Nat may have seen his Jewish heritage as a national, cultural business but he was enough of a snob to recognize pedigree when he saw it. And Miriam had more than Jewish lineage; she had Zionist credentials too.

The Weinberg family had wandered the globe – her mother ended up buried in Beirut. Miriam spent her childhood travelling across Europe, as her father sought a doctor who might cure her brother's rare eye disease. They settled in Edinburgh until she was sixteen, when the father turned his attention away from his son's ailments and towards his daughter's marriage prospects. He was

keen to do things the old way, picking a husband for her. She wanted none of it, writing to an aunt in America to plot her escape. She arrived in St Louis, then went to Brooklyn, New York, to take up a place her aunt had secured for her at nursing college. There, and now called Marjorie, she heard the call of Henrietta Szold, one of Zionism's most celebrated heroines. An activist and scholar, Szold was especially keen to boost the health of the people of Palestine. She set about recruiting nurses for Eretz Yisrael, moving there herself in 1920. Miriam turned up for an interview, only to be told her journey had been wasted: they were taking only Jewish nurses. Apparently she did not look Jewish, a fact that has been recorded and passed down the generations – whether as a source of humour or pride is not clear. Anyway, Miriam got through and was among the twenty nurses who formed Szold's very first batch. (Szold's Hadassah women's movement went on to become the biggest Jewish organization in the world; the Hadassah Hospital in Jerusalem, of which Miriam Weinberg could have considered herself a co-founder, became the finest medical centre in Israel and perhaps the entire Middle East.)

When Nat met her, in the new Jewish city of Tel Aviv – a place with no past, filled with new, white buildings and obsessed with the dazzling, modern future – he did not take long to decide. He had a rival, an Italian lieutenant seconded to the British forces who would march up and down past the nurses' hostel, trying to make Marjorie take notice. But Nat brushed the Italian aside. He had made up his mind. Unlike Ethel, here was a woman who shared his passion for Palestine: they could plan their future together. They had not been courting for long when they went for a stroll on Tel Aviv beach, gazing into the Mediterranean blue. He took his officer's cap off his head and placed it on hers. 'You know, everything that is under my cap belongs to me,' he said, by way of a proposal. They were married in March of 1921 and rewarded with a child nine months later. They would call their honeymoon baby Yehuda Baruch, names rooted in the Hebrew words for 'Jew' and 'blessing'. The child's British birth certificate, however, records him as Julius Benedict. Later Nat would explain to his son that he was doing him a favour: Nathan Isidore had been a handicap, it was so Jewish. Not that he had ever considered changing his name, but the birth of a child was the chance for a fresh start. His son would be freer.

Nat was making his dreams real. By the time he turned thirty, he could look on his life with satisfaction. He was building the Jewish homeland by creating a new Jewish family and believed his work would allow him to achieve the same goal – all the while rising through the ranks of the British civil service.

His first job in the Palestine administration was in the department he would serve for more than a quarter of a century. The Zionist movement's prime objective, as Nat had stressed in those arguments back in London, was the creation of a Jewish majority in Palestine. That could only happen through mass Jewish immigration and Nat was now stationed at the one post where he could realize that ambition. In 1921 he took up a position in the Department of Immigration.

Everything was fitting into place, from the bottom to the top. To Nat's delight, his overall boss, Palestine's first High Commissioner, was, as promised, Herbert Samuel. The military and Whitehall had objected to the appointment of a Jew with Zionist sympathies, but Samuel had prevailed. He disembarked from a British battleship at Haifa on 1 July 1920. His arrival was hailed by the Yishuv, then numbering fewer than 80,000, as an event of almost biblical moment, the first Jewish ruler in Palestine since Horcanus II, whose reign ended forty years before Christ. When, a few weeks later, Samuel set out on foot – respecting the Sabbath by refusing to use his car – for the famous Churva synagogue in the Old City of Jerusalem, the response was ecstatic. As he entered through the Jaffa Gate and headed towards the Jewish Quarter, crowds filled flower-decked streets. Spectators broke out into spontaneous applause and cheers.

Inside, the synagogue was packed and the mood expectant. Before long, the visitor was summoned to the Torah in traditional fashion but with a new formulation – '*Ya'amod! Ya'amod! HaNatziv Ha'Elyon* . . .': 'Arise! Arise! Let the High Commissioner be upstanding.' As Samuel arose, so, in his honour, did the entire congregation. He made his way to the *bimah*, the platform from which the Torah is read, and began reciting, in Hebrew, the blessing for one who is about to read from the holy texts. He was to deliver the Haftorah, the passage from the Prophets that serves as a kind of supplement to the main Torah portion of the week. There he stood, the British High Commissioner in a great synagogue, chanting in Hebrew. And his was no ordinary text. That week's Haftorah was from the Book of Isaiah, the same words which open Handel's *Messiah*:

Comfort ye, comfort ye My people, says your Lord. Speak to the heart of Jerusalem and say to her that her time [of exile] is over; that her sin has been forgiven . . .

A shudder went through the congregation. Samuel already embodied their dreams, but now he was voicing them too:

Every valley shall be exalted, and every mountain and hill shall be made
low: and the crooked shall be made straight, and the rough places plain
. . . O Jerusalem, that bringest good tidings, lift up thy voice with strength;
lift it up, be not afraid; say unto the cities of Judah, Behold your God!

Everyone in the room felt it, a charge of emotion. An aide to
Samuel was moved to describe a 'golden moment' in which the
Jews in the synagogue felt 'as if the hour of redemption had arrived'.

Nat could not help but be swept up in the euphoria. Buttressing
Samuel's own instincts was a League of Nations mandate that
incorporated Balfour's promise, turning what might have been a
British whim into an international obligation. As a matter of policy,
Palestine's masters were to oversee the creation of a Jewish national
home – including the admission of the Jewish immigrants who
might build it. Samuel himself had spoken of facilitating Zionism's
goals on immigration, not by opening the gates to the Jewish masses
in one tidal wave but through 'cautious colonisation' of Palestine
by Jews. Nat's task in the Department of Immigration would simply
be to help that along.

All was in perfect harmony, the British administration and the
Zionist movement working together as allies. A quota of Jewish
immigration, known as the Schedule, was agreed between them,
with the task of selection and allocation of visas effectively contracted out by the British government to Zionist officialdom. Would-be
immigrants to Palestine applied not to the British consulate but to
their local Zionist office for an entry permit; if the Zionists said yes,
the British merely had to wield the rubber stamp. The Zionists did
not resent the limit set on numbers; they agreed that Palestine
should only take in the Jews it could absorb. If too many came, and
economic ruin and destitution followed, the rest of the world's
Jews would stay away. Britain and the Zionists saw this issue the
same way.

In 1921 Nat had barely settled into his bureaucrat's chair as the lead
immigration officer in Jaffa, the main port of entry for new arrivals,
when trouble struck. A May Day street fight among Palestine's young

Jewish pioneers, intoxicated with the conviction that they were building a socialist Utopia in the Levant, got out of control. Originally a clash between Jewish socialists and communists, who had been handing out leaflets, in Arabic and Hebrew, calling for a rebellion against the British and the creation of a Soviet Union of Palestine, it soon turned into a battle between Arabs and Jews.

Jewish witnesses spoke of a terrifying rampage, starting in Jaffa and spreading beyond, with Arab men beating Jews in the streets, bursting into buildings to murder the Jews cowering inside. Armed with clubs, knives and swords, they killed Jews wherever they could find them – slaughtering children, raping women. Survivors, many of them refugees from places like the one Nat had left as a boy, feared the pogroms they were meant to have left behind were chasing them into their new home.

Except this time the Zionist leadership would not sit and take it. Close to its ideological core was the belief that Jews would no longer play victim but be a nation strong enough to defend itself. (The Yishuv's national poet, Chaim Nachman Bialik, had written a poem lamenting the passivity of the Jews of Kishinev, who had taken their punishment in 1903 with next to no resistance.) Gone would be the powerlessness of diaspora; the new Jews of Zion would fight back.

Under the guidance of Ze'ev Jabotinsky, the polemicist and leader of the hardline revisionist school of Zionism, Jews armed themselves and headed into the streets bent on revenge. Now Arab witnesses described a pogrom of their own, with Jews looting Arab shops, breaking into Arab homes looking for people to beat and kill. Once again, according to Arab accounts of the time, children were among the victims; once again, they said, corpses were mutilated.

The motive of the rioters was not difficult to fathom. Indeed, the mob's initial target had been Jaffa's Immigrants' House, a hostel for newcomers, many of them young. The raid there had claimed the largest number of Jewish victims, the killing apparently aided by the enthusiastic participation of several Arab policemen. The rioting had spread to Jaffa port, Nat's own patch, where Arab boatmen declared they would no longer unload ships full of Jewish arrivals.

In hindsight, Arab opposition to Jewish immigration seems straightforward: surely they feared their country was gradually being taken from them, right before their eyes. In fact, not everyone was far-sighted enough to realize what was happening. Sometimes it was just the behaviour, the habits, of these newcomers that offended the Arabs. Deeply traditional, many complained about the morals of Jewish women: the way they dressed, the way they worked in the fields as the equals of men. In Jaffa, Arab opinion was shocked by the sight of Jewish youngsters canoodling on the beach, even skinny-dipping together in the sea. Others complained of Jewish radicalism, the immigrants' import of foreign ideas, typi-fied by those Jewish Bolsheviks trying to stir the Arab peasants to revolution on May Day. Samuel knew that only one thing would placate Palestine's Arabs and within a few days of the riots he announced it: a freeze on Jewish immigration.

For a pro-Zionist like Samuel, it was a hard call. The Arabs who had opposed his appointment already distrusted him as a Zionist. Now the Zionists branded this British Jew a traitor for blocking the path towards a homeland. He was, they said, rewarding terror, responding to an Arab-initiated bloodbath by appeasing Arab demands. It caused Samuel heartache to be condemned by his own people. (This was a man whose last act as High Commissioner would be a request that he be allowed to stay on in the country, to remain a private citizen in the Jewish national home. His successor, Lord Plumer, strongly objected and Samuel returned to London.) But he happened to believe that it was in Zionism's own interest to reach an accommodation with Palestine's Arabs; if a slowdown in immigration calmed Arab nerves, that too, surely, was the act of a conscientious Zionist. Moreover, Samuel had other responsibilities besides the Jewish renaissance. He had to protect all those living under the British crown, not just the Jews. In his words, he was 'not commissioned by the Zionists but in the name of the King'.

Nathan Mindel would doubtless have said the same thing had he been asked, as the senior immigration man at Jaffa, to stop boatloads of Jews yearning – as he had yearned so badly – to come to Palestine. But Nat received new instructions. He would not stand at the dockside, turning back the ships. He would go to the source of the human flow, his mission to slow it down if not to stop it outright. He was off to Europe, to cope with some of the 3,000 immigrants massed in various ports across Europe, clutching papers but suddenly denied entry to their promised land. His destination was the Italian port of Trieste.

There he found families who had given up their homes and were now living with nothing; many had made the journey all the way to Palestine or Egypt, only to be refused permission to disembark and sent back to Trieste. Packed with him was a memo of strict instructions, spelling out the different categories who were to be denied admission. He was to send back everyone except those who had set out before the freeze and had the most unanswerable claims. His instructions were unbending: 'Those who do not satisfy you will be refused . . . Persons who are old, incapacitated or who are not in a position to be self-supporting, and whose breadwinner is not already in the country must be refused . . .'

Worse, Nat was also to act as an officer of the thought police. Given the way the Jaffa riots had begun, the British authorities were especially keen to keep out communists. The president of the Arab executive, Musa Kazim al-Husseini, had been firing off letters blaming the Balfour Declaration for the injection of Bolshevism into Palestine, carried like a bacterium by Jewish immigrants. Samuel was sympathetic and, in that spirit, the first page of Nat's instructions for Trieste included the request that he interrogate all applicants to determine 'whether the person is desirable politically i.e. has Bolshevik or other undesirable tendencies'. He was even to create some kind of 'intelligence organisation', in order to work out which Zionists were plotting to get around the British rules. Nat was being asked to spy on his fellow Jews.

But he was not unduly troubled. In Trieste, he did his job

professionally, complying precisely with the rules – and still managed to admit seventy-one of the seventy-five cases he handled. Even when he came across a new batch of forty applicants who had arrived in Trieste after the freeze, he made a big show of complaining to the Italian authorities – but still let in twenty-four of them. (Perhaps he was moved by the fact that they had made the journey to Trieste all the way from Riga and Kovno, once his own part of the world.)

It was not always easy, but Nat was confident that his Zionist and British duties could be reconciled. Trieste was no great trauma; he did not think too long or hard about those he had to turn back. Perhaps he had forgotten his own restlessness in London in 1918, when he too had had to give up on Palestine, selling umbrellas and dreaming only of going back to the Orient. His biggest complaint about the Trieste experience was his hotel: there had been a waiters' and servants' strike and the food had been terrible. (This was no one-off dispute: Nat had walked into a period of unrest that seethed throughout northern Italy in the 1920s and would culminate in the triumph of fascism and Benito Mussolini.)

To get back to Palestine, Nat joined an American ship, the SS *Pocahontas*, at Naples. On board were, among others, a lively group of US Jews heading for Palestine as immigrants. But when they reached Kantara in Egypt they encountered an unforeseen problem. The British immigration official on duty was wrapping up for the day; if they wanted to enter Palestine, they would have to come back tomorrow. Nat was having none of it. He promptly put on his jacket, pulled rank and went behind the desk to stamp the immigrants' papers himself. Among them was a young idealist from Wisconsin, Goldie Myerson, heading to Palestine to start a new life. She would eventually change her name to Golda Meir and become the future state of Israel's fourth prime minister. (She never forgot that British official and what he did for her; his name would be on her admission paper for ever. Decades later, when she was already one of her country's most powerful figures, she celebrated the anniversary of her arrival – and made sure Nathan Mindel was there.)

Nat returned from Italy as confident as ever that he could, as the Yiddish phrase has it, dance at two weddings – one British, the other Zionist. There were strains, of course. The Zionists were constantly trying to stretch the immigration rules, always trying to squeeze in one more person – often with great ingenuity. Nat's department grappled for years with a favourite Zionist trick deployed by migrants the world over to this day: the fictitious marriage. Young women would come into Palestine swearing that they were about to marry the man of their dreams, only to leave Haifa dock and start new, single lives. Or there were the bigamists, Jews from Yemen keen to bring in multiple wives despite the rules that allowed only one spouse per husband. The Brits suspected a ruse; Zionists insisted it was just a difference in culture. Or there was the 1924 affair of the bogus rabbis: a sudden surge in arrivals under the provision for Jewish religious leaders. Merchants, furriers and locksmiths from across Europe were mugging up on their liturgy and posing as men of the cloth to get round the British authorities and into Palestine. Nat's job was to stop them, to choke off all but the British-approved routes into the country.

In 1922 his department received a tip-off (from the Chief Rabbi of Beirut, of all people) that a Zionist ring of human smugglers was operating across the Palestinian–Lebanese border. They were sailing past the official entry ports of Jaffa and Haifa, docking in Beirut, bribing port officials, then travelling overland before crossing into Palestine at Jadida or Metulla. Nat had to interrogate one of these illegal immigrants, reporting to his boss that this was no random incident but rather an organized movement. Nat recommended cooperation with the French masters of Lebanon and Syria as the only way to effect a crackdown. He was duly commended for his efficiency.

And, through it all, he continued to insist there was no contradiction. Miriam would bait him over it. 'I don't understand you,' she would say. 'You tell your brothers all the time, ' "What we need is Jewish immigration, we must have a Jewish majority here." ' And every time we come up with some ingenious plan to get more people in, you and your British chums stop us! Really, Min, I don't know how you do it.' (He was never Nat at home but Min, for Menachem.)

'Because these are not the kind of people we need here: liars and cheats. If we're going to build our new Judaea in this country, it will take a much better class of human material. We need men of honesty, strength and character – not whatever scum washes up from Eastern Europe.'

'Oh, and I suppose the British are the judges of that, are they?'

'No, but if their – if our – rules keep out the physically and morally unfit, then that can only help our cause.'

Such talk was not unusual. A wide streak in the Zionism of the time was the belief, heavily influenced by the Soviet dream of forging a heroic new man, that a return to Palestine would create a 'new Jew'. Gone would be both the pasty-faced bookworm of Eastern Europe and the effete, bourgeois Jew of the West; in their place would come a strong, lantern-jawed pioneer, a hoe in his hand and a song on his lips. The Palestinian Jews would be a new breed, free of the neurotic hang-ups of the urban, diaspora Jewry which they had escaped. They were about to evolve to a higher stage – into what the Zionist essayist Max Nordau called *Mushel judentum*, Muscular Jewry. Jabotinsky, who had inhaled deeply the nationalist vapours of Weimar Germany and fascist Italy, put it squarely: 'There is a need to create a new Jewish frame of mind, I am almost prepared to say a new psychological race of Jews.'

So Nat did not mind applying the rules strictly. When occasionally he allowed his Jewish heart to overrule his British head, he only regretted it. He once had a call for help, a call from what must have felt like another life. Two cousins from Vilna – the nearest big city to Dunilovich – from his mother's side of the family, were desperate to get to Palestine. Nat surely recognized his own story in theirs, for he did all he could. He sponsored them and brought them to Palestine. The two Wexler boys became instant Hebrews, changing their names – which Nat never did – to Yitzhak and Hanan Ben-Sinai.

Later Nat, who was nothing if not a skilled bureaucrat, was thumbing through the files when he spotted that one of them, who he knew was a bachelor, had brought in a 'wife': a fake marriage. Nat was livid. He felt his trust had been violated; he had vouched for someone who had deliberately deceived the British government. These were not the men to build Nat's new Judaea; he was ashamed of them. He put all family sentiment to one side and refused to speak to his cousins for nearly thirty years.

Nat was not to be disheartened, though. If he had loyalty to two masters, they were at least allies not enemies: the British and Zionists were not quite as far apart as later Israeli mythology would suggest. Thanks to the Balfour Declaration, the two shared the same horizon: they were both pursuing the creation of a Jewish national home in Palestine. They might disagree over pace, scale and details, but on ultimate goals they were broadly agreed.

Nat looked upward and saw the close cooperation between the two sides. He noted the extraordinary access granted to Chaim Weizmann, able to sit with Lloyd George, Balfour and Churchill – the three top men in the Cabinet – all at once. He saw much of the avalanche of correspondence between the Palestine administration and the Zionist movement, a daily blizzard of paper whistling between the two sides, the former constantly keeping the latter informed. And he knew first hand Zionism's power to decide which immigrants were fit for admission into Palestine and which were not. He looked at his superiors. Besides the High Commissioner, Herbert Samuel, there was Samuel's first Chief Secretary, one Brigadier-General Wyndham Deedes, an evangelical Christian Zionist who believed the Jewish return to Palestine was the necessary prelude to the Second Coming. The Attorney-General of the Palestine government was Norman Bentwich, who had been an active Zionist in pre-war Britain. Nat's own boss in the Department of Immigration was Albert Hyamson, another British Jew. Indeed, Britain and Zionism were close enough that the secretary of the Zionist Commission, Max Nurock, could later cross sides to do an equivalent job for the British administration, running the government secretariat. Nat was fully aware of these colleagues, who confirmed a Jewish presence in the Palestine government out of all proportion to their meagre share of the population. In 1921, when Nat won his Jaffa posting, Jews made up just 11 per cent of Palestine's people yet held 25 per cent of the governing posts. Jews, most of them local Palestinians rather than Britons like Nat, were so over-represented in the country's ruling machinery that in 1924 the Colonial Office wondered whether it should impose a limit. They decided against it.

Far from discriminating against Jews, the British accepted that Jews should be represented in every area of official life – including the police force. In 1918 the order had gone out to recruit Jewish policemen in proportion to their share of the population, but the Brits were to be frustrated. The Military Governor of Jaffa reported, 'The Jewish gendarmes have been most disappointing . . . they are either far below the average Arab in general intelligence or else they are impertinent and lazy . . . I really am almost at my wits' end to know by what means I can keep them from walking off their beats whenever they feel tired.' The Zionist defence was that even 'if the Jews on average were perhaps shorter in stature than the Arabs they more than made up in their education and brains'. In Nat's own department, no one could cry anti-Jewish discrimination: three of the five senior officials were British Jews, including himself.

And yet there were times when even Nat's bluff conviction that he could be both faithful Brit and devoted Zionist would be shaken. In the canteen, in the corridor, on the staircase at work, he would hear anti-Jewish talk, as casual as a discussion of the heat. It seemed to Nat that his colleagues regarded the Jews as the source of all the troubles in the world, and certainly in Palestine. He shrugged it off. The military presence in Palestine was staffed, he told himself, by the dregs of the army. They were men with no prospects at home and their anti-Semitism was nothing more than an inevitable trait of the unsophisticated, on a par with bad table manners or slovenly pronunciation.

He had worked hard to develop a thick hide. The last time he had let his ire show had been back in the army in Egypt. 'The thing you have to remember about the Jew,' his commanding officer was saying for maybe the dozenth time, 'is that they are congenitally disloyal. They cannot help it. They wander from place to place with no roots anywhere and will trade national allegiance as if it was something to be sold at a market stall. Likely as not, every Jew in England is spying against us for the Hun.'

'That's a lie!' Nat had said, springing to his feet. 'Jews are as loyal as anyone else. They are proving it in this war!' It was not the first time they had clashed, but this time it was too much. Nat kept up the onslaught, even after the officer started giving him the cold, hard stare. It only ended when the officer moved to place Nat under military arrest for insubordination.

Nat put such things out of his mind, just as he tried hard to ignore the clear signs that his British masters distrusted their Jewish servants. It had become a working assumption in the administration that any Jewish or Arab employees would give their first allegiance to their own community. The British had abandoned any pretence of internal confidentiality, convinced that Jewish and Arab workers alike would seek to funnel nuggets of information they came across to their own side. 'To seal a document or label it "Secret and Confidential" only provoked curiosity,' wrote an exasperated head of CID. The Jews were said to be especially systematic leakers: no matter how sensitive the British document, it somehow found its way to Zionist headquarters. British officials drafted cables back to London on the assumption that they would be intercepted; they conducted phone calls half aware that the legendary 'Shulamit of the switchboard' was listening in.

Repeatedly, Zionism's foes would insist that no Jew could truly serve the crown in Palestine: such a person would always be looking out for Zionism. You did not have to be an anti-Semite to think like that. Viewed charitably, British distrust of the Jews was merely a recognition of reality. There was plenty of hard evidence that Jewish servants of the Mandate did indeed find their loyalties tugged in two directions, while some went further, working clandestinely for what they saw as the cause of Jewish renaissance. That British officialdom noticed the fact could not be attributed entirely to animus against Jews. As far as they were concerned, it was simple common sense that prompted senior politicians in London to maintain a constant protest against the appointment of Jews, just as military commanders had earlier pleaded with Downing Street to send anyone but Samuel to serve as High Commissioner. In 1922 a parliamentary exchange centred on the ethnicity of one appointee, forcing a government minister to deny that the man in question had been born Jewish or had changed his name. A year later, the target was Commander Harry Luke, né Lukacs, nominated for a top job in Jerusalem. One official dashed off a helpful note about Luke: 'The only objection I can see is that he is of Jewish extraction, but he is certainly not a professing Jew and does his best to keep his origin well concealed.' Another official was less forgiving: 'I think that Mr Luke's Hebraic blood is a fatal objection to him.' It goes without saying that Arabs in Palestine agitated against senior Jewish appointees, arguing that such people could not be trusted to arbitrate fairly between the two populations but would always lean towards the Zionists.

Some of this murky water lapped up against Nat's own desk. In 1923 his boss, a Major Morris, devised a scheme to tackle the immigration problem at source by installing inspectors in the European cities which Jews were leaving for Palestine: Warsaw, Vienna, Constantinople. Morris suggested Nat for one of the jobs, but the High Commissioner refused: he could not have Jews. Word of this reached one of Nat's two senior Jewish colleagues in the Department of Immigration, Dennis Cohen, who 'flared up' and promptly resigned. Weizmann himself was outraged, feeling that Cohen had been punished for his sympathy for Zionism: 'It seems a terrible thing that the few friends we have in the Administration are being gradually frozen out and in a way they suffer for their friendship to us.' Nat wondered about resigning too, but soon put the idea out of his mind. He had a family to feed; quitting was out of the question.

In any case, his life as a British official was too good to give up. Paid on a completely different scale from the Palestinian Jews around him (to say nothing of the Palestinian Arabs), he and Miriam could afford to live in one smart neighbourhood after another. They had a house, not an apartment, with a small garden and a yard. He wrote home, bragging of the 'kitchen/dining room, sitting room, 3 bedrooms, small library and bathroom with real running water from a tap. You can scarcely imagine what a bath in a real bathroom means in Jerusalem – a luxury only attained by the plutocrats.'

The closest they came to a problem was when they lived in the German Colony, the neighbourhood with the best houses in the city. They sent Yehuda to the local kindergarten, run out of a German church, where he mixed with the children of British officers as well as expat Germans. That was all fine until little Yehuda – who, Nat was glad to see, was growing into a spirited, fearless lad – came home singing Christmas carols in German. The Mindels promptly took him out and sent him to a Jewish nursery.

His marriage was happy, with a wife he still regarded as his sweetheart, a son whose value he estimated in ancient Jewish terms as 'far above rubies' and now a new baby girl, Ruth. So what if they did not socialize much: a little tennis in summer, the odd evening with other British Jewish friends? The Jerusalem winters were cold anyway and most people were early to bed. Nat liked to spend what few after-work hours he had with his children, hardening up his boy and taking the measure of his daughter. He thought he detected some early signs of intelligence, as well as a stubborn streak, in her demand to be fed at any time between two and six in the morning. It was like this, rather than at A-list dinner parties or amusing soirées, that Nathan Mindel spent his nights.

He was content; both his home and his city were havens of constancy in a land that was changing before his eyes. 'Jerusalem, dear sleepy Jerusalem', as he called it in one letter to his old friend Sam, remained much as he had first known it. New suburbs had sprung up, the population grown larger and yet 'the character of the place remains unchanged. It is disturbed considerably by motor traffic – old Fords converted into shabby buses – as well as new cars, but they remain exotic. Jerusalem remains much more Oriental than Beirut or Cairo (I don't know Damascus) and yet it is a Jewish city – more Jewish I believe than even New York – in spite of its numerous churches and convents, not to mention the magnificent Mosque of Omar and the Mosque of Aksa in the Temple Area.' He told Sam of the welcome rain, which seemed to wash away the Jerusalem dust. Finally he signed off as Min, explaining, 'I have almost forgotten the use of the name Nat.'

For him, Menachem and Nat had shown they could exist side by side. There would be bumps and grinds, but it could work. Others were never so optimistic. 'A Zionist Jew in office is the servant of two masters,' wrote one senior British official in correspondence with the War Office in London. 'It is an unfair and impossible position in which to place him.' Nat was about to discover quite how impossible.

On 23 August 1929 Friday morning prayers in Jerusalem thrummed with tension. For nearly a year Jews and Muslims had been involved in a stand-off that would recur, in varying forms, for the rest of the century. The argument was about control of, and access to, the holy sites of the Old City. Muslims feared a Zionist plan to take over the Western Wall, revered by Jews as the only surviving remnant of the Second Temple and seen by Muslims as part of the Haram-al-Sharif, the holy compound from where Mohammed ascended to heaven. For months there had been scuffles and violence. In the third week of August a Jewish demonstration was followed by a Muslim counter-demonstration, the stabbing of a Jew followed by the beating of an Arab. By the week's end the mood was edgy. Muslim worshippers came armed with blades that glinted in the sunshine; rumours were churning through the villages surrounding the city that a confrontation with the Jews was coming.

Thanks to a chase here, a scrap there, the prophecy would prove self-fulfilling: both sides would, of course, claim they were hit first and that what followed were acts of self-defence. As it happened, the Jerusalem violence that day was a mere overture to the main performance, whose chosen venue was the ancient town of Hebron.

Jews considered Hebron one of the four holy cities of Israel, claiming a continuous presence there since biblical times. Abraham had bought Hebron's cave of Machpela as a burial site for his wife, Sarah. They, along with Abraham's son Isaac and grandson Jacob, and their wives Rebecca and Leah – Judaism's patriarchs and matriarchs – were buried there. Indeed, when Jacob neared his death he made his twelve sons promise to leave Egypt and take his body to Hebron for burial.

In 1929 the Jewish population of Hebron was down to the hundreds, even if it included a Sephardic community rooted in the town for some 800 years. They were a tiny minority, surrounded by some 20,000 Arabs. Relations had always been good, but from 1917, as the two national movements grew, the tension rising throughout Palestine spilled on to the streets of Hebron. There were reports of day-to-day harassment: beatings, vandalism, the interruption of prayers. Still, no one was prepared for what happened on that Sabbath in late August.

Word of the morning clashes in Jerusalem began to spread; rumour (later proved to be inaccurate) said the Jews had gone on a killing spree. A crowd of Arabs gathered at the bus station, ready to head for Jerusalem. But soon they found a more local focus for their rage: the Hebron *yeshiva*. They surrounded it, hurling stones. A student inside, an immigrant from Poland, was grabbed and stabbed to death. By the next morning, the mood had turned even more vicious. A mob circled a house where Jews were gathered for morning prayers. They stormed it and killed almost everyone inside. The atrocities were spreading across town. Two septuagenarian rabbis, along with five younger men, were castrated; a baker was burned to death on a stove; a local pharmacist, a cripple, was murdered along with his daughter, who was raped. Survivors would later gather photographs of the massacre, lest their word be doubted: the images showed mutilation and torture, with some victims as young as two. When it was done, sixty-seven corpses were left.

Faced with all this, the British police were almost helpless. Vastly outnumbered, the Hebron police chief, Raymond Cafferata, could call on just eighteen mounted policemen and fifteen constables on foot, eleven of whom were elderly and in no condition to take on a mob. They could not protect the Jews on their watch. Cafferata entered one house to find an Arab cutting a child's head off with a sword.

In the hours that followed, the British were in a panic. Beyond Hebron, Jewish revenge attacks were claiming Arab lives, levelling out the tallies of dead and injured on both sides. It was true that there had been some inspiring stories of human kindness amid the degradation. That so many from Hebron's Jewish community survived was down to the compassion of Arab neighbours who hid them from the crowds outside. Some Arab families took in dozens of Jews. But there was too much darkness to dwell on the points of light. The British administration concluded that it had a serious public order problem. The entire Palestine police force numbered just 1,500. Most of those were Arab and wholly distrusted by the Jews, who now believed themselves under attack. (It did not help that Arab policemen had been involved in the rampage at Hebron. Cafferata had caught one of them redhanded, clutching a dagger, standing over a Jewish woman drenched in her own blood. Cafferata shot him.)

Acting High Commissioner Harry Luke – formerly Lukacs – gave the order to enlist and arm suitable administration officials as special constables. They would beef up the mere 175 British officers in the force, adding more of the reliability and impartiality that only the Brits could provide. Among the special constables were those British Jews who served in the administration – including Nat Mindel.

He was happy to do it. He knew what the Yishuv were saying, that the Jews could no longer rely on the British to defend them – they would have to do the job themselves. Here was his chance to do the job, but to do it as an Englishman. As he had fourteen years earlier, Nat joined up to serve King George. He was handed a rifle and given a refresher course in how to use it.

But Luke had not counted on the Arab reaction to his move. A deputation came to see him, incandescent at the notion of Jews being armed: special constables like Nat surely amounted to a British-sponsored militia. How dare the administration arm one of Palestine's competing peoples against the other? Had they not promised to do no such thing?

Under duress, Harry Luke backed down. He may have changed his name; he may have later written an autobiography that discussed at length the ancestry of his non-Jewish mother, detailing her links to Austria's minor nobility, while pointedly saying nothing of his father's origins or even his name. But the man born Harry Lukacs would later admit that the conclusion he came to was not only 'very unpleasant, distasteful' but 'one of the most painful and difficult decisions, if not the most painful and difficult, I have ever had to take in my service'. In correspondence with London, he argued that although the decision was 'an unpalatable one', harsh on the people affected, he was sure it 'was in the best interests of the Jews as a whole'. Arming the Jews would inflame the entire Arab population; it was better for all concerned to remove that 'irritant'. On 27 August he ordered that all Anglo-Jewish special constables be stood down. They were to be disarmed.

The Yishuv were stirred to cold fury. Luke was a traitor who would leave his own people defenceless in the face of a bloodthirsty enemy. They demanded his removal. The Zionist Commission in Jerusalem cabled colleagues in London to coordinate their protests. The Jewish 'specials' were 'absolutely necessary', they wrote, to 'protect Jewish quarters, specially as Arabs had ample Arab police protection'. To add insult to injury, the Zionists were convinced that, while Jews were being disarmed, fifty extra Arab police had just been recruited – including some who were said to have been involved in the Friday riots. And, getting to the heart of the matter, this decision distinguished British Jews from British non-Jews, a 'dangerous innovation for any ministry of His Majesty'.

So briefed, Chaim Weizmann wrote to Colonial Secretary Lord Passfield, who had made his name as the Fabian socialist and pamphleteer Sidney Webb, insisting that Luke's order 'be immediately countermanded'. He said the Arab police had clearly demonstrated their 'unreliability'; to disarm the Jewish special constables at a time like this would only make the Jewish population of Palestine more insecure. Jews should be allowed to play a role in their own defence, and there was no shortage of Jews willing to do their bit – including plenty who had served in the British Army, including some at officer level. He might have been speaking about Nat.

It was no good, though; the decision had been taken. All eighteen Jewish deputies were to present themselves to their commanding officer to hand in their weapons. Among those standing in line was Nathan Mindel.

For more than a decade, he had listened to those, Jewish and Gentile alike, who said Jews like him could never truly serve the crown. He had ignored them. The commanding officer back in Egypt had believed all Jews were spies. He had put it down to the rantings of one bad man. In the Department of Immigration his ultimate boss had scotched a proposal that Nat be posted to Europe on the simple grounds that he was a Jew. He had got over it. In the canteens and salons of Jerusalem, he was ostracized by his fellow Brits because they never counted him as 'one of us'; the credentials of his fellow Jews in the administration were constantly questioned back in London by those who thought 'Hebraic blood' a disqualification.

Nat had known all this for years and had worked hard to shove it to the back of his mind. He had learned not to think about it, to keep his head down, concentrate on his work, take care of his family. But inside his heart lived another man: Menachem, the seeker of Zion. Menachem had learned to accept all he heard too. To tell himself that everything was in the best interests of the Jewish national home, that everything would come right in the long run.

But this was too much. The country Nat had adopted and served, the nation whose shit he had carried by the bucketload, the nation he had begged to join was telling him he was not just different but too different. Nat – the British patriot who had delighted in becoming first one of His Majesty's subjects, then one of His Majesty's officers and now one of his imperial servants – was being told that he could not be trusted with a weapon of self-defence, because of who he was.

He stepped forward and faced the commanding officer. He fixed him in the eye and, in a voice that had been stilled so long, he let out a cry of rage. I protest against this humiliation. I protest against it. This is an outrage and I refuse to accept it. I refuse it. He held his rifle, gripping it at chest height with both hands, as if it were a rail. But he did not hand it to the officer. His eye still locked on his, he raised the gun above his head and, with all his might, Nathan Isidore Mindel smashed it to the ground.

6   We are Invincible!

I would never have recognized him. The Mick Mindel I knew – a great-uncle on my father's side, a generation down from Nat and born to a different branch of the family from those five founding brothers – was short, bald and bespectacled. He even walked with a slight limp, a lurch to the left. Which was appropriate, I suppose.

But he looked nothing like the man in this picture. I say man, though the person at the centre of this team portrait of the 1924 Jewish Athletic Association First Division Cricket Champions is actually a fourteen-year-old boy. He looks older than that, his arms folded, his face unsmiling and dead serious, his hair parted like a young executive heading to the office. He looks tough.

The Jewish Athletic Association sounds like the set-up for a joke. You can imagine Woody Allen explaining that it was a very small organization. Judging by the expressions of the 1924 cricket champions, that would be a mistake. These boys look like they meant business.

As it happens, Mickey was quite the sportsman. He was a skilful footballer, usually playing midfield, and, like a lot of Jewish kids in the East End of London in those days, no slouch in the boxing ring either; perhaps that is where he learned the snarl.

But his greatest prowess was on the cricket field. He was an all-rounder, handy with the ball and a demon with the bat. In the summer of 1923, the *Star* newspaper ran a competition for the best schoolboy innings of the week, with the winner getting a bat signed by Jack Hobbs, then the hero of English cricket. Few imagined that an early champion would be the skipper of the Jews' Free School XI. But when Mickey Mindel, then only thirteen, played a true captain's innings against Lower Chapman Street School – 94 not out – the *Star* had its winner. Waves of pride rippled through the East End; every Jewish boy knew the name of Mickey Mindel. The *Jewish Chronicle* sent a photographer round, so that all Anglo-Jewry could share in the *nachas*, the joy.

Sport might have become Mickey's vocation. He was good enough for Middlesex to give him a trial. They accepted him, but he could not afford to take up his place. He needed to work. Besides, nature did not quite follow the script. When Mickey, who had always been tall for his age, turned sixteen, he stopped growing, just like that. He would not be tall again.

Instead of Lord's Cricket Ground, Mick wound up in the same place of work as most of his peers: the sweatshops. Still a teenager, he became an apprentice cutter – learning one of the most skilled crafts of the tailoring trade. He wielded a slot knife, a badge of some status in the East End; one day, he dreamed, he might even become a designer.

But neither sport nor tailoring could contain all of Mick's passion. For inside that round head, and behind those soon-to-be permanent glasses, raged a fiery spirit that would plunge Mick Mindel into the greatest struggle of the twentieth century. He was to become a leader of his fellow Jews and a champion for what he believed would be a new age of justice for all humankind. Mick became a communist.

He always said his was no overnight conversion. Almost from the day he was born, on Christmas Eve 1909 – a honeymoon baby, arriving nine months after his parents were married – in a one-room flat in the East End, he would see poverty up close. Most of it was from the vantage point of the Charlotte de Rothschild Buildings on Flower and Dean Street, the cramped, infested East End tenement that was the first home for thousands of immigrant Jews, built by Anglo-Jewry's oldest dynasty to house the newest arrivals from the East. Mickey's parents considered this a step up from their first address, but on the walkways and in the courtyards of those buildings, Mickey would see children with no clothes, parents with no shoes, taken in by relatives not much better off than them but who, because they had made the westward journey first, were cast as providers for those who followed.

He did not even need to look outside the tiny window: the same hardship lived in his own one-bedroom flat. His parents, both immigrants from Dunilovich, had nothing either. Their three sons were born and lived in those small rooms: parents and youngest brother, Sid, sleeping in the bedroom, Mickey and brother Jack on a couch in the living room. When their Uncle Harry stepped off the boat from Dunilovich, he lived there too.

Mick did not have to read pamphlets to know about the deprivations of the working class. He saw for himself the bugs that would crawl out of the cracks in the walls, slithering from under the window sills each summer, no matter how often you scrubbed. The walls looked as if they had measles, so covered were they with red spots marking the place where the creatures had been squashed. And the smell! At night those pesky, reeking bedbugs would be at their most ferocious, conspiring to keep you from sleep. Mick's parents would work flat out all day, then lie awake all night. They began each morning exhausted. When it became truly intolerable, or when the twice-yearly fumigation effort got under way, the family would leave the flat and camp outside – sleeping under the stars.

Mickey saw first hand what communist intellectuals would only read about in books. He witnessed exploitation, starting with the garment workers who lived all around. They were paid piece rates, pennies per item, toiling from six in the morning till eleven at night. He heard machinists and pressers complain that they never saw their children awake. And the conditions were desperate, packed into workshops that were nothing more than the front room of a fellow immigrant's home. The work was dirty, stinking and hard. Pressers had to wield fourteen-pound steam irons to force the creases into the collar or lapels of a new suit; in those windowless rooms, the smell of the damp rags would be almost overpowering.

There was no such thing as job security. Tailoring was a seasonal business: for whole stretches of the year, no one bought any clothes so no one made any. During the 'busy', you could work day and night, but the 'slack' could last for months on end. Workers would gather in Whitechapel as if at a Roman slave market. The 'guvnor' would pace up and down, calling for a machiner (female operators of the sewing machines were known as machinists, though quite why no one ever seemed to know) or a tailor or a presser, point a finger at a worker who looked fit and give him a day's labour. In the slack, most would leave with nothing. They would rarely go home, though. Most would hang around all day, playing dominoes in the trade union building on what was then Great Garden Street, rather than face their family and admit they had failed to earn any bread. Or they would get a flash of inspiration and realize that one lucky break could change everything: Mickey would see wives pounding their husbands' chests with their fists, distraught that the men had gambled away what precious few pennies they had.

But not everyone who sees poverty becomes a communist. The difference with Mick was that he was not just surrounded by evidence of the problem; the air around him crackled with talk of the solution. The Mindels and their neighbours may have had little space and no money, but in one commodity they were unimaginably rich: politics.

In the dense, fetid streets of the East End – so narrow the ten-year-old Mickey could hop across the road in two jumps – immigrants formed into the same cells and factions that had animated them back in the old country, anarchists jostling with communists, socialists thrashing it out with Zionists. And much of this rolling, twenty-four-hour argument converged on the fourth-floor flat occupied by Mickey Mindel's parents, Morris and Jessie.

Morris probably imagined his home was such a magnet because of his own scintillating conversation. In truth it was his wife who was the draw. Jessie never really mastered English – she could not even sign her own name, marking her passport with a cross – but she cooked the best strudel in the East End. You could go to Rinkoff's on Jubilee Street, but it would never be as good as Jessie's. She was a powerhouse in the kitchen. She worked for Ostwinds, the kosher caterers, cooking industrial portions of chicken and *latkes* and *kugel* for weddings and bar mitzvah parties, and she deployed the same skills back home. In fact, she cooked exactly the same way whether on or off professional duty. If she wanted to rustle up some dumplings for soup she couldn't help herself: she would make 150 *kneidlach* rather than fifteen. Word got around the Rothschild Buildings: a meeting at the Mindels' would give you a large portion of Jessie's hot food to go with Morris's hot air.

Mickey took it all in – the smells, the tastes, the unique flavours of Jewish diet and debate. He could not escape the politics: even the bread on the table bore a stamp, the mark of the London Jewish Bakers' Union.

In 1917, when he was just seven years old, Mickey noticed a change in the air. The flat was fuller than usual, the discussion more frenetic than ever before. He had nowhere to sleep – his bed was the couch in the living room – so he had no choice but to stay up and listen.

'The future is ours!' he heard one man say in Yiddish, his eyes

Mick's parents: Morris, who always liked a good speech, and Jessie.

ablaze. 'The problem of anti-Semitism is solved!' Mickey could not understand everything, but slowly he got the idea. There had been a revolution back home in Russia.

'We're going back, Morris,' said the man, his mouth full of strudel. 'And you should come too.' He and the others tried to persuade the Mindels that the Russia they had all left behind – of pogroms and press-ganged service in the tsar's army – was now a thing of the past. Only a bright future awaited the Jews in the new Soviet Union.

'Look who's in charge now,' said the neighbour, a fleck of pastry lodged in the corner of his mouth. 'Trotsky, Zinoviev, Kamenev, Radek – most of the central committee are Jews!'

Morris listened to all this with pride; he felt glad that his people were playing a prominent role in the world – and in Russia, of all places, where they had been despised for so long. How wonderful that a Jew like Trotsky, Lev Davidovich Bronstein, was now in charge of the Red Army! For a while, Morris got swept up. He even wrote to the new Soviet Embassy in London, asking that his Russian citizenship be restored. But he never did join his three neighbours, who, true to their word, went back to Russia to join the revolution.

For Morris was not a communist. He was instead a follower of the Bund, the movement which believed in a particular, Jewish brand of socialism. 'Of course workers everywhere must win their freedom, and we support that,' Bundists like him would say. 'But each people, each nation, has its own path. Our struggle and our needs are not the same as the *goyim*'s and never will be. They will never understand or care about anti-Semitism the way we do. International brotherhood and international socialism are all very well as slogans, but the reality is we Jews will always need our own Jewish voice to press our needs.'

Warming to his theme, a Bundist like Morris might say, 'I want to see socialist revolution around the world as much as the next man, but, when it comes, why must Jews assimilate and disappear into the great mass? Why can't we remain distinct and proud of who we are? Why did Lev Bronstein have to change his name to Leon Trotsky, why did Rosenfeld have to become Kamenev, why did Sobelsohn have to become Radek? In a socialist society, why can't Jews be allowed to keep our own ways and maintain our own, Yiddish culture? Our goal should not be to dissolve ourselves into the new Utopia. We should have the right to run our own community – and to be equal with everyone else.'

The demand was autonomy within an equal society, but for Morris it was more than just a political line. Bundism was the driving enthusiasm of his life, a cause to which he had been committed even back in the old country – at great personal cost. In London he was a founder member of the Workers' Circle, a friendly society that served as the Bundists' main organization. Members paid sixpence a week and, if they fell ill, they would get eight shillings back. But there was more to the Circle than collective insurance. Morris helped organize lectures and convene discussions, spending almost every night of the week at Circle House on Great Alie Street. His own children came to believe that Morris would rather spend an evening in the company of the men of the Bund than with Jessie, the twenty-four-hour cook whose arms were permanently striped with burns from the steaming pots and pans that surrounded her to her dying day.

As the eldest son, Mickey was introduced to Morris's world as heir apparent. When Morris paid a visit to the headquarters of the London Tailors' Machiners' and Pressers' Union, he took young Mickey with him, clambering up the iron staircase to see the scene of little Russia within: the samovar bubbling away, the workless immigrants drinking tea through a sugar cube placed between their teeth. And everywhere the guttural, phlegmy '*ch*'s and '*sch*'s of Yiddish.

Morris wanted to teach his son. Emma Goldman, the American feminist, anarchist and revolutionary, came to speak to the Workers' Circle and Morris made sure his boy was there. At first, Mickey thought she looked like another old Yiddish housewife – a real *balabusta* – but then she began to speak and fire came out of her mouth.

Morris was a sucker for a great speech. In 1924 he told Mickey to put on his coat and brace himself for a long walk. They trekked all the way across London, east to west, to the Albert Hall and back, to hear Labour's first prime minister, Ramsay MacDonald. 'This will be good for you,' the father would say, full of admiration for MacDonald and for Labour. 'You'll see what a real political meeting is like. Whatever you do in life, Mickey, I want you always to know what the world is really about.'

The teenager took to it, rapidly developing a knack for argument. One Yom Kippur, a fast day and the holiest of the Jewish year, he saw a group of anarchists outside the Brick Lane synagogue. Now, there was a time, before Mick was born, when anarchism had been the dominant movement among the immigrant Jews of the East End. Part of the explanation lay in allegiances formed back in Latvia or Lithuania; part of it was the anarchist control of the leading Yiddish newspaper, the *Arbeiter Fraint* (the Workers' Friend); part of it was the ferocious energy of the paper's editor, Rudolf Rocker, a blond, German Catholic anarchist who had learned Yiddish and become an unlikely leader of East End Jewry. But perhaps the key to the anarchists' success was education.

Most of those immigrants who came off the boat knew nothing and were desperate to learn. They believed that an education, if not for them, then at least for their children, would be their escape tunnel out of the slums. And the anarchists were the ones who showed the way. They founded the Jubilee Club on Jubilee Street, hosting lectures on art and music delivered by those Jewish intellectuals who had made the same immigrant journey to London. One of these pauper scholars, Frumkin was his name, was devoted to bringing great works of literature to the slum-dwellers. He translated Tolstoy, Dostoevsky and Chekhov into Yiddish, but he also wanted the immigrants to know something of their new land. So the anarchists translated Oscar Wilde – imagine the '*Gevalt!*' let out by a Yiddish Lady Bracknell – and organized tours of the British Museum. For a while, anarchism acted as the unofficial absorption service for a wave of new immigrants. Still, by the time Mickey spotted a handful outside the synagogue, they were a movement in retreat.

'Good *yontuf*,' Mick said, offering the traditional Jewish holy day greeting, aiming to bait the anarchists from the start.

'Good *yontuf*,' one of them replied, the words slipping out before he could stop himself.

'So what's this about?' asked Mick, gesturing at the ham sandwiches each one was holding, rather ostentatiously. 'Snacks on a fast day?'

'This is our demonstration against the orthodox establishment,' said the leader, his chin in the air.

'It's a demonstration of being stupid, that's what it is,' said young Mickey Mindel.

'No, this is a visible manifestation of our stance against all established positions, including the superstition that is religion. Nothing is sacred. All rules are mere human inventions, designed to enslave those who agree to be bound by them.'

'So you don't believe in any rules?' asked Mick.

'No.'

'What about "Thou shalt not kill"?'

'In desperate situations, political assassination may be the only available weapon against the system. Violence and bloodshed can be essential tools in the struggle. Eliminating the right person at the right time can change the course of history . . .'

'But look at you!' laughed Mick, his arm, palm upwards, sweeping across the little huddle of them, munching their bread rolls on Brick Lane. They were pale, thin and reedy. In Yiddish, each one looked a perfect *nebuch*. 'None of you could hurt a fly!'

He chuckled and went briskly on his way. He was not hugely keen to be seen mixing in anarchist company. It was not so much the stance on political murder that worried him, but the anarchist position on sex. They believed – Mick would always lower his voice when saying it – in free love. That had been the kiss of death for anarchism in the Jewish East End: what Jewish mother would allow her daughter to go out with an anarchist? Mickey Mindel did not need that kind of obstacle placed in his way.

Not that he was unsympathetic to all anarchist views, especially on religion. Despite the long hours of Jewish studies pumped into him at school, he found most faith so much irrational nonsense. If ever he talked with a believer, Mick would fast run out of patience. 'You see the world through such blinkers!' he would say. '"Thou shalt make no graven images." Does that apply to paintings? What about architecture? It makes no sense.'

In this too Mickey was his father's son. Morris would take his lad to Sunday morning lectures at Conway Hall, the Holborn meeting place for agnostics, atheists and free thinkers. His father would nod along approvingly. He had little time for the religious. As a socialist, Morris was appalled that the rabbis had raised not a murmur of protest at the sweated conditions making life hell for the Jewish clothing workers of the East End. These workers had once petitioned the Chief Rabbi, begging him to ask the bosses at least to let employees off early on a Friday afternoon, to make it home in time for the Sabbath. The Chief Rabbi had refused.

Morris came to believe that the religious authorities shared the same attitude to immigrants as the venerable families of the Anglo-Jewish establishment: they were embarrassed by them. The old guard seemed to regard these *Ostjuden*, with their scruffy clothes, broken English and radical politics, as just too alien. Perhaps they feared the new arrivals would remind the local Gentile majority how foreign the settled Jews of Britain had once been. The Jewish aristocracy did not want to be tarred with the immigrants' brush. So they channelled much of their philanthropy into cleaning the newcomers up, whether by teaching boys like Mickey how to be good little Englishmen – fluent in the king's language and the rules of cricket – or by offering the residents of Rothschild Buildings 'tidy home' prizes, to make sure they kept themselves and their tiny flats shipshape.

There was personal animus too. Morris earned his living as a bookbinder, a job he loved. He would sew, glue and fold each volume himself, by hand, in his workshop, just around the corner from Princelet Street. He had had no formal education, but he reckoned this was a good consolation prize – to be surrounded by the smell and texture of learning. (On the side, he began his own collection of books. By the time he was done, he had built up a library of Bundist works in Yiddish that would not have shamed a university.)

One of his most regular earners was binding prayer books. He could do them cheaply, in small batches of a hundred at a time – ideal for the *shteibls*, or small synagogues, that popped up on every street in the East End. One order came from his own local house of worship. Morris bound them and delivered them, as requested, but the synagogue never got around to paying its bill. Mickey was about to turn thirteen at the time, the age of bar mitzvah, when Jewish boys are deemed to graduate into men. The *shul* asked Morris to pay for the extra lessons the boy would need. The sheer gall of it, the *chutzpah*, of asking him for money when they still owed him was too much. He had a spectacular falling out with the synagogue and its rabbi. Mick never did have a bar mitzvah. Nor would his brothers.

Morris kept up the old ways, though, chiefly to please Jessie. Theirs was a kosher home, the festivals were marked; but his heart was never in it. He would go to synagogue, but only if he heard a good *chazan* was performing. Morris loved a good tune.

Mickey followed his father on both counts. He learned to love music and he harboured a robust scepticism towards religion. Just as his father had been appalled by the rabbis' failure to speak out against the exploitation of Jewish immigrants in the sweatshops, so Mick would have his own moment of disgust. He saw a sign in the window of a Jewish pawnbroker: 'Will accept *tefillin*.' Since *tefillin* are part of the essential kit of a religious Jewish male, used in prayer each weekday morning, the notion of profiteering from a plight so desperate that someone would be forced to pawn them shocked young Mickey. To him, Jewish tradition surely demanded the opposite: compassion for those in need. That much he remembered from his Hebrew classes. There was the Passover *seder* ceremony, which begins with the cry, 'Let all who are hungry come and eat.' And the obligation of *tzedakah*, which demands that every Jew give a minimum of 10 per cent of his earnings to charity (and much more if he can), not to mention the injunction, repeated over and over throughout the Torah, to 'remember the stranger, for you were a stranger in a strange land'. To see these ideals trampled on so callously by those who claimed to obey them most faithfully meant Mick would have even less time for religious Jewry than his father.

The ingredients were all there: a hatred of poverty, a love of politics and a thick dollop of atheism. Mick had everything he would need to be a good communist. Even so, his life could have turned out differently. His season ticket at Spurs could have become his singular obsession, or his regular appearances on the pitch for Jews' Free School old boys. Perhaps he could have used the school certificate that made him, at least theoretically, eligible for university. (He never did take that up: his family needed him to stop studying and start earning.) Maybe the tailoring might have seized him, nudging him towards his first ambition, to be a clothes designer. Who knows, he might have one day owned his own factory. Yet somehow it was communism that grabbed him. Not through ideology or argument, but the way that causes so often recruit their adherents. They say that people do not believe in ideas so much as they believe in people who believe in ideas – and that is how it was for Mickey Mindel and communism.

He was nineteen when it happened, the year Harry Pollitt, General Secretary of the Communist Party, contested a parliamentary by-election in Mick's backyard of Stepney. Communists descended on the streets where Mick played alleyway football, leafleting, hawking copies of the *Daily Worker*, advertising meeting after public meeting with the candidate. Curiosity led Mick to a Pollitt rally, and he was seduced.

The room vibrated with excitement. The communists in the hall were passionate, excited and, above all, young. They were people just like Mick: the children of immigrants, fluent in English rather than Yiddish, whose zeal to change the world would not be confined to the narrow interests of the Jews. He recognized so many of the faces there. They were kids he had played with, or their parents had been round to his parents', munching his mother's cheesecake and plotting in the Workers' Circle with his father.

Pollitt was an inspiration. 'He sees the world as it really is!' Mick said to himself. 'He has analysed it properly, like a scientist. He *understands*.' When the questions came, Pollitt had an answer to everything. Mick listened to the other speakers as well. They were all so educated, so well versed in history. Nothing was beyond their grasp. He looked around the room. While his parents seemed shaped by the past, the samovar still on the table, here was a generation striding towards the future.

Before he knew it, Mick was drawn in. He joined the Young Communist League and suddenly he was on marches, or doing his shift selling the *Daily Worker* on the street corner, or door to door, to his neighbours in the Rothschild Buildings and on Flower and Dean Street. The more he did, the more he wanted to do; his comrades were fast becoming his best friends. As his father had done in the Circle, now Mick did in the Communist Party – organizing lectures, debates and, his personal favourite, concerts. In the Rothschild Buildings, a meeting might begin with a gramophone recital: the overture to *Egmont*, the Brahms Violin Concerto and *Sheherazade*. They would listen to the music, with a communist message delivered during the interludes. Mick would never feel more at home.

The Communist Party began to take an interest in Mick: he was a talent to be nurtured. They signed him up for training as an activist, sending him to classes in Marxist theory – giving him the further education he had never had. He liked the lessons well enough, though sometimes he heard the talk become so abstract, so light, he could almost see it hovering in the air. The comrades would turn and ask him what he believed. 'When no child will ever go hungry,' he would reply, 'where widows will be provided for, where every woman will have the right to have a baby, where governments will spend more on the arts than on arms, then we'll begin to be a civilized society and a civilized world.' The would-be theoreticians probably found that too earthbound, too naïve, for their tastes, but the talent spotters were impressed by young Mindel's turn of phrase. He did not let on that his answer was not wholly spontaneous, although it was true that he had never heard it put that way before. In fact, he had been translating in his head from the Yiddish. He had been quoting his father.

By the start of the 1930s Mick's life was bound up with communism. In the winter he would play soccer with a Communist XI; in summer it was country walks with the comrades. They had become his closest confidants, those to whom he confessed his most intimate feelings. It was through communism that he discovered sex.

'Under capitalism, sex has been alienated from its natural essence,' a group leader would say in one meeting. 'If people wish to engage in sex, that is not a crime. It is normal, natural and healthy. In the future, the barriers which bourgeois society has constructed around the conjoining of the sexes will all be torn down. Contraception, and the recent work of progressives like Marie Stopes, is showing us the way. Sex will be a matter of complete freedom, free of guilt or unwanted biological consequences.'

'Having sex should be like having a glass of water,' chipped in an especially eager comrade. 'If you have a biological need, you should be able to satisfy it.'

What nonsense, Mick thought to himself, but he said nothing. He was in no hurry to advertise the fact that he was rather more strait-laced than the average revolutionary. His first visit to a communist summer camp had been a shock. When the comrades began to pair off, Mick did not know where to put himself. The truth was, he was still a virgin. For all the talk of changing the world, he could not quite shake off the beliefs that had been etched on him at home, including no sex before marriage. He was twenty-four before he would finally break free and stage that particular, personal revolution.

Through all this, Mick Mindel was still living under his parents' roof. The few hours he was at home, not out flyposting or organizing, would often turn to political discussion.

'The revolution in Russia will not solve all the problems of the world, Mickey,' his father would say.

'You're wrong,' would be Mick's reply, again and again. 'The working class is invincible. Revolution is inevitable. Moscow is only the beginning. A new future is at hand, for Jews and for everyone. Communism will lift us out of this grinding poverty and it will abolish all national and ethnic strife. Anti-Semitism will disappear. It's going to be a relic of the bourgeois past. Don't you see? Communism is the solution to all our problems, as Jews and as human beings. And Russia is showing the way.'

'Listen, I know Russia. I know it better than you ever will from your books and your lectures. Remember, I spent two months in a Russian prison. I know that country.'

Mick fell silent for a second; he could not trump this fact. It was true, Morris Mindel had indeed been jailed back in the old country. His crime had been to distribute leaflets promoting the Bund. It was one of the reasons, besides the pogroms, why he had had to get out.

'It's different now,' Mick said finally, quieter than before. 'Marx says, the contradictions and the crises of capitalism . . .'

'I can't talk like they talk in your classes, Mick, but believe me there are things about Russia that even your precious Communist Party cannot change. You would need another revolution in Russia before the real revolution could begin.'

'I don't know what you're talking about,' Mick would say, shovelling down another mouthful of his mother's potato *kugel*, before heading off for that night's communist gathering.

Morris could only shake his head.

The father must have known he was in an unequal contest for the allegiance of his son. The times were so desperate, only a radical solution seemed up to the task. Carving out a space for Yiddish theatre and song might have been a lovely ideal in its day, thought Mick and his peers, but now there was a global crisis to be reckoned with. In the 1930s Britain, Europe and the United States were in the grip of a depression. Mick could see it right there, on Flower and Dean Street. The men without work, forced to get by on seven shillings a week. They would walk with their heads lowered, humiliated by their dependence on charity: the signing on three times a week, the means-testing to prove they were as poor as they said they were. He saw the families, his neighbours, evicted because they could not pay even their meagre rent. He read of the men all over Britain marching to protest at the hunger that was shrivelling their guts. Mick did what he could to help, organizing a whip-round of second-hand clothes right there in the East End: the desperate helping the destitute. Mick believed that the Jews of Flower and Dean Street and the shipworkers of Tyneside and the miners of Kent were suffering together, all victims of a common enemy whose name was capitalism. It never would have advertised the fact, but the Communist Party was making an Englishman of Mick Mindel: now he cared not only about Jews but also about his fellow countrymen, and his fellow human beings.

Morris could not compete with a world depression for his son's attention. He did not have a battery of charismatic leaders to call on, no one to match the Pollitts, Peter Kerrigans, Johnny Campbells and Palme Dutts that so wowed young Mickey. He could not talk the way they did, impressing believers like Mick with their erudition and their transparent honesty. He did not have a model society to point to either: there was no Bundist republic, hailing itself as a beacon for the cause of international progress. The communists had the Soviet Union; Morris and the Workers' Circle had only their dreams.

But even if Morris had been able to match Mick argument for argument, example for example, he would still have lost – and not only because sons usually want to march one step further than their fathers, whatever the endeavour. The Communist Party offered Mick something Morris and his strudel-eating chums could not: a love affair.

The first Mick Mindel knew of Sara Wesker was her name. In 1926 she became, briefly, an East End celebrity, just as he had been a couple of years earlier when he won the Jack Hobbs bat. Mick was walking down Commercial Street when he saw the *Daily Herald* poster blasting the news: 'Trouser workers strike for a farthing a pair.' The all-female workforce at Goodman's factory had walked out, led by a young trouser machinist called Sara Wesker.

Three years passed before Mick met her. They were both at that election rally for Harry Pollitt, he a curious young neophyte, she a seasoned militant. She immediately set to work on him, urging Mick to join her breakaway United Clothing Workers' Union, a 'red' union tied to the Communist Party rather than the TUC. He muttered something about it not being right: her 'red' union represented those who worked on men's clothes, Mick was a cutter in the ladies' wear branch of the industry, in an era when such distinctions mattered. But Sara kept on at Mick Mindel all the same.

She was hardly a natural draw for Mick. Less than five feet tall, she was arrestingly sallow: Mick thought she was ill. But she always looked that way; the Communist Party grew so worried, they once dispatched her to a Crimean spa in a bid to improve her health.

The Soviet doctors could not find anything wrong. Pale and sickly was just the way Sara Wesker was – though the chain-smoking and the near-permanent bronchitis it brought on cannot have helped.

But when she spoke, Mick felt his pulse race. She was a ferocious speaker, as if the energy of five men was balled up inside that miniature frame of hers. In their communist circle, she was a star – a natural agitator and organizer whom others could not help but follow. No wonder, thought Mick, the Goodman girls had marched behind her in 1926; he wondered how anyone could ever refuse. And she was respected, even by the older generation. She not only understood Yiddish but, unlike Mick, spoke it fluently. She could talk to the old women in the sweatshops, and persuade them to talk to her.

When Mick met her in that 1929 meeting, he was a lad of nineteen and she an accomplished activist of twenty-seven. She became his teacher, allowing him to see the world through her eyes. Such an age gap was unheard of, in the East End as much as anywhere else. Nevertheless, Sara and Mick became a permanent fixture in the Rothschild Buildings – the two of them always together. And eventually they became lovers.

Morris the bookbinder never stood a chance. And yet decades later, when people would ask Mick Mindel why he became a communist, his answer would rarely dwell on the inspiration of the Soviet Union, the camaraderie of his friends or even the bond with Sara Wesker. He would mention instead the threat that loomed over them all – anarchist, Bundist, Zionist and communist – making a mockery of the differences between them. In later years it would seem so straightforward. Why did Mick Mindel become a communist? Because he believed the communists were the only people fighting the greatest menace in human history: fascism.

Mick read enough of the papers to know that nationalism was on the march in Europe. He had watched Mussolini tighten his grip on power in Italy; he had sniffed the wind blowing out of the pubs and on to the streets of the East End. But there is no substitute for the evidence of your own eyes and Mick was about to see the face of danger.

It was sport which gave him his chance. In July 1932 the Stepney Jewish Association, a club with reddish sympathies, was invited to play in a left-organized tournament in Germany. For the lads from Spitalfields, it was a precious opportunity: holidays were rare, foreign travel even rarer. This would be rather more swanky than the usual kickaround on Thrawl Street. For three weeks, they could pretend to be soccer internationals.

Their first fixture was in Cologne, an evening game with a six o'clock kick-off. They were in the dressing room when they began to hear a strange, dull surging sound outside.

'What the hell's that?' one of them would say.

It sounded like a truck or the carcass of a huge beast being dragged across the ground.

'Shhh, listen,' said another, crouching to tighten the laces on his boots. It took them a while to realize the noise was, in fact, a crowd of people, pushing and shoving. 'Crikey, are they all here to see us?'

They stepped outside, Mick and his team mates barely dressed. What they saw was not a group of football fans, excited about a match, but a herd of people in fear of their lives. They were running away. Mickey swivelled around and saw instantly the source of the danger. A clutch of Brownshirts known as the SA, the paramilitary wing of Adolf Hitler's National Socialist Party, were shooting into the crowd – brazenly raising their guns and taking aim.

Mick caught a glimpse of their faces. There was nothing taut or strained: the muscles were relaxed, as if in pleasure. It could have been a Sunday afternoon grouse shoot. It was this laughing cruelty that terrified Mick more than anything he had ever seen. He looked for no more than a second before wheeling around and dashing back inside. But that moment would stay with him for ever.

The team were soon joined in the dressing room by the German organizer of the tour, breathless with fear. 'I am sorry but the match, we are having to cancel it. The police are banning it. The fascists are killing people out there!'

Later, Mick and the Stepney boys were told that nine people had died and twenty-six had been wounded in what was officially termed 'an exchange of fire'. It was said that some in the crowd had shot back at the Brownshirts, though Mick was never sure. As far as the comrades were concerned, the fascists had set out to disrupt a left-wing gathering and they had succeeded.

The team left Cologne and completed the rest of their nineteen-day tour, journeying from one city to the next. But they were no longer there to play football. In each place Mick would probe his fellow leftists about the Nazi danger, pressing them for details. He hardly needed to ask. Wherever he looked there were banners aloft, dozens of them, each one vaster than the one before – all bearing the new shape that Mick's German friends explained was called the 'swastika'.

A few months later Mick was back in Germany. With heroic perseverance, the organizers wanted to have another crack at staging their socialist friendly international. Mindel was picked once again – both for his energy on the field and for his competence in Yiddish, which, the organizers assumed, would translate into proficient German.

He arrived in Berlin at the end of January 1933. He headed out of the railway station into the cold early morning and heard it straight away: the shake of collection boxes. He turned to see a group of Brownshirts staging an apparent charity drive. He could not make out what they were saying, so he inched closer. But when he heard the slogan, and realized what it meant, he froze.

'Passports for Palestine! Passports for Palestine!'

The Nazis were asking Germans to contribute to the deportation of their fellow citizens, the Jews. And people were gladly dropping coins in the box. Mick shuddered. As a boy he remembered walking past the Catholic school, enduring chants of 'Jew bastard!' and 'Christ-killer!' But most of his life, in the cosy enclave of Rothschild Buildings, he had been insulated from anti-Semitism. He had always been surrounded by Jews like him. Now he saw a movement burning with hatred of his people.

There was a tap on his shoulder. It was his student host, a socialist who would face him on the soccer field and put him up for the week.

'I know, I know, it's awful,' he was saying. 'But don't worry. There is no way the German working class will fall for this shit. The Nazis will burn themselves out. No one takes them seriously. Have you seen Hitler perform? The man's a clown. Anyway, you must be starving. Let's get you something to eat.'

They headed down a side street, but reached a dead end. It had been blocked off with a police cordon. 'Don't worry,' said his host again. 'I know another way.' But that too was blocked, this time by a lorry aiming a bright searchlight. People were shouting, some barking orders.

Mick shielded his eyes. 'What on earth's going on?'

'They're saying someone's been killed. I can't tell if it's a Nazi who killed a policeman or the other way around. We'd better get back to my apartment.'

Mick's head was swimming: the tiredness from his journey, the adrenalin rush of all he had seen. He wanted to know everything. His host had invited friends that evening, and Mick pumped them for information.

'What are you doing to stop the Nazis?' he would ask, in one form or other, over and over again. But he was shocked by the response. Instead of agreeing with him, and each other, that the Brownshirts were the enemy and they must all unite to defeat them, these German leftists were constantly fighting against themselves.

'The Social Democrats are social fascists,' one communist student said. 'The gap between us and them is as large as the gap between us and the Nazis.'

'Do you see what I mean, Michael?' His host shrugged. 'You'd have thought no one could say such a thing now, with everything that's going on, wouldn't you? Thankfully some of the people at the top, the leaders, now understand we have to work together.

But the message hasn't quite got through to the troops yet.' He gestured in the direction of his stubborn communist friend. 'You can't even have dialogue with these people.'

'But you could all be so strong!' shouted Mick, bursting with frustration. 'The Communist Party here won 6 million votes. The SPD is powerful. Why not form a united front against fascism?'

'No, it could never work,' said the communist. 'The Communist Party is the true embodiment of the proletariat, and leadership of the class struggle belongs to it and it alone.'

'Ah, and we haven't even told you about the trade unions,' said Mick's host with a weary smile. 'Do you know, Michael, that there is a separate union for the communists, another for the socialists and another for the Catholics – all in the same industry? Can you believe it? If we try to organize a general strike against the Nazis, bringing everyone together, nothing happens. We are paralysed.'

'I can't believe this,' said Mick, as dumbfounded as he had been by the scene at the railway station that morning. 'I just don't understand it.'

'Listen, Michael, you're a worker.'

'I'm a tailor.'

'Swear to me you won't make our mistake. When you get back home, you have to do what you can to unite workers against this menace. Please, promise me. Start with your own industry. Do you promise?'

And there and then Mick made a vow, to become active in his trade union and to strain every muscle to avoid in Britain the divisions that were bringing such calamity to Germany. He and his host shook on it.

The communist was no longer at the table but standing by the window. 'Look over here,' he said, pointing at the street below.

Mick rushed over. The road seemed to be on fire, submerged under a carpet of flames. His eyes adjusted and he realized he was looking at torches – hundreds, maybe thousands of them. Carrying them aloft was a marching column of Brownshirts, shouting slogans and singing martial anthems that Mick could not make out.

Occasionally they would let out a roar at full volume. It was 30 January 1933 and they were celebrating the installation of a new chancellor of Germany: Adolf Hitler.

Mick returned to London with a new and raging determination. Until then he had been involved in politics as much out of habit and friendship as iron conviction. For him, the Communist Party was a social circle, selling the *Daily Worker* on Flower and Dean Street with his closest chums. His favourite party activities had been those involving music or sport.

After Berlin, Mick would say, politics became more important than pleasure. He had seen the enemy and had made a vow to play his own part in taking it on. That Nazism was an ugly, violent force consumed with Jew-hatred, he had witnessed first hand. But, as a communist, he did not want to believe that this was a problem for the Jews alone. He would tell people back home that this was a challenge for the entire working class.

His conversation in Berlin the night of the torchlight parade had taught him another lesson. He concluded that trade unions, solid and united, were the sturdiest bulwark against fascism: if workers were united, no gang of thugs could defeat them. Germany had fallen because it had lost that wall of defence; workers had let their own divisions bring it down. He was now honour bound to prevent any such thing happening on his watch.

His first step would be to join a trade union. He had already refused Sara's enticements to sign up to her red union. He had no doubt now that that breakaway body was a classic case of the German disease, splitting workers off from each other rather than bringing them together. He would have none of it.

No, the group for him was the United Ladies' Tailors' Trade Union. He had tried to join it once a couple of years earlier, but had been rejected. They had told him he was not skilled enough to have a union card and that he should apply again a year later. That was typical of the union: it was more a craft guild than a movement of workers. By the standards of mass labour movements, it was small, never counting many more than 3,000 members, and intensely local. Its members lived in a few neighbouring streets and they were almost all Jewish, many of them immigrants of Mick's father's generation: the union's financial statements appeared in both Yiddish and English.

They were a notoriously difficult bunch to organize. The seasonal shift from busy to slack meant that no sooner had you built a membership than it dissolved and had to be rebuilt from scratch. It did not help that workers were not concentrated in one place – like a factory – where recruitment might be made systematic, but broken up into a thousand little workshops. The clothing industry was all about subdivision, with distinct skills and customs attached to each section. Mick would rattle them off: Savile Row tailoring; mantle and costume (women's outer wear, suits and coats); men's dress and light clothing; shirt, collar, tie and pyjamas; hat, cap and millinery; corsets and overalls. He always tickled people when he listed the last two categories: ostrich feather and fancy, and coffin lining.

Back in the old days, before the First World War, forging a united union had been even harder. Each trade insisted on organizing in its own way: a union for the trouser makers, another for the waistcoat makers. There might be just twenty-five people in a room but, no matter, they would declare themselves the International Society of Tailors. It was in this same era, before the Aliens Act of 1905 cracked down on 'pauper aliens', that wave after wave of immigration flowed into the East End, complicating matters yet further. Each brought a fresh supply of desperate workers only too ready to break a strike if it gave them a crust of bread. The act staunched the flow, by demanding proof from new arrivals that they had jobs to go to. But until then, in the last years of the nineteenth and first years of the twentieth centuries, immigration was as constant as the tides, changing the workforce of the East End with each new wave.

And there was that special Jewish factor, which delighted Mick even as it drove him crazy. To put it politely, Jews were not easily led: they would argue and debate rather than follow any guidance from the top. They had to be convinced of every decision; nothing could happen without an argument. Little wonder that London alone saw dozens of different Jewish tailoring trade unions come and go in the forty years leading up to the Great War, each with its own string of initials, forming an alphabet soup of confusion that would drown any workforce, let alone one whose relationship to English was remote at best.

This was the world young Mick wanted to enter and reshape. He was certain that the Jews were making a mistake. The more fragmented they were, the weaker they would be. There was strength in numbers, even in meagre ones like theirs; a united Jewish union had to be better than two dozen splinters. But Mick wanted to go further. Berlin had convinced him that the Jews could not fight fascism alone. They would have to make common cause with their non-Jewish brothers.

He knew this would be a struggle. The *schmutter* or 'rag trade' of the Jewish East End was a distinct, closed world – complete with its own language, customs and rhythms. The busy periods led up to the fashion seasons, mid-January to Easter and August until the Lord Mayor's Show in November. The rest of the time was slack. It was a cruel calendar, forcing families to stretch money earned during thirty-odd weeks far enough to last all year. Even when they were nominally at work, people could come home with nothing. They might make a single dress, a sample – and then spend the rest of the day waiting around, praying that a manufacturer liked the sample enough to order more.

In 1934, when Mick was finally allowed to join the union, working conditions were appalling. The small sweatshops would be freezing in winter and baking in summer, the rooms turned into furnaces by the hot steam irons kept in an alcove to one side. The light was weak: you could go blind straining to see the stitches on a cuff or aligning the checks on a woman's coat. If a fur collar was required, your heart would sink: that meant using a fur needle, which brought pain and blisters. Or there would be the special orders, the requests to cut the cloth for a woman with fifty-two-inch hips or a seventy-inch bust, a right arm longer than the left or a four-inch hump in the middle of the back. These 'singles' were hated on the shop floor: they took more time but earned no more money.

For all that, the atmosphere in the sweatshops was not hellish. There would be constant banter between the workers, even though they all occupied different notches in a minutely calibrated hierarchy. At the top came the employer, a master tailor whose job was to provide finished clothes to the manufacturer. But there was also a machiner, who would have his own set of workers below him. Cutters, the aristocrats of the workshop, allocated work to underlings too, while pressers would call on the assistance of a second presser and an under-presser, while tailors had under-tailors to help them.

In this complex ecology, everyone knew their place and jealously defended their specialist skill. Pressers had the machismo: operating the Hoffman steam presses was dirty work, requiring brute strength. In the wild East End, they were the gunslingers, each with his own style and his own reputation. As if to make up for the grime of the daylight hours, off duty they were the nattiest dressers in town. The machiners could be tough nuts too: it was not unknown for one or two to slip out from the sweatshop and head to the Whitechapel Pavilion for a bout in the boxing ring. Elite ranking was conferred on the cutters and the general tailors, those whose skills were not confined to one stage of the process but who could 'make a garment through', from start to finish. The women were to be found among the 'felling hands', hand-sewers who attached buttons or finished the hemline on skirts. Earning a third of the men's wages, even for the same job, they were usually young, daughters of immigrants waiting to become wives. Their dialect was East End, a cockney English heavily salted with Yiddish. (Among them were some non-Jewish women, known as 'kippers' because they tended to work in pairs. That was, they said, for safety's sake: they feared the attentions of their male employers or colleagues.)

Mick would listen to them all, hearing their complaints about the piece rates which saw them paid according to how many garments they had finished in a day rather than a fixed, reliable wage. He would hear stories of workers who had asked for a pay rise and been sacked on the spot. He would see the signs above the door: 'No notice given, no notice taken.' Workers had no rights. If they fell sick for a day, they lost a day's pay. Most would turn up for work and carry on, no matter how ill they felt. The economy of the 1930s was weighed down with depression; workers believed they were too weak to demand anything better.

Rebellion was tricky in such a close community too. Mick realized that some sweatshops would be impossible to organize: they were family businesses, with the employer's wife working as a hand, a brother-in-law on the presses and a son learning how to operate the machines. It would not be easy to lead those people out on strike.

Everyone worked at such close quarters; there was nowhere for the boss to have his tea except sitting down with his workers. Everyone knew everyone else's business. Mick would tell the story of the tailor who made the mistake of inviting the boss to his daughter's wedding. The family had saved for years and they made sure to throw a proper party: everyone had a high old time, including the employer. On Monday morning, he called in the father of the bride and fired him: 'The only way you could afford a *simcha* like that is if you're pinching from me.' Perhaps he assumed the tailor was selling 'cabbage' on the side. (Cabbage was important. Say the manufacturer had asked for sixteen coats to be made from a roll of cloth. A skilful cutter could produce eighteen. Those extra two coats would then be sold to a trader at the Petticoat Lane street market, with the tailor pocketing the money. That was cabbage.)

Most days the employers seemed to hold all the power. Yet somehow the workers would find a way to hit back. They would call instant, wildcat strikes. If spirits were high, they would put down their needles, turn off the machines and start banging their tin mugs on the table, singing revolutionary anthems until a representative of the union turned up to argue with the boss on their behalf. While they waited, the youngest worker would be sent out to the other sweatshops with a collecting tin. Most gave, knowing that sooner or later they would be the ones asking for help.

Mick saw all this and wondered why the Jews of the East End had not converted en masse to communism a long time ago. Surely they were living proof of the horrors of exploitation; they could see how capitalism unbound could grind down a human life. And yet communism would never command a majority, not in the *schmutter* trade as a whole and not in the union. Some saw it as less a threat than an eccentricity. Look what happened to Grabel the machiner. He was a red, always complaining about the conditions in the workshop. 'It's too hot,' he would say. 'We must open the windows.' One day, when Grabel stepped out, the others put some night lights under his chair. He came back and started up again: 'It's boiling in here.'

'What is it with you and the heat?'

'I'm *shvitzing*! This chair feels like it's on fire!'

'You're going mad, Grabel.'

It took him two hours to realize what his fellow workers had done.

It was its own world, and most believed the only ones who would ever understand it were those who lived in it. 'No, times are changing,' Mick would say to anyone who would listen. 'We cannot live in our own cosy little ghetto for ever. We need the protection of a national umbrella. We should merge with the National Garment Workers' Union.'

Everyone knew what that meant. The Ladies' Tailors had debated amalgamation at least twice before, always pulling back – usually at the very last minute. They had even tried it once, in 1906, but tensions between the Jews and 'the English' soon broke it apart. There were labour arguments, including the belief that distinct skills merited a specialist craft guild. There were prejudices, chiefly the fear that a national union would demand equal status for female workers, an idea few Jewish men could stomach – tradition taught them that a woman belonged at home. (On the other hand, and barely noticing the contradiction, they also worried that a pool of non-unionized women would be a source of cheap labour, putting them out of a job.)

But none of this was the heart of the matter. 'Only Jews know how to deal with Jewish problems,' was the reply Mick would hear whenever he suggested winding up the separate Jewish union and moving into the larger, British one. His own father, and many of Morris's friends in the Circle and in the Yiddish press, took the same view. 'What non-Jewish officials could negotiate on our behalf? What *goy* would understand why a worker needs time off to sit *shiva*?'

'But we have bosses who refuse that even now,' Mick would say, 'even when it's argued by a Jewish official in Yiddish! We need the muscle of a national union behind us. Besides, new machines are coming which will change the way we work. Soon the sweatshops will be gone and we'll all be in large, mass-production factories. The days of an old craft society like this one are fading. We should negotiate our pay along with the rest of Britain's garment workers. When they get a pay rise, we should get one. When they get holiday pay –'

'Holiday pay? Are you mad? Can you imagine such a thing? Holiday pay!'

The union old guard soon heard of the young firebrand stirring trouble among their members – and a communist to boot! In 1936 Mick was visited by two officials from union headquarters who told him he had joined the union under false pretences. He was a manager, they said, and therefore ineligible.

'A manager? What are you talking about?'

'We have a report that you are involved in employing workers.'

'I'm a *cutter*,' Mick said, furious. 'Cutters allocate work. That's part of the job. You know that.'

'I'm sorry, but that is the final decision of the union executive. We are here to serve formal notification that you are hereby expelled.'

Mick fought back. He tracked down the man who had reported him, an orthodox Jew who soon admitted that he had been 'encouraged' to lodge his complaint. Mick pleaded with him. 'Doesn't the Torah forbid the bearing of false witness?' he asked, suddenly remembering those interminable religious instruction classes at school. 'Isn't that what you did against me?' The man cracked and begged forgiveness, but Mick wanted more than an apology. He marched his accuser down to a commissioner of oaths and had him swear that the charges were false. Mick was reinstated as a union member, but not before his name had once again become a local legend. Twenty-five years old, and Mick Mindel was an East End celebrity for the second time.

More important, he was honouring the commitment he had made in Berlin. He thought back to that evening often. At party meetings in London he would hear what was happening to comrades in Germany: how communists, socialists and trade unionists were imprisoned, harassed, beaten up and worse. And he heard about the Jews, humiliated on the streets, their stores boycotted, their lives made a misery. He read about the Nuremberg Laws of 1935, banning Jews from mixing with Aryans. Now Spain looked set to fall to fascism too, with the country plunged into civil war. What he felt that torchlit night only intensified now. Fascism was getting nearer. Those who wanted to stop it had to stand together.

Mick, whose name now generated something of a buzz, began making speeches around the East End, usually to union branches. 'Spain today, Britain tomorrow,' he would say, alerting his Jewish neighbours to the man who aspired to be a British Franco or even a British Hitler: a former Labour MP with a stylish wardrobe and a nice line in rabble-rousing rhetoric by the name of Oswald Mosley.

Anti-Semitism was nothing new to London Jews. At the turn of the century, the British Brothers' League had campaigned against the 'aliens' entering the country, stealing jobs, they said, and draining the nation's resources. Plenty of trade unions shared those sentiments, building an anti-immigrant, anti-Jewish climate of opinion that finally expressed itself in the Aliens Act of 1905. But the British Union of Fascists thirty years later struck East End Jewry as something far more terrifying. To Mick, Mosley's Blackshirts looked no different from the gangsters he had seen in brown in Cologne and Berlin. They were violent, ready to beat Jewish heads on the street or to put lit rags through the letter boxes of Jewish homes and workshops. And they were confident, convinced that fascism was on history's winning side.

Fascist strongholds popped up all over east London, in Bethnal Green, Shoreditch, south Hackney and Poplar, encircling the Jewish community crammed into Stepney. 'Over there,' the fascist speakers would say, gesturing to an unseen ghetto wall, 'the Jews have got your houses. Over there, the Jews have taken your jobs.' Never mind that the Jews within were living in slums, eight to a room, with bedbugs for company and barely a coin in their pocket. That message – suspicion of the alien – struck home.

Fascism had another appeal too. Mosley offered men who had nothing, hard-luck cases and unemployed drifters, a uniform and a chance to swagger. Once they were losers; now they wore shiny boots, a leather sash and a dashing insignia. Mosley would give them a place to go, taking over disused pubs, even churches, and converting them into military-style headquarters. They would travel around in vans with wire mesh over the windows. A nobody could feel like somebody. In September 1936, after a long hot summer, Mosley called a rally of his troops in Hyde Park and was rewarded with a substantial crowd. Jewish worry turned to fear.

Mick was desperate that Britain should not make the Italian, German or Spanish mistake. He was delighted when tens of thousands of Jews marched through the streets of Hackney to protest against Hitler, but he was adamant that the Jews could not win this war alone. They needed allies.

Driving himself hoarse, he would tell audiences that Jews and non-Jews had to work together. 'We have done it before,' he would say. 'Look at what happened in 1889, when the East End tailors went on strike just a few weeks after the dockers had been out. The dockers won their dispute fairly quickly, but the tailors were not so lucky. You know what those dockers did? They promptly took what money was left in their strike fund and gave it to the tailors! Now that's what I call working-class solidarity. Or look at 1912, when the tailors of the East End went on strike in sympathy with our West End brothers. That proved something to the wider labour movement. We proved our manhood then, didn't we? And wouldn't you know it, but the dockers were on strike that same year as well. And by the end of it, those dockers were really suffering: their families had been without money for so long. And I bet not many of you know this – you won't have read *this* in the *Jewish Chronicle* – the Jewish working class lent a hand of solidarity to the dockers in those dark days. Jewish families took in three or four hundred dockers' children and they fed those children. And the local Jewish shops gave clothes and the bakers gave food. Now that's what I call working-class unity! We owed them for 1889 and we paid them back in 1912. It may have been a long time ago, but the dockers have not forgotten and nor should we. We were there when they needed us, and they will be there when we need them!'

The moment came sooner than anyone expected. Soon after the Hyde Park rally came word that Mosley wanted to stage his largest ever event by parading his fascists right through the Jewish East End. It would be a deliberate provocation, a show of strength calculated to terrify the Jews.

Immediately Stepney hummed with debate. Should the Jews try to stop Mosley or should they keep their heads down and let the event pass quietly? 'Don't play into his hands,' said those in the second camp. 'A fight is what he wants. The only thing we'll get from a battle is a lot of Jewish blood.' The Jewish establishment took the same view. The Board of Deputies of British Jews, the self-styled Anglo-Jewish parliament that dated back to the eighteenth century, urged people to stay off the streets. The Labour Party, which represented most moderate Jewish opinion in the East End, including Bundists like Mick's father, Morris, counselled similar caution.

Only the communists, backed by the Independent Labour Party, demanded that the Jews stand firm. Mick was never prouder of his party than then. Beyond ideology, beyond comradeship, beyond even his love for Sara, this was the reason why Mick Mindel was a communist – because the Communist Party understood, better than any other group, the threat of fascism and was ready to stand up to it. Stopping the Nazis had now become Mick's chief reason to care about politics and, as far as he was concerned, the communists were the only ones prepared to do it.

Committees sprang up all over Stepney, Jews and non-Jews working together to plan their resistance to Mosley. The Communist Party booked the Mile End baths for a large public meeting and each cell of activists went out to spread the word. Mick's patch was Stepney Green. Normally he would have covered the area with posters, but time was short and the moment seemed to call for a dramatic gesture. In the early hours of the morning, he and two comrades headed out, armed with cans of whitewash. In huge letters, they painted their message on the surface of the road. So big, you could not miss it: 'Smash Fascism! Meeting: Mile End Baths, Wednesday, 7.30.'

They stepped back to admire their handiwork when they noticed two uniformed men watching them from the pavement: police officers, one of them an inspector. Mick shuddered. He found himself thinking of his father's stint inside a Russian prison cell. The inspector was heading over, walking across the street in slow, deliberate steps. Mick noticed his truncheon, gleaming under the streetlight.

The policeman stopped, staring down at the message now glowing on the tarmac in luminous wet paint. He stretched out a boot, what Mick took to be the first movement of a kick. But the policeman seemed to be doing something else. He was using his foot to point at the giant '7.30' daubed below. And finally he spoke, a deep cockney, his voice the timbre of beer and pies: 'A.m. or p.m.?' Which is how Mick Mindel came to be illegally defacing the king's highway in the middle of the night, under the supervision of a serving officer of the Metropolitan Police. Neither Mick, his communist comrades nor the inspector left until the letters 'p.m.' were bold and clear for all to see.

By the morning of Sunday 4 October 1936 there was a fever in the air. Starting early, activists from the Stepney committees went into every street, using loudhailers to call the people out. 'Stop the fascists!' they cried, urging the Jews of the East End to halt Mosley in his tracks. People came out to see what the fuss was about; several complained that they had been woken up by all the commotion. But most grabbed their coats and headed out to the agreed meeting point: Gardiner's Corner.

They carried on like that, knocking on doors and calling out the Jews, for three hours, until their throats were cracked. By the time he got to Aldgate, Mick was exhausted. But the sight that awaited him gave him a blast of energy that he would remember for the rest of his life.

The entire area was blanketed with people, a swarming, heaving mass that ran all the way down Leman Street, filling it up like mercury in a thermometer. They said some 300,000 had gathered that day. Mick could not even guess: he had never seen so much humanity at once.

He spotted a familiar face, then another, but it was no good. He could not move. No one could. They were all pressed against each other, elbows jammed into bellies, hands inadvertently pressed on the backs of strangers. It was unlike any other demonstration he or anyone else had ever been on. No one shouted or sang or held up party banners. No one even sold the *Daily Worker*. You couldn't, there was no way to move.

The demonstrators had borrowed the Spanish republican slogan – *No pasarán!* They shall not pass! – and they were as good as their word. When Mosley headed westward along Cable Street, his men got into a fight with anti-fascist demonstrators. Later mythology would come to speak of the Battle of Cable Street, and there was indeed a skirmish there, but the humbler, more heroic truth is that it was not that clash that stopped the Blackshirts. Instead, when Mosley's men reached Royal Mint Street, they saw a crowd so vast it blocked entirely their path up Leman Street. Even the police could see there was no way through. The whole stretch up to

Gardiner's Corner was gridlocked. Through sheer weight of numbers, the Jews and their allies had made good their promise to Mosley: you shall not pass.

The elation that swept through the crowd as they heard of their victory was enough to send East End spirits soaring. For decades that day would be spoken of with bursting pride. It was Anglo-Jewry's Agincourt. Those young men who were not there would be ashamed to admit it, for every person who got squashed in that throng was a hero.

And it was not just Jews. While Mick and his comrades had been waking up the tenements in Stepney, others had headed to the docks to appeal to workers there – many of them Catholics. When Mick saw them at Gardiner's Corner, side by side with the Jewish poor of the East End, his heart swelled. Perhaps they remembered their debt of 1912 and were here to return the good deed. Perhaps, as dedicated trade unionists, they understood the threat fascism posed to them as well as the Jews. It did not matter why. To Mick Mindel, standing on tiptoes to survey the crowd that enveloped him that Sunday in 1936, this was a day to savour. Cable Street vindicated everything he believed. The Jews were not alone; they had allies and friends, and so long as they fought a shared struggle they would win. The Communist Party had shown the way. If Jews fought in the wider battle for universal justice, they would be safe. He was right and his father was wrong. If Jews looked after only themselves, they would be doomed. If they sought to change the world and cared about others, then those others would care about them.

Suddenly, jammed up against Mick was a man clutching a note-book, his head bowed from the pressure of people surging against him. He was a reporter from the *Manchester Guardian* newspaper, collecting demonstrators' opinions on what had just happened. Mick gushed and gushed, talking so fast the reporter could barely keep up. 'This shows that if we stand united we can beat anybody,' he said. 'The working class is invincible!'

7   *Hanging by a Thread*

Very recently a handful of photographs of my mother turned up. Some show her as a teenager at school in costume for a play. She seems to be dressed as a man; perhaps King Ahasueras, husband of Esther, in the Purim story. There is one of her as a baby and a handful of others: the chubby toddler, the formal schoolgirl. These were the first pictures of her as a child I had ever seen.

Growing up, I never found that as strange as I do now. It seemed to fit with the wordless sense I had of my mother's early life: that it had happened in some unknowable, hidden place, full of sadness

and pain. I suppose I thought her childhood was spent somewhere so dark no camera could capture it.

I never wanted to visit that place. I avoided the streets where my mother had grown up, even though, I now realize, they were only a few miles away. My father colluded in this: he was reluctant to visit too. His mission had been to rescue his bride from that underworld and it made him shudder even to glance back.

Yet I was curious. Even when I was very young I would love to listen to my mother's stories of her past. She is a great storyteller, peppering her accounts with sideways observations and Yiddish exclamations, until you cannot help but laugh and cry along with her. They were part folk legend, these stories – packed with characters of pathos and warmth, usually wrapped up with a moral – part fairy tale, telling of a little girl who went on great adventures, travelling far and wide, eventually confronting the one thing that terrifies every child most of all.

She was born Sara Hocherman on 1 November 1936 in Petach Tikva, a small town outside Tel Aviv in what was then British-ruled Palestine. She was two months premature, weighing just three pounds. The doctors were not hopeful. They were stretched as it was; a heavy depression was choking Palestine. Even in good times, they would have struggled to keep such a tiny mite alive. A challenge to twenty-first-century medicine, such an early arrival had next to no chance in the 1930s. 'Her life is hanging by a thread,' they told the child's parents.

The couple prayed and prayed hard. They were used to turning to God, and not only in moments of crisis. They were people of faith, their lives punctuated and ordered by the stipulations and timetables of religious observance. The little girl they had just brought into the world would be raised with the same beliefs. And yet her life would see them tested, almost to destruction. She was a Jew who would grapple with a question as ancient as the patriarchs: how to keep faith in a kindly God when so much of life is cold and harsh? How to stay a Jew when Jews have known such pain?

To the doctors, the baby's parents probably looked like every other young Jewish couple in Palestine: pioneers out to start a new life in a new land. But, in fact, neither fitted the profile of the average *chalutz*, or pioneer. Their past was different to most, and so was their future.

The young mother was unusual because she came not from Russia or Poland or even Germany, which had delivered the Yishuv the bulk of its population. Instead, she had made the journey from one of those countries whose Jews the Zionist ideologues coveted most. The true believers yearned for migrants who would come to Palestine not out of necessity, to escape persecution or destitution, but out of principle. They wanted volunteers from Western Europe and the United States, Jews from affluent, educated communities, who would enrich the new Zion rather than cling to it like a life raft.

These Zionist purists – and Nathan Mindel was one of them – regarded the Jews of the United States as the first prize. If these Jews could be persuaded that America was not the new Promised Land they imagined, not the *Goldene Medina* of emerging myth, and that the real homeland was where it had always been, then what treasure they might bring to Palestine! Rather than arriving at Haifa or Jaffa riddled with consumption, crumbs in their pocket and hollowness in their bellies, American Jews would come laden with wealth, knowledge and energy. They would make Zion what the ideologues insisted it was meant to be: an advanced oasis of Nobel Prize-winning, Jewish genius in an Arab desert of backwardness.

My mother's mother did not come from America but the next best thing. She was from Britain. Compared to the Jewish millions of Eastern Europe or the US, the few hundred thousand people who made up Anglo-Jewry would always be confined to a walk-on part in the Zionist drama. A British accent, while familiar in officialdom, was rare in the Yishuv; my mother's mother was almost exotic.

Back in London, she would introduce herself to non-Jews as Fanny, but everyone in the family called her by her Yiddish name:

Feige. It was pronounced fay-gee, the 'g' hard, as in geese. It sounded like a nickname, but it was not. Feige was who she was.

She differed from the rest of the Yishuv in another way too. She had made *aliyah* once already. In 1926 her father, a milkman based in Old Church Yard in the East End, had packed up his barrow, cashed in the little pile of savings he had salted away over the years and moved his entire family to the Holy Land. Ever since he had arrived in London in the last years of the nineteenth century as an immigrant from Biten, a *shtetl* near Bialystock in Poland, he had made weekly contributions to the First London Achuzah Company, a Zionist scheme which encouraged diaspora Jews to buy land in Palestine. He was not a wealthy man, Feige's father, but he was careful and by 1926 he had become the owner of 112 dunams of land in Karkur, near what is now the modern Israeli town of Hadera.

He began his journey to Palestine full of dreams; he imagined himself the owner of an estate, lush rolling countryside that would burst with the Lord's fruit. What he found was a swamp buzzing with malaria. He and his wife and their eight children, three sons and five daughters, along with his own mother and father, stuck it out for less than a year. The struggle was too much. They headed back to London, utterly defeated. They all wondered, but did not say out loud, whether this was the will of the Almighty. Was God testing them, seeing whether their determination to live in the land of Israel was strong enough to overcome a few obstacles strewn in their way? Was He urging them to try harder or punishing them for trying at all?

Feige's mother, whose health had been shaken by the near-death experience of giving birth to her first child, did not have the strength for Palestine or the stormy crossing back across the Mediterranean. Not long after their return to Britain she was dead. Two years later, her husband himself took ill. 'It's minor,' the doctors said. But he surprised them by refusing to get better. 'He lost the will to live,' they would say later. With his wife and his dream of Zion taken from him, he saw no reason to go on.

All this made Feige a novelty in the Yishuv: twenty-one years old and she was already an immigrant-turned-emigrant-turned-returnee to the land of Israel. Her husband, my mother's father, was just as exceptional.

While most of the Jews of Palestine were newcomers, he was virtually a native, brought up since infancy in Petach Tikva. It was his father, not he, who had been the immigrant, abandoning a life of comfort in Sosnowice in the south of Poland for the uncertainties of Canaan. Yehuda Ze'ev Hocherman had come to Palestine in the 1920s, which put him among the earlier waves of Jewish immigrants. Israeli textbooks tend to imagine these first pioneers as a single, ideological movement made up of avowedly secular Eastern Europeans who came to Palestine to build a socialist paradise. Many of them were indeed like that. But there were exceptions, and Yehuda Hocherman was one of them.

His Zionism was not steeped in the Marxist treatises of Ber Borochov, who argued that Jewish society lacked the 'base' on which all normal human activity, the push and pull of historical materialism, was conducted: namely, a territory. He was not a reader of A. D. Gordon, the Tolstoyan visionary who believed that Jews had become alienated from the soil and, if they wished to heal their broken spirit, would have to till the earth once more, becoming the peasant nation of their ancient roots. He did not join his fellow Eastern Europeans into the intimate *kvutsot*, the tiny communes where, in the name of undiluted socialism, everything had to be shared – from the clothes, including underwear, which hung in a collective cupboard, to each other's bodies. (Some of the more extreme groups held that to form a couple was to claim ownership of another human being, a small step towards property rights and capitalism itself. Therefore, to prevent couples pairing off, members of the intimate *kvutza* would sleep in groups of three: memoirs of the period recall the anxiety and loneliness of that third person as they played ideological gooseberry.)

Yehuda Hocherman was motivated by none of these socialist summons to Palestine. Instead he heard the call of God. He was that rare species in the Jewish world of the time, a religious Zionist.

'This is not Judaism,' his teachers would say, back at the *yeshiva* in Sosnowice, where he first began to dream of Palestine. 'It is for the Almighty to take us back to Eretz Yisroel [as they would have pronounced it], which He will do at the coming of the Moshiach. As we are taught, to return to the land of Israel *before* the Messianic age is to insult the authority of the Almighty. It is to put a stain on His name!' All this delivered in the same singsong intonation the *yeshiva* deployed for all educational speech: each lilt up or down sounding by turns quizzical or regretful. Extra emphasis was provided by a kind of horizontal hitchhiking gesture, the thumb pointing not at the sky, but towards the wall or the belly of the speaker, often alternating, metronomically, between the two.

'But look,' Yehuda would say. 'We are commanded to live in the land of Israel. As it is written, "*Lech lecha*. Go from your birthplace to the land that I will show you." Our sages state that the *mitzvah* of living in the land of Israel is equal to all of the other commandments of the Torah combined. The requirement to live in the land of Israel is so great that once you have entered Eretz Yisroel, you must never leave. We cannot ignore it!'

'Who's ignoring? Did anyone say we should ignore it? *Nechter g'tog* [As night differs from day]. The opposite! We recognize its centrality every day, three times a day! We pray using the same words: "And to Jerusalem Your city You shall return with mercy and You shall dwell in it." And why do you think the synagogue faces east? Is that a coincidence? The builder just chose to build it that way for his health? He built it that way for the same reason every synagogue in the world is built that way – to face Jerusalem!'

'Exactly!' Yehuda would reply. 'These prayers are reminding us, over and over and over again, that our home is not in Sosnowice or Vilna or Minsk or Warsaw or Hamburg or London or New York but Jerusalem –'

'Yes, but only when Moshiach comes . . .'

'But we do not *wait* for the Messiah before we can keep Shabbat. The other way around! We believe that by observing the Sabbath we will *hasten the arrival* of Moshiach. Our rabbis tell us that if all the Jews were to keep two consecutive Sabbaths, then the Messiah would come. Maybe it's the same with the return to Zion.'

'Yehuda Ze'ev Hocherman, do us all a favour. Read Ketubot. It could not be clearer. When Israel went into exile after the destruction of the Second Temple, three vows were made between Heaven and Earth. And the first of those was that Israel would not "break down the wall". What does that mean? It means we must not conquer the land of Israel by massive force. And that is what you are proposing.'

'But the Book of Numbers is equally clear! "And you shall dispossess the inhabitants of the Land and dwell in it." That gives us the authority to do what we need to do.'

'This is not Judaism,' his teacher would say again, the song now gone from his voice. 'Who are these Zionists? They are *apikorsim!*' This word, a Yiddishized version of a Greek term, meaning non-believers or atheists, was about as sharp a spear as he could hurl. He was saying that Zionists were heretics; their obsession with land

– even the land of Israel – bordered on idol worship. 'This is not Judaism,' he would repeat. It was no longer a debating point, but a ruling. Yehuda Hocherman was uttering what amounted to heresy. The academy listened closely to what he was saying. He was, after all, a star scholar, one whose academic prowess had won him, following custom, the daughter of one of the wealthiest men in the region. But this was too much.

By this time he was living with his young wife in a wing of her father's magnificent home – an estate with its own courtyard, servants and a *droshkey*, a horse and buggy ready for use around the clock. Hocherman had what every *yeshiva bocher*, every talmudical student, dreamed of: the chance to study for the rest of his life, subsidized by the fortune of his father-in-law.

But it was not enough. The call to Palestine grew louder. The more texts he read, the more prayers he decoded, the more unanswerable he found it. As a Jew devoted to honouring the Torah he could not pretend that one of its central instructions did not exist. He would have to move his wife and two young sons, Mordechai and Avraham, to Palestine. They would live in the town that was becoming the first Palestinian community of orthodox Jews outside Jerusalem since Roman times. Its very name was charged with future possibility: Petach Tikva, Gateway of Hope.

There Yehuda Hocherman, the Talmud *hacham*, the wise man of Sosnowice, quickly established himself as a man of scholarly authority. He became an associate of the Beth Din, the religious court, acting as a registrar of marriages. His wife, though, did not make the transition so smoothly. Rifka had never been a natural soulmate for Yehuda. She was a simple woman, her mind uncluttered with the intellect that marked out her husband: it was her dowry, and Jewish tradition, rather than her brains which had brought them together. She never learned the emerging language of the Yishuv, Hebrew, clinging instead to Yiddish. She could hardly read, but would instead close her eyes, sit back and ask for one of her children, and eventually grandchildren, to tell her a story. '*Zug me epis*,' she would say, if one came near: tell me a tale. She had a particular fondness for old Hassidic folklore: the stories of learned men disguised as beggars or of pious Jews forever journeying into the forest, legends which hinted at a divine Father sagely watching over all his Jewish charges – especially those who were modest and true to the holy law.

She produced six children, and with each one her health declined. By the time Avraham was a young man, his mother seemed to spend most of her days reclining on a divan, as if convalescing from an illness whose diagnosis was fated to remain unknown.

And through it all, her family back home never gave up the argument they had tried to win before the Hochermans left. Her father even trekked all the way to Palestine just to make the case in person. 'Come home,' he said. 'You do not belong in this land of swamps and disease. And what about all this trouble with the Arabs? Come back to Poland. There you will be safe.'

Rifka told her father she loved and respected him, but no. This was her home now. Her place was at her husband's side. She waved goodbye to him at Jaffa docks as he set off for the long voyage back to Poland. One sister eventually joined her in Palestine, but the rest of her family did not let go. They kept writing from Sosnowice, over the years which turned into decades, pleading with their sister to see sense: come back to Poland, where you will be free of danger. Eventually, by the late 1930s, the letters changed their tone. And in the early 1940s they stopped coming altogether. Rifka was never to hear from her family again.

Of Yehuda's sons, Avraham was the one most like him, intellectually at least. He too was a natural scholar, with a knack for language that made the holy texts open up to him eagerly, yielding their secrets without protest. He relished the fine, hair-splitting disputes contained within each sentence of the Talmud, within each word, often turning on a single letter. The more minute the tension, the more pleasure he would get from teasing it out. He would sit from dawn till night in the *yeshiva*; this was the place where he had spent his childhood and adolescence, and he did not want to leave. The precision of the inquiry, the fervour of the debate, as he and a fellow student would pore over the ancient words for hours at a stretch, sometimes referring their argument to a senior scholar, occasionally to the head of the academy, the *rosh yeshiva* himself – it thrilled him.

Avraham was noticed. The elders of his Gerer sect of Hassidim marked him out as a man of potential. In 1932 the sect's leader, Rabbi Avraham Mordechai Alter, the third Gerer Rebbe – his title recalling the place in Poland where the rabbinic dynasty had been founded – appointed him as an emissary. Aged just twenty, he would venture into the diaspora, give weekly synagogue talks in authentic Torah Judaism to those starved of the word of Ger. The rebbe looked at the map and pointed a crooked finger west of the Mediterranean, west even of continental Europe: Hocherman would go to London.

The East End was the obvious destination: more than 100,000 Jews were there, all crammed into a few dense streets. With *shuls* and *shteibls*, houses of prayer sometimes no larger than a cloakroom, every few paces, Avraham would be lucky to cover a corner of it before his three months were up. He enjoyed it: praying along with the congregation, then holding the floor with his interpretation of that week's Torah portion or, for the more advanced audiences, an extract of Talmud. And people were friendly. On Friday night there would always be someone to invite him back for a dinner of the heavy Ashkenazi food that was fast becoming a rarity in the hot climate of Petach Tikva.

Which is how he came to be sitting across the table from young Feige Bitensky. She had so many brothers and sisters, but somehow she was the one he noticed. With a shyness in her eyes, she struck him as somehow *English*. Maybe it was just the extra little touches to her appearance: the neat row of buttons down the side of her dress or the pin in her hair, but there was something refined about this girl which he liked. 'She looks *edel*,' he said to himself, still thinking in a mixture of Yiddish, Hebrew and English: refined, ladylike.

The attraction was instant and mutual. To her he looked more like a movie star than a *yeshiva* student: dark, clean-shaven and strikingly handsome. He had such confidence too, holding the whole table rapt as he unfurled one choice anecdote after another. He could mould even the most unpromising material into a tale to transfix his audience, and Feige laughed despite herself: she did not want to show too many smiles too early.

He found an excuse to come to the house again, and this time he spoke not of that week's *sidra*, the portion of the Torah read in synagogue, but of Palestine. He knew he was pushing at an open door. Feige's brother Benny had told him the family story that first time they met at the synagogue, before inviting him back home for Shabbat dinner. Avraham knew the Bitenskys had tried to make *aliyah* once already, some six years earlier. He could see the portrait of Theodor Herzl, the founder of modern Zionism, on the wall, apparently left there by his hosts' late father, Yisrael Mordechai, the red-headed milkman whose failure in Palestine had robbed him of his wife and his reason to live. That portrait was a surprise: most of the Jews in Avraham's Gerer sect would have hesitated before revering an avowed secularist like Herzl, the Hungarian journalist turned self-appointed Jewish statesman.

Now Avraham sat around the Bitensky dining table, focusing his charm like a beam of light into the eyes of Feige. 'You would have a wonderful life in Palestine, I guarantee it,' he said. 'You would wake each morning to blue skies and the sound of waves crashing on the beach. You could face the Mediterranean one way and the Jezreel Valley the other. Those malaria days you experienced are in the past now. The earth is fertile and the divine promise is being fulfilled: this truly is a land flowing with milk and honey.

'And Feige, I have big plans for the future. My brothers are builders and we will build a big house, large enough to house even the largest family.' Feige was sure she saw Avraham raise an eyebrow. 'Children will tend to the animals in the morning and play in the sea in the afternoon. It is a new life we are creating in our ancient land, just as HaShem promised.' (He was too devout to call God by his name, so he used the euphemism favoured by the orthodox: HaShem, the Name.)

He seemed so certain, Feige felt he must be right. His confidence was flowing across the table, as if to touch her fingertips. She felt her breath quicken. She thought of the East End: the narrow streets, the dirt that could never be cleaned away, the permanent grey clouds, the rain. And Avraham was not lying when he said Judaism demanded a return to the land of Israel: there were few higher duties than the command to live on that sacred soil. What was so special about east London that she would stay there, in direct disobedience of God? Why not live in the Promised Land, alongside this man with the sparkling brown eyes?

And so, for the second time, she headed to Victoria station, took the train to Dover, then a ferry to Calais, then a train to Marseilles and finally a ship to Palestine. Avraham Hocherman had seduced her. He returned from his three-month sojourn in London having delivered at least one new immigrant to Palestine: his own bride. The couple, both aged twenty-one, married in Ramat Gan, just outside the new city of Tel Aviv, in August 1933.

But Petach Tikva was not quite what she was expecting. True, the place was not the swamp her family had had to abandon six years earlier. But Avraham had built a castle in her mind and this was no castle. It looked more like a hutch than a house. Just three rooms, with a steel roof, it stood low and dirty on the town's main thoroughfare, Ahad Ha'am Street. She felt her heart dipping the first time she walked in.

Still, she had coped with dirt and hardship before. Back in London, she had had to fill the gap left by her parents, cooking, cleaning and keeping house – especially for her youngest siblings, who were almost infant enough to be her own children. That house too could have ended up a dump, but Feige had worked hard and she had never had to feel ashamed of where she lived. She would make the same effort here; with a woman's touch, she was sure she could create a marital home.

The trouble was, she and her new husband did not have this tiny place to themselves. They had to share it with his entire family. In one corner, his father, distant and mostly silent: rather than risk the sin of *lashon hara* – literally 'evil tongue' – and speaking ill of others, he preferred to say little, sometimes nothing. On the divan lay her new mother-in-law, permanently, it seemed, moaning and sighing

My mother's father's parents, Yehuda Ze'ev and Rifka Hocherman.

at the appearance of some new ache or pain. And, all around, her husband's brothers and one younger sister.

The eldest was Mordechai, a scholar like Avraham, who was out all day, doing what, nobody knew. Next came Menachem and Aaron. Less blessed with brains, they worked with their hands instead, making and lifting the crude breeze blocks used on building sites. Feige thought Aaron's skin was the darkest she had ever seen; he was so tall, he loomed over her. Menachem was not built that way: he was skinny, with tanned, leathery skin stretched over his visible bones. That was probably why the brothers worked as a pair, carrying the lead-heavy blocks between them, one at each end. It made the work lighter, but there was a price: they were only paid the wage of one man, which they had to share. (Even the half-loads eventually took their toll. Not many years later Menachem died from a massive heart attack, leaving behind a wife and three young daughters.)

The family did not end there. There was another brother, Naftali, and a sister, Tova. Years later the *shadchanim*, the neighbourhood matchmakers, would do their best for her, eventually finding a husband. But it lasted only a few months. Tova's destiny was to remain at home, the dutiful daughter ready with a glass of tea for her father when he returned from a day at the Beth Din. She barely had a glimpse of life.

Feige was still finding her feet in this new land, and new home, when she realized she was pregnant – it would have been a honeymoon baby, if she and Avraham had had a honeymoon. They had a boy, a curly-headed ball of energy they called Yisrael Mordechai, in memory of her late father, the thwarted Zionist pioneer. The family would always know him as Yisrolic, or Srollik for short.

Feige tried to do her best for him, but she did not know where to start in this shoebox of a house filled with the smell of men. It was all new to her: feeding the baby, coping in the Palestine heat, tending a family not her own, surrounded by a language she did not understand. And then, when Srollik was three months old, she became pregnant again.

Soon she had a daughter, a dark, pretty little thing they named Ronni, after her late mother, Ronya. Feige could contain herself no longer. 'I can't breathe in this house,' she sobbed to her husband, standing just outside the back door, the only place they could be alone. 'I can't even cry in there, there's no room,' she said, knowing that the family inside were listening to every word. She had never known such claustrophobia. There were beds under the beds, which would be rolled out at night. Every inch of floor was accounted for, and shared. 'You have to do something,' she wept, her nose streaming. 'You have to. You have to.'

So they moved out of that house into a place of their own. It was only one room, but it was theirs. Feige believed she had turned a corner; things were looking up. She would make life sweet for little Srollik and Ronni, just you see.

Avraham would go out every day, but, Feige noticed, only rarely would he return with money. Over the years two conflicting explanations arose for this, one for each side of the family. Avraham's brothers would say that he was always willing to work, it was just that there was so little of it about. He was ready to take his turn picking fruit for the equivalent of a couple of shillings – indeed, he once walked all the way from Petach Tikva to Jaffa, just for a day's shift in the orange groves – but, they would say, those opportunities were all too rare. Arab labourers, willing to work for even less money, got whatever thin pickings were going. Besides, the Hochermans would say, Avraham had ambitions to make money without digging ditches. He fancied himself a businessman. He tried running a hardware store in Tel Aviv, but the venture failed. He thought about a stone-quarrying enterprise, but that did not work out either. Later he became a highly skilled polisher of diamonds, but he was always diverted into deals and schemes that came to naught.

Feige's sisters would tell a different story. According to the Bitensky version, there was no shortage of work if Avraham had really wanted it. But Feige soon realized that was the problem: he did not want it. He found physical work demeaning; it was beneath a man of his talents. He would work for a day or two, bring home a few coins, and then spend the rest of the week in his real home: the *yeshiva*. There he could escape life's pressures, letting the hours vanish into the holy texts like water spiralling down a plughole. She could not work out this man she had married. Was he a dreamer, happier to lose himself in his books than deal with real life? Was he just lazy? Did he not care for her or their young family?

Feige was getting desperate. Money was so scarce, there was barely enough to buy food for the children. Yisrolic would tug at her skirt, Ronni would bleat: they were hungry. In the middle of it all, Feige became pregnant yet again, the third time in two and a half years.

She began to panic, scratching at her own skin; there is no panic greater than that of a mother unable to feed her young. She was nauseous each day, craving a chance to rest, to eat a good, hot meal and to be clean. She barely knew it, but she was not suffering alone. In 1936 Palestine faced not only the start of what would become known as the Arab Revolt; it was also bowing under the weight of a grave economic depression. That tended to hit the Arab sector hardest, but the poorest corners of the Yishuv were not immune.

Still, in another sense, the one that mattered, Feige was very much alone. She and her husband were not a couple, battling the odds together. He was not the protector she had imagined those Sabbath nights back in the East End, when he had thrown stardust in her eyes. He did not fight, or even provide, for his family. It was into this world that my mother was born and spent the first year of her life.

One night, as Feige once again peeled and mashed a few potatoes for the children's supper, she found herself consumed with rage. Where was her husband? Where was he when his own children needed him? She scooped up the three kids, six-month-old Sara tucked under her arm, and marched over to his parents' home, the one she had been so relieved to leave behind. She hardly ever went there, but now she marched through those Petach Tikva streets, rehearsing her lines all the way to Ahad Ha'am Street. 'Mr

Hocherman, you have to speak to your son!' she would begin. 'You must instruct him in the ways of a good Jewish man! You must remind him of the solemn contract he signed on our wedding day', when, in the words of their *ketuba*, he had promised to 'cherish, honour, support and maintain her in accordance with the custom of Jewish husbands'. 'He is not doing that! He has broken his vow. He is letting his children go hungry. Look at them!' she screamed in her head, the tears soaking her cheeks. 'Look at them! They need food!' She would say all that, and Yehuda Hocherman would listen. He was a man of Torah and of *rachmones*, of basic human kindness. He would intervene, in the name of Judaism itself.

She knocked on the door and waited. The children, who had been wailing throughout their unplanned walk, had fallen silent now, instinctively quieted by the heaviness in the air. The door finally peeled back. It was Menachem. Feige suddenly felt ashamed; she did not know where to start. And then she caught something in Menachem's face. He was looking down at his feet and she realized he felt the shame too. She wondered how she had passed on her feelings so instantly, how they were so infectious. She was puzzled, until she saw the scene over Menachem's shoulder. Sat at the sparse wooden table was Avraham, his father next to him and Tova standing between them both. In front of them were plates of food. Nothing special, perhaps a piece of carp and a slice of bread, but it was food.

Feige felt her lungs collapse. This was worse than any adultery. To catch her husband like this, his eyes wide with guilt, made the oxygen stop in her throat. He had run back to his mother and father to put food in his own belly while his children grew thinner by the day. He had not looked out for his son or daughter but taken care only of himself. He was not a man at all, she thought. He was a selfish, weak child. In that moment she hated him so much she could not bear to see his face.

She turned around, pulling Srollik and Ronni by their wrists, and clutching the youngest, Sara, tight under her arm. The girls were crying but Srollik was silent, his head down, his lower lip bitten white between his teeth. He was not walking but marching. He was just three years old but he seemed to burn with the anger of a man. Feige felt a stab of love for him; his determination enveloped her.

She returned to the 'flat' and slammed the door behind her. She understood that she was not a wife at all, but a woman alone. The tears were gone now; she could feel her heart hardening in her chest. Her only duty was to these children. She went back to the potatoes, pounding and mashing them with a new ardour. She wished she could make them appetizing; she hammered away, desperate to make them fluffy rather than simply crushed. If only she had some milk or butter or cheese. But there was nothing.

The loneliness was broken by just one person. Her eldest sister, Annie, had also made the journey to Palestine. Not that she had been swept off her feet, like Feige. The opposite: she had been promised to a Palestinian Jew in a marriage arranged by her father shortly before his death. The would-be groom's name was Binyamin and it was dislike at first sight. Annie found him a brute. He was ugly; she recoiled at the very idea of touching him. She pleaded with her father, but he would not be swayed. His answer to his daughter would live on in family legend for generations. 'But he's come all this way. We can't send him back empty-handed.'

So Annie lived in the poverty and hardship of 1930s Palestine too. Travel was difficult, phone lines non-existent, so her contact with her sister was only sporadic. But she had long planned a visit to see Feige and the kids and so pitched up in Petach Tikva shortly after the night of the secret supper.

She was shocked by what she saw. It was not the sparseness of her sister's home that did it, though that was striking even by depression standards. It was the children. They looked pale and sick, Ronni especially. Annie kept looking at this young girl, too small for her age. She seemed listless, her eyes too wide, too liquid. Annie gripped Feige's wrists and demanded to know, 'What on earth is going on here? What has happened to you?'

Feige tried not to tell; she was sure her religious duty was to keep quiet, not to defame the name of her husband. But the tears spoke for her. She explained that Ronni was indeed very ill and that she did not know what to do: the doctors said it was a disease that could not be cured. When Ronni's hair began to fall out they had told Feige to remove it all, but she could not bring herself to do it. 'I know what my child needs,' she sobbed quietly. 'She needs to eat, and I have nothing to give her.' Annie looked around and saw it was true. The kitchen was not worthy of the name. Every cupboard was bare.

Annie left Petach Tikva gripped by sadness. That night, away from her increasingly violent husband, she wrote to the brothers and sisters still in London. The letter was addressed to Benny, the next eldest after her, and probably the most capable of the bunch. 'They are starving,' she wrote, 'literally starving.' Fearing the worst, she added a sentence laden with anxiety: 'I don't know what will happen if we don't do something.'

By the time the letter had been circulated around the family in the East End, it was too late. Ronni Hocherman, not yet two years old, was dead. She left no mark behind; there are no photographs or mementoes of her brief life. No one is sure where she is buried, or even what final illness killed her.

Through all this, Feige never once asked for help from her family back home. Perhaps she was too proud, or too ashamed. But Annie had no such inhibitions, and now the Bitenskys acted. They had no money of their own. As my mother would put it years later, 'They had tuppence ha'penny. They just about had a chair to sit on.' But they did a whip-round and somehow scraped together a small amount of cash.

'With love I enclose a money order from all the family,' wrote Benny to his sister. 'It is sent by all of us, but I must stress an important condition. This money can only be used for one purpose. My dear Feige, you must go to the shipping agent right away and buy tickets for the passage to London for you and your children. If you use the money for anything else, then I have to warn you there will be nothing any of us can do. There is no more money. Please,

Feige, I am begging you. We are begging you. After the –' a word was crossed out, and then another – 'the events of the last few months, you need to come home. With fondest love, Your brother, Benny.'

Feige read the letter over and over again, stuffing it into the pocket of her housecoat, anxious that no one else should see it. Her head was throbbing. She wanted so desperately to leave, to be in a place where her children would not starve: young Sara seemed to have such a tenuous grip on life. She wanted to have her family close by, away from this strange brood she had married into. And, to her shame, she wanted to be away from the house where her first daughter had died. This house felt like the scene of a crime.

And yet she was a Jewish woman, raised in the traditions of piety and duty. Such women did not leave their husbands. How would she get away from him?

She worried away at the dilemma for days, until events took the debate out of her thoughts and into reality. It was evening when her husband, Avraham, suddenly wheeled round, his eyes bulging with fury. 'What is this? What is *this*?' he demanded, clutching the envelope from London. It must have fallen out of her housecoat. Or perhaps she had left it on the table during one of those moments when she had stared and stared at it, hoping that, maybe, if her eyes fixed on it long enough it would tell her what to do.

'Tickets,' she said, without thinking. She was worried the children would wake from all the noise.

'Where are we going?'

'I need to go home. I need to take the children –'

'But this is your home. You belong here with me.'

'I want to take the children to London. Just for a while. Just while we . . . just while you get back on your feet.'

'How much money is there?'

'What?'

'How much? How much money have they sent you?'

'I don't know, enough for tickets.'

Avraham was no longer standing. He sat back in his chair, his eyes back in their sockets. They began to twinkle. His voice was suddenly soft. 'Feige, I have a better idea.'

'I don't understand.'

'With that money, you and I can start a business. We can open a *gazoz*, a kiosk.' They were all over Palestine, little huts on street corners selling flavoured soda water, sometimes with ice. The bigger ones might sell sweets – hard, lumpy things with a sour flavour – but cold drinks were the core product. The Jews of the Yishuv, mainly Europeans unused to the parched heat of the Levant, were thirsty all the time. 'Feige, we'll make our fortune!'

She almost wanted to believe him. His eyes had the sparkle she saw that first night; he talked so well. He could persuade her of anything. 'Who would run it? Who would run this *gazoz*?'

'You, of course! A man cannot do such a thing. But I can manage the accounts . . .'

Feige was no longer listening. She was seeing instead the image now burned into her memory: her husband around his family kitchen table, served by his sister, like a baby in a high chair. She felt the hate coursing through her veins, heading towards her neck.

'NO!' she shouted, the decibels of her own voice making her jump. She had never heard herself shout so loud before. It scared her, her anger towards him. A kiosk! Another scheme, another wild promise. And of course it was she who would have to work from dawn till night, she who would be slicing lemons till her hands were raw, she who would have to smile and serve working men, their brows dripping sweat and their hands covered in grime, men like Avraham's brothers. He would not do a stroke of work. He would stay nuzzling up against his books, while she toiled. And who would look after her children? She would not let Srollik and Sara anywhere near that house of his, so crammed with people. Tova, his sister, was sweet but she would never be able to cope. 'I won't do it! I'm going back home.'

There was something in his eyes that scared her. 'I'll come back,' she said hastily. 'We'll just be a short while, while you have a chance to sort things out, to earn some money. Perhaps I'll be able to bring money back with me. It'll be for the best.'

'You mustn't do it,' he said, almost in a whisper. 'It is forbidden to leave the land of Israel.' He was quoting the words his father had inscribed by hand inside one of his sacred books. 'Once you have ascended to the land of Israel, it is forbidden to step down. It is wrong to leave the land of our fathers. The sages teach us that. *I* was taught that, from when I was a boy! No Jew should abandon Eretz Yisroel. You must not do it. It is a terrible crime.'

He was giving her the creeps. She could not look him in the eye. 'Like I say, it will only be temporary. The children need food. They cannot survive here.'

Avraham looked up at her, his eyes frozen as if in terror.

'You will not survive there.'

'What did you say?'

'It is a crime to leave Eretz Yisroel and you will be punished. You must stay.'

Feige felt dizzy. He had no right to ask her to stay, a wife he had failed so badly. If that was what he wanted, he should have offered to run the kiosk himself, though that prospect probably frightened him even more than saying goodbye to his wife and children. How dare he command her to stay? Still, she was troubled. He was a learned man: was he right that she was risking divine fury? Was he just threatening her?

They stopped talking and the debate became a silent one again, inside her head. She had only to look at Sara, such a skinny, weak child, to know what to do. Or remember Ronni. For their sake she would have to leave. She would come back when the time was right. But now she had to put her children first.

Within a few days she took her two children to the shipping line and handed over the money. From that moment she kept the tickets with her at all times, constantly patting her pocket to make sure they were still there. At night they remained under her pillow, her hand clenched around them like a claw. He would not take them from her; she would not let him stand between her children and survival.

And so, one sweltering day, she, Srollik and Sara packed their bags and headed for the port of Jaffa. The harbour was too shallow, so ships would anchor away from shore and passengers would be ferried to them in small rowing boats. Aboard a filthy cargo ship, they set sail on a long choppy voyage that seemed to take the most circuitous route possible to London. Finally they made it, a young single mother and her two gaunt Palestinian children hoping for a fresh start. It was August 1937.

8 Closing the Gates

The countryside was moving so fast, he could barely take it in. The shades of green, the long stretches of white, his eyes were struggling to keep up: it was all so different from the endless yellow-brown of the landscape back . . . in Palestine. He wanted to say 'back home', but it still did not sound right, even after he had lived there nearly twenty years.

It was 1939 and Nathan Mindel was on a Paris train bound for Switzerland. He had just spent a month in London – he could not quite describe that as 'home' either – visiting his brothers, seeing their children, looking up old friends. These visits always left him feeling melancholy. People were friendly enough, but he could not shake off the sense that he was somehow extraneous. He knew their lives had carried on without him, and would carry on after he had gone. He had once been part of their daily story, but no longer. He did not understand the references that peppered their conversation: he had not seen the latest Gracie Fields picture, he had missed the abdication crisis. He felt like one of the undead, returning to haunt those who believed he had gone long ago.

Still, that was nothing compared to the mission he was on now. The order had come late, asking him to break his journey back to Jerusalem with a stop in Basle for an urgent meeting. The topic could not be more serious. Yet every time he glanced away from the window, with its galloping forests and snow-covered hillsides, and down at his papers he felt his veins throb with dread. It was four o'clock and the wintry sunshine was beginning to peter out. He would be there in four hours.

He tried to focus on the task in hand, but he could not rouse himself. His eyes kept going back to the window. When did things change, he wondered? When did all this start? And the voice in his head came back with a one-word answer: Hebron.

When the call-up came, Nat had been thrilled. To be armed as a special constable, in the aftermath of Hebron, charged with defending the Jewish areas of Jerusalem seemed an honour. Now he would be able to do his bit, his way. He would be protecting Jews – but as a loyal officer of King George. This was how it was meant to be. After all, he believed that Zionism and the British Empire were not at odds: their goals were entirely compatible. Nat had been delighted to hold a rifle in his hands again, a decade after his discharge. And this was no remote Egypt campaign or service in Gallipoli; this was a British fight for his own people.

But once the Arabs had objected, claiming this amounted to Britain taking sides in the Jewish–Arab dispute, the end was obvious. Nat and the other Jewish veterans who had been armed (along with a couple of dozen others) on 23 August 1929 were relieved of their weapons just four days later. Through it all Nat was alone. His wife, Miriam, was in America visiting her family and she had taken the kids with her. Nat could guess what she would have made of it all. She would have assumed he would swallow it, that he would bite his tongue, lower his head and carry on. She would have fully expected him to come home and say that this was for the best, that in the long run he was of more use to Zionism by making compromises on the inside than declaiming his principles on the outside. She would not have anticipated her husband letting his temper get the better of him, and certainly not with such a dramatic gesture of defiance – smashing his weapon to the ground rather than surrendering it to his commanding officer! She would not have expected him to fight back at all.

When she finally found out what had happened, Miriam saw her husband in a new light: as a hero. She had become an ever more devout Zionist, her determination to secure a Jewish homeland uncomplicated by any loyalty to the British king. She may have spent her childhood in Edinburgh, but she regarded Palestine alone as home. The British meant nothing to her save as a means to the end of Jewish sovereignty. So long as they were advancing that cause, she would tolerate them. Otherwise, she was indifferent. She had no sentimental bond to London or the crown. She believed Nat had finally taken sides – and chosen the right one.

Suddenly he was the talk of the town. In Jewish Jerusalem, word spread that 'Mindel was the only one who really protested.' He had stood up for himself and therefore for Jewish pride. Most of those doing the gossiping had little idea that what Nat was standing up for was his own personal creed: that he could be a good Jew and a loyal Brit at the same time. 'How could they not trust me?' he said to himself over and over again that night. 'How dare they believe I would be anything other than a fair and professional civil servant?' For the first time in his life he had been overtly discriminated against because he was a Jew. As the hours passed, his fury only rose.

He lay on the couch, imagining Miriam, always the nurse, soothing his brow. 'Don't worry, Min,' she would say. 'You'll find another job.' Obviously he had to resign his post in the Mandate administration; she would take that much as read. And there would be no objection from her. She would be only too happy to see Min work unambiguously for Zion. Perhaps a job in the Jewish Agency?

Maybe I should, thought Nat, pulling himself straight in his chair. Maybe I should stride into Luke's office first thing tomorrow morning and slap a resignation letter on his desk. He was mentally drafting the opening sentence when there was a knock on the door. It was Albert Hyamson, his immediate superior in the Department of Immigration. Hyamson had once been a Zionist but was now more famous in the Yishuv as a fierce stickler for the rules – Britain's rules. He infuriated the Zionists by rumbling their every trick and zealously moving to close each successive loophole in Palestine's immigration laws. The Jews came to hate Hyamson as a traitor, believing that as soon as they had found a way to get more Jews into Palestine, he would find a way to keep them out.

'Evening, Mindel,' he began, in a voice that signalled he had no intention of coming inside. 'Eventful day.'

'Yes, quite so. Eventful.'

'I'll get to the point, shall I? My view is that it's probably best for you to cool off for a while. Clear the head.'

'I'm sorry, Mr Hyamson. I don't quite understand.'

'I think you need to get away from Jerusalem. Tempers running too high. I suggest you transfer to the office in Kantara. Only temporary, you understand.'

'But why?'

'Because I don't want you doing anything you might regret.' For a moment, Nat wondered if Hyamson feared he was on the verge of suicide. He almost wanted to laugh. Then he realized: his boss meant resignation.

'I see.'

'Good. I'll make the arrangements. Good evening, Mindel.'

And that was it. Hyamson did not declare a view on Nat's gesture earlier that day; Nat guessed that he deplored it. Such histrionics were not Hyamson's style. Moreover, he would have believed that challenging an order, even one to surrender weapons, would only confirm what the British authorities suspected: that the Jews were unreliable. A regular British serviceman would simply have done what he was told. By making a fuss, Nat had confirmed that Jews had an agenda of their own. Hyamson had said nothing of the sort, of course, but Nat was sure that was what he believed.

Nat wondered about resignation. At Kantara, watching the boats arrive and the trains come in and pull out, and all the while fending off the late summer heat, he thought of little else. Miriam was probably right that he would feel freer than he ever had, that he could at last be his own man. But there were other factors to consider. He now had three young children: little Yehuda, a lively boy of eight, and two daughters, Ruth and, the newest addition, Aviva. He had to provide for them. And money in the Yishuv was tight.

He was due a holiday and headed for London. He wanted to discuss his dilemma with the one man whose judgement he respected without hesitation. He asked to see Chaim Weizmann.

A Jerusalem family: Nat with Ruth on his knee, Miriam with Aviva on her lap – and Yehuda in between.

He was ushered into Weizmann's private study on Great Russell Street, the London headquarters of the Jewish Agency. Their conversation was brief but unambiguous. 'If I have any moral authority over you,' Weizmann began, 'then you will not resign. Because, if you do, they will appoint a Gentile in your place. And even the best Gentile in your position would not be as good as a Jew.' The father of diplomatic Zionism had spoken: Nathan Mindel had a duty.

So Nat returned to Jerusalem and to his desk on Queen Melisande Street as if nothing had happened. He carried on shuffling the papers, sending the cables and drafting the regulations just as he had in the previous ten years. His routine did not alter. Up at six-thirty. Two eggs: soft-boiled, four minutes. Toast and tea, and then off to the office by eight. A solid morning's work and then back home for lunch at two, usually eaten in silence. After that he would withdraw to his room and rest for an hour before going out again

– not back to work but to friends to play bridge. He was a bridge addict, quite an accomplished player by all accounts. He admitted it was a drug for him; the bridge table was one of the few places where he found peace of mind. When he returned home at seven, the children would know what kind of afternoon he had had. When he spoke to their mother – 'Julius had a useful opening hand . . .', 'Max opened well but then fluffed it . . .' – they knew the game had gone his way. If he was silent, and the eyebrows loomed large and dark, they knew to tiptoe around him. After supper, either Miriam and Nat would go out to play yet more bridge or friends would come to see them. And that's how it was almost every day.

They told themselves they liked it that way, that they were happy at home with their young family and their small social circle. But, in truth, they did not have much choice. Among Palestine's Jews, Nat was seen as an Englishman. One Flag Day, when young pioneers filled the streets, shaking collecting tins for the *kibbutzim* and *moshavim* springing up around the country, Nat was fumbling in his pocket for change when he realized the volunteers were looking right past him. He stared at them before he understood: they did not expect a donation from this man in a London-tailored suit, this English gentleman. To them, he was part of the colonial set-up. On a good day, that made him a resource to be exploited; on a bad day, he was an obstacle in the way of the Zionist dream.

Which hardly made Nat comfortable in Zionist company. Like most Jews in the Mandate administration, he felt an unspoken pressure to do more for the cause. Officially the Jewish Agency made it a rule never to put a British Jew in a position in which his loyalty to the crown might be questioned. This was not principle but common sense: a distrusted Jewish civil servant would be of no use. But 'advice' was a different matter. Nat might be buying fruit at the Machaneh Yehuda street market when an Agency official would stop by for a chat. 'Look, we hear the Jaffa facility is to be expanded. Who should we approach?' The tacit assumption was that he was an ally.

What complicated matters was that the Agency was not completely wrong. Many, perhaps most, Palestinian Jewish officials in the administration – the 'local hires' – were indeed taking orders from the Zionist movement. They funnelled documents the Agency's way, at least those that had not already been secured through bribery of Arab officials. (The Agency was phenomenally well informed. They even had microphones in key British offices, including the one that housed the Peel Commission, set up following the Arab general strike of 1936 and subsequent violence. The Zionists knew the precise contents of the Peel Report – which called for partition of Palestine into two states, one Arab and one Jewish – long before it was published.)

So Nat could not help but feel like a source to be tapped rather than a true member of the Yishuv family. Yet among his fellow Brits he did not quite fit in either. The policemen, NCOs and 'other ranks' were hardly natural company for a man like Nat. With his university education, he considered himself their social superior. As far as he could tell, most of them lived only for the inter-services football league or for drinking themselves senseless.

The officer class, Nat's colleagues in the administration, was awkward in a different way. After work, most wanted to relax, drink or play tennis – all of which Nat would have found most agreeable. But he did not belong here either. Max Nurock, the Zionist official who rose to high rank in the British administration and straddled the divide rather well, was clear, if brutal, on Nat's problem. At bottom, he would say years later, Mindel was 'an ordinary East End Jew straight out of the ghetto: he looked it and he sounded it'. No matter that Nat's own family back home regarded him as a toff, believing that his perfect posture and diction made him the very model of an Englishman – a view they would insist on for generations – real gentlemen, according to Nurock, could see through that Grocers' school veneer to the true Mindel beneath: a Russian-Lithuanian-Polish-Byelorussian immigrant who had made the best of himself. He would never enjoy the languorous ease of the ex-Grenadier guardsmen, the sons and grandsons of colonial officers, who surrounded him. He could not affect the nonchalance of the gifted amateur which marked out so much of the English ruling class. He did not make playful references to 'sticky wickets' or 'bowling a googly'; if he had, a flicker in his voice would have given him away. He did not have the landscape of Hampshire villages or of Suffolk wild flowers buried deep in his ancestral memory, the way they did. And such unlearned expertise is impossible to fake. Insect antennae able to pick up the faraway beating of a gnat's wings are deaf next to the English ear, with its capacity for detecting the infinitesimal calibrations of class at a thousand paces.

So Nat was left on the outside. He told himself it did not matter. It would, he insisted to friends, be 'very easy to make a splash in the pukka British circles' if he wanted to, but that was not his choice: 'I am not here to remain an Englishman.' Only once a year was he granted entry into the imperial social scene, when his invitation arrived for the High Commissioner's Christmas party. He would feign indifference, while Miriam would protest, using the same words each year: 'Why should we celebrate their Christmas? Would the Jews of Judaea have dined at a pagan banquet with the Romans?'

But the threat of boycott was only ever lukewarm. Despite herself, Miriam would be buzzing with preparations several days before the event, buying new dresses for the girls and maybe even something special for herself. The family would go together, Nat carrying himself a little taller as they walked into Government House. The grandeur of the building made him swell; he liked his children to see the splendour of the empire he served. His was no ordinary job: he was a servant of the king of England! The children loved it. Little Aviva made a beeline for Father Christmas, clambering on to the lap of the luckless British official whose fate it was to wear a heavy costume and suffocating theatrical beard in that snowless Jerusalem winter.

The British were not quite sure what to make of people like Nat. Even regular Palestinian Jews confused them. The great, Russian-born Jewish scholar Isaiah Berlin rapidly got the measure of the relationship when he visited Palestine on a grand tour of the Levant in 1934. 'You have to think of it as a third-rate public school,' he would say later. 'The British officials were the teachers. They were all missionaries, peddling their spiritual goods to the Arabs, who were the pupils, and behaved in an appropriate fashion. Everybody had to be either black or white. Well, the Arabs were clearly black. But the Jews were neither. They formed a separate Jewish house as at, say, Clifton or Cheltenham. And four problems arose. They were no good at games; they were all spotty, that is to say unattractive, rude to the teachers, insubordinate and so on; thirdly, they won all the prizes; and fourthly, if anything went wrong they would go and complain to their parents, who would go and complain to the governors of the school, who would then come back at the headmaster and teachers.'

The British took a rather more charitable view of the Anglo-Jews among them, but they were never quite sure. It did not matter how dedicated his service to the crown, no Jew was exempt from a basic suspicion that he served two masters. Even Max Nurock, he who pitied Nat his East End looks and immigrant voice, was not spared. Despite his Dublin brogue and his first-class education, Nurock could not escape the bureaucrat who reviewed his personnel file in 1936 and declared: 'As he is a Jew he cannot be further promoted in the secretariat . . .' (That prompted a flurry of scribbled asides in the margin: 'I don't think we can say this,' wrote one. 'I certainly hope we shall not say it,' agreed another. 'Certainly not,' confirmed a third.)

Nat soldiered on all the same, doing his best to please his British superiors. But where he had once been able to draw inspiration from his fellow Jews on high, now their example offered only dismay. In the 1920s he had looked to the very apex, to the High Commissioner himself, and seen Herbert Samuel – a faithful Jew and faithful emissary of the king. Now, though, if he gazed upward his eye would be caught by the Attorney-General, whose fate was rather less uplifting.

Norman de Mattos Bentwich would have passed Max Nurock's

accent test. An old boy of St Paul's School in London and graduate of Trinity College, Cambridge, he could mix easily in Nat's 'pukka British circles'. But he was a passionate Zionist – Theodor Herzl had been a visitor to his childhood home – and faced distrust from the day he was appointed. It was perhaps inevitable that the Arabs would resent his position, believing that he could hardly be an impartial umpire in their disputes with the Jews. But plenty of Bentwich's fellow Britons took the same view.

The Chief Justice, Sir Michael McDonnell, led the charge, claiming that the British administration was being 'seriously hampered at the present time by the presence of Mr Bentwich, a Jew and an ardent partisan of Zionism, in the high position of Attorney-General'. (The High Commissioner, Sir John Chancellor, was sceptical of the complaint, suspecting McDonnell was motivated chiefly by prejudice. Both the Chief Justice and his wife were 'devout Catholics', he noted, 'and like all the Latins in Palestine are strongly anti-Semitic'.)

After the Hebron riots, the Arab complaints against Bentwich intensified. The High Commissioner suggested the Attorney-General delegate all Arab-related cases to a colleague; Bentwich refused. Soon the Arabs were demanding his head. A group of merchants cabled the Colonial Secretary in London to 'emphatically request Mr Bentvitch's [*sic*] removal from position of attorney general to give place for Britisher who would not be influenced by Zionists. By this means only Arabs feel they can secure justice and feel confident in judicial affairs.'

When the Arabs threatened a general strike, and an All-Palestine Arab Congress convened by the Mufti of Jerusalem, Haj Amin al-Husseini, called for Bentwich to go 'because he is a Jew, a Zionist, and an enemy of Arabs', the British began to buckle. On 29 November the tension came to a head. An Arab gunman found Bentwich in the government offices in Jerusalem and shot him. He was not wounded badly enough to stop working; indeed, he even took on the case of the man who had tried to kill him, defending him in court.

In a way, that act was typical of Bentwich. He viewed himself as a moderate Zionist; in contemporary terms he would be placed on the far left of the movement. He was a firm supporter of Brit Shalom, the Covenant of Peace, which advocated a less political, more spiritual form of Zionism. Brit Shalom regarded Jewish cultural renewal as more important than the machinery of Jewish statehood. The group, led by Martin Buber and Judah Magnes, envisaged a binational state, making Palestine home to both Jews and Arabs. As Bentwich once wrote, 'It is neither to be expected, nor is it desired that the Jews should occupy the whole country. There is ample room for the children of Esau and Jacob to live together in harmony.'

Yet that moderation did not save him. For Arabs, he was a Zionist and that was grounds enough to condemn him. The British took a similar view. Ultimately they were unimpressed with Bentwich's description of himself as 'a channel of communication' between the administration and the Zionist leadership. As far as the Colonial Office was concerned, his enthusiasm for a Jewish renaissance made his views 'extreme'. And yet he found little succour on the other side, among those the British and the Arabs would have called his own people. The Jews regarded him as so moderate, so willing to see the Arab point of view, that he was all but guilty of treachery. Norman Bentwich, like so many of his fellow Anglo-Jews in the Palestine government, was distrusted on all sides.

London tried to make it easy for him. Once they judged that Arab opinion would be placated by nothing less than his removal, they offered him an alternative berth in the empire. He could be Chief Justice of Mauritius. Or Cyprus. Bentwich rejected both posts. His commitment was to Palestine and he wanted to stay, serving the British government. He believed in the creation of a Jewish national home and so, thanks to the Balfour Declaration, did Britain. He could see no contradiction. But his masters were not to be budged. The High Commissioner told him that the problem would probably not arise in future because 'only Britons' were likely to win senior jobs in Palestine. The implication of that remark was pretty transparent: despite his war record and more than a decade of service for the empire, Bentwich did not even count as a 'Briton'. He told Chancellor directly that this was 'discrimination'. It was clear that the Attorney-General would not go quietly. In London the Colonial Secretary duly terminated his appointment.

The whole affair, and Bentwich's career, had ended bitterly. His wife found their one-time friends in Jerusalem society had turned frosty. 'Once again the word "bloody" invariably precedes the word Jew,' she sighed.

Nathan Mindel watched this drama unfold from below. There were no threatened general strikes demanding his removal; no memos exchanged between London and Jerusalem debating his fate. He was too lowly an official for that. But he cannot have drawn much comfort from Bentwich's story. Just ten years earlier his heart had skipped at the sight of a British High Commissioner called to the law in the Churva synagogue in Jerusalem, hailed like a redeemer come unto Zion. Now the most senior Jew in the administration had been chased out because, in the words of the All-Palestine Arab Congress, he was 'a Jew, a Zionist, and an enemy of Arabs'.

Nat sank himself deeper into his work, his bridge, his routine. His conversations with Miriam grew more infrequent; he knew what she would say and it was becoming harder to argue with her. Occasionally, he would see the men from the Jewish Agency around town, their stride ever more purposeful. They were heading in only one direction, never having to look both ways.

Nat would do what he had to in the office, come home and fall into a heavy sleep. It made up for the long nights when sleep would never come. He struggled to haul himself off to his afternoon bridge game, where he would sit, saying almost nothing. At home, his children began to fear him. Yehuda was especially fragile; the slightest sign of his father's displeasure would trigger tears, which only served to anger his father more. One evening the boy was eating his supper when Nat hissed, 'Stop that.'

'Stop what?'

'That!'

'What are you talking about?' began Miriam, intervening to make peace. But it was too late. The glass had left Nat's hand and was hurtling towards Yehuda's head. It sailed past his ear and smashed on the ground just behind his chair. The boy turned pale, too shocked to cry. Miriam, her voice ice, told Yehuda and the girls to go to their rooms. Calmly, she stood up and went for a broom. Nat stayed stock still, the only sound the crunch of broken glass. Finally, he spoke.

'He was chewing too loudly,' he said. 'Yehuda was chewing so loud, I couldn't stand it.'

His son had a tendency to get under his skin. Nat wanted so much for him, this Yehuda, this Julius Benedict. He hoped the boy would have everything he himself had wanted: easy access to all that British and Jewish life had to offer. He felt Zionist pride at his son's fluency in Hebrew, a language that just a few decades earlier had been a dead tongue heard only in prayer. But he also made sure there were plenty of English dictionaries and encyclopedias at home. He wanted Yehuda/Julius to have both.

The lad had his own ideas. This was the era of the Haganah, the emerging Jewish militia that would one day blossom into the Israeli army. The Haganah, literally the Defence, believed that the British could not be relied on to protect the Jews of Palestine; only the Jews could do that. The very idea was bursting with Zionist confidence. After 2,000 years of weakness, Jews would at last fight for their own lives. The Zion Mule Corps and the Jewish battalions were valuable precedents: they at least proved that a Jewish soldier was no oxymoron. But in those corps, Jews were under the command of others. The Haganah would be a body unseen since the second century and Bar Kochba's revolt against the Roman occupation of Palestine: a Jewish army.

In the mid-1930s, just as Yehuda's childhood was turning into adolescence, his class hummed with excitement. Apparently, they were all to appear before a secret 'appointment committee' after school. This was not some boyish fantasy, it turned out to be true.

Yehuda and his classmates, none older than fifteen, did indeed meet a couple of men in their early twenties for a serious talk. It happened in a yard, behind an empty building. The boys went there sometimes to play football.

'How many of you know what the Haganah is?' the bigger of the two men began. He was tall and, Yehuda could not help noticing, wore an open-necked shirt. His father always wore a tie, no matter the heat. 'You?'

A classmate was offering an answer. 'It is the Jewish army, sir.'

'Jewish defence force,' the man corrected. 'But yes, we are the force to protect the Jewish people. How many of you want to see the Jews free in their own land?' All hands went up. 'And how many of you believe that Jews have a right to defend themselves?' All hands. 'And how many of you are willing to play your part in that mission? Good.

'Let me begin with a warning. This is not a youth club. This is not the Boy Scouts. If you are not good enough, you will not be called, do you understand? We only want those who can help in our struggle, against whichever enemy we may have to face. There can be no room for stragglers. Only the strong are strong enough for the Haganah.'

The boys were thrilled, each one of them straining to repress the smirk of pride they wanted to let out. They did their best to stand up straight and look grave. For the rest of that evening, until the last sunlight had gone, they did what they were told. Running on the spot, fifty press-ups, breaking off into packs of three and 'hunting' the others, more running, this time with twigs as batons, touching their toes. They were exhausted, but none dared exhale so much as a sigh.

At the end, only the whites of his eyes visible in the black night, the second man, who had said almost nothing, gave them one last instruction. 'You are to say nothing of what you did here this evening. The Haganah is above all a secret organization and one reckless word from any of you could endanger your lives.' Yehuda felt his knees wobble.

The next day, the boys exchanged knowing looks; they did not realize it yet, but they were feeling the furtive excitement of adolescents who had just lost their virginity. They imagined they had become men. Over the next days, the boys' glances turned to smiles. One whispered to another and then another: 'You as well? Me too.' But Yehuda heard nothing; no call ever came.

He was a skinny kid and he felt like a loser. He could feel the tears coming but clenched his jaw to stop them. Finally, his mother asked him what was wrong. When he told her, she felt the mixed emotions of any patriotic mother who has contemplated seeing a son off to war: proud, but filled with fear for her little boy. Still, she could see that he wanted to do it so much. 'We'll see what we can do,' she promised.

That night she inched gingerly towards the subject. 'Min, can we talk about Yehuda? About something he wants very much?'

'If it's about the Haganah, then there's nothing to talk about.'

'You know about that?'

'Of course I know about it. I know how that organization works, recruiting in the schools, and so I had a word.'

'*You* had a word?'

'Yes, I spoke to the so-called commander and told him that under no circumstances was he allowed to recruit any child of mine into the Haganah.'

'You did what?'

'I said it was impossible for a man in my position to harbour a paramilitary agent under his roof.'

'But, Menachem, that's terrible. Yehuda thinks he was rejected. He has no idea.'

'Why should he have any idea? This way, he can believe it was a decision taken purely on his own merits.'

Miriam left the room, shaking her head in disbelief and fury towards her husband. She told Yehuda immediately what had happened, but his father's diktat did not deter him. Quite the reverse. If the prospect of a family connection with the Haganah – the relatively moderate force linked to the labour movement –

worried Nat, his son was about to go one better. He signed up with the paramilitary wing of hardline revisionist Zionism, the movement that would one day flower into Israel's Likud party. Yehuda Mindel joined the Irgun.

Now it was Miriam's turn to be shocked. The Irgun did not mess about with mere schoolyard exercises. Just a teenager, Yehuda was part of a cell that wanted to do its bit for armed resistance against the foreign occupier. They needed weapons, which meant paying for them. Because of Nat's colonial salary, the Mindels were far better off than most of Yehuda's Palestinian Jewish classmates, so he was given the task of purchasing a firearm.

It was his mother who found it, letting out a gasp as she saw the pistol hidden under his bed. She ordered him to take it out of the house, 'this instant!' He gave it to a comrade for safekeeping. But once Nat heard about the pistol, his mind was made up: he could not raise his son in this atmosphere. His own child, a Zionist freedom fighter! A terrorist, fighting against the British! Imagine if his bosses were to find out! Nat shuddered at the very thought.

There was only one solution. He would send Yehuda to England to finish his education. Nat fixed on the Perse in Cambridge, a public school for boys – and the real thing, rather than an aspirant imitation like the Grocers'. It was ideal, the best of both worlds. There was a Jewish boarding house, including some boys Yehuda's age from Palestine. But he would be raised as an English gentleman. And the closest his son would get to violence would be on the rugby field.

Even if he had won that battle, Nat would lose the wider war. Eventually his daughter Aviva would defy him and join the Haganah. More unexpectedly, even his own wife broke ranks. Miriam had long been a tireless volunteer, setting up nurseries and lending a hand to youth clubs in the Jerusalem suburb of Rehavia. In 1939, when the Haganah started establishing guard posts all around Jerusalem, they approached her. Would she coordinate supplies to the sentries, ensuring each post had sufficient food, furniture and blankets? She gave an immediate yes.

'Miriam, this is most inappropriate,' Nat had said when she told him of her plans that evening, once the children were all asleep. 'I am a servant of His Majesty's Government. I cannot have an agent –'

'Menachem, you really are the most pompous man alive!' Miriam shouted, standing over him while he picked at supper at the small kitchen table in their flat. He knew she was serious; she only ever called him Menachem when they were having a row. Otherwise it was Min. Never Nat: only the family in London called him that. Or Nathan: that was for forms and British officialdom. She had not finished. 'You work for them if you want to, but I want to work for *us*! I want to fight for *us*!' And with that she slammed the kitchen door.

Nat did not chase after her. There was no point trying to persuade her; her mind was made up and her will was as strong as any man's. That was one of the reasons he loved her. And, he was surprised to note, he felt a sneaking admiration for his wife. He may have taken tea at four, he may have worn whites for a summer game of tennis, but he had not stopped being a Zionist. Half of him felt just the way she did.

In this civil war of the heart, the greatest battleground remained his work. In the 1920s, Nat had liked to think that his 'two masters' were perfectly compatible. From his perch in the Department of Immigration, he could do his bit to nudge along the Zionist cause without ever departing from his duties as a British official. Just look at what he had achieved in Trieste. Thanks to him, nearly a hundred Jews had made it to Palestine who might otherwise have been shut out and, into the bargain, a bottleneck in the imperial bureaucracy had been unblocked. Everybody was happy.

Now things did not look so straightforward. In the early 1930s, Jewish demand for entry into Palestine had begun to increase. German Jews were especially keen, deluging Nat and his colleagues with applications. Hyamson, who in a different era would be labelled the control freak's control freak, was so distrustful of his own colleagues that he liked to check every form himself. Now he was overwhelmed; by 1934 the department was nine months in arrears. Like everyone else, Nat was getting word of what this new Herr Hitler thought of Jews; reports of Nazi beatings and harassment on the street were spreading. Sitting in his office in Jerusalem, staring at that pile of unprocessed application forms, Nat dreaded to think what a nine-month delay would mean to the people who had written them.

He glanced down at a letter that had come in addressed to Hyamson. It was from a Jerusalem lawyer, seeking advice on a matter of 'exceptional character'. Unusually, the lawyer had withheld the name of his client.

> *A lady has just arrived from Germany where her husband has been a practising lawyer at Worms. He has been a member of the Labour Party and the majority of his clients belong to the working class. On September 1st he was sent to a concentration camp and is now held there as a political prisoner. At the same time, financial measures were taken against him which make it appear unlikely that he will be able to save any substantial part of his capital from this catastrophe, even if he should succeed in being released from prison . . . My question is: Is there any possibility for the lady concerned to be granted permission to remain permanently in Palestine . . . What could be done in order to bring the husband to Palestine in case he should succeed in being released from his imprisonment?*

Nat scanned the rest of the letter. The lawyer was asking for Hyamson to let these people in under the category reserved for 'capitalists' – those people with £1,000 at their 'free disposal'. This category, known fittingly enough as A(i), was proving useful for German Jews. Initially the new Nazi authorities were reluctant to let Jews out with £1,000 worth of assets: they wanted their money to stay in Germany. But the Jewish Agency had found a way round that obstacle, and the Nazis had accepted it. Jewish would-be emigrants were allowed to buy £1,000 worth of German goods – thereby boosting the economy of the fatherland – which could then be exported to Palestine, so meeting the British requirement for A(i) immigrants. A shipping company called Ha'Avara, or Transfer, was set up solely for this purpose and thousands of middle-class Germans began to use it.

Not that that would help this poor soul in the concentration camp. Nat had read about these places. It had been one of the first things Hitler had done: Dachau was opened just a few weeks after the Nazis had come to power in March 1933. Nat could not imagine what such a place was like. He looked back at the file and saw, stapled to the lawyer's letter, a reply from Hyamson: '. . . if either he or his wife can show that he is in bona fide possession and freely disposes of a minimum capital of £1,000 . . .'

Nat slammed the file down on his desk. That bastard! Hyamson had ignored the plea for mercy the lawyer was making to him and simply repeated the rules and regulations, with all the pity of a speak-your-weight machine. The man was in a concentration camp, for God's sake! How on earth could he freely dispose of anything, let alone 'a minimum capital of £1,000'? Had Hyamson no heart? What kind of Jew was this?

Nat shot up from his desk and strode towards the door. He stopped as soon as he had opened it; he didn't know where he was going. He had a good mind to confront Hyamson, to grab him by his lapels and shake him. Could he not see what was happening?

Even non-Jewish officials in the administration had been sounding the alarm about Germany within weeks of Hitler's accession. 'Affairs in Germany are I fear bad,' Eric Mills, then in charge of the Palestine census, wrote to Norman Bentwich in May 1933. Men like Mills, who would replace Hyamson as Nat's boss at immigration, recognized the danger to Jews, but they stopped short of seeing Palestine as the natural refuge. 'It seems to me to be short-sighted to think that Palestine can accomplish miracles of absorption on behalf of the distressed Jewry of Europe,' Mills wrote, adding this prescient postscript: 'I suppose Austria is likely to follow Germany in these matters and this will add to our local difficulties.'

He had been right, thought Nat now, as he looked out at the Swiss countryside, covered in a blanket of January darkness. It was the first week of 1939 and Austria had fallen a matter of months earlier. Life for the Jews was just as 'bad' as Mills had feared, probably much worse. What were they calling that shocking business a couple of months back? Kristallnacht, the night of broken glass. The Nazis had staged a modern pogrom, just like the one the local nobleman had warned his father about all those years ago. Except the Nazis did things on a huge, modern scale: ninety-one Jews had been killed, with hundreds more injured; as many as 1,300 synagogues had been burned, with countless Jewish cemeteries and schools trashed; 7,500 Jewish businesses were destroyed, while 30,000 Jews were rounded up and sent to concentration camps – all on a single night.

Nat thought of that man, the unnamed client in the lawyer's letter. What had become of him? Was he still in a concentration camp? Where was his wife? He looked down at the file outlining the business to be done in Basle, now just a few minutes away. Mills had asked him to travel there on a matter of the highest importance, and there it was in the flat prose of a Colonial Office cable: 'Mr N I Mindel who is an Assistant Commissioner in the Department of Migration in Jerusalem . . . has been asked by the Head of his Department to visit Basle on his way back from leave, in order to discuss with the British Consul there various questions relating to the handling of applications by German Jews for entry into Palestine.'

This was it, then: his mission. He knew what he had to do. He should stride in there, roll up his sleeves and he and the Consul would work through the night devising an airlift of the Jews of Germany, spiriting them from the hell of the Third Reich to the safe haven of Palestine. It would be a latter-day exodus, with himself as Moses and the Consul as his Aaron.

That was what he should do – but not what he would do. For the rules on immigration had changed these last few years. In the middle of the decade the administration had actually let in more Jews – the figure rising to 66,472 in 1935, the highest number since the Balfour Declaration. There was plenty of demand, with Jews desperate to flee the Nazis' clutches, and the system still allowed a steady supply of entry visas. The old rule, linking the number of immigrants to the economic capacity of the country, continued to apply. The Zionists, using every wile their imagination could dream up, were by now skilled at ensuring both that 'capacity' was defined generously and that plenty of Jews came in 'off' the labour schedule, classified in categories granted entry regardless of the economic health of Palestine.

But from 1936 – when Sara Hocherman was fighting for her life in a Petach Tikva clinic and Mick Mindel was pumped with the adrenalin of victory at Cable Street – the picture changed. The Arab Revolt had begun, a sustained period of violent assaults on Jewish and British targets. 'Most of the attacks involved land mines, bombs, gunfire and ambushes on the roads or in isolated settlements,' Israeli historian Tom Segev would write some six decades later, in a description humming with echoes of his own time. 'A person taking the children to school had to weigh the possibility that the school building would be set on fire. Sitting in a coffeehouse, a man could not be sure there was not a bomb under his chair.'

What was unfolding was an insurgency by Palestine's Arabs against what they believed was an attempt to seize their country from right under their noses. The way the Arabs saw it, the Zionists' chosen weapon for this invasion was neither cavalry nor tanks nor fighter planes, but ships. And not warships either, but humble vessels loaded up with civilians. 'Every day the ships bombard us with hundreds of Jewish immigrants,' wrote Khalil al-Sakakini, a Christian Arab teacher, writer and Jerusalemite. 'If this immigration continues, Palestine's future is very black . . . there is no choice but to rouse ourselves . . . there is no choice but to act.'

The heart of the Arab grievance was Jewish immigration. If the

Arab Revolt was making a single demand on the British authorities, it was, as it had been back in 1921, to halt the influx of European Jews. For a while, the administration insisted it would hold the line. The British Empire was not in the habit of being blown off course by a mere uprising of the natives; it would not surrender to the demands of terrorists.

But that resolve became ever harder to maintain. The attacks were a daily occurrence, so that by 1939 a tally for the previous decade would record 10,000 incidents and a death toll of 2,000. At least half of that was made up of Arabs; an estimated 400 Jews were killed. Crucially, though, the Arab Revolt also claimed the lives of some 150 Britons.

That was not the only reason why the Mandate government was anxious to calm Arab anger and bring the rebellion to an end. By 1938 most British policymakers knew that war with Germany was looming. The Middle East would, as always, be of strategic significance; control of Palestine would matter. It was obvious that the Jews would back the British: they could hardly root for the Nazis. But the Palestinian Arabs could not be taken for granted. Arab support would have to be won, and if that meant thwarting Jewish demands for immigration then so be it. In the words of the Prime Minister, Neville Chamberlain, 'If we must offend one side, let us offend the Jews rather than the Arabs.' (The effort failed anyway: by 1941 the Mufti of Jerusalem would be in Berlin, taking tea with Hitler.)

So the door through which Jews had come running for their lives began to close, and among those duty bound to push it shut was one Nathan Mindel. A serving officer in the Department of Immigration, he was charged with implementing the new approach. It was spelled out in black and white in a paper by the Colonial Secretary, Malcolm MacDonald, in September 1938: 'Policy in Palestine on the Outbreak of War'. It proposed a total freeze on Jewish immigration for the duration of the coming war, in order to win Palestinian Arab support. Once victory over Hitler was won, argued MacDonald, then the policy could be reviewed – but not before.

That was how things stood as Nat's train drew into Basle station. He looked down again at the bald document on his lap, setting out the purpose of his visit: 'to discuss with the British Consul there various questions relating to the handling of applications by German Jews for entry into Palestine'. Except there was only one real question: would the British rulers of Palestine allow the Children of Israel to enter the Promised Land? Would they open Zion's gates, knowing that the lives of those Jews depended on it? There was only one answer – and Nathan Isidore Mindel, who had fled persecution as a child, was the person who would have to give it.

9   A Pact with the Devil

Mick Mindel was now an East End star. Still only in his twenties in 1936, he could claim the wisdom of an elder. Had he and his comrades not sounded the first warning of Mosley and his fascist bootboys? Had not Mick and the Stepney communists demanded resistance when the Jewish old guard had called for quiet, make-no-fuss acquiescence? Had not the Battle of Cable Street provided the sweetest vindication?

Well known as the man the union could not expel – he had even had the *chutzpah* to cite ancient Jewish law in his support – Mick was a celebrity in the small, intense world of the Jewish clothing trade. When he made his formal political debut, seeking a place on the social committee of the United Ladies' Tailors' Trade Union, he breezed to victory.

As a bridgehead towards the revolution, the 'social' might not have looked like much, but Mick took full advantage of his opportunity. Organizing the union's May Day festivities, it fell to him to select the guest speaker. Suddenly, the obvious choice was a luminary of the Communist Party.

Above all, the young Mindel gained a vantage point from which he could see his community, and especially its senior members, up close. For the building on Great Garden Street that served as union headquarters was more than a cluster of offices: it was a working men's club, debating chamber and village square all rolled into one. If the Romans had their baths, the men of the *schmutter* had Great Garden Street.

They had nowhere else to meet. A workforce scattered across hundreds of sweatshops – in cramped living rooms or around a master tailor's kitchen table – had no other focus. There was no factory floor where a shop steward might organize his members.

So machiners or pressers would make a trip to the union building, to pay their seven pence in weekly dues or renew their membership card, and stay a while. There was a bar, but this was a Jewish trade union: it did not serve beer, finding more call for tea, pickled herrings, potato *latkes*, *platzels* and bagels. Dominoes were laid on by the union (Mick tried to reach out to the younger generation by bringing in a billiards table: *schlepping* that thing up the stairs would stand out as one of the toughest tasks of his union career). The old timers, still sipping their tea through a sugar cube, saw the union the way they had once seen the synagogue – as the centre of communal life.

And, just as it was in the old country, it was a place free of women. Mick would argue the point over and over again: 'We have to recruit women into the union, for their sake and ours!' He would point out that unequal pay both impoverished women and threatened men, tempting employers to replace male workers with women available at half the price. Still the old boys would not listen. They wanted to protect their privileges – 'Such privileges!' Mick would say with a 'Feh!' in his voice – but the young Mindel reckoned they just enjoyed having no women around. He would study the faces of these men, all of them variations on his father's, and see a look of relaxed calm visible nowhere else, not at work, not at home and not in the street. These men would sit back, playing idle dominoes, wearing an expression of soft contentment. There were no *goyim* and no women and they could be themselves.

For Mick, the real action came at the meetings: general ones open to the whole union on Sunday afternoons, assorted committees on weekday evenings and, best of all, the executive, Thursdays at eight. All life passed through those sessions, Mick reckoned. There might be a report on a strike, like the one at Gotkin's shop. 'The pickets request a car or motor cycle to follow the employer,' the executive would be told, 'as there is ground for suspicion that the work in dispute is being taken outside.' Spying on a boss? By motor car? Mick was thrilled.

Or they might have internal matters to discuss, like the time the treasurer of the Christmas fund was accused of dipping into the seasonal pot a trifle too early – and for his own benefit. None of these Jews, these Applebaums and Ginsbergs, seemed to find it odd that a union whose accounts appeared in Yiddish had a Christmas fund. Not that any one of them would himself have celebrated Jesus' birth by cooking a turkey, singing carols or filling a stocking with Santa's gifts for the children. Perish the thought. But Christmas was a day on the English calendar, like Whitsun or the Lord Mayor's Show. They were parts of English life whose origins and meaning might be utterly alien, but which had to be mastered if these new Britons were to have any chance of getting on in the new country. So they spoke of Christmas Eve or Easter as if they were natives.

The agenda was not always parochial. There might be a request for solidarity from a fellow trade union. Mick was delighted when the Ladies' Tailors lent their weight to, say, the London cinema strike. The projectionists had walked out over pay, conditions and their right to be recognized as a union. For their strike to work, potential filmgoers had to resist the temptation to see the latest Clark Gable picture and refuse to cross picket lines. 'The Fascists are gloating over this strike which, they say, is forced by the Jewish Cinema Proprietors and broken by the Jewish Masses,' thundered a pro-strike leaflet distributed by Mick and a clutch of other Jewish trade unionists. 'It is therefore the duty of every Jew to nail down the Fascist lie by refusing to patronise scab cinemas, whether under Jewish proprietorship or not, and by supporting the heroic struggle of the Electrical Trade Union.' For pauper workers whose sole source of escapist pleasure was the occasional glimpse of Fred and Ginger, this was quite a sacrifice. But Mick demanded nothing less.

The executive would often have a guest speaker, like Comrade B. Emanuel, the secretary of the Central Organization of the Bund, who came with fraternal greetings from the organized Jewish workers of Poland. He appealed to the executive for moral and financial support for their 'combat against Fascism and Anti-semitism'. The minute-taker faithfully recorded that Mr Emanuel sought help for the Bund 'to continue its socialistic work which is now more than ever necessary and which serves as an inspiration to the whole International Proletariat'.

They may have been a craft union with a mere 3,000 members, but the United Ladies' Tailors' did not balk at such talk. They believed, communists like Mick especially, that they were indeed part of a global working-class movement. Their war was on several fronts, from Gotkin's shop to the Whitechapel Palace cinema, from Warsaw to Madrid. (Members of the United Ladies' Tailors' Trade Union were grindingly poor, but they still had a whip-round for the Republican wounded of Spain for every year of the civil war, eventually saving up enough cash to send an ambulance.)

Even when there was not yet another meeting, Mick could not stay away from Great Garden Street. When his own work, measuring and cutting, was done, he would be straight there, burning with one topic more than any other. Any stray conversation with a union member would soon turn into a debate on it, though it was hardly a dialogue. Instead Mick would deliver a one-way stream of argument, methodically setting out his case – the case for workers' unity, as he put it. What his enemies called the case for betraying Jewish independence.

Amalgamation – merging the Jewish union into the wider, national movement – was the question of the age. Mick, Sara and the other communists in the union had successfully headed off an earlier suggestion that the union should merge with their immediate employers, the master tailors – the very subcontractors who owned the workshops where the members sweated their lives away.

'That is a travesty of trade unionism!' Mick bellowed at the plan's advocates. 'Imagine, a union with *employers* in it!' he would say, fairly spitting out the word as he held court at the 'bar', among the bagel munchers and domino champions. 'It's an unnatural alliance. How can you be in the same union as the man who has a right to sack you? It would amount to a no-strike clause!' Those lessons in beginners' Marxism had paid off.

Now Mick and the comrades were on the offensive, pushing their own vision of the Jewish working-class future. By 1937 Mick decided he needed a sturdier platform than organizing speakers, concerts and entertainment. He stood for election as vice-chairman, and won. Now he would have an important role in the union: chair of the complaints committee. Just as a Westminster chief whip learns the innermost secrets of his fellow MPs, so Mick Mindel suddenly became privy to every rattling set of bones in every cupboard of his fellow union members. Men his father's age came to him for redress, telling their life stories in the process. The presser who had lost his job because he was having an affair with the boss's wife; the felling hand, responsible for the manual sewing of seams and hems, too blind to see the chair he was meant to sit on but who insisted he was still fit for close-up sewing – they all came to Mick. He was becoming a leader.

The union old guard could see what was happening. At executive meetings, the young deputy seized every moment to needle his immediate superior, usually on the issue of amalgamation – all of it faithfully recorded for posterity in the minutes. 'Mr Chairman, I would like to bring to the attention of the executive reports I have received of threats to break away from this union, should we take the next obvious step in our development. Can I call on the Chairman to guarantee today that he and his associates will stop sowing seeds of discontentment among the membership and will instead unite together on the policy of amalgamation?'

The head of the table was a cloud of huffs and puffs, but Mindel was not to be deterred. 'While I have the floor can I also put on record my regret at the Chairman's recent failure to attend meetings both of this committee and of the complaints committee, which I believe show he is not so much concerned with the work of the union as with his personal squabbles, using political issues as a vehicle for petty, personal ambitions.' The secretary struggled to keep up, what with the banging of fists on the table provoked by that last remark and the pace of Mick Mindel's flow, but he got the thrust of it, and lodged the excoriating words in the minutes – for the chairman to sign.

It was only a matter of time before Mick cleared out the aged men above him. In 1938 he ran for the top job in the union. His manifesto could not have been clearer: 'A vote for Mick Mindel is a vote for amalgamation.'

The campaign was one long row. Tailors would argue the question for hours on end, their fellow workers putting down their lead iron or giant scissors to join in. It continued at homes, over borscht and gefilte fish, and on the porches and over the stairwells at Rothschild Buildings, neighbours clashing with neighbours. At Great Garden Street, there seemed to be no oxygen in the air, just talk about the question of the hour: to join or not to join?

Mick had an unofficial campaign committee, made up of his fellow communists. Among them, his most trusted adviser was also his girlfriend, Sara.

'It's clear the main dividing line is age,' she said, absently making tea in the scullery of her tiny, one-room flat. 'Older members are going to be the hardest to win over.'

'Because I'm so young?' Mick was not yet thirty.

'No, because of who they are.' Sara turned around to face him, tea strainer in hand. 'Mick, these people remember pogroms. They came here before the war. Some of them came here in the last century. They don't trust a non-Jewish union. They don't trust *goyim*, full stop.'

'But they must see there's no future for an independent Jewish union! They must see that.'

'Mick, it's not the future they're thinking about. It's the past.'

'Well, what on earth can I do about that?'

'You've got me.'

'What?'

'I can speak to them. In Yiddish. It will make a difference.'

Sara's campaigning, addressing groups of older workers in their workshops and in their mother tongue, was relentless. She was tireless, that compacted energy of hers fearsome when unleashed. But still Mick could not be sure. Not until the day of the ballot itself.

Maybe it was all those cultural evenings Mick had organized, but the United Ladies' Tailors' Trade Union had a distinct knack for theatre. It could have run a simple ballot, inviting members to come to Great Garden Street and pop their vote into a black box. But that was not their style. Instead they staged a night of hustings. It would have been at the union premises, but too many people wanted to come. Instead they gathered at one of the largest venues in the area: Mile End Public Baths.

A thousand workers crammed in that night, waiting to be persuaded. Mick and his opponent, Lew Colton, were given forty-five minutes each. Colton went first. Mick was so seized by the occasion, the sheer number of people packed into row after row and standing all the way around, he could only take in the odd sentence from his rival.

'. . . and that is why our parents and their parents rejected similar proposals before. There are some things that are too precious to give up. This union is the last bastion of independent Jewish working-class organization in this country. Think about that. It brings practical advantages.' And now Colton's voice dipped and he adopted a soft, avuncular smile. 'Who can represent the *yidden* better than a *yid*?' Mick could hear the warm murmur of agreement. He saw a familiar face nodding. It was Kaufman, a friend of his father's. Colton was still talking.

'If we abandon it, we abandon our own heritage. This is not just about pay and conditions at work. What statement will we be making to the next generation? That Jews cannot survive on their own, that you have to become English to get on? That we cannot remain a proud – small, I agree, but proud – group? That we have to dissolve ourselves, lose ourselves in the general mass? Don't let Mick Mindel do it. Don't let Mick Mindel sell the independent rights of the Jewish working class for Moscow gold!'

It was a low blow, utterly predictable from an ex-communist like Colton. But he had planted the suspicion that Mick was taking orders from the party, who were backing a merger in the name of working-class unity. Mick rose, knowing he would have to give the speech of his life. He had not written so much as a note. But he had given this address so many times in his head, he was sure he could just say what he wanted, direct from his heart and his brain.

'My fellow members of the United Ladies' Tailors' Trade Union, let me begin by saying how proud I am to address you. And how proud I am to be a member of this union. It is twenty years ago to this very day that I paid my first visit to the union premises, then on Colchester Street. I was taken there by my father, who some of you know. His name is Morris Mindel, and there is no prouder defender of our Jewish culture and our Yiddish language than him. He taught me the importance of Jewish solidarity and the necessity of a strong union to defend workers' interests.

'But my father also taught me something else. To look at the world around me, to do my best to analyse it and understand it. So let me tell you what I see today. I see an industry that is changing right before our very eyes –' Mick could sense a low groan coming from the middle rows. 'Some of you have heard me say this before,' he said, an ad lib delivered with a modest smile, a neat nod to those who had heard him thumping this drum a hundred times already. 'But I have to tell you, I have got a glimpse of the future and this is what I see.' He paused, just as he had in those silent rehearsals of the mind. And then he belted out his next line: 'The machines are coming! The machines are coming! My friends, the machines are coming.

'You've all seen them, the blind-stitch machine, the basting-out machine, the basting-up machine, the Reese buttonhole machine, the trimming machine. These devices will change everything we do. There will be no sense in small workshops any more. The work will move to big factories, where all this machinery can be used. And that means organizing on a much bigger scale, uniting with other workers in the same factory and in other factories like it. We cannot do that as a small craft union, one that ignores half the workforce – the women who work as hard as we do but get half the pay and threaten our jobs as a result. We need to change.

'Still, even this is not the central issue before us tonight. That has been touched on by my opponent in the regrettable terms of

"Moscow gold" and suchlike. That is an outrageous smear and should be dismissed as such. My first loyalty has been and always will be to the workers gathered in this room. That is the basis on which I seek to be your chairman.

'The issue at hand is the independence of the Jewish working class, and I know that people feel very deeply on this matter. I do too. But let me tell you what matters even more than independence and that is survival. I was at Cable Street, as were most of you. And I swear that we would not have won that battle without the support of comrades who are not Jewish but know an injustice when they see one. Mosley and his thugs wanted to spill Jewish blood that night and they would have – had it not been for the dockers and others who stood at our side.

'It is 1938 and we face a dire threat. The world is in flames, with the Nazis planning havoc in Europe. I have seen them with my own eyes, on my visits to Germany, and let me tell you, these people are deadly serious and they have a lethal hatred of Jews. Can we fight a threat like that alone? Three thousand of us, alone? We need allies, we need comrades, we need strength in numbers, and that means taking our rightful place in a national union!'

Mick had had to battle through applause to get to the end of that sentence. He could feel the room was coming his way. 'And let me say something else about Jewish "independence". None of our parents or grandparents ever imagined independence to mean a ghetto of our own making. Our persecutors made us live like that and we escaped it. That's why we came here! We didn't want to live shut away from everyone else, but wanted to live alongside them. And don't we want that now? We want our children to belong in England, to get along in England. That's why we work so hard to make sure they know the language, or learn how to play football. Or cricket.' A nice touch, that; a gentle reminder of the Jack Hobbs bat. 'Jewish? Yes, always. But part of this country too. And that begins with the union that represents us.'

By the time he was back in his chair, Mick Mindel knew he had won. The room was in tumult, clanging with feet-stamping applause. He watched, drained but elated, as the tellers passed round two iron ballot boxes, collecting votes. Soon he was joined by his immediate supporters, Sara planting a firm, insistent kiss on his lips. When the result came, it broke all records and all expectations. He had won 93 per cent of the vote.

That night, the Mindel camp debated, analysed and revelled in its victory. Everyone had his own pet explanation for the margin of success. Mick's mother believed fate had taken a hand: it was *beshert*, she would say, fate, that he was elected twenty years to the day after he had visited the union as a boy. Mick pretended to dismiss her prattle as old wives' nonsense. But, though he would not admit it until decades later, privately he wondered if his father had indeed played the decisive role. Not by taking him on that tour, but by being the man he was. The older generation of union members had been reassured to think that Mick Mindel was his father's son. They knew Morris from the Workers' Circle, they knew that no one valued Jewish language and tradition more than him. If Morris's boy believed amalgamation was safe, then maybe it was.

What did Morris himself think that day? Mick had no idea. After a victory that electrified the East End, raining congratulations on the Mindel household, Morris said to his son precisely nothing. Not a word. Mick would always tell people he was sure his father was proud of his success. But, even when he was an old man, it would remain a guess.

The roles of the two men were rapidly reversing: Mick was suddenly an elder in his community. Delegations would arrive to see the chairman, asking for the union's help. One came from the Ivrit Be-Ivrit at Redmans Road – where a young Nat Mindel had once been such an eager pupil – looking for money to continue their Hebrew teaching. Others wanted to organize a fund for orphans. A group urged Mick to have the union campaign for Palestine, another for victims of pogroms in Poland. Almost always these petitioners would be older than Mick, bending like supplicants before a boy king. One deputation, seeking funds for the Workers' Circle Yiddish school, included a familiar face: his father.

Workers would invite the new leader to the wedding of a daughter or the bar mitzvah of a son, expecting him to make a speech befitting an honoured guest. One tailor left a note in his will, asking that Mick Mindel ensure he was buried in a Jewish cemetery. In this community of socialists and Bundists, revolutionaries and anarchists, Mick became a kind of atheists' rabbi.

One of the tougher men in town, the weightlifter Charlie Pitcher – Mick's father's age, no taller than five foot but packed with muscle – decided the new boss needed some protection. He appointed himself as Mick's personal bodyguard. Add to that the ex-policeman on the door at HQ – the union took him on after he had been sacked for going on strike – and the young chairman was guarded like a prince regent.

But it was none of these perks of office that gave Mick his greatest pleasure. That came when he was able to fulfil what had always been a key campaign theme. He had jabbed the air a hundred times insisting that the union had to organize women, fighting for the equal pay and equal rights that would improve their lives and remove the threat to their male fellow workers. 'Women are our natural allies,' he had said. 'They work in the workshops, we've got to protect them.' Now he was in charge, he could act. Pushed by him, the union named its first female official. The pioneer was a woman the chairman knew well: Sara Wesker.

Time was short, with a merger to arrange, but Mick did not slacken. He sat down with the Jewish manufacturers to negotiate his way through the long list of demands he had drawn up, chiefly in his head, throughout the 1930s. Close to the top was holiday pay: Mick's members had never had that before, but he persuaded the manufacturers that for one week in August, when the factories shut down, the tailors and hands and pressers could be paid as if they had worked a forty-eight-hour week: three pounds fourteen shillings for the men and one pound ten shillings for the women. They could take the train to Clacton or Frinton or Southend and be paid for it! Mick was garlanded as a hero.

Next he moved to eliminate the piece-rate system: he wanted

people to be paid for a day's work, not per item. And they should have at least some semblance of notice. As things stood, a boss could tell a worker to walk right there and then. Mick saw to it that in a union shop there had to be fair warning. The manufacturers gave some important ground that year, as 1938 turned into 1939. Perhaps they realized that this was the last time they would sit down with their own, *yidden* to *yidden*. From now on, they feared, they would be talking to strangers.

The union itself continued to look out as well as in. It would think nothing of holding an urgent members meeting with two items on the agenda: '1) The situation of the Jews in Poland and 2) The Basque (Spanish) children'. They cared about their Jewish brothers in Europe, but they found room in their hearts – usually equal room – for those who were not Jews but brothers in humanity.

In all this, Palestine barely registered. The union executive might back the odd campaign and there were some Bundists whose Jewish nationalism now channelled itself into the creation of Zion in Palestine. These days an important chunk of the Yiddish press was in Zionist hands too. But Mick was never too diverted by it. He was aware of Zionism churning away, but he only ever saw it out of the corner of his eye. In 1939 he would face it head on.

The invitation came from Sam Dreen, one of the luminaries of the East End. He was a chum of Rudolf Rocker's, the German-born Catholic anarchist who had become one of London Jewry's unlikeliest leaders. Dreen was a solid disciple, but fate did not make his an easy faith to maintain. He became an employer, owning his own small business. That forced him to leave the United Ladies' Tailors' Trade Union and, eventually, it seems to have eroded his anarchist certainty – it is hard to believe in absolute freedom from rules and pure self-government when you have a business to run. So perhaps Sam Dreen was in the market for a new creed. Either way, a new creed found him: Zionism.

When Dreen called, Mick caught the excitement in his voice instantly. 'Mick, I want you to meet someone. He's in London only for a few days and has asked to meet the leaders of the Jewish working class in Britain, which means you, I suppose, I'm arranging it, can you be at Great Alie Street tomorrow at seven o'clock it will only be you, me and two others, and him of course, but it's best if we meet there –'

'Sam, calm down a moment. You haven't told me who we're meeting.'

'Ah! Silly me. Of course, meeting. Yes. It's Ben-Gurion. Ben-Gurion is here!'

Now Mick understood. Sam Dreen had been a faithful lieutenant to Rocker, but David Ben-Gurion was in a different league. This was a mentor who was not just a player in the streets of Spitalfields; he had become the head of a national, maybe even a world, movement. As the founder of Mapai, the workers' party of Eretz Yisrael, and chairman of the Jewish Agency for Palestine, he was the undisputed leader of the Yishuv and was edging Chaim Weizmann aside as the very symbol of Zionism.

They met on a Sunday at the offices of the Workers' Circle. Mick was on time, but Ben-Gurion was already there. He stood up and, to Mick's relief, he was no bigger than Mick. They shook hands and, for once, Mick did not have to tilt his eyes upward. Dreen smiled: my two Napoleons.

Mick took a good look. The face, fifty-three years old, was baggy and creased, with two white horns of hair guarding each side of a bald head. He twinkled, like a kindly uncle from the old country, but when Mick looked closer into the eyes there was a steel, even a coldness there. He felt a shiver of something like fear.

Ben-Gurion did not wait for the meeting to be called to order, or to be invited to speak. He got straight to business, offering not so much as a sentence of small talk. Mick was still standing when he began. *'Ikh hob dikh gevolt zen vayl du bist der onfirer fin dem Yidishen proletariat in dem land.'*

Mick jolted. He had not expected this, though quite what language he imagined Ben-Gurion would speak he did not know. Russian would not have done much good, nor Hebrew. It was obvious he would speak in Yiddish. Mick felt seven years old again, hearing matters of world moment discussed in a language he understood but could not easily speak.

'I wanted to see you because you are the leader of the Jewish proletariat of this country.' Mick tilted his head and exhaled, as if to say I don't know about that, but the gesture of English modesty was wasted on the Palestinian. Ben-Gurion carried straight on, alternating by sentence, sometimes even by clause, from Yiddish to English. 'I am calling on Jewish leaders throughout Europe and delivering the same message: there is no future here. You must tell those who follow you, Jewish workers, that their destiny is in Palestine. There Jews will, at last, be in control of their own destiny. We will not live as guests in other peoples' countries as you do here or as I did in Russia. We will be the majority, forming our own government and taking our own decisions, for the first time in 2,000 years. The days of exile are ending. At this very moment, young men and women are constructing a Jewish society which will be normal. We will work the land, we will control the means of production, we will not be confined to the margins, but will form the economic base of our own society.'

Mick wondered if the great Ben-Gurion gave this spiel to everyone, or somehow knew that the young man before him was a communist and was therefore calculatedly pressing all the right buttons. *Means of production.* Mick would be flattered if that were true, but he doubted it. He knew Ben-Gurion, like the rest of the men in control of Zionism, was a socialist even if not a full-blooded communist. He had vaguely heard the argument that Zionists were good Marxists because they understood that, if the Jews were ever to have a revolution, they first had to have their own country. Maybe that's what Ben-Gurion believed too.

'This is no longer about forming Utopia. This is about survival. A homeland in Palestine is the only hope for the Jewish people. It is the only place we can live. You can see what is happening in Europe as well as I can. Jewish life here, in *golus*, in exile, is doomed. Our only future is in Palestine. But the Yishuv is struggling, Mr Mindel. We depend on new energy, and that means new people:

fit, young, new people. The ragged, the desperate and the old we have no shortage of. We need the strong. You are how old?'

'Twenty-nine,' Mick said, his voice uncomfortably close to a croak.

'Twenty-nine.' Ben-Gurion was leaning forward now, almost tilting out of his chair. 'You are the man to do it. You are a young man and you can lead the young. Go from here and urge them to sell up, sell whatever they have, and take the next ship to Palestine.'

Mick imagined agreeing to Ben-Gurion's request. He pictured himself won over by the old man, setting out to persuade the Jews of the East End to change their lives, to make a fresh start. Even if he wanted to do it, how would he ever find the eloquence to stand in front of the bulk of his members – men in their forties and fifties – whose horizon stretched no further than whether there would be any work to do tomorrow? How would he stand before them and tell them to cross Europe and the Mediterranean Sea for a new life in an utterly alien land? How would he face people who had weathered a depression that had ground them down for nearly a decade and tell them that now they had to steel themselves for yet another sacrifice? How would he tell those who had fled pogroms for a new beginning here in London that they had to pack their bags once again? He knew what his members wanted: a roof over their heads, a kitchen they could keep clean and walls that did not slither with bugs. They wanted a decent school for their children, so they at least might have a shot at something better than stitching a fur collar or pushing a punishingly heavy iron. They did not dream of the cool stones of Jerusalem or the birthplace of the prophets; they dreamed of getting out of Stepney, of having a house with a small patch of garden, perhaps in Essex or a north London suburb somewhere, of a son trained to be a doctor. Their heads were full of this land of promise, not the Promised Land. How could he, Mick Mindel, who prided himself on his knack for voicing the hopes and anxieties of the people he represented, come to them with such a fantasy, a vision so completely remote from their daily lives?

Besides, he was a communist. He had listened closely to the debates on the Palestine question, including the formal communist vs. Zionist showdown at Shoreditch town hall when Willie Gallagher took on Rabbi Maurice Perlzweig of the World Jewish Congress. Mick had rooted for Gallagher and reckoned he had had the better arguments that day.

The communists believed that Zionism overlooked the locomotive of all human affairs: class. Jewish workers surely had more in common with Arab workers than they did with Jewish bosses; Zionism asked for national unity when every good Marxist knew it was proletarian solidarity, across the nations, that mattered. Leaders like Ben-Gurion called themselves socialists, but they seemed to envisage socialism and capitalism existing alongside each other in the new Zion. Two systems in one country: no communist thought that could ever work. No wonder Zionism's greatest backers were among the middle class. It was a bourgeois idea and a distraction from the real interests of the workers.

What was more, said communist doctrine, a Jewish state would inevitably be religious – and religion was the opiate of the people. Most Jewish communists, however attached they might be to Yiddish, to the tales of Shalom Aleichem or the songs, plays and music of the old country, had little patience for belief. They accepted the Marxist teaching that faith in a supreme being was nothing but a soothing illusion, an almost deliberate attempt to divert working people's gaze from the injustices of their daily lives. The rabbis were pedlars of superstition, nothing more. And if there were ever to be a Jewish state they would surely dominate, just as they had whenever Jews had governed themselves before. Behind the ghetto walls of the past, the rabbis had kept Jews in line. Their grip only loosened when the walls came down, when suddenly they had to compete with a thousand other forces of modern life for Jewish attention. In a Jewish state, the walls would be back up.

But the argument that struck Mick with greatest force was that Zion would not solve the Jews' largest problem. 'A Jewish homeland will not be a cure for the disease of anti-Semitism,' communist speakers would say. 'It will instead be a kind of hospitalization of the Jews, a medical refuge. It may give temporary relief but it will never get to the root cause. Those Jews who live there will be fleeing from the problem – but the problem will remain, in the world outside.' The only way to solve it would be a radical change in the way human life itself was organized, bringing justice to all, including the Jews. Anti-Semitism was just one more deformity in the world. It would vanish in the revolution, and the people to make it disappear were the communists.

'I have great respect for you, Mr Ben-Gurion,' Mick began finally, 'and I am honoured to meet you here today. I have listened closely to what you have said and I have no doubt that in the weeks and months to come the members of the union I represent will consider seriously your point of view. I bring you their fraternal greetings and, of course, their good wishes for their fellow workers in Palestine. Once again, it has been a great pleasure to meet you.'

He could see the disappointment on Sam Dreen's face. Mick had spoken as if this was a Thursday night meeting of the United Ladies' Tailors' Trade Union executive rather than an encounter with a latter-day Moses. He had not risen to the occasion. Maybe Sam thought Mick was deliberately being rude, as if to show his disdain for the bourgeois nationalist ideology of Zionism. He certainly had not fallen to his knees before Ben-Gurion and sworn his dedication to the cause, as Sam realized at that moment he had hoped Mick would.

Ben-Gurion was too good a politician to reveal himself as clearly. He stayed in his chair, leaning back in it now, and, smiling, gave Mick a small nod – a gesture that simultaneously combined polite thanks, recognition that his request had been rebuffed and a signal that the meeting was over. Mick rose, reached for Ben-Gurion's hand, shook it, offered a guilty nod in Dreen's direction (though without looking at him) and then moved for the door.

Once he was out, he closed his eyes and took three deep breaths. He had, he now realized, been quaking with nerves. The Yiddish had intimidated him; so had the pretence that he and Ben-Gurion were meeting as equals; so had the wildness of the old man's request. Mick had spoken briefly in part to keep his ordeal to its shortest possible duration. And he had felt too overawed, too outgunned to say what he really felt. The truth was, he could not call on his fellow Jews and trade unionists to ship out because he himself did not want to go. Mick Mindel lived in London and, he realized that day, sitting eyeball to eyeball with the future first prime minister of Israel, he wanted to stay. His ambitions were in Britain. He wanted to be part of that society, even to belong in it. That, after all, was one of the reasons he had joined the Communist Party. There, among his comrades, he was not only a Jew; he could be English, fighting for the future of the country that was now his home. He was not about to give all that up for a Jewish-only enclave in Arabia. His ancestors had lived in ghettos for too long. He was damned if he would volunteer to live in one now, even a large one of the Jews' own making, under the warm Levantine sun.

Word soon spread: Mick Mindel was the man who had dared say no to the king of Israel. In communist circles, he was a hero. Like the titans of the Bible who prove their faith by resisting great temptation, like Joseph fending off the advances of Potiphar's wife, his own conviction had been tested. He had faced Zionism's most powerful advocate and stood firm. His trust remained where it had been for a decade. Mick felt as strong in his conviction then as he had that day in Cable Street. It was the comrades of communism, not the false prophets of Zion, who would bring deliverance.

But, like Job, he would not be tested just once. It was the summer of 1939, August, barely a month or two after the meeting with Ben-Gurion. Mick, who still worked in the daytime as a cutter, had returned to the home he now shared with Sara Wesker and her family after an exhausting twelve-hour shift. He was turning his front door key when he heard the sound of the wireless, louder than usual. He called out to Sara, but heard no reply. He tried again, and again nothing. The moment he was out of the tiny hallway, he could see why. Sara was huddling by the wireless, her ear next to it even though the voice was loud and clear. She did not look up; her eyes were frozen. Her face, always sallow, was now a deathly white. Mick felt his heart surge in panic, yet she was clearly not ill. He began to speak – 'What's –' – but Sara hissed him hush.

The room was filled by the voice of the BBC: '. . . standing under a portrait of Vladimir Lenin, Foreign Minister Molotov signed the pact in Moscow on behalf of the Soviet Union, while Germany was represented by Foreign Minister Von Ribbentrop. General Secretary Stalin looked on . . .'

Sara had her head in her hands, moving it from side to side. She began letting out a low noise, a sound Mick had never heard from her before. It was part wail, part growl – an animal wounded and angry. The wireless would not stop.

'The text of the non-aggression pact between the two governments is as follows:

'Desirous of strengthening the cause of peace between Germany and the USSR . . .

'Article I. Both high contracting parties obligate themselves to desist from any act of violence, any aggressive action, and any attack on each other, either individually or jointly with other powers.

'Article II. Should one of the high contracting parties become the object of belligerent action by a third power, the other high contracting party shall in no manner lend its support to this third power.

'Article III. The governments of the two high contracting parties shall in the future maintain continual contact with one another . . .'

Mick felt dizzy. It was hot outside, he was sweating, he needed to sit down, he needed to drink water, he needed to think. There was obviously some mistake, some terrible act of deception designed to break the will of communism. Perhaps there had been a coup and the BBC was broadcasting propaganda.

'Both parties shall settle these disputes or conflicts exclusively through friendly exchange of opinion,' the voice was saying.

Friendly. Mick put his hand on Sara's shoulder and she at last raised her face. Her eyes were red raw, her cheeks wet; she seemed to be trembling. He felt his own innards dissolving.

They stayed there, Sara still holding the wireless, Mick standing at her side, gripping her shoulders for what seemed like hours. Mick's mind was racing as he tried to explain what he was hearing. Now the BBC was saying the treaty would be binding for ten years, that ratifications would be exchanged in Berlin.

What kind of elaborate trick was this that could pretend the Soviet Union, the beacon of world communism, would make common cause with its sworn enemy? Communism was to be fascism's slayer, not its accomplice. Mick remembered the faces in the crowds at Cologne, the Brownshirts on parade in Berlin, their fists curled around flickering torches. How could his leaders, the men at the front of the liberating column of communism, be partners with these thugs?

That evening Mick and Sara's flat became a *shiva* house. Comrades from all over Stepney would knock on the door, shuffle in and stare at their feet. Few could even speak. Occasionally someone might offer a piece of amateur analysis: 'Now Hitler's got what he wants. He knows now he won't have to go to war on two fronts. He has closed down the eastern front.' 'Maybe it's a ploy?' But no one was in much of a mood for debate. They wanted just to share the shock with others. For ten years they had marched together, the people in this room, selling copies of the *Daily Worker*, handing out election leaflets, sweeping the floors of draughty meeting rooms, arguing the finer points of Marxist doctrine, hiking through the Essex countryside, singing the Internationale – and all of it in the cause of communism, the party and the Soviet Union. They believed that holy trinity would bring salvation, to the human race of course but especially to the Jews. The Nazi beast could drool for Jewish blood all it wanted, it could bare its claws, but there would always be a mightier, more noble creature standing in its way. Communism would keep the thugs of Cologne in their cage. But now St George and the dragon, David and Goliath, were on the same side – and the Jews were alone.

Morning came and it was no lie, no devilish trick by the enemies of socialism. Mick saw the *Daily Worker* and felt his stomach turn. 'Soviet Union and Germany Sign Pact,' read the headline. 'Stalin Present at Vital Meeting: Treaty Valid for Period of Ten Years.' The pact was real and, worse, the British Communist Party had not spoken out against it.

On the first Saturday afternoon after news of the pact broke, a meeting was convened at party headquarters on King Street. Mick and Sara were in the front row; occasionally they would squeeze each other's hand. The first to speak was Palme Dutt, executive committee member and editor of the party journal, *Labour Monthly*. A Swedish Indian by background, he was an exotic figure among the sometimes dowdy stalwarts of the left. He commanded enormous intellectual respect, wearing the proud Marxist tag 'theoretician'. He was one of the very few British party members to count as a substantial figure in world communism.

Moscow had made its decision, Dutt began. It had made it not only as the representative of the proletariat of the Soviet Union but in the best interests of the international working class. Those distant from the decision were in no position to criticize it since they were not fully apprised of the facts and could not reach the objective, scientific conclusions of the leadership. This was the nature of democratic centralism; it required the trust and loyalty of the comrades of the Soviet party and therefore, by extension, of the world communist movement.

'Ours is not to reason why,' Mick whispered to Sara, a sneer in his voice.

Next came Harry Pollitt, general secretary of the Communist Party and a personal hero to the young couple in the front row. They had met at his election rally a decade earlier; his inspiration had brought them together. He spoke for everyone who had huddled together in Sara and Mick's flat that day, articulating the shock they had all felt when they heard the news. Mick and Sara were bracing themselves for the 'But . . .' as Pollitt would finally pivot and join Dutt in defending the mother party in Moscow. But there was no but. He said he could not defend an accommodation with the Nazis; it was a pact with the devil. It was at odds with everything that communism stood for.

Suddenly there seemed to be a heckler. Instinctively people turned around, except the noise was coming from the front. Finally they realized the voice was on the platform and it was Dutt's. He was interrupting Pollitt. It was difficult to make out what he was saying, but the tone was clear enough: Dutt was denouncing the general secretary. His crime had been to disagree with him and therefore with Moscow. Pollitt was now shouting from the lectern, but Dutt was bellowing just as loudly and gesticulating too, leaning out of his chair to brandish a rolled-up tube of papers in his rival's direction. Everyone was too stunned to do anything; certainly no one dared tell the two most senior men in British communism to calm down.

Mick wanted to cheer Pollitt, but he and everyone else in the room stayed strangely quiet. It had been a funeral of a week; most of them were too dazed to say anything. Mick even kept silent when the central committee lined up behind Dutt and voted to punish the general secretary for a violation of party discipline, suspending him from his post for twelve months.

Mick looked around and, almost for the first time in the Communist Party, he felt lonely. Why were all these people apparently able to make a pact with the gangsters of Nazism when he could not? Why did he find the very idea stomach-curdling when they did not? What was so different about him? Surely it could not be the dull, flat fact he had been taught to regard as politically insignificant? Surely it could not be because he was a Jew?

Those seminars in Marxist doctrine had stressed that all people were equal and, to all intents and purposes, the same. The very idea of religions and nations and tribes was so much reactionary nonsense, designed to divide workers against each other. It did not matter what mark had been branded on you at birth, you were brothers under the skin. There was only one race: the human race.

In the communist future, national or ethnic groups would not have to think like groups any longer. In the face of injustice, they would be able to look for protection to their fellow human beings, to the brotherhood of man. That was the theory and, at Cable Street, Mick had seen it work in practice. From now on, it would be like that everywhere. His father and his friends might reckon only Jews could be trusted to fight for Jewish rights in the workplace. Ben-Gurion had said only a Jewish state, with a Jewish government and a Jewish army, could protect Jewish lives. But they were both wrong. Mick had told them so.

Yet here he was, in this hall, with a new, queasy thought snaking through his head. Maybe he could not rely on these people, his communist comrades, to protect him from the Nazi menace after all. Maybe they did not fear Hitler and fascism as much as he did because, in the end, they were not Jews. Maybe the only people who would ever truly care about the safety of Jews were not the brotherhood of man but Jews. There, he had said it. Not out loud, admittedly, but to himself he had uttered a heresy. In his mind he had just agreed with Ben-Gurion. He had sounded like his father.

10   *Hear Our Cries*

She had arrived in a country on the eve of war and yet she felt like a refugee who had crossed the border to safety. At last she could feed Srollik and Sara properly; at last she was in a place she understood, surrounded by people she loved.

Feige had called her cousin Jack, the only person in the family of any means. He owned a factory, making beds and furniture, and even had a car. Much older than Feige, he had always nurtured a soft spot for her; relatives used to joke that he was waiting for her to grow up, so they could marry.

Except he did not wait. He had found a wife and was now the father of two children. But he was the first person Feige called when she arrived in England – she knew he would not say no.

Mindful of his wife, he did not offer to house the Palestinian trio under his own roof. Instead, he threw open the doors to his mother's house in Bethune Road, Stoke Newington, in north London. To Feige, the solidity of the bricks, the greyness of the Hackney sky, the constancy of the rain, were all delights. She was away from the baking claustrophobia of Petach Tikva. Jack would come over and play with the children, and Feige would allow herself a wistful daydream of family life.

It was only a temporary haven. The outbreak of war in 1939 meant she would have to get the children out of London and into the countryside. A single mother who had grown up in inner London and lived, twice, in the dust of the Middle East was now about to try her luck in rural England.

The government wanted all over-fives evacuated immediately – and that meant Srollik. The trouble was, Feige could find nowhere that would take in all three of them. She searched and searched but everyone turned her away. She had no choice: she would have to

Just off the boat, Srollik and Sara.

send Srollik out on his own, like an infant pioneer heading to the frontier. He was handed over to a farmer and his wife in the Hertfordshire village of Kimpton to be a paying lodger. Feige gave the couple strict instructions: the little boy was to be given no meat and especially no bacon. She and Sara would follow as soon as they could find a place. In the meantime, they would be an hour's train ride away, back in London.

Eventually Feige got closer. In the neighbouring village of Wheat-hampstead she rented a room. But it was small, with only enough space for her and baby Sara. Srollik would have to stay with the farmer, making do with visits on Sundays (though not Saturdays, because of the Sabbath prohibition on travel). When his mother arrived at the door, Srollik, not yet five years old, would rush and hug her leg, squeezing so hard it hurt both of them. He would talk and talk and talk, the words tumbling out. Once he detailed what he had been eating, telling his still-orthodox mother of the farmer's wife's lunchtime speciality: rabbit pie. Feige gasped, quickly covering her mouth in shock. Despite her instructions, her son was eating *treif*, food that was defiantly not kosher.

The entire bus ride from Kimpton back to Wheathampstead, Feige tried to think of a way out. She did not want him there; he did not want to be there. What could she do?

She turned the puzzle over in her mind as she carried Sara home, gave her something to eat and tucked her into bed. Much later that evening there was a weak knock on the door. She opened it to find her son, exhausted and dishevelled. He had followed her bus all the way home. He had been walking for five or six hours. She scooped up the panting, scuffed little boy and vowed never to leave him again.

Feige soon found work, as a secretary in a local factory making batteries. Now she had enough money to rent somewhere for the three of them and she found it in Bulls Yard, a row of tiny workmen's cottages that seemed to sink into the River Lea. To Sara, it looked like the picture on a biscuit tin. She loved it, storing away memories to carry with her for the rest of her life. They had a Siamese cat called Edie, whose elegance fascinated the little girl. She seemed like a lady.

In summer the three of them would brace themselves and take a dip in the stream that ran through a nearby field. Srollik would jump in first, paddling away furiously. His mother approached more gingerly, wading in with her clothes still on, all the while holding her daughter close to her chest, doing her best to keep the little one warm. Later she encouraged Sara to swim, holding her under her chin and pulling her along like a tug boat dragging its net. The little girl feared she was about to drown: her breath would quicken. And then she would hear her mother's voice and all would be calm.

Later they might find a meadow for a picnic. One golden afternoon, Srollik thought he would provide dessert by vaulting the wall into a nearby orchard, returning with his sweater rolled up into a tray bulging with contraband apples. Feige told her son she was ashamed of him: it was wrong to steal and he would have to take them back. She did not let on her delight that this young man, her son, was prepared to go to such lengths to feed his family.

On colder days, they would take walks, picking wild watercress and the odd large mushroom. Sara would moan that her legs were too tired to walk any further, and her mother would gather her up, hugging her the rest of the way home. When it rained, Feige would teach Sara to knit. She told her that one day she would be able to make clothes, just like her. Sara would stare open-mouthed as her mother clicked and clacked the needles, crossing here and turning there, marvelling at her skill. Nothing went to waste. When she or Srollik had grown out of a sweater or gloves, her mummy would unravel the wool and turn the long string into something new to wear. To Sara it was magic.

The weekdays were not so happy. Feige would go to the factory, dropping off Sara early at nursery, which the little girl hated. A 1940 kindergarten was a strict affair, where the children had to line up, stand to attention and keep still and quiet. The low point of the day came when the teacher would stand, like a sergeant inspecting

a parade, before her charges, her hand clenched around a dark brown medicine bottle. Inside was cod liver oil, then deemed to be essential for the joints, guts and all-round good health of the young.

Sara retched at the very sight of the stuff. The consistency made her gag; she could not bear the smell. She learned fast that cod liver line-up was a good time to need the toilet, but she could not always escape. The terrifying woman would grab her by the wrist and drag her back to face the spoon. She deployed all her strength to keep her jaws wired shut, but the teacher would win in the end. And when she did, Sara would be sick.

She could not wait to get out of that nursery and into big school like Srollik. Her brother promised there was no cod liver oil there: she would be happy. As it turned out, she was to taste misery with a new flavour.

Her teacher was tall and thin and very strict. One day after playtime she called out, 'Hocherman!' Less than five years old, Sara still recognized this as something out of the ordinary. All the other children were called by their first names: Mary, James, Katherine. This woman seemed to linger over the word Hocherman, making it sound strange. She called my mother to stand at the front.

'I heard you shouting in the playground,' the teacher was saying.

Sara was confused. She was so new at the school, she barely had anyone to play with, let alone shout at.

'I've told you before,' said the teacher, bringing the hard wood of a ruler down on to the flesh behind Sara's knees.

The little girl yelped, 'I wasn't shouting,' which only brought the flat, sharp stick cracking down harder.

It went on like that every day for a year, or so it seemed to my five-year-old mother. Decades later she would think about what had happened: the only Jewish girl in the school, the only Jewish family for miles around, the only girl known to the dinner ladies as No Meat, and she was singled out for humiliation and punishment. Even at five she was aware of being treated differently and therefore being different. It was not an awareness she could have articulated, of course, but she understood it physically. The flesh behind her knees understood it.

Sara complained to her mother, whose answer also stayed with her for years: 'Well, you must have done something to deserve it.' So she never mentioned it again. Instead she lived in fear of school, hating the class she was in and dreading the next one up. The teacher there looked even scarier, a woman as wide as a couch, with harsh, ugly features. Yet there was a surprise. This fat ogre of my mother's imagination turned out to be full of care and love and took a special shine to little Sara, who suddenly started to do well with her sums and her reading and writing.

And that was life in Wheathampstead. There were reminders of their unusual family situation, like the afternoons – rare – when their mother would sit Srollik and Sara down and make them send postcards to their 'Daddy'. Sara could only imagine what this man far away might look like or who he was or why she was meant to love him.

There would be days during the school holidays when, with their mother still having to work, the children were farmed out to one of the village's better-off families to play and have tea. Their house was big and comfortable, the mother tall and somehow substantial. 'Butter or jam?' she asked one teatime. Sara said jam and that was what she got: a piece of bread with just jam on it. She wanted to cry. She thought she was going to get butter *and* jam. At that moment she wanted her mummy so badly, but her mummy was not there. And Sara had to go back to this house and this lady, somebody else's mummy, every day.

One time Sara took ill and Feige left Srollik to look after her. When Feige came home she found her youngest child all but knocked out, unconscious in her cot. Srollik was standing over her, clasping an empty bottle of cough medicine: he had been giving his sister a swig of the mixture every few minutes. He was seven years old and he thought he had been a very good boy.

He had big responsibilities. When Sara was deemed old enough to take Hebrew classes, it fell to Srollik to escort her on the bus to St Albans, the nearest town with a large enough Jewish community to have a *cheder*. The boy had strict instructions not to leave without her; over and over he told her to meet him after class. But Sara took herself to the bus stop and some well-meaning adult had bundled her on, saying, 'This is your bus,' and she had gone home by herself, crying all the way because she was without her brother. And meanwhile Srollik was back in St Albans, terrified, walking up to policemen asking, 'Have you seen a little girl in a blue dress?' And back at home Feige was going out of her mind until finally an ashen-faced Srollik turned up at the door – without his sister – and when he saw Sara sitting there, somehow magically already there, he sighed the sigh of a man of eighty and said, 'Such a lot of troubles for such a little boy,' and his words became a kind of family motto for decades to come, even among people who had never heard that story.

Despite her mother being away each day, despite the Daddy she did not know, despite the cod liver oil and the cough mixture, Sara loved Wheathampstead. She loved the river that bubbled past the cottage windows; she loved the bushes, their branches studded with berries; she loved the smell of fields and hay; she loved it when her mother tucked her up at night. If anyone had asked her, she would have wanted to stay there for ever.

But Sara was not involved in the discussion when Benny, still the responsible brother and de facto head of the Bitensky clan, told Feige it was time to come back to London.

'Feige, it's nice here and you've done the cottage very nicely,' he began. It was Friday night, after the kids were in bed. (Someone from the family came up to the cottage almost every Shabbat. They told themselves they were doing Feige a favour, keeping her company, but they were also relieved to get out of London.)

'Thank you,' she replied, pretending to take his compliment at face value. She knew he had more to say, but she stayed staring straight ahead, refusing to turn around from the sink and the dishes. She did not want to encourage him.

'It's very pretty. But it's not right for the children to grow up in the middle of nowhere. It's *yennevelt* here.' The back of beyond.

'The children are happy.'

'But you're the only Jewish family here! It's not so nice for the kids to grow up like that, without their own. They're becoming like little farm children, your kids. They know about brambles and cows and pigs, God forbid. What do they know of *yiddishkeit*?'

'Our father knew about cows. There's no disgrace in knowing about cows. And they go to *cheder*.'

'And we all know what a great success story that is. *Such a lot of troubles for such a little boy*.' Feige turned around to face Benny with a mock frown. That episode had already become legend. 'Anyway, it's not just the kids. You need your family around you. Rivvy's a good sister, she comes when she can, but it's a *schlep*. Jack likes to come here, I know, but he has a family of his own. You need us five minutes away. What happens when one of the children is ill, God forbid? Who are you going to leave them with?' Feige thought of the empty bottle of cough syrup, a drama she had kept to herself.

'I know, but they love it here. You should see Sara skip down those country lanes. And after what they went through . . .'

'We all know about that. But it'll be better for you in London. Feige, you know we're right. It's for your own good.'

And so Sara packed her knitted teddy away into the suitcase that was always under the bed and the three of them – four, counting Edie – left Bulls Yard for the last time. Sara said goodbye to it all: to the row of cottages, to the alleyway and to the green door that led on to the main street, to the River Lea, even to the outside toilet. She ran from one to the other, touching each place as if its memory would burn into her fingertips. This was the first home she could remember. Now barely five years old, she had spent half her life there.

Children, especially young ones, are meant to forget easily and move on. But Sara pined for Wheathampstead and not only because it was the prettiest place she had ever seen. It was also an earthly paradise compared to the hellhole she landed in next.

Benny had arranged rooms in Hunton Court, a dead end off Hanbury Street, near Brick Lane, in the East End. The smell of human defecation was so sharp, it seared the septum. There were people upstairs who seemed to regard the stairwell, and maybe even their own living room, as one big latrine. Outside brought no respite. Being a dead end, the side of the house became an improvised urinal for all comers, especially after chucking-out time. Even by the putrid standards of the East End's poorest streets, this place stank.

The children missed the air and space of the country. Edie had been sent back to Wheathampstead within days of her arrival in the city: she was a cat with class and the stench of Brick Lane was not for her. Srollik now hankered for a dog, constantly pestering his mother. He found an ally in his young and persuadable aunt, Rivvy. 'They want some nature,' she would tell her sister, petitioning on Srollik's behalf. 'It's all bricks and dirt here. They want some nature. Let them have a dog.' Finally Feige gave way, and Rivvy, who always turned up with some treat or other, came to Hunton Court with her arms coiled around a puppy.

That did not work out too well. The kids went to school, their mother was at work, so the dog stayed, locked in, at home. When Sara and Srollik came back they only had to set one foot inside before they were sliding from room to room. The floor was so slick with what Feige primly called his 'business' that this puppy did not need to walk anywhere: he just slid. Rivvy had strict instructions to take the dog back where it came from. Now.

Soon, though, Srollik was to become a hero. Not eight years old, he took his responsibilities as the man of the house seriously. And he knew that his most urgent duty was to get his family out of this rotting hole. So when he heard from a friend about an aunt who had a flat on Vallance Road in Hughes Mansions – a mansion! – and the flat had its own bathroom – a bathroom, in the East End! – and the aunt was moving out, he snapped into action. He ran home to tell his mother, who immediately, and using her best office-clerk handwriting, fired off letters to all the relevant authorities. Eventually an envelope came bringing the wonderful news that they, the Hochermans, were to be the new tenants. The three of them danced, literally danced, around that tiny, stinking room.

Hughes Mansions! The name did not disappoint. There was fresh paint on the walls and, at last, Feige Hocherman had a chance to show the world the woman she was. She kept it cleaner than a surgeon's needle, so tidy the walls seemed to squeak. When she could, she would even bring home a couple of flowers, fussing over them until they somehow filled the vase. She and Sara shared one room, Srollik had the other. Not that either of these two places provided the emotional heart of the flat. That was the bathroom.

The instant they had moved in there was a rota. Not for the three of them but for the entire extended family. No Bitensky needed to use the public baths again; they just booked themselves into Hughes Mansions. Every night was the same: a knock on the door from an aunt or uncle, with perhaps a friend in tow. A few pleasantries exchanged and then straight to the tub.

Sara would play with Rivvy, brushing her hair or trying on her big, grown-up shoes. She liked to hang around while Rivvy and her mother chatted; there was certainly no fun to be had with Srollik, who was out on the streets, haring around with the older boys.

The evenings in Hughes Mansions were fun; it was the nights Sara could not stand. First would come the noise, the droning moan of the air-raid siren. Next would come the hand on the shoulder, her mother shaking her awake. Still dozy, clutching her sheets and blankets, they would head for the cold stairwell. Down they would go, her mother shouting for Srollik to hurry up.

'Get down from there,' she would say, as Srollik clung to his perch on the landing, gripping the outside railings and craning his neck up towards the sky.

'Coming,' he replied, still staring. He would be watching the dogfights, planes diving and looping, their engines whining, each hurling fire at the other. Sara would blink at the sight of the flames, her eyelids shuttering again and again at all that orange. She was desperate to get away, tugging at her mother's sleeve. 'Let's *go*.'

She would be heading down the stairwell, her mother still shouting for Srollik to catch up, and each time they reached another landing the little girl would glimpse more burning. There were flames wherever she looked. The whole world seemed to be on fire.

There were a few public shelters nearby, several of them in warehouse basements. Sara found these almost as much of an ordeal as the raids themselves. All those unknown, bleary faces huddled in the dark: old men shrouded in blankets, mothers cradling wailing babies – it was a scene from one of those witches-and-ghouls fairy tales she found so terrifying. She shivered into her mother's chest, begging her to make it stop and take her back to bed.

But the raids were nightly and soon Sara learned not to fall asleep. She would stay awake waiting for the siren, twitchy as an alleycat. She would be exhausted the next day; Feige would see the charcoal lines under her eyes. She faced what was now a familiar dilemma: she hated to uproot her children yet again but how could she keep them here?

If she had asked Sara what she wanted, she might have been

surprised by the response. For, despite the bathroom and the vases of flowers, Hughes Mansions contained some demons for her young daughter. It was not just the nightly stampede to the shelters. The stairwells had also brought an unhappiness she had kept bottled inside, revealed to no one.

No more than six years old, Sara was walking herself home from school when she noticed him. He was young, in a uniform – he seemed like a policeman, or perhaps a soldier – and on a bicycle. But instead of sailing past, he stopped, right outside her building. As she went inside, she saw him get off the bike and, quite deliberately, prop it up against a wall. He followed her up the stairs.

She walked quicker now, but she could hear his louder, faster footsteps coming closer. She tried to gallop up the stairs, but she stumbled and she could hear he was right behind her. She straightened up on the landing, as if to let him go by. And then she saw his face and her body flooded with fear. There was something in his eyes she had not seen before. He began reaching for her, squeezing, pressing and touching. He was pushing at her skirt, and she was wriggling, squirming to get away. She knew she did not like it, she did not want this man touching her, and suddenly she was screaming as loud as she could and the man jolted back – as if shocked by the noise. And in that moment she ran to the side of him, then up the stairwell until she was finally at her own front door. She closed the door behind her, her heart thumping with terror. All she could think of was the man's face, the odd, distant look in his eye, the uniform, the bike placed so carefully against the wall. She saw her mother and knew straight away: she would never utter a word about it. Not to her aunts, not even the lovely Rivvy, not to Srollik and not to her mummy. She was too scared to say the words out loud. She would not speak of it for another sixty years.

There was much to escape. Which made Sara Hocherman and her brother prime candidates for the Avigdor High School, formerly of Stoke Newington in Hackney but now relocated to the Bedfordshire village of Shefford.

Plenty of children became evacuees. It was rarer for an entire school to move itself out of the city and start again in the country-side. And this was no ordinary school. Avigdor was the personal fiefdom of Rabbi Solomon Schonfeld, who inherited it from his father, its founder. As early as 1938 he had understood the mortal danger confronting the Jews of Europe and had transformed himself into a one-man rescue agency. He crossed again and again to the Continent, plucking out as many Jewish children as he could. He cut through bureaucracy, soothed diplomatic niceties, arranged transport – anything it took to pull young Jews from the fire he knew was about to engulf them. In one transport alone, in November 1938, he led 200 children from Austria to England. The parents took their young to the Vienna railway station themselves, promising they would see each other again soon, urging their kids to write often, not to crush the biscuits in their bag and to wrap up warm against the cold. They could not come too, since Britain's hospitality was only extended to these kindertransport. So Schonfeld became known as the Pied Piper; and those who anticipated the coming catastrophe saw his school as a Noah's Ark.

A troupe of 500 orthodox Jewish schoolchildren arriving among the white-painted cottages and green shutters, vicarages and rec-tories, pubs and bowling greens of a village like Shefford, which had never known any Jews, would always have caused a shock. That over half of them, thanks to Schonfeld, were foreigners, some with only a word or two of English, only widened the gulf. The villagers had few points of reference. On the day of their arrival, one churchgoing woman was overheard calling to her husband, 'Tom, come quickly, the Children of Israel are here.'

The newcomers had gathered in the market square, where they were to be divided up and allocated to foster families. 'I would like to have four little girls,' said a Mrs Mitchell, getting proceedings under way. Others took six or one or three. The rector's wife set an example by volunteering for one of the least popular job lots: seven boys, all teenagers. Mr Taylor set a record by taking eight children, from ages seven to seventeen, and all from one family.

Everybody did their share, the parson and the baker, the headmaster and the milkman, the antiques dealer and, yes, even the pig-food collector. Before long, the market square was empty and Shefford was full of Jews.

By the time Sara and Srollik arrived in 1942, this island of Jewish orthodoxy was well established. They had sorted out the problem which surfaced on day one, when the foster children offended their hosts by refusing to eat the ham omelettes or bacon sandwiches that had been so generously prepared for them. From then on, all meals were taken at the school. And they had even found a building to teach in, after the old cinema they had first used for lessons was burned down. Slowly Shefford's villagers and the Children of Israel were getting used to each other. *Tzitzit*, the ritual fringed garment worn by orthodox boys, could be seen hanging on many a washing line. Moss, the village grocer, now stocked kosher margarine because so many 'parents' requested it, in preference to seeing their charges eat dry, unbuttered bread. The villagers even grew familiar with the mysterious logic of Jewish religious observance. One mother knew to switch off the light in her lad's bedroom on Friday nights. If she did not, he would sleep with it on, rather than violate the Sabbath by using electric power to turn it off. And, in an act hailed as a miracle by Avigdor's teachers, when the local fire brigade came to hose down the blazing cinema, they first made sure to rescue the scrolls of the *sefer torah* within.

None of which stopped Shefford feeling strange to Sara Hocherman when she first arrived. She liked the countryside; it reminded her of Wheathampstead. But she was seven years old, away from her mother for the first time, and she was anxious. After the bus journey from London each child was handed a piece of paper with the address of his or her new foster parent. Once again, she and Srollik were to be separated. He was dispatched to a hostel full of other boys. She was to go to 24 Clifton Street. It was across the river, in the next village. Sara did the walk to Clifton by herself, found the house and pushed the garden gate open. There were rose hedges on either side, taller than she was, and she liked the smell.

The door was open, so she walked in, immediately captivated by the ornaments on the shelves and especially by a shiny box on a sidetable. She opened it to take a closer look.

'Hello there.' Sara wheeled round, pale, and immediately blurted out an apology.

'I was just looking at the box . . .'

'That's all right, dear,' said the lady, who looked old, her hair fine and grey. 'You look around as much as you like. Now, what's your name?'

'Sara,' my mother answered, barely audible.

'And I am Miss Slater and I think we will get along very well.' The truth was, the moment Miss Slater, who would always remain a miss, had seen the little girl in a mauve coat, standing on tiptoes as she peered into the mother-of-pearl box, she had fallen in love. She had long given up on sharing that cottage with a child; she and her sister were the village's old maids, known by that label to all who saw them cycling here and there – maybe even to holy communion through the morning mist. But now their house, their flower garden and their pear orchard would light up with the glow of a child.

For Sara, it was a new world to negotiate, full of new things to be scared of. At seven o'clock each morning she would have to walk herself to school; weekends too, to ensure she never risked the food of Miss Slater's non-kosher kitchen. That walk was fine in spring or summer; Sara quite liked it, swinging her satchel, singing one of the tunes Aunt Rivvy had taught her back in London, listening to the unfamiliar music of birds and insects. But in winter, the same lane looked altogether different. The trees now struck Sara as looming, baleful monsters, their bare branches gnarled, clawing arms. She was sure she could see their mouths gaping in a shriek, their screams carried in the wind. So Sara closed her eyes and, counting three-two-one out loud, would make a run for it – only daring to peek once she had put the trees' wails and flailing arms behind her.

Once at school, the little girl was a free agent. For this was secondary school and she was too young for even the youngest class (she was only admitted at all because of Srollik and her mother's determination that the two should stick together). So Sara was allowed to wander from lesson to lesson. She tended to hang around Mr Eiserman's music class a fair bit; she understood what was going on there, with no hard books or long words to read. She would sit quietly as the older children blew their recorders and dinged their triangles in an attempt at 'London's Burning'. When it was over, Mr Eiserman gave house points for the wind section, house points for the percussion 'and a point to Sara because she sat quietly and was so good'. She became well known in the school, a kind of mascot who would either be drawing in a corner or else trailing after the school secretary on an errand. Fair and blonde, she even had a nickname: *shiksele*, the little *shikse*.

But it was not easy to be the smallest child in the school. Each pupil had a government-issue ration book. The teachers took everything save the E-coupon, the one that entitled children to buy sweets. That was torn off and handed to each child, to be redeemed at the local shop. Without it, the only available delights were Ovaltine and cough sweets. The E-coupon was a treat and gave the children the frisson of spending power.

Not Sara, though. Every week it was the same story. The coupons would be handed out and, within seconds, the older kids would snatch hers clean out of her hands. She could not turn to her big brother; Srollik was rarely around. Often his classes were in one of Shefford's chapels or parish halls (with no building large enough to contain them all, the Avigdor children were scattered throughout the village). Sara had to take defensive measures of her own. She deployed the old cod liver oil trick, rushing to the toilet within seconds of the E-coupon handout. To no avail. When she got out, the hoodlums of the sweet ration trade were waiting for her.

Still, there were times she was glad those older lads were around. Whatever peace adult Shefford had made with its alien guests, young Shefford was not always so sure. Sara had her own taste of it from the boy who lived opposite Miss Slater's cottage. His name was Peter and he was always pestering Sara to come over and take a look at his pet rabbits. She had trouble understanding him at first, his accent was so far away from the Jewish, East End melodies that had always surrounded her. But she finally deciphered what he was asking.

'Where are your horns? Don't you have horns? I thought all of you lot had horns. Where are yours?'

As she sputtered that she was the same as everyone else, she felt a stinging sensation – like a ruler slapping the skin just behind her knees.

Friday nights were often the hardest. As the Avigdor kids trooped out of school, a crowd of the local toughs would be waiting for them in gangs. At first it was just chanting – 'Hey, Jewboy', that kind of thing. Then it was attempts to grab the caps off the boys' heads. Before long, there was shoving and worse. All the children were scared, but a girl as young as Sara was terrified. The attackers seemed to be like monster-children, perhaps sent as a spell by the evil, swaying winter trees.

One night they saw a whole crowd of them, bigger than ever, ready for an assault. Before she knew it, Sara felt a strong hand on each arm and her feet lifting from the ground. She glanced left and right and saw two of the oldest boys in the school – to her, they were men – one on each side. Appointing themselves as the little girl's protectors, they had picked her up and were now running. She was flying along the street, slicing through the whirl of skirts and fists and caps as the Avigdor kids all rushed to get away. When they reached a row of houses, one of her two escorts began pounding on a door to be let in. Once inside, they called the police, but it was too late. Some of the Avigdor children had been badly beaten; one boy was found with his shirt in shreds and his arms pocked with cigarette burns.

The older kids plotted retaliation. Their leaders were the Polish boys, some nearly sixteen, who were parentless and wild. (Srollik would sometimes tag along with this crowd, agreeing to whatever antics they put him up to. A favourite trick was to stand at the first-floor window overlooking the bus stop, urinate on the people waiting below and then duck back inside, escaping detection: piss down ginger.) On the chosen day, the Poles turned up at the Shefford school and staged a revenge attack. Now it would be the turn of the 'Yocks', not the Yids, to play victim.

There was so much for Sara to be scared of, whether it was Peter and his rabbits, the rough boys of the village or the Hitler that used to visit in her dreams. So she found it a comfort at Pesach time, when she would hear the story of the Children of Israel, who wept at their suffering under an evil Pharaoh and whose cries were heard by God, who, with a mighty hand and an outstretched arm, rescued them from torment. The *seder* may not have been where she wanted it, back home in Hughes Mansions with her mummy – instead it was with the family of the school Hebrew teacher, who lived near Miss Slater – yet God was the same. He was big and strong and good and would save the Jews, eventually. If they cried loud enough, prayed hard enough, he would smite all their enemies – the Shefford boys with the cigarettes, the Germans, all of them. She knew it.

She knew it in the springtime at Pesach, and she knew it eight months later, at the midwinter festival of Chanukah, when the teachers would tell them again and again the story of brave Judah Maccabee and his proud defence of the Jews. She knew it when her eyes flickered in the light of the six-foot *menorah*, made entirely out of empty tin cans painted gold. She looked at the blaze of candles, their brightness kept within by the wartime blackout curtains, and thought of God, who made the miracle of the Maccabees' oil – a supply for one day that lasted for eight. He had looked after them and he would look after her.

In the meantime, there were more direct comforts. Soon after Chanukah came Christmas, which the Avigdor children knew was not for them. All the decorations in the village, the holly, the lights, the songs of sleigh bells, they knew to be forbidden. These were the trappings of another religion; to recognize them was a step towards apostasy. They could not be persuaded that 'Jingle Bells' or mince pies were British, rather than Christian, traditions; that distinction would have been lost on the teachers as much as the pupils. The instruction was to turn a blind eye and a deaf ear to it all. Santa Claus and carol singing were as *verboten* as a ham omelette. Even the word was best avoided. If it had to be referred to, *Kratzmach* was an acceptable, Yiddish substitute or Xmas – handily avoiding the C-word.

So Sara's stocking had to remain a secret pleasure. Miss Slater had always been careful to respect her charge's religious differences, but there was a limit. Christmas was Christmas. So long as that child was under her roof, there would be a stocking at the end of her bed on Christmas morning.

At first Sara did not know what she was looking at; she had never seen such a thing. But when she twigged, she clasped both hands together and let out an 'ooooh' of excitement. She knew it was wrong, but she could not help it. She touched the stocking, examining it from all angles, prodding to see what might be in it. She put her ear next to it and gave it a shake, finally lowering her nose to inhale the scent. It was tangy and spicy and stirred some long-buried memory. She thought instantly of Srollik, her mother and, though for too fleeting a moment to grasp, someone she imagined was her father. Carefully she opened it up and let the contents fall on to the bed. Nuts of different shapes, large, dark brazils and gnarly, wrinkled walnuts, came tumbling out, followed from the bottom by two tangerines and an orange. They never had oranges at school; the war had made them a rarity. In fact, she was not sure she had so much as seen an orange since she had come to Britain. And yet this fruit did not look unfamiliar. She held it to her nose and that feeling, that memory, of her mother and Srollik and more, came back to her. She still could not quite place it.

Sara waited for Miss Slater to wake up so that she could say thank you. To the old lady's surprise, the little girl had not broken into any of her Christmas goodies: she was waiting for permission. So on Christmas morning, Miss Slater – pained that she could not cook this little girl a juicy, succulent turkey – watched as her Sara methodically worked her way through a tangerine, lingering over each segment as a connoisseur might savour a fine wine.

My mother would not forget that morning, nor the afternoon a few months later when her excited landlady was waiting by the front door when she got back from school. 'Now run into the garden,' Miss Slater said, her voice higher than usual. 'Hurry up now! I want you to see something, just by the flowers.'

Sara looked around, searching for a visiting cat or perhaps an injured bird. What was Miss Slater talking about?

'There,' she was pointing. 'Just there, look.' And now she saw it. Four large letters in mustard cress, spelling out a word: S-A-R-A. The little girl could not speak; she was overwhelmed, with gratitude for Miss Slater, with surprise, with the novelty of such a fuss made for nobody but her. She stood there, staring at those letters for what seemed to Miss Slater like hours. And not just that afternoon, but the next day and the day after that.

She could have hugged this sweet lady who seemed so fond of her, though she did not and never would. Sara was happy in that house; she thought her landlady was nice. She would chat away, happily gabbling while Miss Slater combed her hair, tying it up in one of her own ribbons. But the little girl always held something back, Miss Slater could feel it. She would always be Miss Slater to this tenant child; she would never be family.

The greatest joy in Sara's life came from the visits of her mother. For reasons the little girl did not understand, Feige could only visit once a month, if that. Maybe she was busy in London, working hard at the factory by day, cooking and cleaning for the others by night. But a month is a long time for a seven-year-old. She would wait on a Sunday by the bus stop, willing that moving thing there, that one far in the distance just coming over the hill now, that one, to be her bus. But it was only another car. Oh, wait, there it is now, look, that big one – that must be it! But it was only a big Bedford van. And then, when disappointment was creeping into Sara's heart, it would appear: a Green Line bus, spilling out its passengers, and there, in her elegant coat, was the most beautiful lady in the world and Sara wanted the lady to scoop her up and spin her around in a hug that would last for ever.

They would cross the road to the school to pick up Srollik and go on to Miss Slater's, all three of them chatting away, Srollik running ahead then sprinting back, tugging at his mother's arm, swinging it one moment, tunnelling underneath it the next. 'Mum, Mum, look!' he would be saying, before showing her some new feat of daring: a handstand, a running leap over a fence. 'Oh, Srollik, no!' Feige would gasp, meaning it but also obliging the urge of her son, the desire of boys throughout time, to shock his mother with his courage.

Sara would be holding Feige's other hand, pulling on it ever so gently, as if to slow her mummy down, to walk with her at *her* pace. She would speak quietly, forcing Feige to crane down to hear her: that was good, her face so close. Sara would want to play with the brooch on her mother's coat; or tell her about the cress in Miss Slater's garden; or the point awarded by Mr Eiserman for being good. There was so much to talk about; the pictures she had drawn at school, the creatures she had seen in the wood, the friends she had made, all the days that had passed since she had last seen her mummy.

Now they were inside the cottage and Sara could feel the happiness spread throughout her insides. Miss Slater liked Feige and the two talked easily; it made Sara warm. Besides, she loved this bit, when her mother unpacked her bags. Miss Slater would disappear and come back with the special tin, the one that stored whatever treats Feige might bring. Sure enough, out came two little bags of toffees, one for each child. Srollik wolfed his straight away, but Sara held on to hers – as the serial victim of E-coupon crime, sweets were precious gems to be guarded. They would stay in the tin, the only supply of food – *Kratzmach* oranges and nuts apart – allowed to Sara in this non-kosher house.

The day would pass too fast, Sara and Srollik dragging their mother all around the village to see the landmarks of their young lives. Sara would walk taller than ever, her little chest puffed out:

she was proud of the beautiful lady who was her mummy. If they came across a teacher, Sara would be especially excited; she wanted everyone to know.

Sara would dread dusk, when her mother would have to round up her bags, thank Miss Slater and return to the bus stop. The two children would wave her off and keep waving till the bus was back over the hill, its lights distant dots and then gone. Miss Slater would always beg her to stay. She enjoyed young adult company in the house and knew how much it meant to Sara. And very occasionally Feige would put aside her commitments back in the East End and say yes.

To her daughter this was the greatest bliss life had to offer, sharing her room with her mummy. 'Oooh, now this is a *mechayer*,' Feige would say at intervals throughout the night, deploying the Yiddish word reserved for physical pleasure, especially relief. (Soaking your feet in a bowl of hot water after a day spent walking in the cold, that's a *mechayer*.) In London she was used to sharing her bed with one of her adult sisters, and the beds were never as comfortable as this one; nor did they look out over lawns, hedges and flowers. Feige thought of Wheathampstead and a future with her children in a cottage somewhere pretty. Once the war was over, maybe she and the kids would live somewhere like this.

By the spring of 1945 plenty of people were thinking that way, looking ahead to life after wartime. The staff of the Avigdor High School were beginning to wind down, believing that the end of their Bedfordshire sojourn was approaching. The immediate focus was on Pesach, the sixth time the school would spend the festival in Shefford.

The Hocherman children's plan was to be back home at Hughes Mansions for the *seder*, the first-night meal that launches Passover. The whole family would be there and now, with the air raids all but stopped, it was safer to return. But on post day came bad news. It was a letter addressed to Srollik, from his mother:

My darling children, I know how much you have been looking forward
to spending Pesach here, and I have been too. But I really think it's for
the best if you stay at school, just until everything is all sorted out. You
enjoyed the sederim *there last year, and I'm sure they will be just as*
nice this year. Don't be too disappointed. To make up for it, I'll come
and see you on Sunday and we can have a lovely day together then.

Looking forward to that very much, and remember, eat well and,
Srollik, be polite and do as your teachers tell you!

All my love,

Mummy.

Feige felt guilty about that letter. Maybe she was being over-
cautious. Everyone knew the war was nearly over; the air raids
seemed to be a thing of the past. That was certainly the mood as
Vallance Road readied itself for Pesach, the season of liberation and
renewal. People were coming home, either from the countryside
where they had been evacuees or from the front. The East End was
in festive mood, as if impatient to throw off the gloom of the
previous five and a half years.

There were only two discordant notes. The pang of conscience
Feige felt at her decision to keep the children in the country, and
Yiddi, her pious, older sister, kept telling her of an odd dream. She
had found herself suddenly sitting bolt upright in bed and shouting,
'Feige! Get away from the window!'

Otherwise, Hughes Mansions was buzzing with preparations for
Pesach. As always, Jewish families heard the religious demand to
remove all traces of *chametz* – leavened bread – as a summons for
a mammoth spring-clean. All the regular dishes, pots and pans were
packed away and nominally 'sold' to a non-Jewish neighbour. (In
their place came crockery and cutlery that were used only for the
eight days of Passover.) Every floor was then swept and swept
again, every surface cleaned and bleached. To round off the process,
there was the ritual of *bedikat chametz*, the search for *chametz*
conducted with candle, feather and, of course, prayer book.

All that happened at Hughes Mansions, with Feige scrubbing

harder than most. Everything had to be ready in time for the first *seder*, on Wednesday. She wished her children could be there for it. As she fell into an exhausted sleep, she realized it had now been years since she had heard her little Sara ask the Four Questions, beginning *Ma nishtana ha'lila hazeh?* Why is this night different from all other nights?

It was probably around that time, as Feige and Rivvy lay sleeping in the flat in Hughes Mansions, Rivvy closest to the window, that the V2 launch team came on to the dawn shift at their base near The Hague. Their daily task was to fire what Joseph Goebbels and his propaganda ministry had insisted on calling the Vergeltungs-waffe 2, the reprisal weapon 2 – though what exactly it was avenging remained unstated.

The V2 was the fruit of nearly two decades' research by Germany's finest scientists and its transition from wild-eyed scheme to operational weapon was a source of great Nazi pride. In Wernher von Braun's rocket, with its black-and-white chessboard pattern, they were convinced they had devised the weapon of the future: it was Flash Gordon made real.

By March 1945, the rocket had been in active service for the best part of six months, pummelling cities in Belgium and liberated France. Antwerp had taken severe punishment and so had London. The team on duty this early morning, 27 March, would have checked the logbook and seen the tally. This would be attack No. 1358 on the capital. There was no shortage of rockets: a constant flow came from the V2 production centre at Dora, the underground slave labour camp near Nordhausen in Germany. Management at Dora ensured there was no slacking – even if that meant 10,000 slaves dying of overwork or at the hands of their captors.

The launch process was now fairly streamlined. First, a thirty-truck convoy bearing men, equipment, fuel and the missile would reach the staging area, where local crews fitted the warhead, weighing in at some 2,000 pounds. Then each launch team would transfer 'their' missile to a dedicated *Meillerwagen*, on which it would be towed to the launch site. Any place would do: the

Meillerwagen were so small and nifty, a humble forest dirt track was fit for the task. There it would be set up on the launch table, fuelled and fired.

It raced through the air, higher than any plane and faster than the speed of sound. No wonder the Germans loved it: it was silent where traditional bombers were noisy. Its predecessor, the V1 flying bomb, announced its arrival with a characteristic buzzing sound. The V2 flew so fast, it gave no warning before impact. There was no chance of defence.

So Feige and Rivvy would have heard no air-raid siren and, their family hoped, they would have had no moment of panic as they tried to hide under the bed, cower under a table or find some other feeble shelter from the plume of lead and fire that would descend upon Hughes Mansions at 7.21 a.m. precisely.

Yiddi heard a distant thud while loading the shelves in the grocer's shop she ran with her husband, but thought nothing of it. But then word reached her: they had struck Vallance Road. She ran, bleating a kind of involuntary moan that sounded with each step. There were crowds, and instantly she was asking friends, 'Has anybody seen Feige? Has anybody seen Rivvy?' And, to strangers, 'Has anybody seen two young ladies?'

She thought she would find them; there were so many people there. She saw a coat and hat and shoulders that looked like Feige's and she called out, but it was not her. She found herself remembering what Feige had once asked Yiddi's husband, Max: 'What will happen to my children if something happens to me?' And Max had said, 'We won't all be killed together. If you won't be here, we will be here, or you'll be here and we won't be here.' She suddenly pictured Srollik and Sara and immediately screwed her eyes shut to push such nonsense out of her mind. She had to find them, had to keep on shoving her way through the throng. They would probably be just around this corner, helping the wounded. That would be typical, Feige and Rivvy, sleeves rolled up, doing their bit. She saw a man beckoning over a team of rescuers, a look of exhausted joy on his face: he had heard the voices of his brother and sister through the rubble. She saw the men dragging behind packs of dogs, trained to sniff out any sign of life. It would not take long to find them.

Soon Max was with her and he gave their names to the officials, who said they would let them know. Later that day, one of the rescue workers tapped Max on the shoulder and led him away. Yiddi could not hear what they were saying, but she could read her husband's face. Max was nodding and she knew. She felt her heart cave in.

They asked Max to identify the bodies. It was easy. 'They had hardly been touched,' he would tell Yiddi later. 'Hardly touched at all. A little bruise on Rivvy's head maybe. Hardly touched. As if they died in their sleep.'

In all, 130 people were killed by that rocket, the very last V2 of the Second World War. Even though the weapon was notoriously inaccurate, its guidance system too primitive to hit specific targets, the Nazis would have been delighted by their luck on 27 March 1945. The V2 made its exit by killing 120 Jews. Whole families were wiped out that night at Hughes Mansions. One grandfather buried two sons, two daughters, a daughter-in-law and a grandson. One returning soldier lost his parents, two brothers, a sister, sister-in-law and two nephews. Another had begun his leave from active duty just twenty-four hours earlier, only to be killed with his family.

They buried Rivvy and Feige the next day and that night the family sat down for the *seder* – to praise God for his mercy in delivering their Jewish ancestors from evil and to thank him for saving them from suffering, hearing their cries and seeing their tears.

11   *Neither Here nor There*

The end of the war was a relief to the whole world, but in the Jewish community of Palestine the joy was especially sweet. The battle for North Africa, and Rommel's initial string of successes there, had panicked the Yishuv. There were times when it seemed possible that the embryonic Jewish national home was about to be overrun by the Nazis. It was a prospect too appalling to contemplate. Jews who had fled persecution would instead have run right into it, their haven would have become a trap.

For once sharing in the collective mood was Nat Mindel. He was as delighted that this war was over as everyone around him. He had been too old for military action but the war years had been an ordeal all the same.

In 1942 his son had gone missing in the Western Desert in Libya. Having completed his schooling at Cambridge, Yehuda had returned to Palestine to study but had enlisted in the British Army almost straight away, signing up to the Royal Artillery. Nat had been proud of his boy, wearing, as he had once worn, the uniform of a British king. He pounced on Yehuda's letters from the front; he even allowed himself the odd covert smile of pride when he remembered the lad's impatience to join the Jewish paramilitaries of Palestine. A pistol under the bed!

But in July 1942 came the telegram saying his son was unaccounted for. From then on there was no word. For two months it continued: no letters, no cables, nothing. Nat and Miriam hungered for news and yet dreaded it. The slightest rattle of the letter box could be an envelope bearing the mark of the War Office: *We regret to inform you.* Without news they could at least hope.

Finally, in mid-September, there was a letter. It came via the Apostolic Delegate, the Pope's representative in Jerusalem. Gunner

Mindel was held in Italy as a prisoner of war. He stayed a captive for nearly three years after that, mostly in Italy but later transferred to the senior partner in the Axis, Germany. That is where he was when the Russians liberated him in April 1945.

Those years had cost Nat and Miriam dearly. They were told the Nazis treated British prisoners of war relatively well, that they adhered to the Geneva Convention: food, Red Cross parcels and daily exercise. But there was no telling what they would do to those obviously identifiable as Jews. (Indeed, in the closing months of the war, about 350 American PoWs with Jewish-sounding names were separated from their comrades and dispatched to Berga, a labour camp and satellite of Buchenwald. They lived in appalling conditions, forced to work twelve-hour shifts in quartz mines, where about seventy died in just two months.)

The anxiety about his son gnawed away at Nat, but he could hardly find solace in his work. That too was devouring him. For 1939 had brought not only the outbreak of war but also the White Paper. It had come within months of Nat's Basle meeting, a statement of British policy in Palestine which sought to placate the Arab anger which had boiled throughout the 1930s. First, it promised that Palestine would become an independent state within ten years. The Zionists hardly welcomed that. They knew they would remain a minority in such an entity, all hope of creating a Jewish state dashed. Second, it restricted Jewish purchase of Arab land and property. Third, and most significant, it put a cap on Jewish immigration. Over the following five years, no more than 75,000 Jews were to be granted entry to Palestine, ensuring that Jews would not make up more than one-third of the total population. Any increase beyond that quota would have to be agreed first by the Arabs. Few could have known then that a five-year limit would be in place for almost the entire duration of the war, so closing Palestine to Jews at precisely the time they needed a refuge most.

The Yishuv had often declared its official outrage to Britain, but this time the anger reached a new pitch. Ben-Gurion denounced the White Paper as 'evil'. 'Satan himself could not have created a more distressing and horrible nightmare,' he told his diary. The Yishuv was on fire with fury. Demonstrators, already desperate at the plight of European Jewry, likened the White Paper to the Nuremberg Laws and Colonial Secretary MacDonald, the paper's author, to Adolf Hitler. At least two Zionist leaders were visited by young activists ready to volunteer to stage their own suicides in the House of Commons, perhaps taking Neville Chamberlain with them.

The Zionist right wing now regarded Britain as a direct enemy of its cause and began an armed campaign against it. Groups like Etzel – the Irgun Tzva'i Leumi or National Military Organization – targeted symbolic government locations, even planting mines in Jerusalem's central post office. By 1944 Etzel had made a declaration of war against the British, promising 'war to the end'. A faction yet more militant, Lechi – the Lochamei Herut Israel or Freedom Fighters for Israel – twice tried to assassinate the High Commissioner, Harold MacMichael, and eventually succeeded in killing Britain's man in Egypt, Lord Moyne.

Since all this activity was as much a challenge for the leadership of the Yishuv as it was an onslaught on the British, Ben-Gurion had to respond. His answer caught perfectly the dilemma of Palestine's Jews, who loathed London's new policy and yet looked to Britain to save the world from German fascism. In what was destined to become the soundbite of the age in Palestine, he declared, 'We shall fight the war as if there were no White Paper, and the White Paper as if there were no war.'

And caught in the middle was Nathan Mindel. A Zionist who twenty years earlier had bombarded friends and family with his hopes for Jewish redemption, insisting that Jewish immigration was their only hope, was now charged with curbing the very influx he believed would save his people. Nor was he a mere official in the British Department of Immigration, required to enforce the White Paper and its limit. By July 1944, at the height of Etzel's anti-British campaign and as the Nazis were squeezing the last breath of life out of European Jewry, he was the man in charge.

Until then immigration had been linked to Palestine's economic capacity: Jews could come in numbers as large as the country could absorb. Now the rules were tightened and unyielding: only 15,000 Jews could find a home in Palestine each year, no exceptions. Nat could not repeat the results he had pulled off in Trieste or throughout the 1920s, where his answer had usually been yes. Now the British answer was no to all but a very lucky few. And it was Nathan Mindel, the new acting Commissioner of Migration, who had to deliver it.

He would wake each morning with a double dread: his first thought about Yehuda – Gunner Julius Mindel, according to the War Office – and his second about the day ahead. The forms, letters and cables piling on his desk kept him busy, but he could not escape their central message: no entry. He would walk to work avoiding the glances of Jewish Jerusalemites as he turned down Queen Melisande Street. To them, even to walk into that building was to consort with the enemy. To implement a policy deemed as cruel as the Nuremberg Laws made him a traitor to his people.

His family ran from him. Yehuda was God knows where; Ruth, his older daughter, was now focused entirely on her future with the rather dashing Captain Hillel Beham, serving with distinction in Nat's old unit, the Royal Army Medical Corps; while his youngest, Aviva, had fled the family home in her mid-teens for a pioneer's life in the north of the country, on Kibbutz Ma'agen Michael. The house felt empty, especially now that Nat had taken to closing the curtains at midday, to keep out the sunlight. Miriam tiptoed around him, but she could not conceal her disdain, even contempt, for her husband's work. In the old days they had at least rowed about it. Now it was too late. There was a silence between them.

He did not need to have this distance between his wife and himself explained. It was the same gulf that separated him from most Zionists, and he knew its shape well. At the start of 1943 he had stared into it.

Nat had been dispatched to Tehran, then under shared Russian and British control, to defuse what was fast unravelling into a humanitarian crisis. More than 1,000 Jewish children and some 800 adults had wound up there with almost nothing to eat and only the hospitality of Tehran's Jewish community as shelter. They had arrived after hitching a ride with one of the most curious migrations of the war. Shortly after Hitler broke the Nazi–Soviet pact by attacking Russia in 1941, Stalin decided to release the tens of thousands of Poles he had previously locked up in Soviet prison camps, many of them refugees from the Nazis who had fled eastward in 1939. He reckoned his captives would be far more use as part of the Free Polish Army then taking shape under the guiding hand of the Allies. He laid on ships to ferry the former inmates via the Caspian Sea to Tehran, where the new Polish force was assembling. Stowed away on that voyage were those 1,800 exhausted Jews.

The Jewish Agency was already on the scene in Persia, with a Palestine office up and running. They wanted the children to be granted entry into Palestine; they knew that nowhere else would have them. The British embassy in Tehran was overwhelmed with the bureaucratic challenge posed by a block application for 1,800.

They needed a specialist and Nathan Mindel was named as special emissary in the winter of 1943.

The two men from the Jewish Agency braced themselves. They knew of this Mindel by reputation. 'A Jew of English extraction, he strictly enforced the limitations of the inimical immigration laws, and for this reason was considered an enemy of the Zionist endeavour,' one of the Agency men, Avraham Zilberberg, would later record in his memoirs.

The two men arranged to see each other over tea at Café Polonia, at the heart of Tehran's rapidly expanding Polish quarter.

'So, Zilberberg, what's the story here?' Nat began, keen to take charge.

'It's simple enough. We have more people than visas. I don't have enough immigration certificates for the people who need to get out. And sometimes even those with certificates are denied visas. When I ask why, I am given no reason. The British authorities don't even try to hide their hostility to us and to what we are trying to do here. Any excuse they can find to make things difficult, they find it.'

Nat was only half listening. Over Zilberberg's shoulder there was a couple laughing and flirting over a large, shared slice of gâteau. She was striking, her dark hair set off by thick red lipstick, sharp, defined cheekbones and eyes as deep as mineshafts. Her features were heavy, like those of many Jewish girls from Eastern Europe. The man with her was in British uniform, an officer and no Jew.

'There is another category that has caused much trouble,' Zilberberg was saying. 'Many of our young women, some of them single, most widows, have found work with the Polish Army, as secretaries or nurses. The Polish officers constantly make advances to them, harassing and pushing them. Those who refuse, the Poles have been handing their names to British officials, naming them as communist agents. That's grounds enough for the British consul to deny them a visa to Eretz Yisrael.'

By now the couple were getting up to leave. The lipstick woman nodded at Zilberberg on her way out.

'So who's she?' said Nat, doing his best to sound official.

'She is a refugee from Poland, waiting like all the rest to get to Eretz Yisrael.'

So she *was* Jewish, thought Nat, and cavorting like that with a British officer. 'Do you mean to tell me that you are doing all this for people like *that*? These are the people you want to bring to Palestine?' Nat's views about the moral character of the new Jew who would build the new Judaea had not shifted much in twenty years. 'Is that all that Palestine is lacking, more prostitutes for the Tel Aviv beachfront? Is that the gap you're hoping to fill?'

Zilberberg pulled back as if he had seen a cockroach crawl across the sweet pastry set before him on the table. He was stunned by what he had heard.

'Listen, Mindel. I think you and I should talk to each other man to man, Jew to Jew. Do you have any idea what that woman has been through? She was a respectable girl from a well-to-do family in Warsaw until one day the Germans decided to blow up their house. They were left with nothing: no money, no possessions. She was wearing a nightdress when it happened and that's all she had in the world. She was the only one to survive. So she begins her journey through the seven circles of hell. She somehow gets from Warsaw to Lvov. And from there she flees east, by train in a sealed cattle wagon, for thousands of kilometres. The cars are packed with Jews who have next to nothing to eat or drink. And she ends up, with barely enough rags to cover herself, in Siberia. She has escaped, but she is tired and dirty, and when the train pulls in at some remote station she has to get out and wash in front of men – and she does it, just to feel a little cleaner.

'And these men, some of them are savages, you know? Full of lust and they –' Zilberberg was looking for the right word – 'they fall upon her. What can she do? She is weak and alone and starving. And then this girl hears of the transfer to Tehran and she has the wit to know she needs to be on it. And somehow, even though the Polish Army is not exactly in a hurry to help Jews, she gets here. And here, for the first time since she was a teenager in Warsaw, there is plenty. There is food and drink and, at last, an *ease* she has not known for years, not when she was running from one camp to another in Siberia. So a woman like this meets a cultured gentleman, whether he's a British officer or someone else it doesn't matter, she meets a man who extends a warm and helping hand. She goes out with him for a decent meal. Maybe he even takes her to the theatre or to the pictures. Now tell me, Mindel. Why should I, or you, who have not been through the seven circles of hell, treat this woman as a whore? What right do we have to stand in judgement over her? What right, Mindel?'

The British official was pale, Zilberberg could see that much. His eyes were cast down, staring at the table, concealed behind those wire-brushes of eyebrow. Zilberberg was not sure what he was thinking. Perhaps, Zilberberg wondered, he had gone too far. Perhaps he had offended Mindel. But the man from the Jewish Agency gambled and carried on.

'All this woman, and others like her, want is to reach Eretz Yisrael, see if maybe some family have survived and made it there. They want to start a new life. Some of them had this dream of Zion even before the war. Some speak Hebrew. If they are not allowed to make *aliyah* now, you know what will happen. The British – you – will send them, along with all the other Poles, to Kenya, to East Africa. And they will be lost to the world.

'She is a person, Mindel. This woman has a name. She is Miriam Bar-Mandelbroit and she is no whore. She works hard for a living. She is the pianist at the local Polish Officers' Club and you can imagine –'

'What did you say?'

'Excuse me?'

'Her name. What did you say her name was?'

'Miriam. Miriam Bar-Mandelbroit.'

Nat raised his head, his eyes meeting Zilberberg's for the first time. He seemed to be looking clear through him, at some distant landscape. Zilberberg was uncomfortable in the silence.

'Do you know this woman?'

'No. I know a Miriam, that's all. I know a Miriam.' He paused and finally came to, focusing clearly on Zilberberg now. 'Tomorrow is Sunday,' Nat said, 'so we won't be able to do much. On Monday I will look into the matter.'

'Let's not wait,' Zilberberg said. 'Let's not waste tomorrow. I'll give you a tour.'

Never before had Nat felt more like an emissary of the British Empire. He was hailed in the refugee camps of Tehran like a visiting viceroy, crowds surging around him. Each time he peered inside one of the refugees' huts, there would be a new swarm of noise, a new surge of shoving. 'Mr Mindel is an official of the British government. He has come from Jerusalem to understand your situation,' Zilberberg would say each time. 'He will do all in his power to help you.' Nat felt gauche in his suit and tie; he felt too tall.

As he turned to leave one hut, he could feel a tight grip on his arm. He looked down to see a silver-haired woman, her eyes soaked in tears yet to fall. She talked fast, in Yiddish, saying she couldn't bear living like this, in a camp, and she needed to get to Eretz Yisrael *now*. Suddenly Nat, who had so far offered little more than a nod here or a murmur there, asked her where she came from. 'I lived in a town near Vilna,' she said, quieter than before.

'I did too,' said Nat in Yiddish, sending a wave of shock through the ring of people around them. They almost seemed scared. He might as well have levitated, or pulled a dove from his pocket. 'My father was a tailor in a little village not far from Vilna before we all emigrated to England.' Zilberberg was staring at him now. 'Who knows, perhaps it is the same place.'

The old woman started describing her home town, a smile of disbelief on her face. 'Once a week we would travel to market. We came to buy food, but the farmers would not sell to us. They said we were "competition".'

Nat nodded and listened and finally, to her and Zilberberg, announced, 'I will do everything I can to enable you to travel to Palestine as soon as possible.'

Next day, Nat took Zilberberg to see the British Consul. He all but ordered the diplomat to convert all Jewish Agency-approved certificates into visas for Palestine. If there were any political or security questions, he was to refuse an application only after he had first discussed all details with Zilberberg or his fellow representative of the Jewish Agency.

Lest there be any doubt, Nat also paid a visit to the local head of British intelligence, with Zilberberg still in tow. The office was tucked away off a Tehran alleyway, in a private house surrounded by high walls. They rang the bell on what appeared to be the only entrance, a narrow gate, which was eventually opened by a wizened Parsee. The servant made a good pretence of having no idea what the men were after, until Nat finally mentioned the name that brought the requisite flicker of recognition. They were led through doorway after doorway until they met the station chief himself. He was pleasant enough and once again bowed to Nat's request that no case recommended by Zilberberg be delayed.

By February 1943 the temporary Jews of Persia were on their way to Palestine. The Yishuv was waiting for them. The story of the Tehran refugees, especially the children, had become a national obsession. Some had been orphaned in the original long trek eastward from Poland, escaping the Nazis; others had lost a mother or father in Soviet camps; and still others had left behind in Russia parents who, believing this was their last chance to keep their children alive, had handed them over to the nuns and priests who ran the Polish orphanages, begging them to take their young to Tehran. Now their children were ready to travel to Karachi, to sail from there to Suez and finally to Palestine by train. They were 1,230 in all, 719 of them orphans.

Over the next few years Nat would love to read stories in the papers about the Tehran children, how they were getting on in their new homes. Sometimes there would be a special feature marking the anniversary of their arrival, and he would linger over the photographs showing suntanned teenagers picking tomatoes on some kibbutz up north. He was proud of them, and therefore of himself.

But these moments, when the black curtain would peel back, were brief. At the first crack of light it would fall shut again. No sooner had a warm thought about, say, Tehran entered his head than its shadow would chase after it. For every Tehran child now alive in Palestine, how many were not here? He thought back to that day in Basle. What had he been able to do? Perhaps he had flushed out the odd blockage here and there, but the tunnel itself – the escape route from Germany to Palestine – had always been too narrow.

It was right to stick to the rules, he would say to himself when these moods struck. It was right. If the system functioned properly, there was still hope, at least for some people. If he had blithely broken all the rules, allowed the system to break down and descend into chaos, then the government would probably have closed the gates of Palestine altogether.

But then the memo would appear before his closed eyes, the words swimming in the air: '. . . in order to discuss with the British Consul there various questions relating to the handling of applications by German Jews for entry into Palestine'. In a rare cinema visit with Miriam, which he instantly regretted, he had seen the newsreel shots of Belsen, liberated by British troops, and of Auschwitz, taken by the Soviets. There had been gasps in the theatre, some wailing too from the countless people in the Yishuv who had left people behind in Europe. The walking cadavers in the newsreel footage could have been anybody's brother or wife, a cousin, a friend from school days. So could any one of the corpses, piled like so many discarded mannequins. The words would not leave him: 'the handling of applications by German Jews for entry into Palestine'.

He tried to tell himself that perhaps this was some kind of awful winnowing, that the Jews had just experienced a Darwinian process of selection, separating out the 'acceptable material' from the rest.

But he would see the names of the cities, towns, villages and *shtetls* whose Jews had been liquidated and know it could have been Dunilovich. It could have been him.

At moments like those he never felt more of a Jew or more of a Zionist. And yet, the Zionists did not feel the same way about him. Thanks to the White Paper, Zionism regarded Britain as, at best, an obstacle, at worst an enemy. Nat may have ached with the rest of that cinema audience at the news from Europe, but if they had known of his day job they would not have counted him among them. They may even have turned on him. He was a collaborator.

Life at work was not much easier, even if it was sweetened by the arrival in June 1946 of a letter from Buckingham Palace, informing him that His Majesty was minded to appoint him as an Officer of the Most Excellent Order of the British Empire in the forthcoming honours list, should he choose to accept. He knew it was ex officio, an award attached to his civil service rank and granted automatically, but he still felt his heart warm with pride. Dunilovich was a long way away.

Not that the glow would last long.

'They're bastards, that's what they are. Animals, every last one of them.'

'You know what they say about a Jew? That he'll stab you in the back as soon as look at you.'

It was the morning of 22 July 1946 and the two squaddies guarding the entrance to the Department of Immigration were discussing the sole topic of conversation in Palestine: the bombing the previous day of the King David Hotel, headquarters of the government secretariat. Ninety-two people had been killed. The men behind it were from Etzel, seeking revenge for what the British had code-named Operation Agatha a month earlier. After a wave of terror attacks, the British had decided a crackdown was in order and the weekend was the time to do it. Using more than 100,000 soldiers and policemen, they surrounded dozens of Jewish settlements, imposed a curfew on Tel Aviv and Jerusalem and made no fewer than 3,000 arrests, rounding up several top-ranking officials of the Jewish Agency. Agatha was the harshest attack yet by Britain on the Yishuv and the Jews of Palestine instantly branded it Black Sabbath.

'Now, the Arabs may be a bit oily, but they wouldn't do something like this. Ninety-two people, eh? Ninety-two!'

Nat tried to shrink himself as he headed past the two guards for his office. But he felt their eyes on his neck as he walked; he knew what they would say once he was out of earshot: 'He's one of them and all.'

He had hated Black Sabbath. A curfew made a suspect of everyone, including him. He was appalled by the King David bombing, and appalled again a week later when the Etzel hanged two British sergeants, retaliation for the hanging of three Etzel members in Acre prison. He had fought in the same army as those boys. What were his people doing, fighting his nation like this?

He felt lonely. The children were not around; from Miriam there was only frost. Even his bridge circle was shrinking. He had only ever felt truly at ease in Palestine among people like himself, British Jews serving the administration, but now he was one of only a very few left. Hyamson had long gone, converted by his experience as a Zionist hate figure into a spirited polemicist against the concept of a Jewish state. Some had retired and were back in England, like his first boss, the first High Commissioner, now in the House of Lords with a title that vividly reflected his two lives, Lord Samuel of Mount Carmel and Toxteth. Some had shed their former British allegiance and were now fully absorbed into the Zionist scene: Norman Bentwich had become a professor at the Hebrew University. Nat was one of the few still trying to dance at two weddings.

It was too late for resignation now, he thought. Such a gesture would look futile and narcissistic. Better to see out his twenty-fifth anniversary and retire at fifty-five, according to civil service convention. That way he would get his pension.

So on 31 March 1947 he worked his last day. He signed a few papers, received a pat on the back from the High Commissioner and left the Department of Immigration for the last time. The

Palestine Post recorded the occasion, just as they had gazetted the key milestones in his long civil service career. 'The departure of Mr N. I. Mindel reduces still further the small number of senior Jewish officers in the Administration,' the paper mused. 'The Jewish official does not have an easy task, and in recent years, under the White Paper, his function certainly was not to be envied. Yet the Government and the country have been well served by its Jewish servants . . . Mr Mindel had an especially difficult post in charge of immigration. He filled it with ability and integrity and earned general respect.'

He would not have had long to serve anyway. Eight months after Nat cleared his desk at Queen Melisande Street, the United Nations General Assembly voted by a margin of thirty-three to thirteen to partition Palestine into two states, one for the Jews and one for the Arabs. There were ten abstentions, one of them from Britain.

Like every Jew in Palestine and throughout the world, Nat sat with his ear pressed to the wireless that night. The BBC relayed each vote as it happened: 'Union of Soviet Socialist Republics? Yes. United States? Yes.' Once the gavel went down and the vote passed, Jerusalem erupted. The streets filled, horns sounded and they really did dance the *hora*.

Nat was not one for street parties, so he watched. He remembered the young Nat Mindel, so full of infatuation for his Belle of the Orient, upbraiding his brothers and school chums for their lack of Zionist fibre. Come and build our Promised Land, he had cried. Now here it was, within reach. And yet Nat could only look on, as if this were happening to another nation. Those dancing crowds, swigging from bottles of local hooch, were cheering the imminent end of the British Mandate. Soon they would see the back of the hated Brits! And that half included him.

Barely six months later, and the crowds were back. With the British Mandate over Palestine due to expire on 14 May 1948, Ben-Gurion scrambled to declare the establishment of a new state. Despite the mockery Nat had made of the idea some thirty years earlier, the new Prime Minister announced that the Jewish national home in Palestine was hereafter to be known as Israel.

As it happened, Nat was not even in the country to see the new state established. He was abroad, on a mission for the American Jewish Joint Distribution Committee – a relief organization usually referred to as the Joint – doing what he had always done, processing refugees. This time the dispossessed were European Jews now held in camps in Germany. But, once again, he was antagonizing the Zionists. The Joint, based in Frankfurt, and the Jewish Agency, based in Munich, had struck a deal according to which the Joint would not automatically funnel all refugees to America or Britain, but would ask them first whether they wanted to go to Palestine. Officially, that was all the interviewers had to do and Nat followed those instructions to the letter.

But the Jewish Agency officials on the scene saw it differently. They believed these refugees should be gently, and not so gently, directed towards Palestine. That was where they were needed, after all. One of the most outspoken advocates of such pressure, who repeatedly took Nat to task on the issue, was an Austrian-born kibbutznik and Agency emissary by the name of Eli Zamir. He suspected that Nat's reluctance to push potential migrants towards the Jewish homeland was born of something other than a desire to implement his instructions precisely. He wondered if Nat Mindel harboured a kind of elitist Zionism, one that placed greater premium on the quality of the population than its quantity. Mindel seemed keen for Zion to be a centre of Jewish brainpower, inhabited by professors and poets rather than primitives from Poland whose sole motive was the need for shelter. Those in the former category would get a nudge towards Palestine from Nat Mindel, suspected Zamir; those in the latter could go somewhere else. The 21-year-old Zamir did his best to shake the senior man, but he did not succeed. Still, Nat did not forget him. Not least because Eli Zamir would soon marry a fellow kibbutznik, Nat's younger daughter, Aviva.

By the time he returned to what was now Israel, Nat was ready to offer his skills and experience to the new state. A lifetime of service in the administration of Palestine, helping create the machinery of statehood which the Jewish Agency had inherited so smoothly, would surely have its reward. He fancied a job in the new Foreign Ministry, perhaps heading its consular department. Now that the Jews were to decide for themselves who deserved a visa to enter their own country, he could imagine no better candidate.

He was to be disappointed. In just the few months he had been away, almost all senior positions had been filled. Ben-Gurion was not just the father of a nation, he was also a practised party politician with decades of favours to pay back. He bestowed his patronage on loyal comrades of his Mapai Party, as well as on the legions of bureaucrats of the Jewish Agency. They had toiled in the shadows as a government-in-waiting for long enough; now they would have a chance at the real thing.

There was nothing left for an ex-British civil servant, a man whose position and temperament had held him aloof from the networking and politicking that were determining rank in the new Jewish state. He had just one contact, a Canadian Jewish Agency official, Bernard Joseph, who had been smart enough to reinvent himself as Dov Yosef. He was now Minister of Supply and Rationing. He had always had a soft spot for Miriam, maybe even a crush, and now he promised to find something for Nat.

A man with twenty-six years' experience, in a country full of novices, might have expected a top post, perhaps as director general, the Israeli equivalent of permanent secretary. But the best Yosef could do for Nat was a job as a district inspector. He would have to enforce compliance with regulations on food, merchandise and raw materials.

It was boring and Nat hated it. In August 1949, after just three months, he sat down to write a formal letter of resignation to his friend and patron. The letter, from an Englishman to a Canadian, was, of course, in Hebrew. 'I personally feel a sense of revulsion from the daily work,' he explained. He did not relish cracking down on black marketeers and the like. He could not stand being a snoop:

'At heart, the work is detective and I cannot put my heart and soul into police work.' Besides, he could not deny it, he missed the more elevated perch he had enjoyed under the British. 'For more than a quarter of a century, I have been an official of some responsibility at the centre of a department,' he wrote. 'And it is not easy for a person such as this suddenly to come down from High Table to the scrum of the market place.' He then furnished Yosef with a few tips for the better management of the department, a habit acquired from years of writing internal memoranda and a hard one to break. Finally he signed off, M. I. Mindel – Menachem. The letter ran to two pages, but he could have been much briefer. 'This job is beneath me,' would have captured it.

He probably knew why he had not done better. The new Israelis simply did not trust a man who had served the British for so long. Historians would later say the antagonism between Zionism and the Mandate administration was exaggerated, that in reality the two sides had always cooperated, that they had much in common and that the British had, in effect, laid the ground for a Jewish national home. It is quite true that in the late 1940s rival Yishuv factions found attacking the authorities a handy way to prove their Zionist cojones; quite true too that the nascent Jewish state needed a founding myth and a 1776-style battle against King George did the trick nicely. But, for all that, the tension was not invented. It was real enough for those who lived on the fault line. Jews in the Mandate administration were always bound to be torn, serving the 'two masters' identified in that memo to the War Office at the very start. Whatever the future historians of Israel might say, the historians of Nat's own family were quite clear. 'The Jews always thought of him as "that bloody Englishman" and the British always thought of him as "that bloody Jew". And that was that.'

Nathan Isidore Mindel, Menachem to the family he had raised in the Palestine that became Israel and Menachem to the villagers who knew him in the *shtetl* of Dunilovich, died in Jerusalem in August 1961 at the age of seventy-one. The cause of death was leukaemia, but his wife and children would have diagnosed a sick heart. They had seen a man darken with depression for more than three decades. Perhaps ever since Hebron.

Nat had not spent his final years seeing the new Israel blossom; indeed, he never even became a citizen of the new Jewish republic. He was waiting until he could be granted his preferred status: dual citizenship of both Britain and Israel. Partly for that reason, he spent many of those final years back in London. He cut a lonely figure, living in boarding houses or rented digs, angling for an invitation to eat Friday night dinner with a nephew or a cousin. He found the odd bit of work, including a stint at a glass factory; in the evening he might take in a concert or play or listen to the BBC, following the latest news from the Middle East.

He did not want to be there, but he was on a mission. Throughout the 1950s he staged a tireless campaign – lobbying MPs, burying Whitehall in correspondence – on the topic of his own pension. The old Colonial Office insisted that he be paid by the Israeli government, in Israeli *lirot*; he wanted to be paid by the British government in much more valuable sterling. 'It's not just the money,' he would tell his brothers as they begged him to drop it and go home. 'It's the principle of the thing.' They were treating him as if he had been a local hire, a Palestinian Jew. Even if that was partially true, he would say, he had also been something else: a British subject. He wanted the authorities to see that, to understand that of course he was and always had been both.

At the time of his death, Nat's pension correspondence with the British government was still ongoing. They had reached a technical compromise, but the file had not been closed. The core issue remained unresolved.

12   *May Day*

The war years had changed Mick Mindel's life, starting with the move his friends and family had long been waiting for. In 1944 he was finally married – except not to Sara Wesker. Before the war, union business had taken him to the Stoke Newington clothing shop B. Mindel & Co. He had made the Dunilovich connection with the owner, Barnet Mindel, working out that they must be cousins of some remove or other. How strange that they should be reunited here, in London!

Years later he was doing his rounds, visiting factories, suppliers, wholesalers and retailers, when he called in at Goldstein's on Alie Street. As soon as he introduced himself, several of the workers there had the same thought. 'You must come and meet Sylvia. She's a Mindel too! I'm sure you know her already. She's probably family!' The pair shook hands, each explaining their own Mindel lineage. They surprised everyone by insisting that they had not met before, though it did not take long for Mick to make the connection with the Barnet of the Stoke Newington shop. 'That's my father!' exclaimed Sylvia, her eyes bright. But Mick was not really listening. Instead he was taking a good look at this tall, thin, sparkling woman. Sylvia was an officer in the Girls' Training Corps and she was wearing her army uniform. Mick, who had never worn a uniform himself, had to admit to the little rush he felt seeing her framed by its crisp, sharp lines. She filled the room with her talk, charming everyone who came by. She seemed to be a confidante of all around her, whether listening to the romantic latest of one of her fellow salesgirls or trading news with the daily delivery boy.

They all seemed to be in love with Sylvia and it was only a matter of time before Mick fell into line. He asked her to a concert at the Albert Hall and he had never felt so nervous. His heart thumped, out of time with the music, and it galled him that Sylvia seemed so unperturbed. She was relaxed, even nonchalant. It was quite clear that she would not care if he never called her again. She had been in love with another man, Lionel, whose mother had vetoed a marriage (on the barely disguised grounds that Sylvia's family were of too little means). The break-up had left her sick with disappointment; always slim, she had become gaunt. She was still too bound up with Lionel to fall for this over-eager Mick.

That was all right; he would do the falling for the both of them. He knew he wanted to spend his life with this woman who laughed so easily, who made even strangers feel like family. All the determination he had once deployed to take over and transform the United Ladies' Tailors' Trade Union he now concentrated on winning Sylvia's hand in marriage. When she was thirty and he nearly thirty-five, she finally relented. Mindel married Mindel and the two branches of the family, sundered by time and geography, were reunited not in Dunilovich but in Stoke Newington, north London.

The way Sara Wesker's family tell it, the first she knew of this new romance was when she visited communist headquarters on King Street. 'I hear Mick's getting married,' the party's industrial

organizer, Peter Kerrigan, said, by way of small talk. He assumed that Mick and Sara had broken up a while ago. But then he saw Sara blanch, wheel round and head for home. Her niece, Della, found her there, sobbing in the scullery, her arm on the mantelpiece. 'The bastard never even told me,' she was saying again and again. Sara never got over Mick, never fell in love again and never married. Thereafter she devoted all her energies to the causes that had brought them together, the union and the party. They became her life.

The party did not fully forgive Mick either. The comrades loved Sara and resented his mistreatment of her. Worse, he had discarded her for a 'mantle maker's daughter', a member of the Jewish bourgeoisie! Communists regarded this the way their orthodox parents would have seen a church wedding: Mick had married out. What kind of communist would marry a woman who was not even a party member?

The Weskers had their own theories. One imagined that Mick's mother, Jessie the cook, had vetoed Sara on the grounds that she was too sickly to make a wife or future mother: the chain-smoking and permanent bronchial cough had done her no favours. Others would wonder if Mick, who had lived in Rothschild Buildings with both Sara's parents and her sister Ann, had feared the burden of providing for her family. Either way, the Weskers would speak for generations of Mick Mindel and his 'terrible betrayal'.

Sara herself was more forgiving. After a long hiatus, she became friends again with Mick. He would come to see her most weekends, often bringing his only child, Ruth. Sara looked forward to those visits and Mick did too. The bond between them had been too strong to break completely. Even Sara's sisters eventually allowed Mick to be woven back into the Wesker family fabric. When Sara died of a stroke in 1971, Mick spoke at her funeral. He broke down as he addressed her coffin: 'I always loved you, Sara, and I always will.'

The years he courted Sylvia brought more than the joy of romance. They also brought relief. The dilemmas, the soul-splitting, of the start of the war had come to an end. The Nazi–Soviet pact had torn men like Mick in two: their viscera rebelled at the notion of an accommodation with Hitler, yet the party to which they had devoted their adult lives told them this was their duty. As Jews, they believed the struggle to vanquish Nazism was probably the most just cause in human history, yet their communist leaders told them this was an 'imperialist war'.

During that Saturday emergency meeting at King Street, when news of the pact was still stingingly fresh, Mick had come close to leaving the party. He had thought of the amalgamation, how he had flattened Lew Colton and the others who had talked of the needs of the independent Jewish working class, how he had blithely told them no, their future was in the national union. They should entrust their destiny to their fellow workers! Watching Pollitt suspended for the crime of standing firm against Hitler made him wince at the memory.

But other speakers had come forward that day, mostly to endorse Dutt and the Molotov–Ribbentrop pact. Moscow was still an enemy of fascism, they had said, of course it was. But there were facts, objective realities, to be taken into account; the Soviet Union had to think about the short term as well as the long term. Through all this guff, Mick had seized on what sounded like a fair point: perhaps the Nazi–Soviet pact was a tactical ploy, designed to give Moscow the time it needed to prepare for war. No one had said so explicitly – they could not, since officially the USSR and the Nazis were now 'friendly' – but the implication was, 'Don't panic, this is just a trick to fool Hitler. The war against fascism goes on.' Besides, the Soviet Union was to be communism's model state. It had to be protected at all costs. If that meant an alliance with Lucifer himself, so be it.

So Mick and Sara did not shout and scream or shake their fists at Palme Dutt and the platform that day. They did not even walk out when their mentor, Harry Pollitt, was suspended. They told themselves the pact between Nazi Germany and their beloved Soviet Union was for the greater good. Sometimes Moscow moved in mysterious ways, its wonders to perform. If ordinary believers like them could not always fathom the purpose, that only showed the limits of their imagination. So long as they kept the faith, revelation would come eventually.

In the meantime, Mick, Sara and their friends kept telling themselves this was merely a clever ruse by Stalin, enabling the Soviet Union to gird itself for eventual war with Germany. Mick put the pact to the back of his mind and did his best to pretend it did not exist. For him the Nazis were the enemy and always would be.

He had the union to attend to. His flock were now officially known as the Mantle and Costume branch of the National Union of Tailors and Garment Workers, but they were still his flock. Through them, and his place on the executive of the merged, national union, he was able to do his bit for the war effort. Women were needed in factories, whether to replace men who had been sent to fight or to manufacture the essentials of war, from munitions to uniforms. Mick became the link between Whitehall and those workers, hearing where the women were needed and sending them where they had to go. (Dealing with government was something of a culture shock: at one meeting Mick mentioned the potential risk of black marketeers profiteering from cabbage. 'Cabbage?' inquired the gentleman from Whitehall. 'That is surely a matter for the Ministry of Agriculture.') Mick approached his task with enthusiasm, working so hard there was no time left for party activities. Which suited him just fine.

Then came June 1941 and Operation Barbarossa, Germany's attack on the Soviet Union. Winston Churchill announced that from now on Russia was to be considered an ally. The Prime Minister had barely sat down when the Communist Party leapt into action. In the Jewish East End it was as if they had been in cold storage for two years, with most party members too demoralized, even ashamed, to do anything. Now they were ready to thaw, to come back to life.

Mick felt as if the rocks had been taken out of his backpack and he could walk lightly again. All was in harmony once more: he was a British Jewish communist and the British, the Jews and the communists were on the same side, united in the battle against fascism.

Suddenly Russia, a semi-enemy during the war and an unpopular cause before it, was the friendly giant in the East and a brave brother in arms. The papers were full of the heroics of the Red Army. (Russian soldiers were always the focus of the new friendship; Soviet socialism barely got a mention.) Mick even found himself on a Red Cross committee with the Prime Minister's wife, Clementine Churchill, raising funds to send medical supplies to Moscow. For all Mick knew, the future Lady Churchill did her bit by hosting society luncheons; he relied on the old strikers' technique, passing a tin cup around the factory floor.

The Soviet Union, so long an obscure passion of Mick and the comrades, was now a mainstream interest. Stalin, once reviled by the establishment, was now Uncle Joe in the Fleet Street press. Everyone wanted to be an expert. At one of Mick's regular meetings with the military, a high-ranking officer began to sound off about Britain's new partner.

'This Red Army, strong in numbers of course, but I'm not sure they have the stomach for the long haul.'

'Oh, really?' said Mick.

'Yes.' *Yarrs.* 'I fear they won't last two months. In fact, I'll wager they will be defeated in seven weeks! Yes, I suspect Mr Hitler will find it light work pushing back our red friends.'

'I think you'll be proved wrong.' All eyes were now on Mick, the trade union official who had dared contradict the uniform. 'The Red Army is made up of brave fighting men. They are well equipped and they are ready.' Mick was thinking of the two-year pause the Molotov–Ribbentrop pact had bought but, fearing some hostile questioning on that score, rapidly moved on. 'And, above all, they are committed. They are fighting for something they believe in. For them defeating fascism is not just a war aim. It is a sacred mission.'

The room was hushed. Mick had broken one of the unspoken but firmly observed rules of these military–civilian liaison meetings:

civvies defer to khaki. He was not fazed, but toughed it out, just as he had learned to do in those countless union meetings at Great Garden Street. Unbowed, he even made a speech about it later that week. 'I tell you what,' he began, leaning down from his podium, as if to have a word in the ear of his audience. 'We ought to get rid of some of these higher-ups in the army and I'll tell you why. Because they will never understand our most important ally in the war in Europe. They will never understand the Soviet Union!'

Victory, when it came, was righteous. Mick believed that a menace he had first spotted in the streets of Cologne thirteen years earlier had at last been slain. And fascism had been defeated the way he always said it would be – with communists in the forefront. Britain was unconquered and free, and it had, in part, Russia and its Red Army to thank. Millions of Russians had died in a war that had shown the world what Marxist steadfastness looked like. The resilience of Stalingrad made Mick proud to be a communist.

The pride is visible in a photograph from that period. It shows Mick chairing a meeting, perhaps of a Russian–British friendship assocation. Hanging from the table in front of him are two large banner-portraits, one of Comrade Stalin, the other of Winston Churchill. Mick is laughing, with a smile wider and easier than the

usual rictus found on the platform of a political meeting. He seems a man utterly at ease. And 1945 would bring further jubilation, thanks to the communist candidate for the parliamentary seat of Stepney. His name was Phil Piratin and he was to be carried on a wave of post-war euphoria, gratitude to the Red Army and old-fashioned *latkes*-and-strudel Jewish campaigning to a victory that would count as one of the great upsets of British electoral history. A communist MP in London! The world, as seen from Whitechapel, seemed to be making a fresh start. After the darkness of those thirteen years, the dawn Mick had yearned for seemed to have come at last.

Yet Mick soon realized that the Stepney triumph was a one-off. The Jewish East End was not about to convert en bloc to communism (they had voted for Piratin partly because they regarded the sitting Labour MP as a useless drunk). Instead a different ideology was rapidly capturing Mick's neighbours and even his family.

Among the Jews, the elation at war's end was almost immediately dimmed by the realization of the Nazis' crimes. In East London, as they had in Tel Aviv and Jerusalem, the newsreels showed the horrors of the Nazi camps. Now people understood what they had been fighting for. They started listening anew to what the Zionists had been saying, albeit from the fringes of Jewish society, all along.

Throughout the 1930s Zionism had repeated its grim warning: the diaspora was doomed, a catastrophe was imminent. Jabotinsky had toured the streets of Poland, reputedly in a van, a loudspeaker bolted to its roof, urging the Jews to get out while they still could. Ben-Gurion had met Jewish trade union leaders, including Mick in London, pressing the same message upon them: leave for Palestine and save yourselves. Zionism had never expected to see its prophecies realized so soon or on such a barbaric scale. Yet now the evidence was in and who could doubt it?

Vindication had to be spoken of carefully, but the Zionist leadership certainly felt it. Events had confirmed their most pessimistic assumption – that the world had no interest in protecting Jews.

Either it killed them directly, a task led by the Germans but eagerly joined by Ukrainians, Poles, Lithuanians, Latvians, Norwegians, Hungarians, Greeks, the French and myriad others, or it tolerated their murder. Governments in London and Washington had known what was happening, they had seen the aerial shots of gas chambers and crematoria, they had heard first hand the testimony of those who had seen one train after another arrive at Auschwitz or Treblinka or Majdanek or Sobibor full of people, only to leave with their once-crammed cattle carts empty. They knew of these vast factories, whose only product was human ashes. And yet they had never made the destruction of such places a priority. Jews had pleaded with both Churchill and Franklin Roosevelt to bomb the railway tracks to Auschwitz: that at least would halt 'production' for a day or a week or two. It would save lives. But it never happened. The Allies' only mission was to win the war. Anything else was a distraction.

From this day on, the Zionists argued, Jews would go begging for their survival to no one. They would defend themselves with their own army behind their own borders. They would be 'guests', dependent on the goodwill of strangers, no more. The loss of 6 million Jews proved it as clearly as anything could be proved: the Jews needed a home of their own.

'I don't understand you, Mick, I really don't,' his father would say as they argued the point for the thousandth time. 'What more needs to happen before you'll see what is as plain as day to everyone else?'

'I'm not against a Jewish presence in Palestine –'

'*You're* not against anything. It's "the party" I'm talking about. What *you* think is irrelevant. Because I'm not sure you think anything for yourself any more. Whatever the party tell you to say, you say. You're like that puppet on the radio. What's his name? Archie Andrews, the ventriloquist's dummy!'

Morris had found Mick's tolerance of the Nazi–Soviet pact impossible. He could not understand it, or accept it. And Mick was too loyal a comrade ever to air his own doubts in front of a non-party member like his father. No matter how anguished he had been after 1939, he had shown his father only the public face of communist unity.

This debate on Palestine was no different. If his father had not interrupted him, sending Mick into the kitchen to snaffle up a last piece of strudel and give his mother a peck on the cheek before saying goodbye, he would have maintained his usual posture. He was about to parrot the communist line that Palestine was best resolved by the formation of a binational state, Jewish and Arab workers creating their own secular, democratic republic.

He would not have voiced his own worries. Yes, communist Russia had finally come to the rescue and saved the world from fascism. It had done so at a painfully high price, paid in its own blood. But it had been too late for three-quarters of European Jewry. Six million was such a colossal figure, no one could begin to digest or understand it. Nor could he escape the fact that Stalin had been prepared to cut a deal with Berlin when Hitler's antagonism to Jews was already well known. What if the Germans had not miscalculated and never attacked the Soviet Union? Would Stalin have joined the fight voluntarily? The Zionists said that Russia entered the war the same way the US did, only when it was attacked. It had not taken up arms to save Jewish lives. Indeed, if Jewish survival had been the sole issue at stake, neither the Soviet Union nor America would have done a thing. Mick hated to admit it, but on this he feared the Zionists were right.

He remembered his own arguments in the union hall back in the 1930s: the future was in the world, not in some self-made ghetto in the Middle East. That would only ever be a hospital not a cure. He had had the nerve to say something like that to David Ben-Gurion himself! But would not a hospital have helped the Jews of Poland in 1942 and 1943? Would not a hospital, even if that was all it was, have saved the Jews of Hungary in 1944? He thought of what he had told Ben-Gurion and shuddered with relief that he had not been the leader of the Jewish workers of Belgium or France or anywhere else in Europe. For what weight would be on his conscience now? Ben-Gurion had thrown him a lifeline and Mick had thrown it back in his face. He was lucky. The English Channel and the Royal Air Force had saved British Jewry. But now he knew: the Nazis would have had their corpses – his, his brothers', his father's, Sylvia's – if they could have. Many years later, at a museum in Jerusalem, he would see the document that served as Hitler's shopping list, agreed at the notorious Wannsee conference of senior Nazis. There, among the Jews of France, Holland, Poland and Russia, was 'Great Britain – 300,000'. It was one of the few Jewish communities in Europe the Nazis had not been able to tick off their list.

Events made things easy for Mick; the decision was taken out of his hands. On 29 November 1947 Andrei Gromyko, ambassador of the USSR to the United Nations, voted yes to the proposed partition of Palestine into two states. He affirmed the original communist position, that a binational state remained the ultimate ideal, but now acknowledged that partition was essential. The decision may have been rooted in Moscow's own strategic gameplan for the Middle East, but that scarcely mattered. World communism had given its official, ideological approval to the concept at the core of Zionism. As Mick would later joke, Gromyko had made it kosher.

And he was relieved. Mick would only ever be a reluctant Zionist. He could not get excited about the creation of a new state, with borders and armies and passports and flags. Such nation states were meant to wither away, to be replaced by international brotherhood. For 2,000 years, Mick liked to think, the Jews had set a lead: they had lived as an international civilization, without the mechanics of statehood. Some day all peoples would be that way. Now the Jews were retreating from that ideal, putting themselves and their own interests first, ahead of the needs of workers everywhere.

Still, the slaughter of so many Jews had taught him an unwanted lesson: that the Jews might one day join a grand, global experiment in territory-free, state-free, unarmed living – but they should never again be the first to try. Now they would have a state just like everyone else and, thanks to Gromyko, Mick Mindel could be glad they did. (Eventually he would even visit the new Israel, taking holidays there. He struck up a particular rapport with Sylvia's cousin Ruth. She was the daughter of Sylvia's uncle Nat, famous in the family as the man who had served the British Empire in Palestine and been decorated for his trouble.)

For a short period, after the UN vote, Mick could feel comfortable. For once, his parents and his party comrades were in official agreement. The Jewish state, whose birth had so delighted mainstream Jewish opinion, looked set to become a useful friend of the Soviet Union. Mick was pleased to hear of the kibbutzim where a portrait of the benign Joseph Stalin hung protectively over the communal dining room. His fellow Jewish communists noted with a warm glow that it was arms from socialist Czechoslovakia which had kept the new state alive during the war of independence.

But the spell was not to last. In late 1948 a rumour began to spread among the Jewish comrades, started by those with contacts back in Russia. 'Have you heard what they're saying about the Jewish Anti-Fascist Committee?' one asked Mick.

'No, what?'

The JAC had been an inspiration for Mick. Created under Stalin in 1942 to drum up international Jewish support for the Soviet war effort, especially in Britain and the US, it had become a powerhouse of Jewish culture and Yiddish literature. With its own weekly newspaper and regular wireless broadcasts, it put out the word that anti-Semitism had been abolished in the Soviet Union, that the Red Army was poised to crush fascism and that a great Jewish renaissance was under way in Russia. It was led by Solomon Mikhoels, a much-loved Yiddish actor and director of the Moscow State Jewish Theatre, and by the writer Itzik Feffer. The pair had visited London as part of a seven-month tour of North America and Britain, drawing euphoric crowds. In the East End, memories of the old country were still sharp; to see these two Russian Jews was to glimpse the past. But the visitors' pride and patriotism were something new. That, and the very existence of a Jewish cultural organization backed by the state, convinced many in the East End that Mother Russia was no longer the abusive parent they had left behind.

'You haven't heard? They're saying Mikhoels has been assas-sinated.'

'Who by? Fascist agitators?'

'Mick, they're saying he was killed by agents of Stalin.'

Soon it was confirmed: the Jewish Anti-Fascist Committee had been disbanded and most of its members arrested. The line from Moscow was that this was the start of a new campaign against 'cosmopolitanism'. But Mick knew the code: *bezrodny kosmopolit*, rootless cosmopolitans, meant Jews.

He talked about it with his kid brother Jack, who admired Mick so much he followed him into both the Stepney Jewish football team and the Communist Party. 'Maybe this is what's needed to destroy capitalism,' Jack said. 'If this is what's required, we have to support it.' Mick would have found a more complicated way of saying it, but that was essentially his attitude too. He stayed with the party.

In the summer of 1952 it became even harder. One August evening fifteen eminent Yiddish writers were falsely charged with treason and espionage. They were all executed in the basement of Moscow's Lubyanka prison in what would become known as the Night of Murdered Poets. The Jewish Anti-Fascist Committee, which had numbered just twenty, was finished; most of its members, including its chairman, were dead. As for motive, some suspected that Stalin's paranoia, perhaps even his envy, had been aroused by the arrival in Moscow of Israel's first ambassador to the Soviet Union, the rising star (and future prime minister) Golda Meir. In September 1948, during the Jewish New Year celebration of Rosh Hashanah, she had been mobbed on the streets by a crowd of Russian Jews estimated at some 40,000. Such a spontaneous demonstration of political sentiment was unknown in Stalin's Soviet Union. He now saw Zionism as a dangerous rival for the affections and loyalties of his country's Jews.

In January of the following year the *Daily Worker* 'revealed' the Doctors' Plot: nine Kremlin doctors, at least six of them Jews, had been seized, accused of plotting to poison Stalin and the entire

Soviet leadership. All had confessed their guilt. To Mick it reeked of an anti-Semitic sham. He sounded out Peter Kerrigan. Surely he, a sensible, solid fellow, would see through this stunt. 'Mick, we have to accept the evidence of our brother party.' Only Stalin's death that March prevented the doctors' trial and almost certain execution. Later, historians would say that it also prevented the unleashing of an all-out assault on the Jews of the Soviet Union.

Yet Mick and the comrades mourned the passing of the great leader. All their adult lives he had been the north on their ideological compass. Where he had led, they had always followed.

Now Mick would find out the truth. He was holding it in his hands: the *Observer* of 10 June 1956. There in black and white was the text of Nikita Khrushchev's 'secret speech', delivered to the Twentieth Congress of the Communist Party of the Soviet Union more than three months earlier. The new leader had set it all out: the purges, the assassinations, the decades of terror Stalin had inflicted on his own people. Once again Mick could feel the ground falling from under him. As he suspected, the charges against the Kremlin doctors were all false; the men had only confessed under torture.

And in the newspaper were rows of photographs, one headshot after another. Each face belonged to a dedicated communist, many of them veterans of 1917. Every one of them had been murdered in Stalin's purges. One detail leapt out at Mick: most of the victims had been delegates at one time or another to party congresses. Mick thought of himself and the number of hours he had clocked up at party meetings, often as an official delegate: 'That could have been me.'

For many in the party this was the final blow. The invasion of Hungary that same year sealed it; this cause was lost. Their faith was broken.

Morris did not spare his son's feelings. 'Now do you see what I was saying all those years? Now will you have the honesty to admit I was right and you were wrong? Will you at long last look me in the eye and admit it: this Stalin you defended and campaigned for was a *monster*! Just as I said he was!' Sometimes Morris would feign gentleness. 'Look, Mick, we all make mistakes. But the best thing is to face them. You need to do that. You need to admit it – to yourself, if no one else – that it's a blessing your side failed. Thank God! Just imagine what would have happened if they had succeeded: a communist government here or in America! Imagine the havoc, imagine the killing. That's the point, Mick. When you were waving your red flags and singing your Soviet anthems, that country was murdering people in their millions. They were as bad as the Nazis, Mick – and you were on their side.'

That last barb was too sharp. Of course Mick was racked by the very thoughts his father was voicing. But Stalin as bad as Hitler? That was too much. Despite all that had happened, Mick could not shake the memories of the fascists he had seen so close in Germany, or his certainty that, had it not been for Soviet Russia, Hitler would never have been defeated. For all the cruelties and tyrannies of Stalin, the loss of up to 20 million Russian lives in the war was not a sacrifice that could be ignored. And what of the hundreds of thousands, maybe half a million, who had escaped from Poland to Russia? For all their suffering, those people, many of them Jews, survived. As Mick would say whenever he had to defend his decision, 'You cannot ignore it.'

Besides, he remained what he had always been: a sentimental, almost utopian socialist. He believed no child should ever go hungry, that bread should be free for whoever needed it. No, he was not dreaming. He had seen something like it, they all had. The war had shown what a country could achieve when it pooled its resources, when the animating spirit of the society was cooperation not competition. The women who sewed and stitched uniforms were not adding to the profits of some capitalist fat cat; they were working for the collective good. Why could they not repeat that now, in peacetime?

So Mick never tore up his party card. For that he paid a heavy price, and not only in the bruises inflicted on his Jewish soul by communist Russia's serial crimes. In 1948 he had sought the leadership of the National Union of Tailors and Garment Workers. After four years on the national executive he was a serious contender. In an earlier round he had beaten all the union's lead London officials. But he was black-marked from the outset as the communist candidate, too identified with the wrong side in the Cold War to be general secretary. This was the era of the 'Black Circular', when communists were officially barred from high office in the trade unions. The union's establishment, to say nothing of the wider union movement and Labour Party, were determined that no red should get near the top job. In the final vote, Mick Mindel came third out of seven candidates. Communists accused the machine of rigging the ballot to keep out their man, but Mick accepted the result.

His consolation prize was to work under the new general secretary, but only on condition that he renounce his communist activi-

The man from the union: Mick and the Morris Minor that took him to see every clothing worker within a seventy-mile radius of London.

ties. It was written into his contract. Mick signed it, though how sincerely is not clear. The Communist Party were quite happy with covert activism, especially in the trade unions. They would not have minded a public disavowal, so long as they knew they could still count Mick as a comrade. Which they could.

So Mick embarked on the job that would consume the rest of his working life. He became the union's full-time official for London and the surrounding counties. Every clothing worker in a seventy-mile radius of the capital was to look to Mick Mindel, some 30,000 people. And full-time meant full-time: his contract specified that he be on duty twenty-four hours a day.

From that union perch he saw the transformation of a workforce he had once led and the slow disintegration of the community, the miniature world, that had reared him. The one-room sweatshops were disappearing, replaced by factories. And these were no longer in London. Manufacturers had had to move out during the war and they stayed out, preferring the cheap rent and breathing space of a Luton, Margate or Eastbourne to the cramped side streets of Stepney. The Jewish East End had lost its economic heartbeat.

The Jews themselves had changed too. Young men came back from the war with the same spirit as their fellow returning soldiers. They were no longer content to accept the fate of their parents. They wanted better prospects than the *schmutter* could offer. Many became taxi drivers. Others joined the post office or the insurance industry: they wanted the security and pension the clothing trade had never promised. All wanted to put the bomb-damaged East End, with its memories of squalor, Mosley and wartime, behind them. They were heading for the greener lands of suburban Essex and, for the better off, north-west London.

Mick stayed, still living with Sylvia in the flat where she had grown up on Stoke Newington High Street, but the workers he represented were changing before his eyes. Now they were from the next wave of immigrants, and the wave after that: first Cypriots and Turks, then West Indians, then Asians.

Each one gave Mick a new education. Special care was required in those factories where Greeks and Turks operated the machines together: industrial harmony required the skills of international diplomacy. In the black factories Mick had to persuade the management that some things were non-negotiable: if the test match was on and the West Indies were batting, the machines had to stop. Other bosses needed to learn that, if they were to communicate with their workers, they would need to put up notices in four different languages.

The Wynona Corset Company in the west London suburb of Southall was typical. In 1973 there were 150 women working there, alongside three male design-cutters. Not one of the women spoke English. Mick reckoned the managers were using that fact to exploit them – without language they could do little to fight for their rights.

Mick was dismayed by what he saw. The women were on the same piece-work system – paid a flat rate per dozen, no matter how long it took – he had striven to abolish some thirty-five years earlier. When new garments arrived, the manager would ask one woman to do the stitching and time her. From that he would work out the rate for a dozen. But the workers suspected the bosses were fiddling the timings. For some reason it would always take them longer to get through a dozen than the management had budgeted for.

Mick remembered that sort of trick from the old days. The only solution was for the women to be able to speak up for themselves. He needed to find a crack in the language barrier. How could he represent them if he barely understood them? And then he met Shanti Sharma.

Back in East Africa she had been a teacher; her English was fluent. Here, on her first day in the factory, her fellow workers had pressed her to join the handful of women who were already members of the national union. Mick suggested she become a shop steward, offering to teach her all he knew. The management were not pleased.

The two hit it off. Each week Mick would visit with new advice on the art of negotiation. One winter, when the women were shivering over their machines, Shanti asked the boss to switch on the heating. He refused, claiming it was too expensive. 'Right, that's it,' she told the workers. 'Coats on and go to the canteen.' Within half an hour, Mick was there and the boss had backed down.

'You did the right thing,' Mick told her. 'But you didn't need me. You can do this yourself. You've got what it takes. You're firm and the women listen to you. That's all you need, a commanding voice, and you have it.'

Mick suggested that Shanti should teach the rest of the women English. That way they could all speak for themselves. The management hated the idea, but she did it anyway, half an hour a day in her lunch break. By the time Mick retired in 1975, every woman in that factory was a member of the union. They were paid properly, they were warm in winter – and they all spoke English.

The Sharma family stayed friends with the Mindels for years. When Shanti's two sons wanted to continue their education, Mick Mindel was their referee. Mick, who had always wanted a son alongside the daughter he loved, was especially fond of Shanti's eldest boy, Rajesh. When he went to Bradford to study to be an optician, Mick drove him to the station and waved him off. His parting words were the same ones he had given to Rajesh's mother so many times: 'You can do it.' For Mick, it was obvious. If the Jewish experience was worth anything, it was surely worth sharing with others. That was why he sat on government-sponsored wages councils, seeking to ensure fair pay, for some four decades. And that was why, when he heard of immigrants or asylum seekers, from Yugoslavia to Sierra Leone, having trouble staying in the country, he would lend a hand. Jews like him had been there; if they could help, they should.

He had suffered his disappointments, just like anybody else. But the greatest one was not a setback to family or career. Rather it was the cause for which he had been ready to give everything. His youth had been dedicated to communism: it had given him friends and a first romance; it had endowed his life with meaning and purpose. He had made great sacrifices for it, including, eventually, his relationship with his father. Morris could not stomach Mick's apologism for Stalin and, in the final years of his life, father and son barely spoke.

And yet, in the end, he was so badly let down, like a lover betrayed. Communism had promised him the sun and the stars but had given him only the familiar brown earth of reality. All the vices these revolutionaries had diagnosed in others, they carried themselves. They had made a pact with the anti-Semites of Nazi fascism, as he never thought they would. Worse than failing to protect the Jews, the Soviet Union became their enemy. He had once believed his comrades would save the world and protect his people, yet they had done neither.

But the strange thing about Mick was that he never allowed himself to become bitter. His heart had been broken but he repaired it and lived again; he was not a sour or splenetic man. On the contrary, he was always a gentle presence. As a union representative, he enjoyed good relations with the employers and managers he had confronted in pay talks and strike negotiations: they found him straight and patient. I saw some of that in the family, my great-uncle Mick playing the role of conciliator. I remember a summer afternoon at a great-aunt's house. We were all sipping tea, but there was a haze of tension in the air. Present was a cousin who had 'married out', there with his children, who were strictly, under Judaism's rules, non-Jewish. Mick could tell that some of the relatives disapproved, or at least felt awkward. He decided to make a speech. Not a pompous address but a softly-spoken toast – to togetherness and to the bonds of family, which matter more than any difference. He dispelled the tension and a warm glow descended on the summer garden, one that did not fade with the afternoon sun.

So Mick was never eaten up with resentment, not even of the communist movement that had disappointed him so grievously. He spoke fondly of his comrades, of their idealism, of their *certainty* as they mounted barricades and whitewashed the ground beneath their feet. Those had been the best days of his life and nothing could ever take them away. And he never stopped believing that the world could be a better place, that if the Jews had a mission it was surely to help that process along – never just to look after themselves.

And, if you asked him in a whisper, he would admit that he had never really stopped being a communist. He had nothing to do with the party any more. His old *Daily Worker* habit – buying two copies, one to read, the other to support the cause – did not survive the paper's death and resurrection as the *Morning Star*. But he still believed in a world where widows would not starve, babies would have enough to eat and governments would spend more on orchestras and opera than tanks and missiles. Whatever the party had done, whatever the failings of other communists, the communist ideal was in his marrow, part of who he was. So if the Moscow State Choir or a troupe of Georgian dancers were in town, performing at the Albert Hall, he would take his daughter to see them – just as his father had once made him listen to Ramsay MacDonald. When a lean-to in the backyard was overtaken with mildew, ruining all the books and records he had stored there, Mick could save only one: the Red Army Choir's recording of '*Berezia*', 'The Birch Tree', a wistful song of longing for the Russian homeland.

By 1994, at the age of eighty-four, he had contracted cancer. It struck in his gullet, preventing him from eating. Within weeks he was shrinking. His eyesight began to fail too, so his books and papers had to give way to the radio. In his hospital bed in April of that year he listened to the news of the first democratic election in post-apartheid South Africa. Ill as he was, that made him smile.

Mick Mindel died on May Day, the festival of workers' liberty. He had left strict instructions that there were to be no prayers, none of the religious mumbo-jumbo his father had taught him to leave behind all those years ago. Instead, and in complete violation of Jewish tradition, his body was cremated.

But Mick's body did not leave the world alone. Up until the last minute, his coffin was wrapped in the splendid red banner of the United Ladies' Tailors' Trade Union, the movement of Jewish workers he had once led. Its slogans enveloped him to the last: 'For a Socialist Commonwealth, Toiling Tailors True Together!'

13   *The Cork*

When Sunday came, Sara and Srollik were going to protest to their mother about this great injustice. Other children had gone home for Pesach and they had missed out, forced to spend the *seder* with their teachers rather than their family. They headed to school for breakfast and, before they could take up their positions at the bus stop, they were handed a message. Their mother would not be coming that day after all: she had a cold.

Sara was distraught; she cried and cried. But it was more than disappointment. It was as if a cloud had descended on her, not looming overhead but down here, engulfing her. It was March but it felt like November. She cried all day long.

Soon there was some consolation: they would go instead to stay for a few days with their uncle Benny, who had been evacuated with his whole family to the Hertfordshire village of Buntingford. Srollik and Sara were cheered by that prospect: whenever they visited Benny's family, their cousins would always make a fuss, enveloping them in a big hug of greeting.

But not this time. The moment Sara and Srollik appeared, the kids scattered at top speed, as if someone had just set the clock ticking on a game of hide-and-seek. Sara did not understand why the children were all running away, and why some were looking back over their shoulder and staring.

Immediately, Benny ushered them away from the house. 'Let's go for a little walk, just here,' he said.

Sara liked this lane, which had brambles and berry bushes on each side. She was imagining blackberries when she heard Benny's voice waver.

'I'm afraid your mummy's gone to heaven.'

Sara turned to him and said, 'When will she come back?'

Benny looked like she had never seen him before, his nose red, his eyes glittering, and he said, in a voice he hoped was gentle, but which sounded all wrong, 'I'm afraid you won't see her any more.'

The little girl began to scream, a barking, animal scream, not a long, sustained wail but a series of short stabbing noises that frightened Benny. Soon she was lying in the lane, her eight-year-old body taut and stiff, rasping that noise, over and over again.

Benny was crying, sobbing the way he had expected the children to sob, but now he noticed Srollik, still standing and making not a sound.

Srollik had said nothing. He was not crying even now. This ten-year-old man was white, a ceramic, porcelain white that would terrify anyone who saw it. Benny was murmuring, 'Come back, come back,' picking Sara up from the gravel, holding her hand and nudging Srollik back towards the house.

By this time the cousins had returned from their hiding places and were in the garden, staring at Sara, Srollik and Benny. One of the children, David, could not help himself and muttered something to Srollik. He may have said, 'We know about your mum,' or 'You haven't got a mum,' no one knows, but Srollik flew at him, this David who was much older and towered over him. Srollik grabbed him, shoving him against a tree, and began to punch and punch and punch until David was bleeding everywhere, from his nose, his ears, even his eyes. They were all too paralysed to do anything. There was no one to stop Srollik pulping this boy but Srollik himself and he would only stop when the job was done. (Two years later David drowned. He was fourteen and, though the two events were unconnected, his mother never spoke to Srollik again.)

Sara's tears would not dry. She cried all night and throughout the next day, and kept on weeping all the way back to Shefford the day after that. One unspoken sentence repeated itself again and again in her mind. She would never have dared say it out loud, but why did this have to happen to her? Other children had *two* parents. Now she did not even have one. Would it not have been fairer to do this to a child who at least had a daddy to look after her? Sara had no one.

Within forty-eight hours of her walk down the lane with Benny, she was back in the guest room at Miss Slater's. Her aunts and uncles had worries of their own. The older siblings, Yiddi and Benny, had to house the younger ones, along, in Benny's case, with his own children. So no one thought to take in Sara and Srollik, an eight- and a ten-year-old who had, in effect, been newly orphaned. They were sent back instead to their lodgings with strangers.

The demands of Judaism provided scant comfort. The Avigdor High School determined that Srollik, as the only surviving male present, should recite the mourner's *kaddish*, the memorial prayer that the bereaved read in each of the day's three services, every day for a year. It is poignant enough to see a grown man in synagogue, his face stubbled and eventually bearded in compliance with the tradition that bars mourners from the razor, utter the words, *Yitgadal v'yitkadash sh'may rabba*, the opening of the *kaddish*'s cascade of devotion for a supreme being who deserves to be 'blessed, praised, glorified, exalted, extolled, honoured, elevated and lauded'. But to hear those funeral sounds from the lips of a ten-year-old boy, it was too much.

Orthodoxy also rules that the bereaved must, for a year, abstain from any activity that might be considered needlessly pleasurable. Dancing, music and entertainment are all out. This rule came down on the Hocherman children just as the war was ending, when the Shefford kids were at last able to emerge from behind the blackout curtains. There were, for the first time in six years, school outings, trips to the theatre and cinema. But not for Srollik and Sara. For them, special arrangements had to be made. On those days out, they were separated from the other children and sent to a family nearby. Sara would play listlessly with the handful of toys on offer mainly out of politeness; she did not want to disappoint. Still, she and her brother could not escape the sense that they were being singled out for a punishment.

Of course the worst day was 8 May 1945. Shefford, like the rest of the country and much of the world, erupted into joy and celebration. It was the end of the war, Germany was defeated and Britain turned into one spontaneous street party. Publicans flung open their doors, strangers hugged and Sara and Srollik could not have felt more alone. The little girl wept hard that VE day. How could the world cheer when her mother was in a grave whose earth was still fresh?

That summer, if a few distracted seconds passed thinking about something else, Sara would jolt with a start, remembering the granite fact all over again: *Your mummy's gone to heaven.* No night's sleep ever changed it. She still went to class, still learned her times tables, still learned her poems off by heart, but she could not escape what Benny had told her. It was the stone that made her heart sink to the bottom of the sea.

Those around her offered little comfort. Children at school either did not know what to say or else were cruel. One older and particularly vicious child, Frances, found sport in extracting tears from Sara. 'Why don't you cry?' she would begin. 'You haven't got a mother. You know your mother has been killed. Why don't you cry? What's wrong with you?' Eventually she would get what she wanted.

The adults were lost. Apparently under instruction from Sara's family, Miss Slater made a house rule of never mentioning the little girl's dead mother. The fact of her death and her past presence in life were equally unmentioned and unmentionable. When Sara was with Benny or the cousins, the same edict applied. The name 'Feige' was never uttered. Occasionally voices might be lowered and Sara would hear the Yiddish 'Zie': *she.* But her name, never. Sara and Srollik soon got the message; the taboo spread to them. Fearing there was something wrong, forbidden, in speaking about their mother, they did not even talk of her when they were alone.

So Sara had to remember her mother privately and in secret. She would doodle notes on her exercise book: sentences about Mummy, drawings of her, the letters of her name. And at night they would talk. Sara would address her night-time prayers not to God, but to the woman she had snuggled up to in that very bed. She would look out of the window, up towards the sky, where Benny said she had gone, and would tell her mother all about her day, who her friends were, who had picked on her and which teachers were kind, and she imagined her mother nodding gently and tucking her into bed.

Finally in August 1945 the time came for Schonfeld's Avigdor High School to leave Shefford. The whole village turned out for a farewell ceremony, in which the headmistress, Judith Grunfeld, promised that word of Shefford's generosity would travel all the way to 'God's throne': 'While on the Continent children were starved to death and massacred throughout these last grim years, this village gave them sunshine and a warm welcome.' She told the villagers that, just as God promised Abraham, 'Those that bless thee shall be blessed,' so Shefford's people had earned divine approval by their care of 'these Children of Israel'. Schonfeld himself said that Shefford provided further proof that Britain had shown 'more fair play to the Jew than any other country in the world'; he hoped that the Jewish homeland in Palestine would remain under the benign authority of the crown.

There were songs, dances and sketches too, including the performance of a minuet by four girls, including my mother. The *North Bedfordshire Courier* reported that a poem of thanks, 'To Our Foster Parents', was read by the youngest girl in the school, 'little Sarah Hockermann'.

Some of the temporary Jews of Shefford would try to extend the rural fantasy they had played out there. Reunited with their parents after the war, they would move out of the East End and start new lives in what, by comparison, were the bucolic idylls of London surburbia.

Others simply had to go back, and my mother was among them. Feige's sister Yiddi offered to take her and Srollik. It was her duty. She may have had a house full of dependants, assorted in-laws and siblings – though no children of her own – but she was adamant. The house was on the corner of Warden Street, one of the tenement

Yiddi and husband, Max.

lanes of Whitechapel. At the front was the shop, with a compact living room at the back. Off that room was the scullery, a tiny square with a sink, a little cooker and a minuscule counter for the preparation of food – more a cupboard than a room. Upstairs two more rooms for everyone to sleep in, and that was it. The whole place was so cramped that if the family gathered in the living room they could not all sit down; instead, two or more would have to perch on the stairs, each step serving as a substitute chair.

But this was not the feature that would most strike a visitor to Warden Street. No, that delight lay through the scullery and out into the yard, a patch no bigger than a modest porch, which separated the house from the outside toilet. This was a yard that, once seen, was never forgotten.

It was covered entirely by a wire mesh, about a foot above the ground. Inside the enclosure lived a family of . . . chickens. They were there as the brainwave of Yiddi's younger brother Sonny, for whom nothing was ever easy. He thought a chicken coop out back was inspired: the animals would provide a ready supply of eggs, a precious commodity in austerity Britain. And, when the time was ripe, the birds could be slaughtered for meat.

Except Sonny made two miscalculations. The first was that the chickens of Warden Street never laid a single egg: he had bought only cockerels. Second, he had nailed the mesh at a fine height for young chicks, but not quite high enough for the adult cocks they became. Impeded by the low ceiling, every last one of those chickens grew up with a crick in its neck, its head on one side.

Maybe that was what made them so angry, for these creatures were vicious. If a delivery man or travelling rep made the mistake of asking Yiddi to use her 'facilities', they would soon learn just how vicious. No sooner was the scullery door open than the birds would mount their attack, squawking and pecking at the ankles of whichever luckless visitor was clambering over them to reach the WC.

Sara was to get used to such eccentricity in her new home. Her aunt Yiddi, Feige's older sister, could not have been a straighter arrow. The worker of the family, she had been bringing in a wage for years. When the Palestine experiment failed in 1926 and the Bitenskys returned to London, it was Yiddi along with brother Benny who were the breadwinners. She worked in the same office at the De Yonge's wholesale department store in Houndsditch for over ten years, eventually rising to the rank of head cashier and book-keeper, with six girls under her: four ledger clerks, a typist and a junior. Now she single-handedly ran the Warden Street shop, starting her day at five with a round of domestic chores before rushing to open up the store – cutting and callousing her fingers on the raw, splintering wood and twisted wire of crates holding tea or tins – and ending it with the clearing up of an evening meal sixteen hours later. Somewhere in that day she managed to fit in a religious fervour which outstripped all her siblings. She observed the rules of *kashrut* to the footnoted letter, and had a deep and wide repertoire of *tehillim*, psalms and prayers, she could recite from memory.

No, the eccentricity of Warden Street did not come from Yiddi, but rather the family into which she had married. In a moment she would consider *beshert*, meant to be, she met Max Pugachow at Victoria station on the very day she and the Bitensky clan had set off for Palestine. He was there to see off his grandfather, who was also about to make *aliyah*, though not so much to start a new life as to end an old one: he was going to Jerusalem to die. Yiddi took an instant shine to the old man's grandson, remembering their brief encounter at the railway station through the long months in the Levant. She rejected one Palestinian Jewish suitor, confident that one day she would be reunited with Max.

He was lucky she was so in love, for there was much to deter a less forgiving prospective bride. One source of shame was his father, who had been in jail not once but twice. The first offence would, in time, enter family lore, recounted as a warm tale of the old country. The story goes that Mr Pugachow Snr had a club foot – a disadvantage in most situations, but in tsarist Russia a potential asset. He carved a nice niche for himself in the medical business, though not as a doctor. When Jewish men were conscripted into the army, facing the nightmare of twenty-five years of forced military labour, they would first have to pass a physical examination. But if Pugachow went in their place, pretending to be them, his club foot would guarantee instant discharge. It was proving to be quite a fruitful business – until one sharp-eyed tsarist doctor asked the dreaded question: 'Haven't I seen you before?' He was thrown into a Russian jail.

Once in England, he again chafed against authority. He told the police he had no idea the two men lodging in his house were operating a still, fermenting their own illegal whisky. But the police did not believe him. They threw him into a British jail, where he stayed until he was dead.

Perhaps this was why Max was eager for the fresh start offered by a fresh name. He eventually became Max Dove. He liked it; he was proud to be a naturalized British citizen and saw no reason why he should not have a robust English name to prove it. But there were new difficulties to live down in his own generation. For Max was the only one of five children to be unscarred by serious mental illness. One sister and brother, Minnie and Menashe, were, in the language of the day, badly retarded: they had the mental age of very young children. Menashe, whose two left feet were not metaphorical but literal – he had to have shoes specially made – learned enough to do simple deliveries and, in later life, to serve as the *shammas*, the beadle, of the local synagogue: opening it every morning, arranging the prayer books. Minnie could do very little. But the others had grave problems.

With Pinny, it began with a compulsion. He insisted that his mother make him not just one cup of tea but seven, all lined up in a row. Or he believed his clothes were not fastened tight enough, that perhaps a button was left undone and he wanted there to be no gap, no space, so he would demand that his mother, a Yiddish-only immigrant from the *shtetl*, sew the clothes he stood up in, stitching one garment to the other, making a perfect seal. He stood there, like a gentleman in a tailor's shop, his exhausted mother running a needle around his arms, ankles and neck as if he were a mannequin.

Pinny fell in with a bad crowd, becoming an errand boy for a gang of East End criminals; he was fearless and they liked that. He would be gone all night, until the police brought him back next morning. Max could not stand it, the prospect of another jailbird in the family. Maybe that was why they had Pinny certified and taken off to an institution. His mother found it painful to say goodbye; despite the tea-making and the stand-up tailoring, Pinny was still her son.

She would pine for him, eventually prising him out of the asylum for a weekend back home. But it never worked. He would be out of control within hours, running wild. On those days, it would fall to Yiddi to resolve the crisis. As if managing a siege, she would first clear out the house, leaving just the two of them inside. He would know his time was up and would beg for mercy, dangling out of the window: 'I'll be good, I'll be good, I promise. Please let me stay.' The whole street would turn out for the spectacle, some laughing at the show, others scared. Yiddi would do her best to talk him down, to soothe him. (Max was nowhere; he could not cope.) Eventually a van would pull up and men in white coats would take over, Pinny's protestations now raised to a scream. They would drag him, squirming and yelling, into their van and back to who knows what kind of hell.

Moshe was a different story. Throughout childhood and adolescence he shared with Max the honoured status of normal child. He did well at school; he learned to play the piano. He was the youngest and, by all accounts, a fine-looking lad. But at eighteen he broke. The signs were there, but no one picked them up. He began washing his hands obsessively, scrubbing them again and again. He took himself for a long walk to Westminster, trying to push his way into Downing Street. Yiddi always reckoned it was the filth of the house that did it: lodgers who cut their toenails on to the floor, too many people crammed into too small a space. Others said he was surrounded by too much craziness to stay sane: the antics of his siblings, the constant noise, cracked him. He, like his brother, would spend the next fifty years in an institution, locked away from the world.

Somehow Max had emerged from this gene pool intact but not, perhaps, entirely unscathed. He had his own *meshugas*, his own minor lunacy, which the young Sara, who now lived under his roof, would come to know only too well.

Maybe it was fear of debt, which could bring prison, or perhaps a determination to avoid the poverty which had blighted his family, but Max had a sickness when it came to money. He could not part with it; to take his leave of even a coin brought him pain. While Yiddi worked in the shop, *schlepping* boxes and crates, he would stay in the back doing the paperwork – and counting his money. The linoleum covering the floor would be torn into shreds; it was several years overdue for replacement, but Max could not bring himself to pay for it. For Sara's journey to school, from Whitechapel to Clapton on the 653 trolley-bus and Clapton to Stoke Newington on the 106, he gave her exactly seven pennies – thrupence ha'penny for the fare there, thrupence ha'penny for the fare back. Once Sara complained that she was getting hungry during the school day, that the lunches were not filling her up. She took some fruit from the house, perhaps an apple to keep her going. 'You can take as much bread and butter as you like,' he told her, 'but you are not to take any fruit.' Fruit was too expensive to waste on a hungry child.

My mother's ninth birthday came in November 1945 and it went unrecorded: no card and no gift. The government distributed a meagre pension for bereaved children like Sara and Srollik, to pay for their keep. Guardians were entitled to hold on to the money, but some preferred to save it up for the children themselves. Not Max. He kept it all; the kids never saw any of it. It was, my mother would say years later, Max's *crank*, his weakness.

There were points of light, *Kratzmach* one of them. Children on the orphans' pension would get a five-pound Christmas bonus to buy clothes, so that was the time Sara and Srollik would be entitled to a new pair of shoes. Max would take the boy; Yiddi would go shopping with the girl. Sara loved these outings and would pick out the prettiest, daintiest shoes she could find. Yiddi would shake her head; they were too impractical. But how could she refuse this little girl? Yiddi would remember her sister Feige, her brooches and buttons, and conclude that Sarah had something like a right to hanker after such charming footwear. It was her inheritance.

The gloom also lifted whenever the name of Rothman was mentioned. The Rothman family of cigarette manufacturers approached Avigdor, now returned from Shefford to its pre-war home in Stoke Newington, and announced their desire to give something to those less fortunate than themselves. The school must have nominated the Hocherman children as the most deserving cases. And so it was that a limousine pulled up outside the Dove residence in the East End, bringing out the same street audience that would gather to see the forced return of Pinny to the asylum. A chauffeur in peaked cap knocked on the door at Warden Street, asking for Miss Sara and Master Israel Hocherman. My mother allowed herself to disappear into a fairy tale as she stepped into that car, her face pressed against the window as it glided west across London to the distant planet of luxurious Kensington. The Rothman flat seemed a bejewelled cave of treasure; the carpet was so thick, Sara's feet seemed to sink with each step. There was a little girl,

Virginia, and a boy, Jimmy, who might as well have been royalty. Jimmy had his very own microscope and let Sara and Srollik take a peek. It was a glimpse into another world.

But such afternoons were rare. Comfort came instead in smaller parcels. When the family moved to Turner Street – a larger house but no more spacious, since Max and Yiddi were joined by several of their adult siblings – Yiddi would manage both to run the shop, still in Warden Street, and somehow to provide for the children. She would dart between the counter at the front and the scullery at the back, serving customers, each one of them calling out some new demand – 'Mrs Max! Mrs Max!' – even as she stirred a barley soup, handing out change, then rushing back to ladle the soup out, slicing some cheese to order, then covering the tray, handing it to Menashe with clear, monosyllabic instructions, and then sprinting back to the cash till. Menashe's two left feet slowed him down and, in winter, the food had usually cooled by the time it reached them, but Sara and Srollik gobbled it up all the same. Young as they were, they could see their aunt loved them and wanted to enfold them with warmth; but she had too much work to do and too little time.

So Sara learned to comfort herself. When she won a prize at Avigdor for coming top of the class, all the other children had parents there to see them collect their awards. Sara looked out across the faces in the hall and not one belonged to her – nobody there. She felt her eyes itch. But she told no one about it. Yiddi was either too busy or too exhausted; her young aunt Rochel was kind, but she had her own life. So at night my mother would look out of the window, towards the stars, and talk to the only person she imagined really cared about her. And she would never be top of the class again.

What Sara and Srollik would not know until much later was that all through these years their father, Avraham, had been bombarding Yiddi and Max with letters, demanding they send his children back. 'This time, things will be different,' he would write. 'I promise.' More or less explicitly, he would vow to put bread on his children's table, to earn the money that had been so absent a decade earlier.

Max, especially, was not impressed. He remained convinced that this Hocherman had failed his sister-in-law Feige. He had failed in the most basic duty of any man: he had not been a provider. Perhaps Max did not notice that it was his wife, Yiddi, who was providing most of the bread in his household and cooking it too, for he considered himself a man who had discharged his responsibilities honourably. Business was doing well. He had closed the corner shop on Warden Street, known universally as Mrs Max's, and now opened a grocery and off-licence on Brady Street: Medina Stores, named, in Zionist aspiration, after the Hebrew word for 'state'. 'Don't come to me with your hard-luck stories,' he would murmur as he read Hocherman's letters from Petach Tikva. 'I was dealt a worse hand than you, or anybody else. Your father was a Talmud *hacham*, mine died in clink. But I have made something of myself. What have you done?'

In Max's eyes, Sara and Srollik's father had compounded his crime by sending money to provide for his children just once in all the years they had lived in England – and never since the death of their mother. Five pounds, one time only. 'What kind of man is this?' Max would ask Yiddi, as she wrung out that day's laundry and he sat in his usual chair, his hand wrapped around a glass of lemon tea. 'And what kind of place would we be sending them to?' He remembered the pre-war reports of the shack that had housed two elderly parents and six other adults. Maybe there were nearly as many people sardined into Turner Street, but this was different. For one thing, Max's home was no shack: it was a solid house. Besides, he had had that conversation with Feige: *What will happen to the children?* He had told her not to worry: if she died, he and Yiddi would still be around. He understood that now as a promise he could not break.

The letters became more persistent. 'You've stolen my children!' Avraham wrote. 'I've lost my wife, but I will not lose my children. You must send them back.' Yiddi hesitated. He is their father, she would think to herself. But she held firm. She had an idea what they, what Feige, had been through in Palestine and she did not dare put them through it again. Besides, the children had already moved so many times, how could she force yet another upheaval? Eventually, she wrote to Petach Tikva herself.

'The children are settled here,' she began. 'They have been on the move nearly all their lives – from Petach Tikva to London to Wheathampstead to London to Shefford to London again, and they have lost the only parent they have ever known.' She paused, before crossing that last line out. '. . . they have lost their mother.'

Now the ante had been upped. Avraham's mother replied to Yiddi's letter, making this a battle of matriarchs: 'How can you do this to my son? How can you keep him from his children?' And then, in a line designed to strike Yiddi at her weakest point, 'If you were a mother you would understand.'

The exchange continued like that for months, becoming ever more bitter. Max and Yiddi were at a loss, eventually seeking the advice of a rabbi. He suggested they yield to the children's father. Yiddi wrote the letter: 'Obviously I cannot take your children from you. I have been thinking throughout only of what is best for them. But ultimately you are responsible for them. I will send them to Palestine – but only when they are able to travel on their own. Yisrael may be at that age now, but Sara is too young.'

She regretted that promise almost as soon as she had made it. It was obvious that these kids needed stability and permanence. Their roots were so shallow, yet here she was, pulling them up once again. Sara was not yet eleven; maybe Yiddi could put off the move for years.

But then Srollik had his bar mitzvah, marking his official transformation from boy to man. Since Max would spend no money on a celebration, it was a modest affair: the high point was the gold watch that arrived as a gift from the Rothmans. Still, it counted as a turning point. For the orthodox and literal like Avraham Hocherman, Srollik was now an adult. He could travel to Palestine and be responsible for his younger sister. When David Ben-Gurion rose to his feet on 15 May 1948 and declared the establishment of a new Jewish state, Yiddi wept, but only partly from joy. She was delighted that the dream nurtured by her dead father, the milkman who yearned for Zion, had been realized. But she also knew that she had run out of arguments in her battle with Avraham. The Jewish nation was being reborn; the flower of Jewish youth was needed to nurture its growth. How could she keep these two natives of Eretz Yisrael away?

Yiddi carried it around like a lead weight for days, worrying how she would break it to the children. Srollik, she guessed, would be pleased: he was brave, with a lust for adventure. He fancied himself a kibbutznik, working the land like the farmers he had seen in Wheathampstead and around Shefford. Besides, he and Max were chemically incompatible: one would ignite the other. Srollik had long been desperate to get away.

Sara would not take it as well. She had flourished in London, doing well in her studies and, more important to her, becoming the most popular girl in the class. She was good at ball games, with a knack for juggling that made her a playground star. There was something else too. Unusually for a child, she was not selfish. She was good at putting herself second, at doing whatever others wanted to do. Unlike her classmates, she did not have to be taught how to share attention; she did not need to discover that affection is never automatic but has to be earned. These were lessons she had learned long ago.

When Yiddi told her of the new plan, Sara had to work harder than ever to console herself. She could barely stand Turner Street; she was ashamed of it, devising all manner of ruses to ensure her school friends never visited, never saw it. But she had made a life of sorts. She could daydream on the bus; she had friends to play 'five stones' with; the teachers, some of whom remembered her as the *shiksele* of Shefford, liked her. Now all that would be lost. She asked her mother for advice and, by way of reply, a picture formed in her head of a pretty house in a sunny country with a father who would love her. She saw him smiling, opening a big front door. The house was white, along with all the others in the neighbourhood. And outside was a garden with flowers, just like Miss Slater's.

She would miss Yiddi but she would be away from the grime of the East End. Above all, she thought, it would be lovely to have a daddy.

They were to travel with Youth Aliyah, an organization that specialized in sending displaced teenagers, many of them refugees or children orphaned by the Holocaust, to Israel. There were not many British children in that category; still fewer able to buy their own tickets for the boat, as Sara and Srollik were thanks to the fund set up for them by Mr Steckel, the factory owner Feige had worked for until her death.

In 1949 the day came and Yiddi was hushed. The journey from Turner Street to Victoria station seemed endless. No one was able to say a word. Sara noticed Max staring straight ahead, as if he had swallowed something rotten but could not spit it out. 'You don't like my father, do you?' she asked finally, surprised by her own courage.

'No, I do not,' he replied, and Sara caught Yiddi shooting a glare at her husband and at that moment, really for the first time, the little girl began to feel nervous.

Soon they were loading their cases on to the luggage rack, Max passing them to Srollik, who had leapt on board first. And maybe it was the sound of the guard's whistle or the sight of Sara in her little coat, but Yiddi could contain it no longer. Now her eyes were speaking: they were pouring out the tears, faster than she thought possible. She wanted so much to control them, not to let Sara see her sobbing like this, and now, of course, the girl was crying too, and Yiddi held her hand up to the window but it was too late. The train was moving and Sara kept thinking that she had never seen her aunt like this. Yiddi, who had the strength of a bison and who worked as if down a mine, weeping until her face was contorted. Yiddi had promised her sister to care for her children and somehow, even with the shop and Max's blighted brothers and sisters, she had done that. They had eaten well enough, had had a roof over their heads and gone to school. But what was to become of them now? Who knew what would happen? It was out of Yiddi's hands. She had given them up and now she had no idea when she would ever see them again.

Inside the train, Sara was crying just as hard. She clung to the promise Max had made a few days earlier: if she hated it in six months, she could come home – he would go to Israel and haul her back himself. But the tears would not slow. Eventually Srollik, who, like older brothers throughout time, had made a vocation of bullying his younger sister, pinching her, thumping her and stealing her packed lunch, turned to the weeping girl and said, 'Don't worry, sis. I'll look after you.'

From the train they boarded a ferry to Calais and on to Marseilles, to Villa Gabi, a large estate thrown open by a philanthropist to serve as a kind of reception centre for young immigrants. At the entrance all the children were handed a small piece of soap, and that was that: from then on they had to look out for themselves. Sara was shown to a dormitory and that first night she screwed up her eyes in prayer. She was like the Children of Israel and this was her journey through the wilderness, she told herself. They too had despaired, but God had not forgotten them. He would not forget her. He was testing her, making certain that she would not abandon Him. That was how He worked: sending hail and thunder and plague and rewarding those who stayed true.

The next day she made a friend, Ruth, an Irish girl her own age who was running away after her mother had had some kind of breakdown, culminating in the extremely rare step of a conversion to Christianity. The two girls were both so relieved to have found each other, they could not be separated. For three weeks in that Marseilles villa, while Srollik was off with the older kids, they were soldered together. When the time came to leave and board the ship for Palestine, they were glad to have a hand to hold. For the *Artza*, or *Homewards*, terrified them both.

A rusting old hulk, the corrosion visible even to the untutored eye of a twelve-year-old girl, it had no cabins – just hundreds and hundreds of bunks, stacked four high, in the belly of the vessel. The ship was already teeming with people unlike any Sara had ever seen. There were children from North Africa; Yemenites with dark skin, long, spiralling *peyot*, or side curls, and dazzling, embroidered costumes; Eastern European orphans who moved like zombies, no light in their eyes, and others as alert as wolves, turning and twitching as if on the hunt for their next meal. Sara suddenly remembered Peter, the little boy who kept rabbits in Shefford. She almost missed him. How funny that she had once found him strange.

There was little sanitation on board and plenty of the passengers were not used to twentieth-century lavatories anyway; they did not know how to use them. Soon the pipes were clogged and overflowing with sewage. No one could sleep down there, so the two girls followed everyone else to lie on deck.

Sara's stomach was heaving. It might have been the lurching and rolling of the ship, the battery of injections pumped into her veins before she left England or the still-fresh odour of human excrement, but she was sick. Srollik found her, as green as mould, on the deck and ran to fetch her a blanket. Sara clung to that piece of cloth, willing herself to get warm and fall asleep until she was shoved awake at five by sailors anxious to scrub the decks. Each morning the same thing happened, inaugurating another day of vomiting and prayer for release, until finally it was over. They had docked at Jaffa, in the new state of Israel.

They were loaded on to lorries and then transported to a camp for new immigrants. The older kids immediately set off for new lives, many snapped up by kibbutzim, the communal villages intent on making good Zionism's founding promise, to build a Jewish Utopia that would fulfil the Jews' highest destiny: to serve as 'a light unto the nations'. Others waited for the nascent Israeli bureaucracy to decide what to do with them. And some, like Sara and Srollik, waited for a parent to take them away.

There was no build-up, just a gesture from the staff at the camp, beckoning her to come and meet someone. As she moved closer, all Sara could see was a strange sparkle. She squinted in the sunlight, before recoiling: it was a mouth full of gold teeth. She was frightened and, when the mouth came towards her, she realized in an instant that her dreams would not come true.

'How you are?' he said in wonky, accented English. 'Your voyage, good? It was good?'

Srollik managed some chatter, but Sara could only mumble. There had been no hug, not so much as a touch; just those metal teeth and now these words. This man could not be her father. He was a stranger and, Sara knew then, she did not love him.

Her father turned away to sign some forms and Sara began to cry.

'Don't worry, sis,' Srollik said again. 'I'll look after you.'

'I don't like him. I don't like him,' she was saying, between sobs. 'I don't want to go with him. Don't make me go. I don't like him.'

'Don't worry. I'll look after you.'

And so she sniffed deeply and followed Srollik outside to join their father. They climbed into a taxi, and Sara thought of the last car ride she had had, that limousine to Kensington, and she felt the tears start again. From the passenger seat at the front, her father was swivelling round, pointing at her glasses. He made a face to show he disapproved of them, that he found them ugly. 'This they sent from England?' he said, with what he supposed was a smile. But if it was meant as a joke, Sara did not laugh. She was old enough to realize that disappointment is rarely one-way; her father felt it too.

They arrived at Ahad Ha'am Street and the gold teeth were glinting again. 'Remember? You remember?'

But Sara remembered nothing. She had been less than a year old when she had left this place more than a decade earlier and she had no memory. There had been no photographs and no stories told by her mother to turn into the implanted remembrances children take to be memories. It was unfamiliar and its misery completely new.

There was no white front door and no white fence. Just the stony, pebble-dashed exterior, the thin black roof and a narrow path through an overgrown, nettled yard to get to the back door. When she peeked inside, Sara buckled. She thought she had seen a beast – a man wearing little more than a vest, with the hugest, barest feet she had ever seen. His face was gentle enough, but the rest of him was dark and terrifying. Like her mother before her, Sara was convinced this man – Avraham Hocherman's brother Aaron – was some kind of bear.

Soon the house filled up, with her father's parents, more of his four brothers and their sister, Tova. Only she and Avraham spoke any English, but neither of them could manage more than a few words. The rest rained questions on the children in Yiddish or Hebrew, neither of which Sara could understand.

They showed the new arrivals where they would sleep. In a three-room house, every inch was accounted for, beds under beds. In this room her grandfather slept on the left, an uncle on the right, and she was to sleep on a small bed between them. The little girl's lip wobbled; she wanted so badly to go home. She longed for Yiddi.

The more she saw, the more desperate she felt. She considered herself a hardened veteran of foul conditions but nothing had prepared her for this. Next to the toilet was a bucket for the paper. They did not flush it away but stashed it there, and, as far as Sara could see, no one ever bothered to throw it out. The used paper just sat there, stinking and swarmed by flies. Inside, the house gave little respite. The brothers, sometimes the grandfather too, would routinely spit on the floor, leaving suppurating mounds of mucus and phlegm for the children to slalom around.

Food was in short supply. On a good day, her father might give her a few pennies to buy some breakfast. Then she would cross the road to the shop that sold a local delicacy she loved, *labneh*, a kind of cross between Greek yoghurt and cream cheese whose smooth, fresh taste would stay with her for life. If there was change to spare, she might treat herself to some halva, the ultra-sweet confection that would crumble in her mouth and stick, deliciously, to her teeth.

At home, there were few such pleasures. Sara's grandmother

spent most of her days recumbent on the divan. Her cooking extended to *lokshen*, the traditional noodles that complement a Friday night chicken soup. In Petach Tikva, though, *lokshen* was no complement: it was the starter, main course and dessert. That was all there was.

Sara ate it at first, but she soon lost her appetite. She had seen food move: rice kept for days that had become infested with maggots. In the heat of summer, it became worse. The house felt like a zoo. Turn on the taps in the bathroom and a slug would slither out; the buzzing of flies in the toilet could be heard from ten paces; and all over were cockroaches, not coyly hidden under a sink or behind pipes, but bold and brazen, leaping from floor to wall as if they were the landlords and these filthy humans their mere tenants.

So Sara refused what little food was put before her, barely touching even the plate of carp that constituted the big Sabbath treat. *Edel gipacht* they called her, Little Miss Ladylike, as if she were too good for them. But she could not do it; she could not brush away a maggot and eat the rest. She got by instead on a diet of oranges and black bread, hopeful that the outer layer of peel or crust had shut out the contaminations of the house.

Not that everyone starved. On the contrary, Sara soon learned that the eight adults around her were very careful to feed themselves. She discovered secret stashes of food, a bag of sugar behind a bookshelf, an apple under a pillow – private supplies not to be shared with each other and certainly not with these two child strangers from England. One day Sara caught her grandmother munching an apple, the old lady shoving it down the side of the chair as soon as she saw her grandchild, hoping the fruit had not been spotted.

'Menachem buys the apples,' the grandmother said, her face reddening. By now, Sara had picked up just enough Yiddish to understand. 'He thinks I need them because I'm not well. I'm not well, Sara, you see. I'm not well.'

It was every man for himself on this raft. The austerity measures imposed by the new state's Ministry of Supply and Rationing entitled children to a quarter-chicken once a week. Srollik and Sara had to collect it and cook it themselves; no one would help and, if they did, there was a risk the children would lose their bounty. They were learning.

Maybe if she had been younger, maybe if she had never left, maybe if Feige had never taken her away, she would have grown used to it, the way children do. But Sara could not adapt to this place. Not to the live fish in the bath – carp kept in water, ready to be skinned and gutted alive; not to the chickens, their legs tied together before slaughter, which also took place in this bathroom. Sara could not adjust to any of it.

Nor, it seemed, could Srollik. Despite the London injections, Srollik got sick very quickly. He had a headache he could not shift, his hair fell out, his cheeks turned ghost white. It was typhoid and it confined him to hospital for three months. Sara felt for her brother, prayed for him too – to God and to her mother – but she also envied him a little. He was away from *there*.

Sara wrote to Max, seeking to redeem the promise he had made back in Turner Street. 'I hope you will not mind me writing to say that I am not very happy here and I miss home. I don't like the food and my tummy aches all the time. It hurts very badly and never seems to get better. There is no room for me to sleep and I can hardly understand what anyone says and it's too hot, so please can I come back home to you and Auntie Yiddi?' She told Srollik, still laid up in his hospital bed, what she had done and his response was instant: 'Forget it.' He was right. She sent the letter and Max ignored it. He never replied.

Soon Sara had medical problems of her own, that stomach cramp that would not ease. She told no one, because there was no one to tell. She had started at the local school but that was no good: she did not understand a word. She was picking up Yiddish from her uncles and grandmother, but Hebrew remained a cacophony of '*ch*'s and '*sh*'s that made no sense. In London, Sara had been loved, juggling and catching her way through the school break times.

Now she sat alone, deaf and dumb. The other children thought she was backward, an idiot who understood and said nothing.

Still, the health visitor who came to the school did not need Sara to speak. The cursory examination she made of the little girl's body told her all she needed to know. Within days, she was knocking on the door at Ahad Ha'am Street.

Sara's father answered. He would work here and there polishing diamonds, but these days he spent much of his time at home, studying. For hours he would analyse in the most infinite detail the holy books which teach a Jew how to behave, not in the next world but in this, the texts which instruct a Jew in the sacred business of human relations and of right and wrong. In this area, as a field of intellectual inquiry, he was an expert.

The health visitor aimed most of her questions at Sara's grand-mother, who soon began to cry. 'What can I do? The girl won't eat. She won't eat. We look after her, but what can you do with a child who refuses to eat?' Sara dared say nothing, but she squeezed her own hands, willing her mother to send a message from heaven into the heart of this visiting angel. But there was no time. Once the grandmother's tears were flowing, Avraham decided he had had enough. 'No more questions!' he said, rising to his feet. 'That's it! No more now.' And he shooed the woman out of the front door. Sara thought of the Children of Israel in Egypt and how they had had to wait so long for God to hear their prayers.

Two days later the woman was back. 'We're not here to admon-ish you, Mr Hocherman. We want to help. It seems to us that you're not really in a position to look after your daughter. We believe this child is ill and we want to help. There is a residential school not far from here, a boarding school. There she will have a chance to get well. I'm very sorry, Mr Hocherman, but Sara cannot stay here any longer.' Avraham's mother listened but said nothing; she just cried into her handkerchief.

At last there was someone to look after Sara Hocherman. The school was well run, funded by the religious Zionists of American Mizrachi. Some of the girls were refugees who had come to Israel the way Sara had: on board rusting ships operated by Youth Aliyah. But others were relatively well-to-do, their parents prepared to pay fees for a wholesome, orthodox education.

Sara was dispatched immediately to hospital, where they diagnosed a stomach parasite that had burrowed its way into her intestines. The symptoms were dramatic weight loss and a tendency for sudden attacks: her temperature would shoot up, her face would lose all colour and she would keel over. They continued for months, these attacks, even once she was discharged from the hospital and transferred to the school infirmary.

Every day Sara felt grateful to be in a place that was clean. If there was an aroma, it was the chemical lemon of disinfectant. In charge was the house-mother G'veret Davitz, Mrs Davitz. Small and neat, her hair permanently scraped back, she radiated a strict cleanliness. She demanded the girls get up at six-thirty and that they take their share of *toranut*, chores, before their classes. Their duties would change each week – washing the floor in the bathrooms and along the hallways, making the beds in two rooms, eight beds in all – and the girls' performance would be inspected, as if they were buzz-cut recruits in the army.

But G'veret Davitz was more than a sergeant major with a mop. Despite the severe hairstyle, she could warm the chilliest room. She understood these children of grief. A Jew from Holland, her husband had been a victim of the Nazis. She had come to Palestine with her daughter, resolving that she would give her child two parents' worth of love and that there would be some left over, for the children who had none.

She took good care of my mother, encouraging the other girls to show similar kindness. When Shabbat came and tradition demanded a change of clothes, it only took one Friday night for Sara's dorm-mates to notice that she owned nothing but the one flimsy summer dress she wore every day. From that week on, and every Shabbat thereafter, there would always be a skirt or blouse left on her bed. Later a parcel full of second-hand clothes came from London: Srollik had written to Yiddi and she had done a whip-round, tapping anyone she knew with a twelve-year-old daughter. Most of the clothes were too wintry for baking Israel, but Sara was glad to have them all the same.

All this – fighting the disease in her gut, learning Hebrew and settling into this new place – left little energy to notice the shifting landscape through the infirmary window and beyond. But occasionally the birth of this new nation would intrude into her life. She could not help but notice, for example, the day in 1950 which marked Israel's second birthday.

It was a street party as loud and heartfelt as the VE Day that had brought such tears five years earlier. Sara detected the same emotion: the relief of those who had narrowly escaped death. They danced everywhere, the houses emptying of people, the streets and roadsides swelling instead. Sara staggered out to see it all and the joy infected even her. In 1945 she had stood outside the mood, grieving for a mother who had been buried little more than a month earlier. But now, on this Yom Ha'atzmaut, Israeli Independence Day, she was surrounded by people who, she knew, had escaped places even more desolate than the one she had left behind. She had no mother, but they had no parents and no siblings. She had lived in poverty and squalor; they had breathed the fumes of death. She understood why they were celebrating and her heart could not help but join in.

Almost a year Sara spent in and out of that infirmary, enjoying chats with G'veret Davitz, visits from the other girls and the escape of an English classic or two. Her Hebrew was now proficient but English was the easiest language to read. She would lose herself in the romances of the Brontë sisters or Jane Austen, the adventures of Pip and David Copperfield. She had only ever been a little Jewish girl in England; now in Israel, this Jewish country of Yemenites, Poles and Germans, she realized that she was also rather English.

By the time she was thirteen, she was getting stronger. She was now out of the sickbay, fit enough even to seek out some adventures of her own. A couple of girls invited her to see the new country. They went hitchhiking, hopping from one kibbutz to another,

Looking out on the new Israel: four of G'veret Davitz's girls in Tel Aviv. Sara is on the far right.

sleeping in a barn or haystack. The country was small enough then, with a Jewish population barely over a million, to feel like a snug village. Sara and her friends would pitch up in the collective dining room of a kibbutz and be invited to share a meal as if they were family.

In all this, Avraham Hocherman was invisible. Despite the final demands he had sent Yiddi, insisting on the return of his children, he was now barely involved. He came to the boarding school only rarely; when he did it made an impact on his daughter that she would never forget.

'So this is your room?' he said, his eyes scoping up and down Sara's dorm.

'Yes, this is it. Shall we go?'

'No, let me see where you live. I want to see.'

Sara was in a hurry to bustle him out; she did not want her friends to see that mouth full of gold teeth.

'OK, that's it,' she said, once he had paced around long enough.

'I thought we would take a walk.'

'I can't,' she said. 'I have this homework to do. It's hard. It will take all afternoon.'

'That's OK, I'll help you. Now, what is it?'

Sara was reluctant. Her father was of another world; what would he know of literary criticism? 'It's by our national poet, Chaim Nachman Bialik. It's called *"Ha'Matmid"*, "The Talmud Student".' As she said the words, she realized. The poem might as well have been about him, Avraham Hocherman, the lifelong *yeshiva bocher*.

> With pallid face tight drawn, and puckered brows
> He keeps his incommunicable guard,
> And in the Talmud, all his soul
> Is lost and locked, for ever and ever.

He sat himself at his daughter's desk and scribbled furiously for no more than ten minutes. 'There,' he said. 'It's done. Let's go for that walk.'

Later Sara copied out her father's writings, word for word, and handed it in.

When her teacher finally gave the essay back, she asked Sara to stay behind.

'I want to know who helped you with the criticism exercise.'

'No one, miss. I did it myself.'

'Sara, you're not in trouble. I don't mind that you got help. That shows initiative. I very much want to know who helped you. I need to know whose work this was.'

'Well, my father sort of gave me an idea.' Softly now.

'Please tell your father he has a remarkable gift. This is a quite brilliant piece of work.'

It was the only moment in Sara's life when she would feel proud of her father, but it would instantly turn bittersweet. For how, his daughter would always wonder, could this man be so capable and so clever, and yet do so little with his life? How could he have been blessed with such a fine brain, only to waste it?

It was rare for Sara to think about her father. Mostly he was unseen and unheard. She could go on her kibbutz-hopping jaunts, staying out all night, with no trouble from him. He would have been pleased by one thing, though. His teenage daughter was a pious kind of rebel: she would never hitchhike on Shabbat.

But she did take risks. She would visit Jaffa at night, spotting the knots of Arabs at the quayside who seemed to be eyeing her and her friends with a gaze she had not known inside the high walls of the Mizrachi school for orthodox girls. Dressed modestly, their sleeves long, they were unused to these stares, these calls in broken Hebrew: 'You come with me.' It was like the time they had hitchhiked and jumped off at Nazareth. They could not get another ride and began to feel edgy. All they could see were Arab men, no women, hanging about, suddenly materializing out of alleyways and storefronts. None of the girls knew any Arabs; neither they nor their teachers nor parents would ever have had a conversation with one. To Sara, they were utterly alien and instantly menacing.

Suddenly a van pulled up, a door was flung open and Sara was hurled into the back. 'Are you crazy? What are you doing here? Where are your parents? Are you crazy?' A Jewish Israeli had been driving through Nazareth and scooped them up, just in time he imagined.

In 1951 Sara Hocherman turned fifteen and it was time to leave school. Srollik heard a job was going with the British Olim Society, established to absorb the few thousand British Jews who had now 'ascended' to Israel. They needed someone able to type in both English and Hebrew and, thanks to the Mizrachi school and its idea of suitable careers for women, Sara was now just such a rare creature. She went for an interview and got the job before the school term had even finished. Still, Sara did not celebrate. She knew there would be a big cost.

She was too young to find a place of her own. She would have to go back to that house in Petach Tikva and, she knew with dread certainty, it would not have changed: the moaning, sick grandmother; the filth; all those men. She was a teenage girl, part of the group that cherishes privacy as sacred, and she would be living in a three-room shack with a stinking toilet and a slug-ridden fishtank for a bathroom.

Sure enough, all G'veret Davitz's good work and the year of convalescence in the infirmary were soon undone. Sara fell ill. Her skin turned yellow and her hair came out in clumps; her innards seemed to be in violent rebellion. She had typhoid, jaundice and dysentery, all at the same time. Her father did not act and he did not help. She would see him in the house, either sleeping or studying his holy books. They would nod. Occasionally, he would be out, doing an hour or two of work to pay for a meal.

Her new colleagues did their best to look after her. Sadie, the secretary, liked Sara and her young friend Rachel: she called them 'the kids', the two office juniors who were forever giggling and whispering together, who would promise to be friends for life – and who would keep their promise. My mother would call Sadie 'plain', but that would be one of her trademark charitable euphemisms. The truth is, Sadie was ugly and she knew it. She was an unmarried woman who wanted to be married, who would gamely turn up at dances, silently urging the men there, 'Please don't look at my face, look at my feet!' She was quite the dancer, this Sadie.

The boss noticed Sara too. What struck Shlomo Temkin most was that his newest employee seemed to be shrinking before his eyes; he saw she was sick. Once Sadie had told him of Sara's home life, he realized that releasing her from work would be no blessing – she would only have to find a job somewhere else. So he issued my mother with a perk available to no other employee: vouchers redeemable at the neighbourhood canteen. He made sure she used them too. At one o'clock each day, Temkin would make an announcement over the office intercom: 'Has Sara gone out yet? Sara, have you gone for your lunch yet? I don't want to see you still here. You have to eat!'

She managed to do some work too. Her favourite duties were as a delivery girl. She loved to be out on her own, pacing the streets, seeing the bustle of this new city. Once she had a parcel to drop off at Tel Aviv's newest landmark, the luxury Dan Hotel on Ha'Yarkon Street, overlooking the Mediterranean Sea. Sara took the scenic route, strolling along the beach, gulping in the sea air. And once inside the hotel! The magnificence of it: the shine and polish of those floors; the overstuffed bowls of oranges; the breakfast tables bowing under the weight of fresh *labneh*, ripe tomatoes and a dozen varieties of warm bread. 'One day,' Sara said to herself, 'one day.'

By now Srollik was back in England. He had started his compulsory army service in the new Israel Defence Forces but had been discharged on medical grounds. He could not stay on Ahad Ha'am Street a moment longer. Just as once he had clashed with Max, now he and his father inflamed each other. Finding work in young Israel was not as easy as the Olim Society brochures made out. He decided to hop on a ship back to London, just for a while.

Once there he wrote to his sister, suggesting she do the same. 'You could do with a holiday. And there's still money in the Steckel fund.'

And so, with the money left in trust by her mother's kindly wartime employer, Sara took a train to Haifa docks. She had already said goodbye to her father; he did not come with her. Alone she boarded a Zim passenger ship for London. Her ticket was for three months.

Still sick, Sara found the journey almost as hellish as the one she remembered more than six years earlier. This time, though, she had nothing inside her to vomit. She had become what her boss in Tel Aviv always said she was, a bag of bones.

The London of 1955 was even greyer than she remembered; Turner Street shabbier, if that was possible. She was thrilled to see Yiddi. When they hugged, Sara shook with tears – she had not been hugged like that for so long. Yiddi cried with her, ashamed at the skinny thing she held in her arms, confirmation of her greatest mistake.

Max's welcome was predictable. Sara was now an adult; if she was to live under his roof, she would have to pay rent. So she got a job, illegal, off the books and paying next to nothing, while she waited for a work permit. Once it arrived, she found something better and thought she might share a flat with one of the girls in the office. But she knew Yiddi would take it badly; she would feel as if she had failed Sara again. So Sara did what she thought would please others.

She considered going back to Israel, she really did. But she had made a vow to herself: she would not return the way she had left, without a penny in her pocket. She would not set foot in that land except as a *mensch*. So she took what opportunities she had in London and waited to see what fate turned up.

The break came with a job at the Israeli Embassy in Kensington. Her ability to type in both English and Hebrew, left to right and right to left, was still rare, almost a party trick, and highly employable. It was a long journey to the embassy but she liked it: a stroll in the gardens at lunchtime, a peek in the window at the fine shops, it suited this *edel gipacht*.

Yet she could not help the embarrassment, even the shame, at where she lived. She would go out at the weekends, usually to a dance organized by a Jewish charity and advertised in the *Jewish Chronicle*. There she would see young Jewish women from north London who seemed as elegant to her as Chelsea debutantes or Home Counties aristocracy. Sara imagined them before they had set out, turning and twirling before their full-length dressing mirrors – not using a cracked medicine cabinet on the kitchen window ledge for a reflection. For Sara's powder room was the Turner Street kitchen. There was no bath, of course, just a tin tub. To use it, Sara had to lock all the doors, fill the bath from the Ascot gas water-heater, soak, and then bail out the water by hand. If that was too hard, there were always the public baths.

One evening it was too much. Trying to apply mascara by squinting into the splintered mirror, she noticed a slow black trail snailing down her cheek. She was crying at the pity of it all. She turned to her aunt Rochel and let it all out.

'Those other girls look so beautiful and look at me! How can I go out like this?'

'You know what, Sara? You look a million dollars. Those girls at the dances would swap with you in a minute, never mind how you have to get dressed and made up. Look at you! You have nothing to be ashamed of. Nothing.'

Sara liked that thought and lived by it. At the embassy she looked as presentable as the girls from Finchley or Hendon; no one would have guessed her day had begun in the rougher parts of the East End. She had become skilled at covering her traces; she had inherited her mother's knack for conjuring grace out of deprivation.

So it was that by the time she met a young journalist bursting with ambition, by the name of Michael Freedland, she could pass herself off as a confident young woman. He asked her to dance; she was never left sitting for long. At the end of the evening he asked to see her again. They had a first date on a Saturday night, a trip to the West End to see the desert drama *An Eye for An Eye*, and when he asked to see her the next night too, she replied that she rarely went out with the same boy twice in one weekend. He gulped. But she was just as surprised as he was; it was an act and she was shocked she could play it so well.

He was keen, calling the next day. She liked the look of him, perhaps a little too thin but with a full head of dark hair. And he spoke with such purpose. He was from a provincial town, Luton, working as a reporter on the local paper, but he had big dreams. He talked of Hollywood and the movies, of national papers and American presidents. He was interested in the world and determined to make his mark on it.

And he promised to take Sara with him. Other boys had taken a shine to her before, only to lose interest once they discovered her home address. But Michael did not care that she ended their dates in a shabby corner of east London. He did not even seem to notice. Instead he would be standing on the doorstep at Turner Street a minute after sunset at the close of the Sabbath on a Saturday night.

(Neither Max nor Yiddi ever asked how he had transported himself from Luton to Whitechapel in sixty seconds, for surely he would not have dared travel on the Sabbath.)

But maybe the moment she knew she would marry Michael Freedland came when they talked about their childhoods. His had been happy enough: two traditional parents, strict but loving; a tight-knit group of pals from the synagogue youth club; a place at the local grammar school and an obsessive's interest, developed young, in newspapers, politics, the music of Al Jolson and the movies.

When Sara told him her story – and she told only a fraction of it – his mind was made up. He could hardly bear to hear it and Sara winced to give the details, but he knew enough: 'I want to give you all the things you've never had. All the things you deserve.' And so their future together began.

★

I know my mother sometimes thinks of her life as divided into three sections: a happy period of about twenty years sandwiched between two spells of suffering or, put another way, a long stretch of illness and misery broken by two decades of pleasure. The age of contentment began soon after she met my father in 1957. They married in Stoke Newington in July 1960, though not before overcoming some resistance from Michael's family. On his mother's side, the Mindels, there had always been a fair smattering of snobs. They were not so sure about this East End sparrow landing in their nest. They were proud to have got out of the slums as early as they did and feared young Michael was stepping down a rung in the Anglo-Jewish evolutionary ladder. One particularly haughty aunt publicly scolded my mother for eating from the cheese plate before the main course was over – earning her place in the family's hall of shame for evermore.

Sara had one ally though. Michael's favourite aunt, Sylvia, was

married to a man who earned his living fighting injustice and he could never quite kick the habit. When Mick Mindel saw the reception the family's newest would-be member was having, he detected a cause to be championed.

'You should give the girl a chance,' Mick would say to his sister-in-law Lily, as she wondered whether her son Michael was making the right decision. 'What does it matter where she comes from? Sara's a fine girl. And to have done as well as she has from a background like that, well, that makes her twice the person.'

Mick spoke up for Sara, recognizing in her a fellow graduate of the East End school of hard knocks. He did not know the half of it, but she was grateful all the same. Mick was a fierce atheist, Sara still meticulously observant, but the two would maintain their mutual affection for decades.

So she was pleased that he was accorded a place of honour at their wedding celebrations, rising to give the toast to the parents of the groom. But the man who followed him to the top table intrigued her. Great-uncle Nat sounded fascinating: an immigrant made good who had left England for Palestine during the Great War. He had been asked to give the toast to the state of Israel; then just twelve years old, the phrase still had a ring of novelty. 'Above all we wish her peace,' Nat said, as he raised his glass. Mick stood up, reflecting on the years he had spent opposing the very idea of the Jewish state that was now a reality. Sara joined the toast too, remembering the land where she was born, the land where her father still lived. For that one brief moment – the only time they were all together – they were thinking the same thought: Nat, Mick and Sara, dreaming of Israel.

For Sara, it was as if her life was beginning. She and Michael bought a small house together in the modest suburb of Kenton. It was tiny, but she could not have been more proud. She had told him that all she wanted was a garden and a bathroom and now she had both – with her own front door to boot. She scrubbed the floors, washed the curtains and polished every visible surface. This would be her home, the first that really deserved the name. Now she could be a *person*, no longer dependent on the generosity of others but able to extend some hospitality of her own. She loved people to visit, she loved to be on the other side of the front door.

One of her first guests was that great-uncle of Michael's, Nat, who had made the toast to Israel. She was expecting someone heroic, what with his OBE and all. But the man who arrived cut a cheerless figure. Alone and away from his family, he was locked in some incomprehensible tussle with the government over his pension. He talked endlessly, mainly at the young couple; he was formal, like an officer addressing the troops or someone chairing a meeting. No, she did not warm to him. And within a few months of that Shabbat visit to Kenton, Nat Mindel was dead.

In 1963 Sara gave birth to a girl. Times had changed and she knew she could not call this first daughter Feige, not in 1960s Britain. Her brother, Srollik, now married and also blessed with a daughter, had called his girl Frances. Sara named hers Fiona.

Another baby girl, Daniela, followed thirteen months later and, in February 1967, a baby boy: me. My mother had given up her job as soon as Fiona arrived. She had not hesitated and never once regretted it. She was determined to be a full-time, twenty-four-hour-a-day, 365-days-a-year mother to her children. She would not sleep a night away from them; nobody would ever have to take care of them but her. If they woke in the dark, she would be the one to cuddle them, and if they needed to talk, she would listen. No child of hers would ever have to gaze out of the window, talking to the stars.

Those were the happy years. Michael was doing well enough for them to move to green and wooded Elstree, a Hertfordshire suburb of London. He now had his own programme on the radio, a magazine show about Jewish life. He had had to change to be with his wife. Growing up, he had never strictly observed the Sabbath but he did now: he taught his children to switch no lights on and never to use the phone. They learned that Friday night was always a home night, no matter what their school friends might be doing.

Sara had what she wanted: a loving, hard-working husband and a wholesome, Jewish family.

They were even able to take the odd foreign holiday, including a few trips back to Israel. On one, they stayed in the Dan Hotel in Tel Aviv. It was Sara's first visit since she had delivered a parcel there a quarter of a century earlier. She had kept her promise to herself.

She also visited the shack on Petach Tikva, but she did not stay. She came as a guest and left when she was ready to leave. She dressed up for those visits, jewellery, the works. She wanted them to see that the *edel gipacht* had made something of herself after all.

They were strange encounters, these. Michael would shift in his seat, his eyes darting around the room, occasionally exhaling through his nose in what sounded like a snort of impatience. He was speaking the international body language of discomfort and something else too: anger. He was angry at what these people had done to the wife he loved so much; he wanted to whisk her away from there as quickly as he could, lest they get close enough to inflict any more damage. He also suspected they looked down on him, with not a day of *yeshiva* education to his name. He wanted to shout, 'I live in the twentieth century and I am in the world. Where are you? And what did all of your books and your *halacha*, your Jewish law, ever do for this woman? Nothing. Not a fraction of what I have done for her.'

But body language was all he had, and not only because he spoke no Hebrew. His father-in-law, Avraham Hocherman, had no speech at all. Sometime in the early 1970s, he had fallen silent. He would gesture towards his throat as if it was an unavoidable medical problem, but doctors never could find out what was wrong. They suspected the old man had taken a decision never to speak again. Those who saw him on the streets of Petach Tikva, a Hassid in wispy, grey beard, shuffling along clutching the pencil and notebook that served in place of his tongue, would never have guessed that this man once captivated audiences with his storytelling and teaching, and that he once swept a young Englishwoman off her feet with a soaring comet of words. On her visits, Sara would speak slowly, waiting for his written reply, and she would be polite. But, if you overheard her, you would imagine she was a kindly social worker checking in with a client or perhaps a distant cousin in town for the weekend. They did not speak as daughter and father.

Sara would be relieved to leave. She loved Israel and wished only well for it. But Petach Tikva carried too much dread in its name. She had a life elsewhere now, with a wide circle of friends and even a part-time job in journalism, editing the children's page of the *Jewish Chronicle*. She just prayed that the bubble would not burst.

Then, in November 1979, her head began to ache. Something was pounding her brain like a jackhammer. She tried to sleep it off, but when she got out of bed she tottered like a drunk, keeling over. The room was tipping. Her ear was aching too. Michael tried to be helpful, bringing regular cups of tea, but they did no good. Each day was worse than the one before.

My prime focus that month was my part in the school play. Twelve years old, I delivered my lines the way the teacher had told us to, ensuring I made regular eye contact with all parts of the audience. Except for me the move came naturally. I was scanning the rows of seats looking for my parents. Halfway through I spotted my father, but with an empty seat at his side. This was grave. My mother did not allow moments of childish glory to pass without a full parental presence to share the joy.

Initially her local doctor had suspected mental exhaustion and stress – code, it seemed, for housewife boredom. 'I'm not saying you're nutty,' he said, 'you just need to rest a while.' He was only moved to act when his patient's face started changing. My mother's mouth began to twist, stretching upward as if to reach her right eye. 'Well, you couldn't have done that yourself,' the GP quipped, before suggesting she head straight to the local emergency ward. She could not make it down the stairs to the car; one of my father's friends carried her in his arms. My father could not bear to do it himself.

There she was pumped full of a series of powerful drugs – all of them wrong, as it turned out. They accelerated the illness rather than repelling it. The GP finally relented and contacted a specialist. This man refused to make an appointment to see my mother. From the few details he had, he knew there was not time. Instead he dispatched an ambulance to bring her immediately to the (archaically named) National Hospitals for Nervous Diseases.

There a consultant recognized a rare form of the neurological disease encephalitis. A virus had begun in her ear, burrowed its way through the middle ear, which controls balance – hence the walk of the drunken sailor – and on into the peripheral nervous system. Now it was eating away at the outskirts of the central nervous system itself, moving like a bush fire, hacking down whole fields of nerve tissue as it advanced. Messages were rerouting wildly, like phone calls on an overloaded switchboard, so that the eye and the mouth would suddenly be tied together, tears coming whenever my mother began to eat. The doctors took my father to one side. They would do their best, but no one had survived this disease in twenty years.

Once she was trolleyed into an operating theatre, except this was not for surgery; it was for a lecture. The senior professor wanted his students to see this rare case for themselves. A photographer was on hand to record the moment for publication in a scientific journal.

Somehow the virus was halted in its tracks and slowly my mother began to stabilize. She could eat, though her wayward mouth made that a challenge; it was now the wrong shape. She could sit up, but each tiny movement of her head would set off a neurological chain reaction, sounding a series of explosions in her head as loud and sustained as a city firework display. Walking was a fairground ride: somehow she had to put one foot in front of the other even though the ground was undulating or spinning.

She came home but was effectively bedridden. She tried to pretend otherwise, for her children's sake. Eyeing the clock, she would haul herself up at four in the afternoon, fighting the dizziness and the nausea as she clung to her bed and slowly got dressed. Somehow, perhaps one step at a time and on her bottom, she would get downstairs. She wanted to be there when we arrived home from school. Once we had seen her and she had heard the outlines of our news, she would yawn and say it had been a long day, perhaps it would be good to have a lie-down just this once. (The words did not come out easily; her mouth was bent the wrong way for speech too.) For years I fell for this ruse, believing the thirty minutes I had witnessed marked the last phase of my mother's active day rather than its entirety.

It was probably around now that the anger grew. In 1945 Sara had wondered why children with two parents had been allowed to keep both when she had lost the only one she had ever known. Now she puzzled over the divine joke that had thwarted her one real ambition. She had vowed to be a present, constant mother and she had been granted little more than a decade and a half in the role. As a child she had known surrogates and strangers and now – she could hear them, at the front door – they were in her house, carting a vat of chicken soup or bagloads of shopping to feed her children.

She began to think God had made a concession in what was otherwise a cold plan. She was obviously preordained to live a life of suffering and, perhaps in a moment of mercy, he had decided to give her twenty good years' respite. That furlough was now over and it was back to the harsh sentence of grief, pain and heartbreak she had known before. This was what she would think, horizontal in the daytime, waiting for her children.

I knew some of this from the long evening talks I would have with my mother when I would perch on the end of her bed, like a hospital visitor. She knew I was too young to hear it, but she could not help herself. She needed to speak. She needed to voice her rage at a God that had forced her to endure a childhood of loss, tricked her into believing she was to live happily ever after with a devoted husband and loving children, only to prove that happiness was a mere interlude. She knew she should not, but she could not stop.

She told her sixteen-year-old son that sometimes she wanted to end the pain once and for all. She told him she had tried.

There was much I did not understand in that period, but one thing in particular stands out. I remember that parcels used to arrive for my mother from Israel, postmarked Petach Tikva. They were from Avraham, her father, letters recommending alternative therapies and diets that would make her well. He enclosed packets of herbs that she was to brew into a tea; seeds to sprinkle on her food. In defiance of the doctors and secular science, he insisted this was the cure she needed.

Sara would give a thin smile at the sight of these packets, which would pile up unopened. She was surprised, and even oddly touched, that her father was so bothered; she never knew he cared. It was the first time he ever had.

But there was something else too. She looked at those green leaves and her father's scribbled recipes and thought: after all those years of study, of poring over those holy texts, this is what he comes up with. This. He had eaten so well from the Tree of Life, as orthodox Jews call the Torah, he had gorged on it, but what wisdom had it given him? Quackery. The same mumbo-jumbo she might have gleaned from some spiritualist crank. Is this what a lifetime spent peering into the heart of Judaism's eternal mysteries had given him?

She had stuck by God as a child and as a young woman. She thought the suffering was some kind of test. And she kept her faith for those twenty golden years of marriage and motherhood: they confirmed that God had looked out for her in the end, perhaps even that she had met the challenge he had set for her. But she could not explain this punishment, to be struck down by a neurological illness, reduced to the life of an elderly invalid at the age of forty-three.

And so, gradually, her faith began to ebb away. If she needed a confidante, she would speak to Yiddi, who, now widowed and freed from the grind of running Mrs Max's corner shop, had become as loving as any mother and as devoted as any grandmother. Sara no longer looked to the stars for company; her concerns were right here on earth.

Over the next twenty-five years she did not exactly recover. Instead, my mother adapted to the damage the disease had wrought in her brain. She learned to walk straight, even on ground that seemed to turn like a gyroscope. The National Hospitals arranged plastic surgery, so the mouth and eye meandered no more. She spent fewer daytime hours in bed and eventually none. After ten years weighed low with unhappiness, she began to believe again in a future. The strength which had seen her fight off typhoid, jaundice, dysentery, poverty, abuse and virtual orphanhood returned. The cork bobbed back up.

Through it all, one thing has never changed. My mother still maintains, more or less, the practices of an orthodox Jew. She lights candles every Friday night, eats only those foods allowed under Jewish law and sits in a separate enclosure for women when she prays in the synagogue. Whatever her private views on God and belief, some things never change. When Pesach comes, she does what her mother did that night in 1945: she scrubs and wipes and polishes. She does it with a vigour, an intensity, that can seem almost frightening. If she could take a flamethrower to her kitchen, scalding off every last mite or crumb of dirt, she would. She cleans and cleans and cleans. Everyone who knows her says it. There is no cleaner place in the world than Sara's home.

PART THREE

Reckonings

14   *Nat and the Dream of Both*

A Jewish man is keen to join a golf club with a restricted-membership policy. His application proceeds well and at last he comes before the selection committee.

'What is your name?'

'Smith.'

'Your father's surname?'

'Smith.'

'Do you have any special dietary requirements we might need to tell chef in the clubhouse?'

'Only that I eat bacon every morning for breakfast, preferably with a side order of cream. Oh, and I love all kinds of shellfish.'

'What is your favourite holiday?'

'Easter, with Christmas a close second.'

'And finally, Mr Smith, what is your religion?'

'Why, *goyische* of course!'

There are a thousand variations on that theme, each one aiming at the same target – the Jew so eager to reach the finishing tape marked 'acceptance' that he trips and stumbles – and each punching home the same pessimistic moral: that the Jew bent on assimilation will always fail. He may get close, but he will always be exposed in the end.

Nat Mindel and his immigrant brothers changed their names, shed their old-fashioned, tribal garb and traded their old language for a new one. My generation, the fourth to Nat's first, have had to do nothing quite so radical, but the impulse remains the same, albeit in milder form: the urge to drop the outer signs and habits that seem to stand between us and the country we live in. The requirement to eat kosher food is often an early casualty: it can be annoying to order from only a quarter of the menu or to refuse a meal prepared by a kind host. It is similarly inconvenient in today's professional workplace to have to knock off early on Friday afternoons in winter and to rule out Saturdays in order to respect the Sabbath. Nor is it easy to stand out on a commuter train by wearing a skullcap. Most important of all, who can deny the power of love? When a Jewish man or woman falls for a non-Jew, they have to weigh a heritage of which they may know only little against a passion that may never come again. Is it any wonder that everywhere but Israel nearly one in two Jews marries 'outside the faith'?

I have had to make my own decisions on all those dilemmas; some of them have pressed in very deep. My guide has been the experience of my family and also the story of my wider clan, the Jewish people itself. Not that the record is encouraging.

It shows first that the urge to blend in is enduringly powerful, even when that means ridding oneself of all outward signs of difference. In its most extreme form it is an attempt to shake off one's heritage, to escape one's very identity. Is it any wonder that Harry Houdini, the greatest escapologist the world has ever known, was in fact Ehrich Weiss – a rabbi's son from Budapest who sought to pass himself off as an all-American lad from Appleton, Wisconsin? A jobbing magician, fame came when he conjured an act from a centuries-old Jewish fantasy: to slip the bonds of birth and escape.

The record shows something else too. That when assimilation fails, it fails badly. The Jews' persecutors have rarely extended clemency to those who strove to disguise themselves, no matter how dedicated their effort. In the late Middle Ages, the Marranos, the secret Jews of Spain, whose outward appearance was indistinguishable from that of Castilian Catholics, were suspected all the more. A few centuries later, German Jews became the most assimilated community in Jewish history. Emancipation saw them shave their beards and lop off their side curls. They ate what others ate, they worked on the Sabbath – whatever it took. In the first half of the nineteenth century, one in three German Jews converted to Christianity. They married Gentiles and took the sandpaper to any remaining rough edges, including their own names: Hershel became

Heinrich, Itzik became Hitzig. They were shedding their Jewish skins, all the better to swim upstream. But it was in vain. Their children, even their grandchildren, were still branded Jewish enough to die.

This is not to deny that many of Germany's assimilated Jews made good and happy lives for themselves in the nineteenth and early twentieth centuries; nor is it to suggest that the Nazi war against the Jews was somehow preordained, that German Jewry should have seen it coming. It is merely to note that even the most strenuous efforts to conform have rarely brought ultimate safety.

And yet the cruel joke of assimilation is that even when it succeeds, it contains a kind of failure. Take Moses Mendelssohn, who in 1743, as a fourteen-year-old boy with a hunchback and a stutter, entered Berlin through the gate reserved for Jews and cattle. He went on to become a philosopher and man of letters, admired as the father of the Jewish enlightenment. He set in train the shift that saw Jews become German in language, costume and even values. Jewish integration into German life was so complete that, a century after Mendelssohn's entrance through Berlin's Rosenthal Gate, only four of his fifty-six descendants were still Jews. According to the historian Amos Elon, 'When the last died, many of the Mendelssohns attending the funeral witnessed a Jewish rite for the first time in their lives.'

This paradox – the loss that comes with success – is not confined to the Jews. On the contrary, it is one of the Jewish experiences that might most resonate with today's other diasporas. Often they face the same temptations, a whole new society laid out before them, exotic in its difference to themselves. They can dive into it, submerging their whole being in its novelty, sinking deep into the look, the language, the literature, the smell, the possibility. *East is East*, a film about British Pakistanis in 1970s Salford, follows Tariq, a young man who has to choose between the lure of miniskirts, disco and modern hi-fi and the Islamic dictates of his disciplinarian father. The old religion cannot compete. Tariq becomes Tony.

There is a gain to this change, as every Moshe who became

Morris can testify. The world seems to open up, to them and to the generations that follow. Some make it work, with no regrets; eventually they or their children or their grandchildren blend in completely, their ethnic origins a fading, maybe even unknown fact about their family's distant past. But others will feel a cost. Tony will miss Tariq: the warmth, the continuity, the certainties of the closed community he has left behind. And if his motive was a dream of safety, the hope that Tony could elude the prejudice and menace that would have haunted Tariq, he might be disappointed. The Jewish experience since the eighteenth century suggests, depressingly, that the attempt to mingle into the crowd is not much of a strategy for survival.

Not all of this was so clear when Nat, Barnet, Louis and Simon – formerly Menachem, Berel, Levi and Shimsel – lifted their chins, straightened their backs and held still for their formal portrait, the one that sits now on my mantelpiece. But, a century on, that is how it looks to me. I have seen how the great experiment in assimilation worked out.

So I have chosen something different. I do not follow orthodox custom by refusing to work at the weekend, nor do I wear a skullcap anywhere but the synagogue, but I do restrict myself to kosher food. I live and work in the mainstream of national life, but I publicly identify as a Jew and have never hidden it. My social life is wide and varied, but when it came to marriage I was glad to fall in love with a woman whose heritage I share. What it amounts to is a decision that says, I want to take part in British society, but I don't want to disappear. I want to assimilate, but only so far.

I now realize that my great-great-uncle Nat, the immigrant who left Russia for England and England for Palestine, felt the same way. He was not prepared to accept the usual either/or choice. He would not stay in the all-Jewish *shtetl*, not in Dunilovich, not in London, not even in Palestine. But nor did he want to dissolve himself into the non-Jewish society all around him, even though, in England, that door was open. He did not want to be either Jewish or British. His life might have been easier if he had chosen one or the other. When he was a student at University College, London, stepping out with his non-Jewish girl, he could have shed his past and climbed ever upward. Or in Palestine, he could have quit – over Hebron in 1929 or the White Paper ten years later – crossed sides and become a full-blooded Zionist servant of the Jewish Agency. But my great-great-uncle was not interested in either/or. He wanted both/and. He wanted to be both Nat and Menachem.

I am like him. Perhaps I learned it from my father, who saw no reason why he should not have two careers at once – one as a chronicler of popular movies and music, the other as an observer of Jewish life. Maybe it was Nat's legacy, silently working its way through the generations. Wherever it came from, I have always lived in two worlds: school and synagogue; Oxford and Habonim; Britain and Israel. Sometimes the contrasts are stark. I remember smiling at the improbability of a single morning in the late 1990s which began with a face-to-face background briefing with the British prime minister and ended with my crossing London, west to east, to visit my beloved great-aunt, the woman who had raised my mother and become a surrogate maternal grandmother to me. Yiddi, whose husband, Max, had died a quarter of a century earlier, had not left the East End; she lived in a spartan flat in Myrdle Street, off Commercial Road. A couple of friends were there, fussing over tea and crumbly kosher biscuits, each of them with voices that still carried the melodies of old Europe, the rhythms of the *shtetl*. Yiddi's friend Ginny was explaining why she was not keen to go on a pensioners' outing to Hatfield House, a stately home in the Hertfordshire countryside.

'Why would I want to go there? They're all the same, these old houses. "On your left is a portrait of the Third Earl of This, and here's a painting of the Fourteenth Duke of That." It's just pictures of their family! Why do I need to see pictures of *their* family? They can come here and look at my family if they want. "This is my *booba*, this is my *zaida*." Why not? What's the difference?'

I would enjoy this talk and feel entirely at home, wrapped warm by it. And yet an hour earlier I had sat in Downing Street, discussing the finer points of Britain's programme of devolution with the Prime Minister and I had not felt out of place there either. I wanted to inhabit both places. I liked being both.

But this duality comes at a price. Nat/Menachem knew that, and he paid the price in full, never winning complete acceptance in either of the two worlds he hovered between. Admittedly, his was an extreme case. His was not the bothness of most diaspora Jews, who have to balance between the country they live in and the community they come from: he wanted to be British even though he no longer lived in Britain. His demand – to be a trusted servant of the crown in mandatory Palestine – was far more extravagant, more complex, than the request made by most ethnic minorities in modern, diverse societies. Nevertheless, there is something in his story that I sense in my own. I feel it most keenly on those days when I am simultaneously denounced by both sides – anti-Israel activists condemning me as a 'Zionist apologist for war crimes' even as Jews identify me as a collaborator with our people's mortal enemies. That's when I remember that Nat was branded 'that bloody Jew' by his British colleagues and 'that bloody Englishman' by his fellow Jews.

During his first years in Palestine, he told himself that his two masters were compatible: since Britain supported the Zionist pursuit of a Jewish national home, by serving one he would be serving the other. I now see what he did not: that that was either hopelessly naïve or a bad case of self-delusion. Of course, realpolitik and the requirements of 'fair play' in the treatment of both peoples under British rule, Jews and Arabs, would ensure that not every British decision would coincide with Jewish interests. Jewish and British needs would diverge eventually and when they did, when Britain's rules seemed to be keeping Jews out rather than letting them in, he felt himself divide. Today I can look at the position of Britain (and of the *Guardian*, for that matter) on Israel and see no great contradiction with my own views. I love Israel, I want it to survive and thrive – but I believe its best hope is a return to the borders it held in 1967, the year I was born. As it happens, that is the British position, and the *Guardian* position too.

But what would happen if that changed, just as London's policy changed in Nat's day? What if the world became so frustrated with Israel's continued refusal fully to withdraw that it imposed stinging sanctions? And then, if that did not work, it decided to back its stance with the threat of force? What if Israel became what Serbia was in the 1990s, an international pariah and eventual military target of Britain, the United States and Nato? I find such a thought awful to contemplate. I know that I could not regard the Jewish state as my enemy, but nor could I turn against the country that has raised me. Bothness would be impossible; I would have to divide myself in two.

Luckily, these are remote hypotheticals, as far away as the playground question that school chums used to ask of me and the other Jewish kids: 'If Israel and Britain were at war, whose side would you fight on?' But for Nat these questions were not hypothetical. And what shocks and impresses me, all these years later, is his refusal to give an answer. He would not make it easy, would not jump one way or the other.

I hope that I would be like that, that I would defend my bothness. A lot of today's Jews must share that sentiment, including the majority who have chosen to remain in the diaspora rather than move to Israel, where they could, if nothing else, be one thing rather than both. Wherever Jews have lived, there have been some who refused to stay put on one side or the other: they wanted to live on both sides of the boundary, hopping back and forth.

Again, as Nat knew so intimately, such duality does not come cheap. Even when your two allegiances do not tug in opposite directions, as they eventually did for him, there is the constant pressure, the almost neurotic desire, to prove your commitment to each side, lest the either/or merchants doubt your fidelity. I am thinking of the motivation behind *The British Jewry Book of Honour*, a 1922 volume that faithfully recorded the Jewish contribution made for His Majesty in the Great War. (There, in a group portrait on page 312, looking rather pleased with himself in his crisp uniform, complete with cane, is one 2nd-Lieut. N. I. Mindel.) But I am also thinking of the Reich Union of Jewish Veterans, whose chairman wrote to the office of the new Reich Chancellor in October 1933, offering to fight for Herr Hitler as devotedly as they had once served the Kaiser and declaring their wish 'to mobilize themselves entirely for the Fatherland'.

The pressure to prove your loyalty is one kind of obstacle to bothness, but there are others. After all, moving between worlds is not solely a matter of personal choice: the different worlds have to let you in too. There may be plenty of British Bangladeshis or French Algerians who would love to shift freely between their ethnic community and the wider society but find they are hardly accepted by the latter. Old-fashioned suspicion of the outsider, xenophobia and racism are often to blame. But sometimes politics plays a part too, just as it did for Nat. It cannot be easy for Muslims in Western countries, for example, to feel 'both' when the nations in which they live are waging war against Muslim states with which they so strongly identify. Direct conflict of that kind tends to pull bothness apart, testing it to destruction. Witness the Japanese-Americans whose dual identity is rich and vibrant in the twenty-first century, but was torn in two during the Second World War: they were interned in camps after Tokyo's attack on Pearl Harbor, rounded up by the US authorities as suspected traitors. Conflict forces the one question that duality cannot stand: whose side are you on?

When bothness is possible, however, the rewards are great, starting with the ability to enjoy both the possibility of the world and the warmth of the tribe, without giving up either. There are other gains too. I think of myself as having at least two or three different loyalties: I am Jewish and British and European. Each one of those ties connects me with several million others across the globe. If I am travelling in, say, Cairo and come across a synagogue, I will feel a bond with the handful of elderly worshippers I find there, even though I will never have met them before. If I am in

California and find a bar showing England's national football team playing in the World Cup, I will feel an instant unity with the people gathered there too, even though they are all strangers. This kinship with unknown others is an uneven thing, open to abuse, but there is no denying its power, even its beauty. The individual with multiple ties is simply richer in kinship than one who has nailed his flag to a single mast.

I believe there are some lessons here, for Jews and for everyone else. The first is an assertion that complexity and plurality are strengths rather than weaknesses. Purity is the province of the fundamentalists; only they dream of a pure ideology, religion or race. In the real world, away from the fantasies of fanatics, we have to live with impurity. Jews can make a start by becoming more tolerant of the differences among themselves. For all the alacrity of their demand for pluralism in the countries in which they live, they have been slow to make their own communities truly plural. Rival denominations do not always accept the legitimacy of the other; the observant or conventionally orthodox sometimes look down upon those they regard as too lax. They have operated as if there is only one way to be Jewish, when everything in our history points to multiplicity. I wish this would change. If our message to Britain or France is that there is not only one way to be British or French, we need to apply that same logic to ourselves. That means more tolerance and fewer denunciations, less willingness to ostracize those on the other side of an argument. If I have a view you do not like, then it means we disagree; it does not mean that I am no longer a Jew and no longer a person.

The logic of hybridity surely extends to Israel too. It has long been a paradox that the very demand Jews have made of liberal societies since the French Revolution is, to put it kindly, as yet unfulfilled in the Jewish state. Jews in the diaspora want both a full role, free of discrimination, in the countries in which they live and the right to maintain their different identity. Israel's Arab citizens, those Palestinians who live within its internationally recognized, pre-1967 borders, surely have the right to expect nothing less. It is true that they have greater liberty in the Jewish state than they would in any of its Arab neighbours – they have the vote; an Arab judge sits on the Supreme Court – but few would maintain that they enjoy full-blooded equality. Jews who have fought so hard for the right to be both should be the first to understand those who want to be both Israeli and Arab. If it is complex and fraught, that should come as no surprise. Not to the Jews who have lived as a hybrid nation for most of our long history.

We need to make a change in our own hearts too, accepting our own bothness, which is harder than it sounds. For minority communities, it will mean a recognition that many among them, especially the young, will move in more than one circle – that inside every Tariq will be a Tony. Such a move requires great honesty. Take the age-old charge of dual loyalties. It has extra potency now, in the post-9/11 era, as Muslims in Western countries face constant demands to prove their fidelity to the societies in which they live. For Jews the question has intensified too. In the past, they might be accused of allegiance to both their country and their community. Now, if the charge is raised, it is that Jews are guilty of a divided loyalty to two states, the one in which they live and Israel. Traditionally, Jews have responded with outrage, insisting that it is wildly unjust to allege such a thing. This might be a mistake. Perhaps it would be more honest to admit that, yes, Jews have more than one allegiance. We do have a bond with Israel, not identical but similar to the tie which might connect a Korean-American to Korea or a British Pakistani to Pakistan. The crucial point is not that they and we have this link, but that it need not detract from our ties to the land in which we live. A person can, in other words, be loyal to two or three or four identities at once.

What of everyone else? If duality truly is an enriching force, then societies need first to accept it and then to welcome it. They would stop asking people to choose, accepting instead that dual or multiple allegiances are just part of what it is to live in the twenty-first-century world. In devolved Britain, it would mean losing the hang-up over whether a Glaswegian feels Scottish or British, understanding instead that he feels both, to different degrees at different times. In contemporary France, it would mean dropping the ban on outward symbols of faith as some kind of threat to the republic. It is surely too thin a notion of Frenchness which says a Sikh man cannot wear a turban, a Jewish man a skullcap and a Muslim woman a *hejab* and still remain French. In multi-ethnic Britain, it would mean no return to the 'cricket test' laid down by the 1980s Conservative Norman Tebbit. If British Indians root for India against England, then the British majority should let them. If they did, those Indo-Brits would be rather more likely to cheer for England against Australia the following week. Identities are like that: multiple, overlapping circles, which expand and contract depending on circumstance. None cancels out the others; each only makes the whole larger.

Surely this should be the message to the Muslim communities who live in countries where Islam is a minority faith. It would understand that at times of direct conflict any dual identity is put under impossible strain. But it would also see that, outside those periods of war, a different conversation is possible. One in which Muslims are not told to choose between the Muslim way and the British or French or American way, but are encouraged to develop an allegiance to Britain or France or America even as they retain their bond with the 'old country' or with the wider Muslim world. Identity is not a zero-sum game. People can have more than one. If that was true in Edwardian England, then it is even truer now in the twenty-first-century globalized village.

I found one source of inspiration for all this in the United States. Despite all its failures, indeed its crimes, in handling those who did not *choose* to come to its shores – including both the Native Americans, who were already there, and the African-Americans, who were dragged across the ocean in chains – I was struck when I lived there by the country's ability to absorb those who had made the immigrant's journey of choice. It ensures that when they or their descendants look at the collective culture, they see a little bit of themselves – or at least some of their symbols: Jews note their fellow Americans chomping bagels or using the word 'schlep'; Hispanics know they have converted the nation to the taco and entered the word 'siesta' into the language. These may sound trivial, but they are the source of a quiet pride: minorities calculate that if their customs have been absorbed into the wider society then so have they. The logic is simple enough: people feel as if they belong in a place where the collective tapestry includes a thread or two of their own.

As a new society, the US has few of those thick layers of native culture that can be such a barrier to the newcomer. Instead it proposes a set of ideas: anyone who signs up to them can join. As then President Bill Clinton put it once, 'If you believe in the values of the Constitution, the Bill of Rights, the Declaration of Independence, if you're willing to work hard and play by the rules, you are part of our family and we're proud to be with you.' The American promise to minorities is a uniquely powerful one: you can join us without losing yourselves.

Today's United States not only accepts hybridity, it all but enshrines it in the form of the hyphenated identity. Those with roots in County Kerry, San Salvador or the *shtetl* need not abandon their heritage; they do not have to choose between their new land and the old country. They can be Irish-Americans, Hispanic-Americans or Jewish-Americans, that little hyphen doing the enormous job of stapling together what, for some, will be their past and their future, for others their ethnicity and their citizenship. The US may not be the first society to have pulled it off and no one would deny that it can become badly strained. But that hyphen might be one of America's greatest gifts to the world, the licence that says there need be no conflict; you can be both. The Indo-Brits have adopted it; let the Turkish-Germans or Greek-Australians be next.

That can be a hard case to make, especially when different loyalties collide, as they do in times of direct conflict – pitting a minority's new land against their old, their actual home against a spiritual one. Even in circumstances less clear and less grave, holding on to bothness can be difficult. Traditional Jews suspect that it may be sustainable for a generation or two but not for much longer. Over time, they say, the Jewish element becomes ever more diluted until it has faded away completely. By way of proof, they ask how many dual-identity Jews have Jewish grandchildren. They maintained the balancing act in their own lives, runs the argument, but they could not pass it on.

Like the man in the joke about the golf club, or the Asian Kapoor family who insist their name is pronounced Cooper, it can seem less of a headache simply to plump for one thing or another: in those cases, to attempt complete assimilation; in others, to stay in the walled city. Some have tried to solve the problem by neatly separating the two, perhaps in the spirit of the old slogan: 'Be a man in the streets and a Jew at home.'

My great-great-uncle did his best to follow that advice. At the office he was a 'man' of the British Empire. At home he was a father who inculcated Jewish pride in his children. He was Nat and Menachem. But the line separating the two became ever harder to police; the streets intruded into home and home into the streets. Modern psychiatry tells us such attempts to split the self in two are not only damaging but doomed. Yet that wisdom was already there, buried deep in Jewish tradition. For Jacob and Esau were twins, two halves of the same self. They fought and competed even before they were born: wrestling in the womb, Jacob grabbed the heel of his brother as Esau emerged first. They lived opposite lives. Jacob is depicted as cerebral and a homebody, while Esau is physical, a hunter who ventures out into the world. Esau offers an early example of assimilation: he marries 'out', taking as his bride a Hittite. (As if to prove how little changes, Esau's choice of partner causes great 'grief of mind' to his parents, Isaac and Rebecca.) Jacob makes no such move.

After his act of deception, stealing the blessing that rightfully belonged to his brother, Jacob flees. They spend many years apart until finally he hears that Esau, joined by 400 men, is nearby. He fears for his life, praying for divine protection. When Esau approaches, Jacob throws himself to the ground, bowing seven times.

But the story has a twist. Esau does not attack Jacob, even though his brother wronged him. One does not kill the other. Instead, Esau runs to meet his brother. He embraces him, his head cradled on his neck; he kisses him. The two men weep.

Esau is Jacob's shadow. Where Jacob is fair, Esau is dark. Jacob stays at home; Esau roams outside. Jacob's wives are Jewish; Esau's are not. The Torah tells us that these two cannot be separated, they are part of a whole. The self can no more be divided than there can be sunlight without shadow. Rebecca's womb contained not one or the other but both Jacob and Esau. This is the Jewish story: to be both.

15 Mick and the Revolution

I interviewed my great-uncle Mick when I was about seventeen years old. I had spoken with him often, but only then had I sat down with a tape recorder. We were face to face in the living room at 28 Stoke Newington High Street, the flat above a Radio Rentals shop that he had shared with my great-aunt Sylvia for nearly fifty years and which had served as the family home for her branch of the Mindels since her childhood. My father's mother, Lily, Sylvia's sister, had grown up there; my father had visited often as a child. His sharpest memories were of the table set for *seder* night, each chair plump with extra cushions, to fulfil the injunction that to-night, being different from all other nights, Jews demonstrate and celebrate their freedom by leaning relaxedly rather than sitting bolt upright.

There was plenty of history in the room, even more when you glanced at the copy of *The History of Socialism*, Volume V, which Mick had at his side. We sat down, he with a Scotch, I with a notepad of questions, and we talked. Listening back to the tape now, I am predictably embarrassed by my younger self. This adolescent version of me fails to follow up the half-thoughts Mick leaves hovering in the air; he does not pick up conversational cues and clues. He is too busy banging his own drum, insisting that his Utopia of the time – a socialist Israel embodied by the kibbutz – is a much worthier goal than the working-class struggle in Britain. My seventeen-year-old self does not see that Mick has had this argument a thousand times before, most heatedly a half-century earlier with his own father: the particular cause of the Jews versus the universal cause of humankind.

Nevertheless, and mainly unspoken, there is a deep agreement between us. It is the reason why I have come to talk with him. For this is the mid-1980s, the high-watermark of Thatcherism, and there are not many people like Mick around – at least not in the Jewish community. So I am glad to hear that things were once very different, that the dream that tugged at young Mick Mindel had pulled at a thousand or a million Jewish hearts before. Anti-Semites keen to target Bolshevism as a Jewish-made product – when they were not casting the Jews as the arch-controllers of capitalism – were never short of ammunition. The founders of nineteenth-century German socialism were Jews; Moses Hess could claim to be the first German communist. Besides Karl Marx, the Jew haters could also point at Ferdinand Lassalle, the first organizer of German workers, or to Eduard Bernstein, theorist for the reforming wing of German socialism, or to Rosa Luxemburg, a founder of the German Communist Party. When Munich briefly rejoiced in its very own Soviet Republic, its head was Kurt Eisner, backed by three other Jewish comrades.

The pattern was repeated in Austria, Hungary, Romania, Poland and of course Russia itself. At times the 1917 struggle between Bolshevik and Menshevik resembled a Jewish civil war: Trotsky, Sverdlov, Kamenev, Zinoviev, Radek and the others lined up against Axelrod, Deutsch, Martov, Dan, Liber and Abramovich.

I was thrilled to read that as communism marched across the globe in the nineteenth and twentieth centuries, Jews were often at the head of the column. I knew Jews had been prominent in capitalism, with the Rothschild family as the archetype; I knew too that plenty of Jews had been, and continued to be, guilty of exploitation of their workers. Nor could I gloss over the fact that Jews had been lead players in movements of the right as well as the left, while others had sided with the most reviled regimes: in 1860s America Judah Benjamin served as Secretary of State to the slavery-preserving southern states of the breakaway Confederacy; in 1960s South Africa one Percy Yutar acted as chief prosecutor of Nelson Mandela and the rest of the anti-apartheid leadership at the Rivonia trial. Still, I was content that such examples tended to leap out of the historical record as exceptions rather than the rule. The more common pattern was of Jews in the vanguard of movements for 'progress'. The pattern was most visible in the communist period, but it existed and exists both before and later, in Europe and beyond. Name almost any struggle for rights or justice, almost anywhere, and you will soon find Jews.

In the United States, the trade union movement was founded by Jews. The first president of the American Federation of Labor was Samuel Gompers. In 1934 the Jewish Labor Committee led the charge against sweated conditions in the garment industry and, in the process, began negotiating America's first modern labour laws. Thirty years later Jews joined black Americans in their movement for civil rights. In 1964 over half of the white volunteers who went to Mississippi to demand racial equality were Jews; the same proportion of civil rights lawyers in the American south were Jewish. And when Martin Luther King marched for justice, bound to him, arm in arm, was Rabbi Abraham Joshua Heschel, one of the pre-eminent scholars of modern orthodoxy. When the agenda shifted to women's rights, Jews were once again in the forefront: Betty Friedan, Gloria Steinem, Andrea Dworkin. Today's new generation of feminist leaders is no different.

In South Africa, a white campaigner against apartheid usually turned out to be a Jew. At that same Rivonia trial, five of the six whites in the dock with Mandela were Jews: Lionel 'Rusty' Bernstein, Dennis Goldberg, Arthur Goldreich, James Kantor and Harold Wolpe. The leader of Umkhonto weSizwe, the armed wing of the African National Congress, was the Lithuanian-born communist Joe Slovo. Even in the Arab world of the 1950s and 1960s, parties of progress contained disproportionate numbers of Jews in their leading ranks. Among Egyptian communists, Henry Curiel was a dominant figure, eventually assassinated in Paris, while Yusuf Salman, known as Abu Fahad, was a founder and leader of the party in Iraq – until he was hanged for his views in 1949. Jewish communists like him came under great pressure to convert to Islam, to demonstrate their solidarity with their Muslim comrades. Most refused, insisting that their faith was neither Judaism nor Islam but Marxism. (As it turned out, they were persecuted on two of those three counts anyway – as Jews and as communists.)

Given that history, it is hardly surprising that those left-wingers who migrated to the right, America's neo-conservatives – many of them ex-Trotskyites with no loss of appetite for world revolution – should also include several Jews on their founders' roll: Richard Perle, Irving and William Kristol, Paul Wolfowitz and Norman Podhoretz, to name a few.

It was this Jewish attraction to grand causes, aimed either at ending an immediate injustice or at changing the very order of human society, that appealed to me. It still does. Maybe it was the influence of Mick and his wife and comrade, Sylvia; perhaps it was down to my father, who defined himself as a socialist before he left school and still wears a red tie on polling day; or maybe it was his father, my grandfather, David Freedland, who used to urge me as a child to eat up my grandmother's barley soup – lest I 'put the barley growers out of work'. Whatever the source, I cannot remember a moment when I did not believe my place was on the left – and when I did not regard that as a peculiarly Jewish obligation.

Some will find that surprising, but such a view is hardly a stretch; it requires no imposition on to the Jewish story of something that does not belong there. On the contrary, it is quite possible to see a progressive streak running throughout, right from the very start.

For how does the narrative of Judaism begin? In contrast with most faiths, it starts with the story of the first man and woman. It does not begin with the first Jew. Adam and Eve – not Abraham, not Jacob, not Moses – are the first characters in Judaism's story. The message is plain: we are first and above all human beings. What we have in common with others is more important than what separates us. Implicit is a profoundly enlightened notion: everyone counts, not just our narrow group.

The radicalism of the opening story does not end there. For Adam and Eve, and therefore all humankind, are created in God's image. That means that to kill a human being is, in effect, blasphemy: an attack on God himself. This simple idea – that all human life is sacred – represented a new departure for the world. Until then, life was dispensable; indeed, many pagan traditions believed that the gods craved the sacrifice of human blood. But the Jews declared human life holy. To save a single life was to save the whole world. Such a concept could not help but be the foundation stone for an entire system of ethics. For if human beings shared the spark of the divine, they had not only to be spared from murder but to be treated with dignity and respect.

As the Jewish story unfolds, the moral message sharpens. What is one of the first things every Jewish child learns about Abraham, the first Jew, even though it is recounted nowhere in the Torah itself? We learn that his father was a maker of idols and that, one day, Abraham entered his father's shop and smashed the merchandise to pieces. He is an iconoclast, a revolutionary.

Abraham is involved too in a revolutionary act. He becomes the first father to circumcise his son, as a gesture of devotion to God. The political significance of this might not be obvious to us, but the ancient Greeks understood it immediately. They vehemently rejected circumcision because, they argued, the human form was born perfect and not to be tampered with. Jews held that true perfection comes only when God and humanity work together, as partners. The underlying Jewish belief is that the world is not yet complete: all of it, including ourselves, needs fixing. Viewed like this, the *brit milah*, or circumcision, ceremony that had entered my son Jacob into the Jewish people had also sent this message: nothing and nobody is perfect; our task is to make the world a better place.

Judaism even captures this mission in a slogan: *tikkun olam*, repairing the world. Originally a mystical idea, it holds that heaven and earth have been rent asunder and need to be put back together again. It is here that I find Judaism's driving purpose. The phrase 'chosen people' has always aroused Jewry's enemies. They assume it means that somehow the Jews reckon they have been picked out for first-class, luxury treatment – a divine upgrade. But that is not how most Jews understand it. Chosen for what? some ask, noting that if Jews have been singled out for special attention it has usually been of the negative variety. Others play word games, suggesting that what the phrase really means is that the Jews are a *choosing* people. But the interpretation I prefer is that Jews have a project: to do what they can to repair the world. It is the commission of this duty that might make the Jews the 'holy nation', the 'light unto the nations' of our own sacred texts.

Not that this is solely a matter of theology. History also had an impact. Perhaps the central Jewish narrative is the story of the exodus: Jews were slaves in Egypt until Moses led them to freedom and to their own promised land. The story is retold annually, at the *seder* ceremony which launches the festival of Passover – my favourite night of the Jewish year. Ceremony is not quite the right word: it is conducted not in a synagogue but in every Jewish home, around the dinner table. When it works, it combines a good meal with a kind of informal teach-in, as readings, song and, above all, food are used as visual, aural and olfactory aids. I remember my childish eyes watering as I bit into a slice of raw horseradish, a bitter herb to evoke the bitterness of slavery. Next would come a hard-boiled egg mashed up in salt water, a reminder of the Hebrews' tears of suffering. Then we would dip a finger in a glass of wine ten times, one for each of the ten plagues visited on the Egyptians, the series of disasters which finally persuaded Pharaoh to heed Moses' call: Let my people go.

As educational formats go, it is without rival. I am not the only one to find the *seder* the source of some of the strongest Jewish memories. Even those who have long separated from formal Judaism have only to experience again the sights, sounds and smells of the *seder* to summon the most intimate remembrances of family and childhood.

The result is that the exodus is seared into Jewish consciousness; it is the story that defines us. Throughout the *seder* the Jew is asked to identify directly with those who were slaves in Egypt – 'This happened to *me*' – and to glory in the justice of their rebellion. We are never to forget.

This has had a profound effect on Jewish thinking. It is quite possible to see the entire battery of Jewish laws and teachings – including the Torah itself, the five books of Moses handed to the Children of Israel on Mount Sinai immediately after the flight from Egypt – as a response to the experience of oppression. (Of course, orthodox believers would allow no such historical gloss on the writing of the Torah, for which they credit the Almighty as sole author.) Put simply, the central myth of Jewish folklore is a rebellion against human suffering. That should put the loathing of slavery, an intolerance of injustice, at the very centre of our culture. Witness the Sabbath: a compulsory day off no boss can deny his workers. In the ancient world, where slavery was commonplace, such an idea was truly revolutionary. In modern times, it still holds – as a declaration that no human being exists for work alone. For one day, Jews are commanded to step out of the rat race, turn off the mobile phone and break from the stresses of contemporary life. In times both ancient and modern, the Sabbath is more than a day off: it is a fundamental declaration of human freedom.

As befits a former slave nation, the call for social justice runs throughout Judaism. The demands of *tzedakah*, usually translated as charity but whose actual meaning is justice, are stringently illustrative (even if not unique to Judaism). Jewish tradition requires the giving of at least a tenth of one's income to the poor – and not as a magnanimous act of generosity but rather as a basic human obligation. There are strict rules too to prevent the humiliation of the recipient: in the Second Temple, rooms were constructed with one door for the wealthy to leave donations and another for the poor to pick them up. The two would never catch sight of each other, denying glory to the one and shame to the other. The notion of *pe'a* requires Jewish farmers to leave a corner of their field, and all its crops, to the poor. *Leket* demands that any fruits or vegetables that fall to the ground during the harvest also be left for those with the least. Every seven years there is to be an economic sabbatical, including an amnesty on all debts. Jewish judges even have instructions on how they are to rule in labour disputes: they must give the benefit of the doubt to the employee, since the employer is less likely to remember the contested incident. Most modern Jews may not know of these specific laws, but the overall message gets through.

Subsequent history ensured that Jews' understanding of oppression rested on more than the memory of the Egypt experience alone. Repeated persecutions reinforced the Passover message, some of them earning their own place in the Jewish calendar. The candle-lighting festival of Chanukah recalls the Maccabees' revolt against foreign rule and oppression. Even the song, dance and drunken revelry of Purim is a commemoration of a Jewish uprising against Haman, the wicked vizier of fifth-century-BC Persia who plotted to destroy the Jews. Somehow all this has an effect. Marking those festivals year in and year out, whether at home or in the synagogue, guarantees that even those Jews living eons later in comfort and safety have an inkling of what it is to endure tyranny.

I like to think that Jewish tradition equips Jews for political agitation in other ways too. While most faiths make much of the individual's relationship with God, Judaism prefers to operate in groups. No prayer service can take place without a *minyan* of ten Jewish souls to make it quorate. Even the study of the holy books is assumed to be a collective activity: tradition has Jews learning in pairs, wrestling over every word.

Judaism inculcates another essential reformist trait: scepticism. A faith which has its leading protagonists engaged in argument not only with each other but with God himself – witness Abraham's negotiation with his maker to spare the doomed people of Sodom and Gomorrah – is one that does not hesitate to question authority. Argument is enshrined in Judaism's holy texts, to the extent that it is impossible to speak of a single 'Jewish view' on anything. Judaism is no monolith, but is made up of as many different branches, denominations and interpretations as there are Jews. The Talmud, for example, is not a book of laws, etched in stone and beyond dispute. It consists instead of a never-ending argument, laid out across the page. A small chunk of text sits in the middle, surrounded by commentaries written over the centuries, each generation adding to or contesting the stance of its predecessor. Challenging the established view is all but a religious commandment. Others might disagree, but the Jewish teaching that has stayed with me constantly places its emphasis on good questions rather than cosy answers; it seems to prefer doubt to certainty. And never is this laser beam of scrutiny fiercer than when it is trained on the Jews themselves: from the prophets onwards, self-criticism is a perennial Jewish habit.

Perhaps most important, Jews are trained to believe in progress. Judaism does not hold that humanity's greatest chance is behind it: we are still waiting for the arrival of the Messiah. Judaism is restless, constantly assuming that tomorrow can be better than today or yesterday. It does not insist that humankind is blighted from the very start by the original sin of its past, nor does it say that justice is attainable only in the next world. It looks to today and tomorrow.

There is a paradox here, one not easily explained. Jews are forward-looking, yet they are also the people of long memories. Without a land of their own, they could not build castles or cathedrals to enshrine their past. They had to carry their collective story in their heads. So Jews made remembrance, of their own history and of their dead, a sacred act.

Yet at the same time Jews kept their gaze focused, almost neurotically, ahead. I know that my older relatives, the children of immigrants, only rarely heard their parents speak of the old country: they had come to Britain or America and did not want to look back. (The contrast is great with the Palestinians, who may have lived for decades in Lebanon or Syria or the US but never stopped dreaming of their original homes in Palestine. Of course the historical circumstances were dramatically different, but Jews cannot relate to this easily: no Jew walks around with the key to his grandparents' house in Vilna, Cracow or Berlin in his pocket. 'We were chased out of there and it's past,' they will say. This is just one of many gaps of understanding between Palestinians and Jews but it could be among the most important. At bottom, many Jews do not understand why the Palestinians have not done what the Jews did – and moved on. The Israeli writer A. B. Yehoshua allows one of his characters to voice the sentiment baldly in his 2001 novel *The Liberated Bride*. 'Why must every one of you live where he or she was born?' Tehila asks of a Jerusalem Arab. 'What babies you are, missing Daddy and Mommy's home when you're parents and grandparents yourselves! I swear, you deserve a spanking not a state.')

All this, along with the memory of Egypt, could have instilled in Jews a radical cast of mind that looked only inward: an antagonism to enslavement of *Jews*, an intolerance of injustice against *Jews*. At first perhaps it did. Until the emancipation of the eighteenth and nineteenth centuries, the Jewish world was all but closed off to the outside. Jews regarded the rest of humanity as remote, even frightening. In this era, *tikkun olam* was a fringe idea, the province of a handful of mystics; most Jews had no grand illusions about changing the world. Liberation changed all that. When the ghetto walls came down and Jews were at last allowed to step out into the daylight, it did not take long for some to wonder how their values might apply to those around them. If there was a job of repair to be done, it would not be confined to their little Jewish community – it was a project for the human race. What had been particular could become universal.

That is how I believe it was meant to work all along. The lessons of the exodus, for example, are surely supposed to be applied universally; why else would the Mosaic books insist nearly forty times that Jews are to treat well the stranger, for 'you were a stranger in a strange land'? The text is insistent: we are required to identify with those on the outside, even when they are not the same as us. Self-interest clearly played a part too. Shut out from the existing social order, Jews had a direct stake in overturning that order. And Jews had few of the ties that kept other groups defending the status quo. Often urban rather than rural, Jews tended to be rooted neither in the soil nor in local tradition but in the ever-fluid landscape of the town and city, making them even more open to change.

One progressive dream seized the Jewish imagination especially, capturing the hearts of many of Mick's East End comrades among others. It was the vision of a world without borders, a universal brotherhood of man. Lenin himself noticed it in 1917: 'It should be said to their credit that today the Jews provide a relatively high percentage of representatives of internationalism compared to other nations.' The fashionable theory of the age was that since Jews had no homeland of their own, they were unfettered by the sentimental patriotism that inhibited other radicals; they would shed no tears for the end of nations.

There may have been something to that. Narrowly national storylines tend to exclude those who are relatively recent arrivals. Look how much Jews struggled to find their place in the German narrative. The more nationalistic the story becomes, the harder it is for the Jews to squeeze into it. But a universal notion – 'One race, the human race', as the old slogan had it – is different. Jews can fit into that quite comfortably.

Isaiah Berlin theorized that this comfort with the universal over the potentially excluding particular was not confined to politics. It also explained the Jewish attraction to science and mathematics. These languages were universal; mastery of them required no thick layers of local, native culture. As he put it, 'In a world of abstract symbols, divorced from national cultures and times and places, the Jewish genius finds full freedom and, consequently, is capable of magnificent creative achievement.' Here, unlike art or literature or music, forms packed with references to native folk memory, 'Jews start not below scratch, but at the same level as others.' Perhaps the Jewish knack for ambitious, capacious 'theories of everything' is rooted in similar soil. It may be no coincidence that Marx, Freud and Einstein, three men who sought to explain the world as a single whole, were drawn from the same relatively small community of Austro-German Jewry. They were keen to write a story that might apply to all humanity, even the entire universe, because such a narrative would at least have room for them and their people. Often, it seemed, the more local German story did not.

There is a less flattering explanation. Perhaps the vision of a borderless, nationless future imagined by some of the most radical Jewish leftists – the likes of Karl Marx and Rosa Luxemburg – appealed because in such a world they would no longer have to be Jews. Peoples would disappear, including the Jewish one. In the twentieth century the radical intellectual Isaac Deutscher spoke approvingly of the 'non-Jewish Jews' – including Spinoza, Heine, Trotsky, Freud and of course himself – who had set a lead by transcending Judaism and Jewry to reach the highest ideals of humankind. Only by shedding their tight, archaic Jewish skins, Deutscher implied, could they make their contribution to the world. As historian Robert Wistrich writes, 'The tragic irony in this situation was that both the Jewish revolutionary and the pathologi-cal anti-semite who feared and hated him, starting from wholly different general premises, desired the ultimate disappearance of the Jew.'

Why would Jewish communists want such a thing? For his answer, Wistrich turns to psychology: the most extreme of these radicals were infected with self-hatred. Their rhetoric – denouncing Jews as clannish, money-grabbing parasites – does indeed suggest they had swallowed some of anti-Semitism's bile. By dipping themselves in the acid bath of revolution, they hoped to strip themselves clean of all Jewish traits. In this, these Jewish revolution-aries had more in common with the upwardly mobile Jewish bourgeoisie than they would ever have wanted to recognize. Except for them socialism, universalism and internationalism – rather than a change of name, a tweak of accent and a Christian spouse – were the way out.

Not all of these socialist assimilationists burned with self-loathing. But, even when they did not, they were determined to switch their allegiance from group to class; their kin were not to be Jews but the international proletariat. As Rosa Luxemburg asked her Prussian prosecutors in 1914, 'What other fatherland is there than the great mass of working men and women?' Two years later she would write to her friend Mathilda Wurm, scolding her for her sentimental Jewish nationalism, 'Why do you come with your particular Jewish sorrows? I feel equally close to the wretched victims of the rubber plantations in Putumayo, or to the Negroes in Africa . . . I have no separate corner in my heart for the ghetto: I feel at home in the entire world, wherever there are clouds and birds and human tears.'

The clash of Rosa and Mathilda was an ancient one, written into Judaism from the very beginning. Judaism's central prayer, the *Shema*, begins, 'Hear, O Israel, the Lord is our God, the Lord is One.' It comes with a universal message – that there is but a single deity for all humankind – but addresses it to a particular people, Israel. The tension is there from the start, universal versus particular, Rosa versus Mathilda. Mick versus Morris.

In one camp stand those who are narrowly Jewish, hushing when the radio brings news from Israel, switching off at word of a massacre in Kashmir or hunger in Africa. They are like the mother in Philip Roth's short story 'The Conversion of the Jews' who, when she hears of a plane crash at La Guardia, scans the casualty list for Jewish names. She finds eight and 'because of the eight she said the plane crash was "a tragedy" '. In the other stand those who follow Rosa Luxemburg, in no hurry to make room in their hearts for Jewish suffering. They are too busy signing up for the Free Burma campaign at their university freshers' fair to join the Jewish Society; every cause in the world is cooler than that of their own people.

I have ended up somewhere in between. I cannot be like Rosa, because I cannot believe in a pure universalism: I suspect that would only mean dissolving myself into the traditions of another people. But nor do I want to be like Mathilda, lending my heart to the Jews and the Jews alone. For I suspect that a zeal for universal social justice has always been inseparable from Jewishness and even from Judaism itself. The scholars say the Jews are a people of three covenants: with Noah, with Abraham and with Moses. The latter bound Jews to the Torah, with all its religious obligations and benefits. The *brit*, or covenant, with Abraham ensured divine protection for his descendants and a promise of the land of Israel. But the covenant with Noah is different. It is an accord with all humanity, a pledge by God that he will never again flood the entire world to destruction. In return, humankind, not just Jews, must comply with the seven universal laws for human conduct laid out to Noah: prohibition of idolatry, blasphemy, murder, theft, forbidden sexual relations and the eating of live meat, plus a demand to establish courts of justice – the so-called Noahide laws. They surely stand as proof that universality is not an optional extra for Jews. It is built into Judaism. As a matter of command, Jews are not allowed to forget the rest of the human race.

So I want to find a path that is both universal and particular. I want to walk in the footsteps of Rabbi Heschel, who did not change his name or pretend to be somebody else but marched arm in arm with Martin Luther King as a rabbi. I want to follow the lead set by the Jewish charities who heed the opening cry of the *seder* – Let all who are hungry come and eat – and invite the homeless to share their Passover meal. I want my people to fight for justice not as individuals of Jewish origin but together as Jews.

I suspect this is why Mick had such fond memories of his days leading the United Ladies' Tailors' Trade Union. It was, in effect, a Jewish union and yet it saw the human race as its business: sending ambulances to Spain, raising money for the striking miners of Kent. Mick was truly himself in those days, serving the universal through the particular.

And, remote and naïve though it sounds today, that was what Zionism was meant to be about too. The first Zionists, who were almost all on the radical left, believed a Jewish national home would not mark a retreat from the world or a shrinking back into the Jewish shell. On the contrary, with a home of their own Jews could at last join the family of nations. They would no longer be the odd one out, but would take their place in the brotherhood of man. On an equal footing they would finally be able to make their contribution to world civilization, not as individuals but as a people. The Jewish voice would be heard not from the wings but on stage, with the rest of the human choir.

Most of the time that feels like a long-forgotten dream, punched aside by the brute reality that across large swathes of the world today Israel is a pariah. But every now and again there is a moment when Jews feel as if the Jewish state has at last enabled them to do their bit for *tikkun olam*. It might be the development of a new medical technique or even the cultivation of a fresh, cross-bred (and typically hybrid) citrus fruit. Or it could be the sight of Snappy, the life-detecting dog and mascot of Israel's crack emergency rescue team, who scampered across the rubble of the bombed US embassy in Nairobi in 1998, sniffing out the scent of survivors, dressed in a blue-and-white doggy vest, complete with Star of David.

This is what I learn now, some twenty years on, when I listen to my conversation with Mick. That to be a Jew is to be both a Jew and a human being. Some try to be one and shut out the other. But it is a dead end. The two are fulfilled together or not at all. For Jews, the covenants of Noah, Abraham and Moses should all be binding: you cannot honour one and forget the other two.

Fittingly, none of this applies to the Jews alone. For many years, all kinds of thinkers and movements have grappled with this tension between the particular and the universal. Whether they were French revolutionaries or Russian communists, they did not know how to reconcile national and group identities with the larger call for human progress. In our own time the question remains just as fraught: if minorities are allowed their own distinct lives, will that not tear away at the fabric of the wider society?

There might be a way to cut through this knot. If the particular is no longer seen as a threat to the universal, but rather as a way into it, as *part* of it, then the two need no longer be in tension. It all depends on how we view our society. If we imagine it like one of those smoothie drinks, produced by crushing a variety of fruits together in a blender, then it is quite true that those elements which retain their distinct edges, which refuse to be blended, will always be an irritant: the ideal is a single liquid, with no stubborn lumps of apple or chunks of banana to spoil it. But if society is more like a fruit salad, then that is a dish that only works if each individual item retains its flavour. No one wants the kiwi and the orange to merge into a pulpy whole; they work together because each element stays unique.

This is surely the way diverse societies, full of different communities, will have to function in the twenty-first century. France seems determined to produce a Gallic smoothie, but the rest of the world is hungry for fruit salad. America may have set a culinary lead in this area, but Britain in its own halting way is slowly getting there. (It helps that Britain has always been a salad of sorts, with English, Scottish, Welsh and Irish ingredients.)

In other words, the particularity of a people should be perfectly compatible with a belief in the oneness of humanity. For most nations hope they bring something distinct, even unique, to the rest of the world. It might be something grand (the Greeks like to think they furnished humanity with the foundations of Western culture), or something specific (the Swiss are proud of the Red Cross and the principle of neutrality that makes it possible), but the core idea is the same. It is that by being itself, by being unique and peculiar, the individual nation enriches the world.

It is a pleasing way to think about identity. In place of the traditional antagonism of local and global, which imagines that adherence to the particular pits one against the rest, comes a much more benign conception. In this view, the more like ourselves we are, the more we fit into the human race. When the Greeks celebrate Aristotelian drama or revere the Parthenon, they are not withdrawing from the world; they are connecting with it. They are adding their unique slice to the global fruit salad.

This works best, of course, when the distinct national contribution is, by its nature, outward-looking. That is how I want it to be for the Jews. They believe they have a specific contribution to make, the task for which they were 'chosen'. It is to spread the wisdom of the Torah, an ethical guide to living. The mission statement is summarized in the two words of the core obligation of *tikkun olam*, repairing the world. When Jews fulfil that duty they are simultaneously being intensely Jewish and, thanks to the nature of the obligation, actively human. Their particular duty has a universal effect.

I do not believe the appeal of this approach can be confined to Jews. For it is not just they who benefit from a collective sense of mission. Surely every group needs to feel it exists for a reason. Otherwise they risk seeing themselves as little more than a bunch of people herded together almost at random, just because they happen to be born on the same soil or, worse, share the same blood. That kind of group can offer to its next generation no purpose for its own survival beyond continuity for continuity's sake: 'You must be Finnish because your grandparents were Finnish.'

But a nation with an animating purpose, that is a different story. Suddenly there is a reason why traditions are worth maintaining; there is an active argument for staying together. Michael Ignatieff refers to this distinction as the difference between civic and ethnic nationalism. The latter is the identity of the *volk*, the group defined solely by blood or soil. Such an identity cannot help but become defensive and, soon afterwards, aggressive: with no driving purpose beyond its own perpetuation, it will always be on its guard for external threats, real or imagined. Those threats will eventually have to be beaten back. The twentieth century drips with bloody examples.

Civic nationalism, by contrast, coheres a group of people around a set of ideas. The group exists for a purpose, to advance those ideas. Membership of this kind of collective is not confined to those of a particular shade of skin or birthplace; it is open to anyone who accepts the key, defining principles. Such a nation sets out its founding texts and insists that anyone can sign up to them, no matter where their parents, or they, were born.

The advantages of such an identity are twofold. First, it is open, allowing for difference among the people who adhere to it. Second, it is positive, endowing all those who are 'members' with the high esteem that comes from involvement in a common cause. If Americans top the world league tables for self-belief and patriotism, there is a reason: many regard themselves as part of a project. However incomplete its realization, however imperfect the reality, millions of Americans do believe they are still engaged in what former US presidential candidate Adlai Stevenson called our 'high adventure' on the earth.

I feel that way about being Jewish. I believe Jews have a project too. That is why they can lack common geography, scattered instead across the globe; why they can be without a single racial or genetic code, including black, white and brown Jews in their ranks – and yet still be a people. They can be this diverse because they share a goal. An ultra-orthodox Jew like my grandfather Avraham would have called it Torah. A communist atheist like my great-uncle Mick would have called it the struggle for a just world. Never mind that, had they met, the two would have argued with each other fiercely, just as the Jewish followers of Torah and Marx always saw each other as enemies. Put to one side the regrettable fact that their heirs – the religious and the secularly progressive – maintain that antagonism to this day, only rarely coming together. To my mind, the ideals of Torah and of a just world flow from the same source. It is our people's driving purpose, the goal that makes us both comfortable with diversity in our ranks and proud of who we are. It makes Jews unique and connects them to the entire human race – all at the same time. Which is why it is so dispiriting when it seems that purpose has either been forgotten or worse.

My guess is that all groups, large or small, need their own animating ideal. Britain used to cohere around the project of empire; since that enterprise faded, midway through the twentieth century, the British have cast around for a raison d'être, a reason why England, Scotland, Wales and Northern Ireland should bind themselves together rather than break apart. A wider version of the same dilemma now troubles the nations of Europe. Their European Union makes good economic sense, but what is the higher common purpose that might make a Belgian or Pole or Italian feel European, emotionally bound to his fellow Europeans? At the other end of the scale, how is the Pakistani patriarch in Bradford to persuade his granddaughter that she should stay in rather than out? What reason can he give her for why his community should survive, even though it might require sacrifices from her?

Groups need a mission, a collective task that can bind them together with rather gentler and less toxic glue than the solidarity of the *volk*. Once they find it, they see the benefits instantly. They are bound closer and more securely together – even as they open outward to the world like a flower, unfolding to face the sun.

The Jews fixed on their mission early, a clue coming even in the sleep of the patriarchs. Jacob had left Beersheba for Haran when he decided to stop for the night. He rested and had a dream: 'a ladder was set on the ground and its top reached to the sky, and angels of God were going up and down on it'. The image of Jacob's ladder has preoccupied scholars through the ages. It suggests a constant, ongoing effort to keep heaven and earth together – even to reunite them after they were rent apart. This is the work of repair demanded by *tikkun olam*, the task of improving the world which would become the Jews' defining project. For notice the angels' direction of travel. Convention would suggest that angels belong in heaven until they come 'down' to earth. But Jacob's angels do not move 'down and up'. They travel 'up and down', as if their starting point is right here on earth. The implication could not be clearer: divine work is done not solely by those sent from on high. It falls to those down here too.

Jews are to heed that message – and not only among their own. That was what my great-uncle Mick believed, and Jacob's dream suggests he was right. For as soon as Jacob has glimpsed the ladder, God appears and makes a promise. He tells Jacob his descendants will spread throughout the world, so that 'All the families of the earth shall bless themselves by you.' They are not going to wander merely to disappear. They have work to do.

16 *Sara and the God-shaped Hole*

The odd thing is that I never found it odd. Even as a child I held in my head two thoughts about my mother without ever thinking they conflicted. The first was that she was religious, in the sense that she was diligent about Jewish observance. More than my father, she was the keeper of the flame: it was she who refused to ride in a car or turn on the TV set on the Sabbath, she who insisted that Pesach be observed to the letter, down to paying four times the regular price for specially approved salt, washing-up liquid and toothpaste – just to be assured that not a microbe passed her lips that was not certifiably kosher for Passover.

The second fact about my mother I grasped only intuitively as a child, holding it more firmly as I grew older. It was that she did not really believe in God. She would never say so explicitly: such a declaration would break her first rule about religious diligence. But I always detected in her a disappointment, a resigned scepticism that spoke of someone who had once believed – and had been badly let down.

Without ever meaning to, I think she passed this on to her children. I have not a single memory of my mother invoking God to us: no 'God wants you to . . .' or 'God will be unhappy if . . .' You would think that a religious woman would speak that way to her children. But not my mother. He, God, barely got a mention. Indeed, I am sure I have a memory of His name coming up and my mother almost rolling her eyes, like an abandoned wife remembering an errant ex-husband. Some of this must have rubbed off on the three of us: if today we were asked whether we believed in a benign, omnipotent supreme being, I suspect none of us would give a straight, positive answer.

In my case, I used to think that was down to a liberal, secular

English education. Rationalism and reason were drilled into me from the start. When my history class studied religion – mastering the conflicting Lutheran and Catholic views on whether the communion wafer was or merely *represented* the body of Christ – it was always on the assumption that the whole business was slightly bonkers. I supposed I had simply absorbed the prevailing wisdom in which I had been taught: enlightened, sceptical, atheist.

Now I am not so sure. For those teenage years were not only filled with classes explaining the finer points of Christian theology. I was also beginning to learn some Jewish history. It strikes me now that hearing of the successive waves of slavery and persecution, the litany of pain and suffering, must have had an effect. At just the age when adolescents are questioning everything – including the childish faith in a white-bearded old man in the sky – I was discovering that my people had been singled out for serial misery. What sense did it make to believe in a God bound by covenant to His people, when the people in question suffered so harshly and so consistently?

But of course something else had happened at the very time I graduated, at least according to Jewish tradition, from boyhood to manhood. A few months away from my bar mitzvah, about to turn thirteen, I saw my own mother come close to death. She was struck down, suddenly condemned to a bed for months that turned into years. Her speech was impaired, her face changed; she seemed to age by twenty years overnight. There had been nothing gradual about this decline. It was as if she had been struck by a bolt from the sky.

Perhaps some would have found faith in this circumstance: miraculously my mother did not die, she survived a killer disease. My father, a helpless, extreme optimist, saw it that way. But my mother did not. She felt her fate was unfair. She had committed no crime, she had done nothing to hurt anyone. If she was guilty of any sin, she had surely paid twice over with the hardship of her childhood. So why this? And why her? What system was it that said those with a happy start should have an easy adulthood, while those who had suffered should suffer some more?

I spoke to my mother for many hours and with great intensity in this period and I now wonder if her doubts, no, her *disbelief* in the possibility of a divine protector, passed on to me. An adolescent ready to discard infantile fancies, exposed to the first glimmers of the wounded history of his people and confronted with imme-diate, personal evidence of the arbitrariness of suffering, was not an obvious candidate for faith in a beneficent God – and so it turned out.

Yet my mother never became any less Jewish. Her habits of observance remained more or less the same; she did what she had always done. I look at the choices of my own life and see that I too have followed her lead, making my Jewishness perhaps the central fact of my identity.

Is this not a paradox? Surely Christians who lost their belief in God would no longer be Christians. Why should it be different for Jews? Is it really possible that you can be Jewish and have no faith? More profoundly, even if you can, why on earth would you want to? What is the point of remaining a Jew without the divine prod of an all-seeing deity over your shoulder?

These are live questions for millions of contemporary Jews who find themselves, for whatever reason, unable to believe in a supreme creator. But they go wider. There are new generations born into apparently religious communities all over the world whose theistic convictions are shaky but who are nevertheless reluctant to leave. They are not sure whether this circle can be squared.

The Jewish experience suggests it can. For Jews are more than mere subscribers to a religious doctrine. That much is illustrated by the simple fact that an atheist Jew is not an oxymoron. Harold Pinter, Arthur Miller and Jerry Seinfeld are unlikely to hold to many of Judaism's traditional beliefs on the nature of divinity. Yet no one would say these men are not Jews. No one would even call them 'lapsed'. They are Jews, regardless of their doctrinal views. This is clearly not true of, say, Methodists or Anglicans or Scientologists. In those cases, if you discard the faith you are no longer part of the group. (Catholicism may be more like Judaism in this respect: the example of James Joyce, among others, suggests that the notion of a Catholic atheist is at least conceivable.)

This makes Jews different and means they cannot simply be branded 'a religion'. There is obviously rather more to it than that. A better description might be to say they are 'a culture'. For many Jews, perhaps most, relate to their Jewishness by means other than religion. It might be their connection to the Jewish past or their passion for Israel; it might be snorting extra loud at the Jewish jokes in a Philip Roth novel; it might be watching a documentary about the Holocaust; it might be volunteering to read out loud to the Jewish blind; it might be eating bagels on a Sunday morning. However it is done, Jews can live a full Jewish life without going anywhere near what might be strictly defined as Judaism. Again, this is not quite the case with Methodists or Anglicans or Scientologists. And yet it could well describe the majority of the Jewish world. Most estimates say that between two-thirds and three-quarters of the world's Jews have moved away from strict traditional observance but nevertheless continue to identify themselves as Jews. It is surely this cultural connection they have in mind.

Indeed, this fits with our history. Many scholars like to suggest that, until the exile from Palestine, Jews were not really Jews at all. Rather they were the Hebrews, a nation living in their national home like any other. When they were expelled by the Romans in AD 70 they hit upon an inspired method of national survival, one that was to endure for nearly 2,000 years. They would distil what had been a national culture into a condensed, portable form no longer dependent on a national territory for its realization. What had been an annual harvest festival, timed for the specific seasonal rhythms of Palestine, would become Sukkot, a holiday that could be honoured anywhere. The national rest day would become the Sabbath, meaningful wherever it was respected. The language, Hebrew, would be codified and preserved in a few core texts. In this way, the national way of life could be contained in the knapsack of the Jews, with them wherever they roamed. And the contents of the knapsack, this distilled essence of Jewish life, would be known as Judaism. To ensure that it was not abandoned, even when Jews had wandered thousands of miles and hundreds of years from the Jewish province of first-century Palestine, Judaism would invoke a more powerful sanction than mere national habit: it would be a matter of religious obligation.

To understand this extraordinary project, imagine France was invaded, the French sent into exile, and a team of clerics rapidly devised a strategy for the survival of Frenchness. They would declare that from now on the wandering French were forbidden by their creator from eating hamburgers. They would be required to gather at least once a week in a special meeting house where they would sing only in French. And they would have to leave their homes for the entire month of August and head to the countryside, just as they had once left their beloved, and now lost, city of Paris. Once a year they would gather for a family meal, serving all the best French delicacies, with much garlic, cheese and wine and climaxing in a toast: Next year in Paris! They could keep this up for centuries, no matter where they lived. They would always be stubbornly, bafflingly French.

That, at least according to this theory, is what the Jews did. They freeze-dried their history into portable granules, compact enough to travel anywhere. They required no great cathedrals or monuments, no territory at all. They did not need walls or borders. They were engaged in an almost unique experiment in human life: to maintain a landless civilization. (This was the lead the Dalai Lama was hoping to follow when he travelled to Israel in the 1990s, seeking the counsel of Jewish leaders. He wanted to see how his people, the Tibetans, could pull off the same feat, maintaining their culture even in exile.)

Not that the Jews saw the experiment as permanent. They never stopped dreaming that one day they would be back in their land, where they would add water to the dusty granules they had carried with them for so long – and watch their desiccated culture flower once more.

Whatever the historical accuracy of this account it is appealing, not least because it seems to fit the way Jews are. For Jewishness does indeed feel, from the inside, more like a national culture than a religion. This even applies to the Jewish religion itself. For much of what is dressed up as religious obligation amounts to little more than collective folk custom, the kind of things nations rooted on their own soil do anyway.

Accordingly, Judaism tends to exert a cultural, national or tribal hold, rather than a doctrinal one, on Jews. A Jew may not believe the Lord physically rescued the Children of Israel from Egypt with a mighty hand and an outstretched arm – but he still loves the curious taste of hard-boiled eggs in salted water or the liquid therapy that is chicken soup with *kneidlach*, flavours forever associated with the Passover *seder*. He may not have faith in an interventionist deity who literally inscribes Jews in the book of life, closing the sacred volume in the final hour of Yom Kippur as He decides who shall live and who shall die, but he likes standing with his fellow Jews for twenty-four hours of collective contemplation as they review the year that has passed and submit themselves to a day of reckoning.

This is not hypocrisy; it is all but built into Judaism itself. Non-Jews, especially Christians, are often shocked when they visit a synagogue for the first time. There is none of the hushed decorum they associate with church. Instead there is a constant murmur, sometimes rising to full-blown hubbub, as fathers chat to sons, women to their friends, everyone with everyone else. Those conducting the service, reading that week's portion of the Torah, will occasionally thump their prayer books, demanding quiet, but the noise level soon swells up again. And why would it not? For the synagogue is not known to Jews as the house of God, but as a house of prayer, a house of study and, crucially, as a *beit knesset*, a house of congregation – a meeting place.

Or listen to the sermon. Rare is the rabbinic address that a non-Jew would recognize as religious. There is not much talk of salvation, redemption, sin or the next world. Rather it is the speech of a leader to his community, addressing their concerns in the here and now. I have heard sermons on the price of kosher meat, media bias against Israel, the standards of Jewish schools and, of course, the politics of the Middle East. I am not sure I have ever heard a sermon on the Jewish concept of damnation or heaven and hell. Truth be told, whatever their outer wrapping, most rabbinic addresses are not usually even about God. They are about people; about the way human beings treat each other.

In that same spirit, Judaism's holy books are packed not with meditations on the precise nature of the divine being – no angels on pinheads in Judaism – but on the rights and wrongs of human conduct. There are no fewer than 613 specific *mitzvot*, or command-ments, mandating the correct behaviour on everything from the appropriate blessing for fruit to the required weave in a coat. The emphasis throughout is less on God than on the relationship between one person and the environment or between one person and another.

Indeed, it is quite possible to discern in the Torah a narrative thrust which takes God ever further away from the action. At the start he is everywhere, creating the heaven and the earth. In the Noah story he is still dominant, commanding nature to flood the entire planet. But by the time Abraham is on the scene, God is no longer a whirlwind. He speaks directly with humanity, even engaging Abraham in negotiation. Moses' God rejects the golden calf as idolatry, as if rejecting deification itself. As the contemporary Jewish thinker Douglas Rushkoff writes, this God next 'sponsors a labour revolt, then crafts a new constitution' in the form of the law delivered at Mount Sinai. Finally, the God of the prophets is less interested in direct worship than in the inner divinity of humankind, while the talmudic God exercises his will only through the ethical actions of his followers. The narrative arc is clear: God is gradually getting out of the way, forcing human beings not to look upward but at each other. Writes Rushkoff, 'The Jewish God's recession from human affairs . . . has been all but preordained by the Jewish religion.'

The Talmud illustrates the point with a beautiful story, one to lift the hearts of radicals and democrats everywhere. It describes a characteristically talmudic dispute, a scholarly row about when exactly a stove can be declared clean. The clash pits Rabbi Eliezer against Rabbi Joshua and the sages. Eliezer brings all the proofs in the world to back his case. But still Joshua and the sages are not satisfied.

In frustration Eliezer declares, 'If the law agrees with me, this locust tree shall prove it!' He is raising the stakes, promising a demonstration from the heavens that God backs him. And behold! The locust tree is promptly plucked out of the ground, like a weed from a window box, and flung far away.

'No proof can be brought from the locust tree,' sniff Joshua and the sages.

All right, thinks Eliezer. I'll show them. 'If the law agrees with me, this stream of water shall prove it.' Sure enough, the stream begins to flow backward. A miracle, representing divine approval for Eliezer! But still the sages are unmoved.

'No proof can be brought from a stream,' they say, shaking their heads.

On this goes, Eliezer prompting the very walls of the house of study to bend in confirmation of his argument. Finally he brings out the big gun. 'If the law agrees with me, heaven itself shall prove it!'

And the heavens shake and an unworldly voice is heard. 'Why do you dispute with Rabbi Eliezer?' booms the voice of God. 'The law agrees with him in every case!' It is the ultimate vindication, the Almighty himself casting his vote for Eliezer. Yet Joshua does not throw himself to the floor in contrition, apologizing for having made a mistake. On the contrary, he rises to his feet and declares, quoting Moses to the Children of Israel, 'It is not in heaven!'

The rabbis then discuss what Joshua means by this 'not in heaven'. They conclude that he is telling God that, ever since the Torah was given on Mount Sinai, human affairs have been for humans to resolve. These matters are settled *lo b'shemaim*, not in heaven, but *kunn b'aretz*, here on earth. In the commentary of

Rabbi Jeremiah, the fourth-century sage who drove his colleagues crazy with his knack for questioning every assumption, it is even more stark. The voice from heaven does not concern us, he writes. From now on the rule is simple: 'After the majority must one incline.'

I can think of no more fundamental statement of democracy than that story. It demands majority rule, even when God himself is in the minority. On one side stand Joshua and the sages, on the other Eliezer and the Lord. And the Lord is outvoted! But it goes deeper even than the democratic principle. That story also presents the case for humanism. It makes human beings, and no supreme deity, sovereign in the world. He may rule the heavens, but down here we are masters of our own destiny.

Even if one does not go that far – and since this is the Talmud, a compendium of argument, every Jew is free to dispute the meaning of that story or cite others – it is hard to escape the impression that Judaism has a rather atypical conception of the relationship between God and man. Some prefer to describe humanity and the divine as partners in creation: He may have started the process, but we continue it every day. This notion of partnership is underlined by the laws that bind Jews (and symbolized by the very first rule, the circumcision which sees God and his children collaborating to 'perfect' the human body). There are two sources, the written and the oral law. The first is the text, including the Ten Commandments, given by God to Moses at Sinai; the second consists of the commentaries, the Talmud and Midrash, authored by rabbis. These human texts, this oral law, is accorded the same holy status as the divinely written. God and humanity are engaged in a shared enterprise.

On this reading, Jewishness is not really a religion at all. It consists of a thick, dense lattice built up over centuries comprising history, music, food, ideas, theatre, literature and every cultural form you can name. Yes, some of it may still share the outward appearance of religion, and many of its customs come with a coating of faith, but there is more to Jewishness than Judaism. Just look at the Jews all around you, living full Jewish lives even if religion plays next to no part in them.

Even if Jewishness were only about Judaism, it still would not be like Protestantism or Buddhism or any other faith. Because Judaism is best understood as a national culture, freeze-dried in the form of religion solely for reasons of self-preservation. And because Judaism translates, even in its own terms, into humanism. And neither of those things requires faith in a supernatural deity.

I think this is why my mother could lose her faith, after severe illness broke her trust in an embracing, protective God, and yet hardly move away from traditional Judaism. Becoming a non-believer scarcely made her less Jewish. And the same is true of me.

I think it might also explain a quirky but fascinating pheno-menon. I once interviewed the founder of the Jews for Jesus movement, a large rabbinic-looking man called Moishe Rosen, who was helping himself to a cream cheese bagel when I came to interview him in San Francisco. I wanted to know how he could square two apparently conflicting identities. He saw no clash. Jewishness was his ethnic affiliation; Christianity was his faith. He was no more conflicted than a Scottish Protestant or a Polish Catholic. He was a Jewish Christian.

But Scottishness or Polishness does not carry with it its own religion, I insisted. Surely to be a Jew was also a religious commit-ment. For some, he said. But many spiritually minded Jews, people keen to think deeply about sin, salvation and the next life, found Judaism lacking. 'There is a God-shaped hole in Judaism,' he declared.

I knew that Rosen was a hate figure among Jews, who regarded him as a traitor. But I could not help thinking he might have put his finger on something. When I interviewed others in the San Francisco congregation of Jewish Christians I heard the same testi-mony over and over: Jewish life, including the synagogue, had dwelled too much on the here and now, on politics, community and history. It did not speak enough about God. I could not argue.

My experience had been similar. The difference was, I liked it that way: it fitted my own beliefs, perhaps even my own needs.

Still, I do not doubt that the frustration these Jews for Jesus felt is replicated among the disproportionately large numbers of Jews who join other religions, especially the smaller ones. The phenomenon of the Jewish Buddhist, or JUBU, is particularly striking, with as many as a third of American Buddhists estimated to be Jewish by birth. Many JUBUs say Buddhist practices help them cope with the Jewish legacy of suffering – and offer a spiritual dimension absent from contemporary Judaism. The God-shaped hole.

For most Jews, however, the cultural, national quality of Jewish life is an asset rather than a liability. It keeps them connected in a way that religion alone would not. It enables them to stay Jewish even if they have no faith.

I would venture one thought, though. This cultural approach to what we usually brand as religion could be useful beyond the Jewish sphere. Other faith communities might see themselves more clearly if they recognized how much of what they do is about community rather than faith. Perhaps they might keep in more of those new generations who often feel compelled to move out: many are the young Hindus and Muslims who feel an allegiance to their people even if they cannot accept the accompanying theology. A cultural, rather than religious, self-description might be more appealing as well as truer to reality.

Majority societies could benefit from such a view too. Instead of regarding, say, faith schools as narrowly theological institutions, they could see them instead as bodies working hard to sustain and renew a minority culture. Judged this way, as ethnic rather than religious places, 'faith' schools might arouse less secular, liberal hostility.

Jews have grappled with such questions for a long time, starting with Jacob himself. The Torah takes us to the night when Jacob is left alone. Suddenly a man appears and the pair wrestle till daybreak, neither overpowering the other. When their fight is finally over, the stranger tells him, 'Your name will no longer be Jacob, but Israel because you have struggled with God and with men and have overcome.'

That, then, is the meaning of Israel: one who wrestles with God. No wonder we struggle with faith and its meaning. The struggle is written into our history, into our very name.

17　The Nightmare That Never Ends

As a student I had friends who dedicated every spare hour to the campus battle against anti-Zionism and, in the parlance of the field, 'combating' anti-Semitism. This was their Jewish passion. In more recent years I have known Jews whose prime form of Jewish identification is detecting prejudice against them, usually in the media. The apotheosis of this tendency is, inevitably, the cult of the Holocaust – the turning of the Shoah into not only a sacral, quasi-mystical event but also the heart and soul of Jewish belonging. There are many who never feel the visceral pull of their people more than when they are in Yad Vashem in Jerusalem or watching *Schindler's List*.

I never wanted to be one of those people. In 2000 I covered the libel trial brought by British Holocaust denier and 'pro-Nazi polemicist' – the judge's words – David Irving. When it was over, I wrote a column welcoming the verdict but hoping that it would at last release my fellow Jews from what had become an unhealthy obsession. I suggested that giving the survivors and victims some peace and quiet would be a fine riposte to Irving, who liked to quip that the Holocaust was 'the only interesting thing that has ever happened to the Jews'. Closing the book of the Shoah would be to defy Hitler's plan for the Jews. He wanted to make us a dead people, I wrote: we should prove we still live.

That was in April. By the autumn of 2000 the second intifada had erupted in all its lethal fury. What followed were uncomfortable years for those Jews, like me, who were keen to accentuate the positive. Jewish communities, especially in Europe, reported a rise in anti-Semitism, linked, they suspected, to both the intifada and the 9/11 attacks. In November 2001 Jonathan Rosen wrote in the *New York Times* of his father, a Jewish refugee from pre-war Vienna, who used to go to bed with a transistor radio, as if listening out for more bad news for the Jews. The 'grumbling static from the bedroom depressed me,' Rosen recalled, 'and I vowed to replace it with music more cheerfully in tune with America. These days, however, I find myself on my father's frequency. I have awakened to anti-Semitism.' In London, *The Times* wrote that Britain had become 'a cold house for Jews'.

I wrote and spoke at public meetings against this kind of panic. It was hysterical, alarmist, to imagine the clock had been turned back to the 1930s. Yes, there was a rise in criticism of the Israeli government: that was hardly a surprise with Ariel Sharon at the helm. But this was not the start of a new war against the Jews.

When the synagogues started to be bombed in Turkey and the Jewish schools burned down in France, this insouciance became harder to maintain. The return of 'dinner-party anti-Semitism' – the longest serving Member of Parliament, the Father of the House, Tam Dalyell, claimed that a 'cabal' of Jews was dictating US policy and had the British Prime Minister in its thrall – was noticeable. The rise of old-fashioned, blood-libel, Jews-are-the-source-of-all-evil anti-Semitism in the Islamic world was well documented and un-ignorable: I had seen the hook-nosed, blood-dripping cartoons myself. Caricatures and tropes that had been common in medieval Christendom were resuscitated and walking again in the Asia and Arabia of the twenty-first century. Occasionally they even resurfaced in their old habitat, Europe.

That anti-Semitism could exert enormous power I knew just from looking at one very unscientific sample: Nat, Mick and Sara. Their lives were all affected, even transformed, by anti-Jewish preju-dice and its consequences. Nat left Dunilovich for England to avoid an anti-Semitic pogrom; he left London for Palestine because he wanted to help build a haven from the Jews' persecutors; he died weighed down by his failure to open Palestine's gates to those fleeing anti-Semitism's newest incarnation, Nazism. Mick dedicated his youth to the fight against fascism and Jew-hatred; his heart was broken when the communist movement he cast as saviour turned out not to be immune to the very virus he wanted to repel. And my mother lost her mother to one of Hitler's bombs. In each of their lives, anti-Semitism was clear and present. It had never gone away.

As with any scientific riddle, scholars have long pulled and tugged at this persistence of anti-Jewish hatred, trying to explain it. They have looked in the obvious places, starting with the historical record. For centuries, Jews' unhappy fate was to be pushed into roles – as lenders of money, tax collectors, agents or landlords – which threw them into immediate conflict with their neighbours. This was rarely a choice. At a time when usury was prohibited to Christians, Jews were banned from other vocations, especially any involving work on the land, and required to lend money. Plenty of rulers found it convenient to have this caste of middlemen, the Jews, functioning as a permanent buffer between themselves and the people they ruled: if the Jews were collecting taxes, it would be the Jews, not the king, who felt the people's anger. The device worked well.

Theology played a role too. In Christendom Jews were the killers of God's son, destined to be punished in perpetuity for the crime of deicide. Never mind that, alone among the gospel writers, only Matthew had the Jewish crowd accept responsibility for Jesus' crucifixion with the indelible sentence, 'His blood be on our heads and on the heads of our children.' The line stuck and new layers of teaching were piled upon it. The myth of the Wandering Jew was created, gloomily telling of the Jew who would suffer until the end of time, roaming the earth and thereby proving the truth of Christ – by illustrating the fate of all those who refuse to let Jesus into their hearts.

For some, though, the sheer longevity of anti-Semitism requires an explanation beyond the conventional realms of economic and religious history. The bleakest theory says it has become nothing less than an essential part of the human condition, as old as the Jews themselves. Were Abraham's heirs not persecuted even in the age of the Bible? Does anti-Semitism not endure even in those places where there are no Jews: Japan or the Philippines? In this view, Jew-hatred is protean, a shape-shifting virus that is always one step ahead of those who would define and eventually cure it. Jews are not despised for what they do; otherwise the hatred would stop when they change, which they have done, frequently. No, there is no logic to such hatred. The anti-Semite hates the Jew as a rootless cosmopolitan when he has no land of his own, and hates him as a colonialist oppressor when he does. The true anti-Semite hates the Jew because he is a Jew.

There are dark days when that senselessness seems to make sense. But it is hard to live in such a world, hard to accept that some forces are impregnable to change or human agency. It is too hopeless, too final. Which might explain why I latch on to a couple of the countless theories of anti-Semitism, grasping for some explanation that might be plausible.

The first centres on the strange persistence not of Jew-hatred but of the Jews themselves. You would imagine they would have vanished centuries ago. They lost their land in the first century after Christ and were scattered to the four winds. They should surely have gone the way of the Minoans or Incas or other conquered peoples and disappeared from history. Yet they refused to die. The nineteenth-century Russian physician Leo Pinsker reckoned this fact alone terrified the Gentile nations: 'The world saw in this people the frightening form of one of the dead walking among the living. This ghostlike apparition of a people . . . without land . . . no longer alive and yet moving about among the living . . .' Dr Pinsker thus diagnosed in humanity a collective fear of the Jewish ghost in its midst – a people without a land was as terrifying as a person without a body – and he called this fear Judaeophobia. His prognosis was not rosy: 'As a psychic aberration, it is hereditary; as a disease transmitted for 2,000 years, it is incurable.'

One can add a second opinion to Dr Pinsker's original examination. Maybe it is not just Jews' longevity, their staying power, that so enrages, or scares, the world. Perhaps it is the knowledge this long collective life has given them. For the Jews are the eternal witness, ever present – albeit on the margins – throughout history.

Who would remember the folk legend of the Moorish queen had it not been preserved in the exquisite Moroccan-Jewish-Spanish ballad 'La Reina Sherifa Mora'? Centuries after they were expelled from Spain, Jews have carried with them a legend from another nation's culture. The Jews are like a tribe of travelling storytellers, preserving in their heads the myths of all the people they have ever known. In the words of the novelist and essayist Cynthia Ozick, 'To be a Jew is to be old in history.'

At the key moments of the past there are the Jews, hovering in the background, peeking through the curtains. This is why Woody Allen's creation Zelig – the outsider at the back of every epochal photograph of the twentieth century – has entered the language. He epitomizes a Jewish role; we are the witness nation. As the maverick Jewish historian Yosef Haim Yerushalmi puts it, 'The injunction of memory falls to Israel, and to Israel alone . . . Only in Israel is the injunction to remember felt as a religious imperative to an entire people.'

Perhaps this is what makes the world shift in its seat. For if we have seen everything, then we know everything. We know where the bodies are buried, now and for ever. Of course knowledge is not handed down genetically, but in this slightly mystical conception, the Jews are the bearers of humanity's memories, including some of the darkest. Whether it was the brutality of medieval England or the bloodthirst of seventeenth-century Ukraine, the Jews saw it first hand. From the slave trade in the West Indies to the Russian civil war, Jews were there.

In the eyes of the anti-Semite, then, the Jews are humanity's bad conscience, constantly reminding the rest of the world of all its misdeeds. Which brings us to the second theory for the persistence of Jew-hatred. This says that, since the very beginning, the Jews have submitted the human race to one long guilt trip. It began with Noah's list of seven universal rules, continued with Abraham's monotheism and seemed to culminate in the Ten Commandments. But the Jews were not done yet. Next came the Jewish revolutionary Jesus of Nazareth, burning up the Galilee with his scorching insistence on human improvement. Another rabbinic figure, Karl Marx, eventually continued the tradition, demanding humankind up-end itself entirely and change from the inside out. Can the Gentiles be blamed if all this constant nagging, this insistence on perfection, drove the world crazy?

Or so asks George Steiner via Adolf Hitler. In his startling novel *The Portage to San Cristobal of A. H.*, Steiner imagines a Führer who has survived the war only to be hunted down in the forests of the Amazon. In the book's closing chapter, he lets A. H. defend himself and his attempted eradication of the Jews: 'You call me a tyrant, an enslaver. What tyranny, what enslavement has been more oppressive, has branded the skin and soul of man more deeply, than the sick fantasies of the Jew? You are not Godkillers, but *Godmakers*. And that is infinitely worse. The Jew invented conscience and left man a guilty serf.'

Steiner's Hitler articulates what no Nazi and no anti-Semite ever would. Out loud, they would only ever blame the Jews for the bad news they had brought, not the good. But this Führer seems to speak more candidly and with greater self-awareness. Could he be right? Could it be that it was not the Jews' flaws that so enraged the world but rather the gifts they came to bring? Might this be the root cause of centuries of anti-Semitism – not that Jews were a nation that dwelled apart, looking out for their own interests, but that they insisted on improving, on repairing, the world? Was this the Jews' mistake, not to have pursued the particular but to have grown obsessed with the universal?

I do not know. And I am not sure what difference it would make if I did. For, even if I were persuaded that Steiner's Hitler is right and that it is the Jews' reforming zeal that so angers the world, I would not draw from that a Jewish obligation to alter our behaviour. Even less would I urge the Jews to lose the thirst for human improvement. We should never give that up; it represents our best instincts. Anyway, the burden should not be on the Jews. For this would be the world's problem, not the Jews' – and it would be up to the world, rather than the Jews, to change.

And that, I realize, is how I see anti-Semitism. It is a problem for the Jews, no doubt; we are the ones who feel its punch. But that need not trigger an introspection by Jews into our own conduct, searching for the habit that so offends our neighbours. Rather it is those neighbours who should be gazing inward, wondering why they are still infected by such an age-old disease. (I see racism the same way: it represents a weakness in the racist, not his victim.)

So I retain my hope that the Jews can avoid making anti-Semitism and the sufferings of the past the central fact of our identity. I want Jewishness to be about more than our enemies and their hatred for us. I do not deny that it exists; I will no longer play it down. But I am not keen to dedicate valuable energy to the search for an explanation, not because such a search is inherently pointless but because that task belongs to the anti-Semites themselves. It is their ailment; they should cure it. We have a different duty.

18   *In Search of Zion*

If hatred of Jews cast its shadow over the lives of Nat, Mick and Sara, so too did the idea which many believed was anti-Semitism's antidote. The dream of a Jewish homeland affected all three of them. One was born there, one died there and the third struggled over the notion his entire life, dividing him from his father and, in some ways, himself.

Like the command to empathize with the world's victims, the dream of Zion was a Jewish response to a past of torments. If one reaction was to channel centuries of grief into a higher ethical standard, then this was the other: to construct a refuge, a haven where Jews would at last be safe. It was a new idea, but also an ancient one – buried so deep in the Jewish heart that it had never disappeared.

For Jews are inseparable from Israel. We are the House of Israel, the Children of Israel, the people of Israel. In modern times, the word has acquired a new meaning. Now it refers to the state of Israel, but the same logic of inseparability still holds. Of course a small but vocal minority retain the principled anti-Zionism of the pre-1948 era. If they are on the left, they might still cleave to the universalist internationalism that once so animated my great-uncle Mick. If they are ultra-orthodox, they might still believe that a Jewish return to the land of Israel is an unpardonable usurpation of divine authority, in common with the rabbis who once argued so spiritedly with my mother's grandfather. But the vast majority of the Jewish world has more than made its peace with the notion of a Jewish state. Some 5 million of them live in it, including twenty or so great-grandchildren of Nat Mindel; most of the rest feel a connection, if not an allegiance, to it. For many it has become central to their Jewish identity, outstripping the Torah, even Judaism itself, as the force that commands their loyalty.

It has also become the terrain on which the Jews encounter the rest of the world. That was the intention of the first modern Zionists, who believed that a Jewish home would act as the portal through which the Jews could, at long last, enter the family of nations. But that is not quite what I mean. For Israel has become a battleground between Jews and the rest of the world. That is literally true in the case of Israel, the Palestinians and the other Arab nations. But it has become metaphorically true of much of the rest of the globe too. Israel – its conduct and its right to exist – has become a constant point of friction between Jews and non-Jews far from its borders. The Jews of the United States have been largely exempt from this phenomenon, thanks to broad American sympathy for Israel. But elsewhere, Europe most notably, Israel has become a source of tension between Jews and their neighbours. Critics are appalled by what Israel has done and continues to do; Jews worry if this reaction is about something else besides current Israeli conduct. One side insists they are merely anti-Israel; the other suspects something more basic, something anti-Jewish. I know this battle well, for I am often caught in its crossfire.

The gap between the two can seem so wide, it is as if they are not even speaking about the same subject. In some ways they are not. One side is sure it is talking only about a small country, fairly far away. The other believes this is not about a foreign country at all; it is about Jews. For it, the state of Israel and the House of Israel are all but synonymous.

I have spoken to people who find this latter sentiment baffling. Perhaps they might understand it of some homeless, stateless Jewish refugee in the months after 1945. But why would a comfortable, third-generation British or French or Argentine Jew feel this way towards another state? What exactly is this Jewish attachment to Israel all about? I am now a little clearer on where it begins – and where it ends.

Its starting point is Zionism's declaration that the Jews are a nation. This is a more radical statement than it looks. The enlightened governments of Western Europe had emancipated their Jews

on precisely the reverse assumption, that Jews were merely followers of a different – and maybe not even that different – religion.
The French Revolution made its offer of equality on the strict
understanding that French Jews were no more a distinct nation
than French Protestants or French Catholics. On the contrary,
the French were one nation, albeit with different tendencies of
conscience.

But Jews are not quite like that. As I have come to understand,
they are not simply subscribers to a faith, like Presbyterians or
Buddhists. They have too many traits that faiths, on their own, do
not exhibit, including elements of shared language, history and
culture. It is also impossible to ignore the Jews' sense of themselves
as a people, specifically a people in exile. Their synagogues always
face towards the Jerusalem they lost. Their prayers plead, three
times a day, for a return to Zion. The annual *seder*, in which the
story of the exodus from slavery in Egypt to freedom in Canaan is
told and retold, culminates in a raucous chorus of 'Next year in
Jerusalem.' It may be merely a hope, a longing, but Jews can tick
the final box in the checklist that defines a nation: they have a deep
connection with a land.

The Jews of the nineteenth century who began arguing this
point were not motivated by a bureaucrat's desire for accurate
classification. Instead they had a hundred motives, starting with
the failure, as they saw it, of assimilation. Jews were contorting
themselves into ever tighter knots to accommodate their neighbours, changing or offering to change even their most fundamental
thoughts and practices – witness the German-Jewish suggestion
that the Sabbath be moved from Saturday to Sunday – and yet it
was not working. Hatred of the Jew endured, often in a form
unchanged since medieval times.

With a heavy heart, Zionism's earliest thinkers suggested the
world was not the fraternal, welcoming place the Enlightenment
had promised. In the words of Moses Hess, a socialist intellectual
and one-time colleague of Karl Marx's, 'The Jews have lived and
laboured among the nations for almost 2,000 years but nonetheless

they cannot become rooted organically within them.' The journey of these proto-Zionists was often the same: assimilated Jews jolted by the stubborn persistence of anti-Semitism. Leo Pinsker was once a leading light in the Society for the Spread of Culture among the Jews of Russia, an organization dedicated to assimilating Jewry into the tsarist motherland. But the pogroms of 1881 – backed by leading newspapers and assisted by the regime – shook his integrationist faith. A year later he authored 'Auto-Emancipation', arguing that Jewish liberation could never come in the form of privileges bequeathed by kings or assemblies. The Jews would have to take their destiny into their own hands.

The archetype of the assimilationist-turned-nationalist is the man venerated as the father of modern Zionism, Theodor Herzl. Hungarian-born, he had long left behind the superstitions and ancient rites of his fellow Jews, becoming an eminent journalist and Paris correspondent of the prestigious *Neue Freie Presse* of Vienna. But when he covered the Dreyfus affair in 1894 – the trial of a French Jewish officer falsely accused of treason – he gave up any belief he still harboured that Jews might survive or thrive in Christian society. He had seen first hand Dreyfus's humiliation, the soldier's epaulettes stripped from his shoulders, and had heard the cries of '*à bas les Juifs*' from the mob outside. Soon Herzl was hard at work on the feverish dream of a manifesto he called the 'Jewish State'.

Other urges rapidly joined the bleak prognosis of the Jews' chances in the modern world. Marxists said Jews needed their own economic 'base', a territory, before they could become a normal society. Some rabbis were convinced that only a return to Zion would hasten the coming of the Messiah. There were Tolstoyan romantics who believed Jews' alienation from the soil was the root of their misery: they needed to get back to their own land. Among some of these reformers lurked an image of their fellow Jews which would have nestled easily in the mind of the anti-Semite: a nation of pale, skinny scholars and middlemen needed, they argued, to be replaced by strong, ruddy-cheeked peasants and warriors. They wanted to rear a new Jew who would be the heir of the ancient

Hebrew. Rosa would become Rachel, Hershel would become Haim. Nat would become Menachem.

This may sound like so much history now, but it is surprising how strongly some of these original Zionist arguments still grip the contemporary Jewish heart. The language might be a world away but the emotion is not.

Take the promise Zionism made to people like my great-great-uncle Nat. It offered to end, once and for all, the neurosis that comes from being split: a man in the streets and a Jew at home. Zionism said there could be a place, far away, where this self-division would end. There your citizenship and identity would be one and the same thing: not French and Jewish or Jewish and Dutch but Jewish and Jewish. No conflict, no tug of war inside the human heart. To live in such a land would be a liberation, said the dream. You could at last be you, defined solely by your character and deeds rather than by a difference you may never have chosen. A black man in a town of white people is forever 'Bob, the black guy'. In a town of black people he is 'Bob'.

There are, even now and even in the super-enlightened nations of the West, Jews drawn to this promise. As a teenager growing up in what I would then have called 'diaspora', I felt torn. I was connected to my fellow Britons, of course. I was (and remain) sentimentally patriotic for the land of my birth. But I felt bound too, in ways I could not always explain, to my fellow Jews. It was tiring when these two ties pulled in different directions, to feel I could not give to one without inching away from the other. A Jewish state seemed to offer an answer.

Part of it was a weariness with living as a minority, of inhabiting a culture that is permanently on the margins. I wanted my habits and customs to be shared by the people I lived among. I would visit Israel and get a kick from seeing Hebrew not confined to the pages of a prayer book, but on street signs and restaurant menus. When Sukkot came, it was not an underground festival known to only a handful but a national holiday. I would notice Israeli parents teaching their children nursery rhymes, humming ditties that commemorate their national history rather than a past to which they felt little or no connection. A Jewish state enabled them to live in the heart of the country they inhabited, not on its periphery. I wanted to live that way.

Zionism strikes a different chord in me today, one cruder and sadder. For Zionism also made a more basic promise: after 2,000 years of persecution, Jews would be safe in their own land. They would not rely on the protection of a benign prince, won through lucre and loyalty. Nor would they depend on the goodwill of the non-Jewish majority, often only granted in exchange for some sacrifice of their own identity. They would at last form their own government and take charge of their own destiny. If they needed to be defended from their enemies, they would do the job themselves.

This is the Zionism that still commands the loyalty of the over-whelming majority of the world's Jews; without any pleasure, I admit I am one of them. They look at the world and believe they need a refuge, a safe place they can call their own. And, if they had ever doubted it, the twentieth century completed the task of persuasion.

It is not a complicated belief. It is a simple one, capable of expression even in a song. In 1948, when the Holocaust was still a fresh memory, Leo Fuld, the self-styled King of Yiddish Music, recorded this tune: '*Vi Ahin Soll Ich Geh'n?*' – Where can I go?

> Tell me, Where can I go?
> There's no place I can see.
> Where to go, where to go?
> Every door is closed to me.
> To the left, to the right,
> It's the same in every land.
> There is nowhere to go
> And it's me who should know,
> Won't you please understand?

Leo Fuld then answered his own question. The year was 1948, so there could be only one answer.

Now I know where to go,
Where my folk proudly stand.
Let me go, let me go
To that precious, promised land.
I am proud, can't you see,
For at last I am free:
No more wandering for me.

Many people would struggle to understand that today. They would appreciate why such a lament made sense in the immediate thunderclap of the Holocaust, but now? Jews wandering around homeless and bereft is surely for the history books. They look at the Jews of Britain or the United States and see communities who are comfortable, settled and at home. So they begin to wonder why Jews need a Jewish state at all. Why not live just as they are, as minorities in the countries of the world?

Jews have an answer, but they are not that keen to voice it. It sounds so bleak, so dismal in its estimation of human mercy. But the truth is that they do not trust hospitality any longer, even from those who seem to be the most generous hosts. In Berlin, Jews were at the top of the professions, at the commanding heights of culture and industry. At a time when British universities were turning away Jewish academics, when American hotels were finding themselves all booked up at the arrival of a Goldberg or Solomons, when France was still the nation of the Dreyfus affair and when millions of Polish and Russian Jews were confined within the pale of settlement, Germany seemed to be at ease with its Jewish citizens. When the Kaiser's commanders rolled east in 1914, they came with this message, delivered in Hebrew and Yiddish: 'My dear Jews, we come to you as friends, our banners bring you freedom.' Germany was admired as the nation that had best solved the riddles of modern Jewish life. It was the America of its day. So if Jews are wary now, even when they seem settled, affluent and unthreatened, perhaps they should be understood. They have seen so many false dawns before, they find it safer to assume it is still dark.

Years of conversation and argument with Jews tell me that they are desperate for the rest of the world to understand this single point. The debate can seem so complex, trading accusations about UN resolutions, rejected peace plans and the latest atrocity, but underneath it comes down to something quite simple. Jews crave the understanding of the rest of the human race. They know that they should be strong enough to take criticism; Israel is a state like any other and it is perfectly right that states are subject to rigorous scrutiny. But they cannot help themselves. Behind so many condemnations of Israel they detect something else, a deeper questioning of Israel's very legitimacy. This instinct is not always off the mark. Many critics do indeed question the right of a Jewish state to exist at all.

This hurts Jews more than perhaps many non-Jews realize. In the old days, say those who are hurt, it was the individual Jew who had no right to exist. Now it is the collective Jew, in the form of Israel, who is to be shunned. Individual or collective, it makes little difference: the Jew is still the pariah. Anti-Semitism has changed shape before, they notice. In a neat trick, they paraphrase the changing message the world has delivered to the Jews. 'You cannot live among us as Jews,' was the early formulation, demanding conversion to Christianity. 'You cannot live among us,' was the next version, as Jews were quarantined behind the high walls of the ghetto. Finally, the Third Reich truncated the sentence still further: 'You cannot live.'

What many Jews hear in the argument that Israel has no right to exist is a new message: 'You cannot live among us collectively.' It is less severe than the formulation of the 1940s, but that offers only relative comfort. The truth is, Jews want to hear a wholly new sentence: 'You can live among us whichever way you like, as individuals in the countries of the world or collectively, as a nation, in a state of your own.' If Jews felt this was the underlying sentiment of Israel's critics, they would listen to them attentively and seriously. But so long as they believe some other attitude lurks behind the critique, their ears clam up. They huddle closer together, seeking to stand strong against the outside.

There may be many non-Jews who genuinely sympathize with the Jewish predicament, but two obstacles stand between them and an embrace of the legitimacy of Zionism. The first is the nagging doubt whether Jews are a nation at all and therefore eligible for the universal principle of national self-determination. They are a religion, say these sceptics; perhaps a race. But a nation? It is surely as mad, and illegitimate, to imagine a Jewish state as it would a Baptist state or a black state. I have heard it argued that a Jewish state in Palestine is as indefensible as a Catholic Ireland or a Protestant France. A confessional state, set up to house a single religion? Not on.

Put aside the fact that plenty of modern states are indeed organized around religion (England with its established Church being one of them). The key error here is a category mistake. The anti-Zionist insists that the Jews are a religion and therefore cannot be entitled to national rights of self-determination. And it is this insistence that sends one scurrying back through the history books. For was this not the wisdom of the French revolutionaries, who believed Jewish individuals were entitled to rights while 'the Jews' were not? Was this not the finger-wagging insistence of Comrade Lenin, who as early as 1903 was declaring that the very 'idea of a Jewish "nationality" is definitely reactionary'? You are not a nation! To you as individuals of Jewish origin, everything. But as a nation, nothing. For you are not a nation.

It is quite true that Jews are not like Scots or Spaniards or Greeks, who tend to live in one place and speak the same language. But such an objection presumes to tell the Jews what they are and what they are not. In today's world we surely prefer to let groups define themselves. Moreover, it rests on an insistence that Jewishness is a narrow matter of faith, a religious leaning and nothing more. Yet I now know that everything about the Jews says otherwise. They are a civilization, a culture, a people and a tribe. Admittedly, it can be frustrating that the Jews do not fit neatly into the box we devise for nations. It is their misfortune to have lived away from their historic homeland for so long. This makes them an unusual, perhaps even exceptional case: a landless people for most of their history. But it seems a rather thin, impoverished theory of national rights that does not have room for an oddity such as the Jews.

Others question Zionism on a second ground. They accept that the Jews might be a nation entitled to self-determination. The trouble is, they say, that right cannot be fulfilled because the nominated homeland is already taken. Another people got there first.

Some Zionists would want to dispute that last sentence and especially that last word. They would open up a long and winding argument on the chronology of ancient claims, insisting that the Jews, the Hebrews, had been there first but had simply been away, in forced exile, for 2,000 years. Scotland would surely still belong to the Scots even if they were booted out of it and took many centuries to find their way back. Besides, say Israel's defenders, it is not as if these critics take an equally hard line on the rest of the world's 'new' societies, those founded by immigrants who displaced the earlier inhabitants. If these doubters denied the right to exist of, say, the United States, Australia, Canada, New Zealand and whole swathes of Latin America, then their opposition to Zionism would be perfectly logical. But Jews meet few anti-Zionists campaigning for the dissolution of those states, so they end up confused. Why has liberal opinion made its peace with those settler societies, most of them born through ethnic cleansing and even genocide, but remained so angry with Israel? Why does the presence of this small, constructed state inflame them so, when the world is full of such entities, all of them forged in blood?

I prefer to locate the argument on different ground. Let us concede that Palestine was inhabited by another people; the Jews still had a right to come back to it. In the mid-twentieth century, theirs was the right, as the Israeli novelist and peacenik Amos Oz once framed it, of the drowning man. That man is allowed to reach out and grab a piece of driftwood, even if another man is already clinging to it – even if he makes this second man budge up and share it. In other words, after the Holocaust, the Jewish people had the right to reach for the life raft of Palestine. If that meant asking, even forcing, the Palestinians to share it, then that too was justified. For the Jews were drowning.

This was not of course how the whole process was experienced by Palestinians, for whom 1948 felt more like a sudden and traumatic dispossession than an act of 'sharing'. (For them the more appropriate image might be Isaac Deutscher's comparison of Jewish refugees from Europe to people jumping out of a burning building: the indigenous Arab population of Palestine were the innocent passers-by on the street below, crushed by the fall.) Even if they were to put that most benign gloss on 1948, what are they to make of 1967 and Israel's retention of the territories it won then and has ruled ever since? Surely that amounts to the once-drowning man grabbing hold of the entire plank of driftwood, keeping it all to himself. (That is certainly Oz's view, which is why he became one of the earliest advocates of withdrawal from those territories.)

Nevertheless, Jews badly need to hear the world, including, ultimately, the Arab nations, accept Oz's fundamental logic – that the Jews have a right to at least some of the land. They long for the family of nations to recognize the legitimacy of their need and so at last to accept the Jewish state among them. The continuing question mark hovering over this matter, the sense that Israel is somehow on probation, its very existence conditional upon a verdict of good behaviour, is what gives Jews their persistent sense of unease. They imagine the world is telling them something: you do not truly belong among us.

This, then, is what the Jews demand of the rest of the world when it comes to Israel: acceptance. But what does Israel demand of the Jews, and the Jews of Israel? If we are asking our non-Jewish neighbours to shift ground, we can hardly exempt ourselves from the obligation.

A start might be a truthful look at the balance sheet, setting out the successes and failures. Triumph has come in an area that only a few of the first Zionists saw as the prime objective of a national home: the revival of Jewish culture. By this measure, Israel's achievements have exceeded the founders' most extravagant dreams. The Hebrew language has woken from its sleep to become the native tongue of millions. It is the vehicle for great novels and radio jingles, for sonnets and graffiti. It is alive. But Israel also teems with Jewish music, dance and art. Some of these might be in their infancy but now, at least, one can speak of Jewish cinema or Jewish sculpture and refer to thematic content rather than mere authorship. Meanwhile, Jerusalem has become the undisputed centre of Jewish religious learning. All this in little over fifty years.

But there are disappointments. With a dream so exalted, high on its belief that it would build a light unto the nations, a Utopia in the Levant to redeem 2,000 years of history, how could it be otherwise? The vision was so dazzling, how could reality ever compete?

So the debit column was always bound to be full. First, the Zionist confidence that a Jewish state would resolve the tension, the neurotic split, between citizenship and identity has proved naïve. Israeli Jews still need two words to describe themselves after all. Sometimes they feel Israeli, sometimes they feel Jewish. Things did not go as planned: most of the world's Jews did not pack their bags and move to Palestine. By their deeds they showed that what they really wanted, and what they today regard as indispensable, is the knowledge that a Jewish state exists – that it is there if they need it. As I discovered in my own life, actually living in the country is a different question. The result is that there are Jews who are not Israelis and, no less crucially, there are Israelis who are not Jews. The first Zionists did not give much thought to either possibility. And so the old mess endures: this remains a people with more than its fair share of names – Israelis, Jews, Hebrews, Zionists – none of them quite interchangeable.

More gravely, Zionism can seem to have failed in even its most minimal purpose. It was meant to be a refuge, the one place in the world where Jews would not be attacked simply because they were Jews. And yet, at the turn of the twenty-first century, Israel had become one of the very few places in the world where Jews were attacked simply because they were Jews. Israelis who wanted to feel safe would holiday in London or New York; diaspora Jews would stay away from Israel, too frightened to visit.

The first Zionists believed they had found a solution to both the neurotic deformities of assimilated life in the West and the ghetto existence of the Jews of the East. Yet they did not plan for an Israel that remains encircled by hostile neighbours, a Jewish state which is all too easily caricatured as a ghetto on a national scale. The construction of a wall – even one nominally built to keep suicide bombers out rather than to keep Jews in – only makes the caricature look more real.

There is another, related truth to face. For many centuries Jews allowed themselves to believe they were an unusually pacific nation: the people of the book rather than of the sword. Jewish power was no more than a fantasy, incubated in childhood tales of Samson against the Philistines, the Maccabees against the Greeks, the Jews against Haman – but never again to become real. The fantasy endured. Even in our own time the tough Jew, the *shtarker*, remained a figure of Jewish dreams. Witness the veneration of the Jewish-American gangsters of the mid-twentieth century in movies like *Once Upon a Time in America* or the rhetoric of the late Rabbi Meir Kahane and his Jewish Defense League, promising a militia of tough, new Jews who would no longer take the punches but throw them back.

We rewarded ourselves with these little daydreams of might. Mainly, though, we saw ourselves as the people of right. For the Jews had a blameless record, an unstained white page in the history book. Christendom and Islam had lengthy rap sheets, records of atrocities to curdle the blood. Denied the means of warfare for two millennia, no army to command and no troops to dispatch, our past was unblemished. We imagined this was part of our collective character.

Since 1948 we have had to think again. Once we have power, we soon learned, we are not so different from everyone else. The occupation which began the year I was born, the checkpoints, the bulldozed villages, the demolished homes, the curfews, the uprooted olive groves, the dead civilians, including children: they all confirm it. A state that once dreamed of being a 'light unto the nations' is capable of acts of great darkness. The Israeli writer and Holocaust survivor Aharon Appelfeld wonders if, 'Maybe we were different because we never had the opportunity until now to inflict cruelty and suffering.' It is, says Appelfeld, a nightmarish thought: that the Jews' long history made them jump to a false conclusion. We told ourselves we were a pacific people; really we were just powerless. Now we know what we are capable of and the discovery leaves a shame that can make the soul sick.

Some of the first Zionists anticipated just such a loss of innocence for the Jews. They understood that statehood would come at a price, that the Jews would be giving something up as well as gaining a home. They may not have used these words, but Zionism was for them a necessary evil. 'Necessary', because without it the Jews would be forever exposed to mortal danger. But 'evil' because statehood represented a step backward in the Jewish, and even the human, story. For two millennia, Jews had tried to live a different way – as a civilization, dispersed across the planet. Not for them anything so crude as borders and passports. (In the Jewish mind, borders were for crossing.) The Jews had tried this new, landless way of living and the world had sometimes indulged it, often been irritated by it and eventually sought to annihilate it. So now the Jews would pick up the tools they had let rust in AD 70 and learn again the mechanics of statecraft. They were an old people and the business of armies and governments did not come easily to them. In critic and essayist George Steiner's enduring image, for the Jews to form their own modern state was like a grandfather playing in a kindergarten.

These reluctant Zionists only came to Jewish nationalism in the gloomy realization that the more hopeful ideal, a brotherhood of man, was impossible. Statehood was a strategy for survival and, eventually, renaissance, not a holy value in its own right. I think I know what they would say today, and they would be right: let us not love the evil. It was necessary, but let us not make a fetish of tanks, fighter jets and border posts. Zionism, these pioneers would insist, was never meant to be a cult of state worship; Jewish teaching and Judaism have rather more to say than mere reiteration of the need for, and value of, Zion. The founders would look at today's Jewish communities outside Israel and, once they had got over the initial shock that they exist at all, would doubtless urge them to have a life beyond herd-like 'solidarity' with Israel. They would repeat that Zionism itself was only ever intended as a mechanism, a way of preserving and nurturing Jewish life, culture and values. They would be disappointed if the Jewish world outside Israel had been reduced to little more than a cheerleading squad for the Jewish state. For them, even the land itself was only a means to the end of national self-government. So let us not worship soil and dust, let us not make an idol of territory. If some of it has to be given up for the higher goal of peace and safe living, then so be it.

Which brings us to the heart of the matter. Perhaps Zionism's greatest disappointment is that the myth it told itself was not true. The old slogan 'A land without a people for a people without a land' was catchy, but false. Another nation dwelled in Palestine. That does not mean Israel is wrong to be there. It has the right of the drowning man. But if that parable is to be Israel's ultimate moral defence, Jews and Israelis must heed its lessons too. For it implies something profound about Israel's creation, a truth too few Jews are willing to see. It says that the realization of Zionism's dream came at a high price. In the parable, the price is paid by the man forced to share a plank of driftwood. In reality, it is what the Palestinians call the *nakba*, the catastrophe of 1948. For them sharing the plank meant flight, expulsion and dispossession, the emptying of 400 villages and the creation of around 700,000 refugees.

Jews and Israelis need to face this truth, to acknowledge that Zionism was realized at a very great cost. Until now they have been reluctant, preferring to pretend that all such talk is anti-Zionist, even anti-Semitic propaganda. This is a mistake. The justness of the cause of a Jewish state is not so flimsy that it tumbles unless one can prove it came without cost. Few moral choices are like that; most entail deliberating between evils, and hoping to choose the lesser. Here, forcing the Palestinians to share their land, dispossessing so many of them, was certainly an 'evil'. Keeping Palestine intact, and leaving the Jews with no national home at all, would have been a greater one. Why? Because partition, the two-state solution, promised two peoples the prospect of self-determination; the status quo ante would have granted that fundamental human requirement to only one. By even the cold moral calculus of utilitarianism, partition was the more just outcome.

The Jewish people ought to confront the reality of 1948, and perhaps another parable, a story from their past, might help. When Jacob sought his father's blessing he did it by pretending to be his brother. He donned a goatskin, to ape the hirsute Esau, and wore Esau's clothes, to carry his scent. Isaac fell for the trick, or played along with it, and blessed the younger of his twin sons. Jacob could tell himself it was fair, because Esau had already sold his birthright to him – in exchange for a bowl of lentil soup. But the truth of both episodes is that Jacob, whose name translates as 'trickster', could only achieve his blessing at the expense of another.

God does not curse Jacob for this; on the contrary, he makes him the founder of the House of Israel. But only after Jacob has faced up to his own conduct, spending that long, sleepless night wrestling with his own conscience, in the form of an angel. In the morning his name changes, from Jacob to Israel. The meaning is clear. Israel could not be Israel until he had scrutinized his soul. Only then was he ready for his journey into the world.

19   *The Gift*

Jacob is three years old. He is still blond, still has wide blue eyes. He runs everywhere, loves anything with wheels and rocks his head back with laughter when he is tickled. He is capable of an undiluted, total joy that is almost unknown in adulthood.

Like any child, he copies the words and phrases he hears us use. 'If you like' is a new one. 'Hakkan mutch' for 'thank you very much' is another. But that goes for Hebrew words too. On a Friday night, when Sarah lights candles and we bless the bread and wine, Jacob has his own stab at the opening of the blessing: 'Brook atta . . .'

I cannot pretend that this does not send a warm pulse of pleasure running through me. When Jacob stood on a chair, his hand in mine, the two of us clutching a candle to mark the start of Chanukah, the festival of lights, I glowed. Why? Because I knew that Jacob was performing a rite that, at that very moment, was repeated around the world: children in Buenos Aires, Beersheba and Brussels, their faces golden in the candlelight, singing a song of gratitude for Chanukah and the resistance it celebrates. And because I knew that this same act would have been performed fifty or 100 or 500 or 1,000 or 2,000 years earlier, more or less the same way. And because I knew that when my mother was a child in Wheathampstead she stood on a chair, her mother holding her hand, lighting candles on the *menorah*, one for each of the eight nights of the festival. I knew that Mick and his brothers, Sid and Jack, would have done the same, perhaps under the semi-sceptical eye of their father, Morris. I knew that Nat would have done it too – with his father, Iddle, in Dunilovich when he was Menachem, and with his son, Yehuda, when he was Menachem once more.

There are people who, hearing of Jacob's infant Hebrew vocabulary or his bedtime reading of the Passover story, would cringe.

How awful to impose a tradition on a child too young to choose for himself! What indoctrination! Many of these same people hold a similarly low opinion of the whole business of group identity. 'Religion has been the source of most of the wars in history,' they declare wearily. 'Nationalism has been the source of the rest.' (Never mind that the cause of non-religious, non-tribal universalism has spilled plenty of blood too, with Stalin the prime exemplar.) These people are convinced that the very notion of defining people as members of one group rather than another is poisonous.

Collective identity and a feeling of superiority are not inseparable, as these critics fear, but the line between them is perilously thin. Cultural preservation can quickly collapse into supremacism, as the Balkans so bloodily illustrated in the 1990s. Throughout that decade the Serbs never saw themselves as aggressors but only as historical victims fighting for their survival. They held that view no matter what the rest of the world said about them.

The line is thin but not impossible to draw. On one side would dwell a positive nationalism whose prime concern is only ever internal: the welfare of its own people. On the other would stand an aggressive nationalism, driven chiefly by hostility to outside others. Of course, the latter often disguises itself as the former, the bully masquerading as the victim. Equally the former can often dissolve into the latter without anyone noticing, as a once-benign movement for national liberation slowly transforms into an iron-fisted state. But even this does not make the two the same. They are different and it is the task of all peoples to police that line vigilantly, to ensure they remain on the right side of it. (Jews and Zionists should take particular note. They must ask themselves every day where Israel stands; whether its project remains one of cultural preservation or whether it has, even while telling itself it is concerned only with looking after its own, inched closer towards oppression. They must ask the question and risk an honest, clear-eyed answer.)

Those nations who watch themselves carefully, striving to ensure their collective pride does not turn into something nastier, are proof that it can be done. And so are the groups – from nations to football clubs – who know they are not the best in the world, who know that in a clash with their rivals and neighbours they would lose, but nevertheless like who they are. They enjoy being together more than they like being apart: we can all think of the loyal fans who turn out week after week to watch a local team get trounced. They have no fantasies of superiority, but they stand together anyway.

Togetherness of this kind is not some innately fascistic sentiment. It can become one, but it can also boil down to nothing more insidious than the human urge to connect with our fellow human beings – that same primate's impulse which makes solitary confinement the harshest of all punishments.

To be part of a nation obviously goes deeper than membership of a football crowd; it provides more than just the warmth of human company. It offers a place to stand in a world that can seem to be spinning dizzyingly fast, a sheltered port when all that was once fixed is now hurtling through the sky as if tossed by a whirlwind. I think this might be why I like to see Jacob lighting Chanukah candles. Everything else around us has changed; technology alone makes Jacob's childhood very different from mine. Circumstance and economics make it entirely alien to my mother's or Mick's. Next to the boy Menachem Mindel in the *shtetl*, Jacob's life might as well be on another planet. But this much they have in common. They too lit candles in December; they too twisted the *dreidel* and sang the Chanukah anthem, '*Ma'otzur*'. There is a comfort in that. All around, the landscape of the world is changing; but this piece remains solid. It is a rock surrounded by quicksand.

This is more, not less, valuable in the globalized world of the twenty-first century. When all can seem blurry and indistinct, it helps to know where you fit. To be a Jew is to know that I am not some random atom bombing around the universe. I belong somewhere. I am part of a family, part of a story.

Which is why it is no surprise that national, even tribal, identities have intensified rather than receded in the era of globalization. Our need is greater now. When the whole world seems to open up, the prospect can be thrilling; the veins throb with the rush of possibility. But it is also daunting: an individual can feel overwhelmed. In the village of his ancestors, one person loomed large. In a planet of 6 billion, he feels lost.

An identity gives him a place. For some it will be a hideaway, somewhere to retreat from the changing world. For others it will be a springboard, a way of plunging into life. Either way, this perch, this place to stand, applies to time as well as space. Identity means that the past is no longer some unknowable void; it is connected to the present. As a Jew I can make out a chain of history, stretching all the way back to Abraham, and know that I am a link in that chain. Identity does that. It says your life does not just begin and end with you. It goes back into the past and reaches into the future. I can open any history book, read about medieval Spain or tsarist Russia and see my own story running through it. This is a blessing. I hope it means that Jacob will be able to look at the world and at history and say, 'I belong. This is where I fit in.'

It can also be a pressure. I remember one of the few times I visited my maternal grandfather, Avraham Hocherman. I was eighteen, spending that year in Israel with Habonim. He still lived in Petach Tikva, in that same one-storey shack that had so appalled my grandmother Feige some fifty years earlier.

I did not look forward to these visits. The cramped room, with lumpy divan serving as a couch; the dense atmosphere, so full of sorrow. As a very small boy I had met my great-grandfather Yehuda Ze'ev in this room. I thought he looked like God, deep into his nineties, hunched and with a snow-white beard. His eyes still sparkled, the same light which, I suppose, had once burned in the academies of Sosnowice.

But that was the past. Now my grandfather was on his own. We communicated through layers of misunderstanding. He was mute, but could write notes in Hebrew, a language I only partially understood. I would speak my answers; he would nod and smile, breathing heavily, sucking his teeth and stroking his beard. He seemed pent up with words, but he could not, or would not, let them out.

Like a commuter decoding crossword clues, I would translate his notes out loud, judging by his nods or shakes whether I was on the right lines. We were on his usual theme, his desire that I study in Gateshead, the town in north-east England which is home to one of the country's largest ultra-orthodox communities and its only internationally esteemed *yeshiva*. I explained that I had a place to study at Oxford and that I intended to take it up. I probably expected him to be impressed, but Oxford meant nothing to him; Gateshead was a prestigious seat of learning.

He was scribbling away. Eventually I deciphered the scrawled note he placed before me, next to the glass of lemon tea. '"Do you understand that you are from a long line of rabbis?"' I said slowly, each Hebrew word difficult to make out even before I tried to translate. I looked up, pleased with my skill. He was nodding: read on. '"This line goes all the way back to *Avraham avinu*, Abraham, our father."' More smiles. I continued, '"But it will all end with you. *Mett.*" *Mett*?' He underlined the word, as if that gesture would somehow pull back the curtain on its meaning. '*Mett*,' I said again. 'Oh, *mett*! Dead! "But it will all end with you. Dead."' Now I understood.

I hope that when Jacob comes to make the big decisions of his life, he makes them for rather more positive reasons than that. I do not want his identity to be decided by Emil Fackenheim's eleventh commandment: 'Thou shalt not give Hitler a posthumous victory' by assimilating out of the Jewish people. I hope that he will have a stronger motive to identify as a Jew than a wish to spite the Nazis. I want him to see that to be a Jew is to hold the deeds to a vast treasury of history and culture and to be a card-carrying member of a movement, a campaign to repair the world, that never stops.

Which is not to say that his people will not sometimes drive him mad. In the orthodox world he will visit synagogues and be bored rigid by services that fetishize ritual over meaning and that no one has had the courage to change. He will see a cultural tradition that has been allowed to calcify into a dogma, often with comically absurd results. I am thinking of the British *dayan* – the chief justice in the religious court – who insisted on wrapping himself in a black plastic bin liner whenever he flew over Israel lest he make contact with particles of air from the cemeteries below. (As a *cohen*, or priest, Jewish law bars him from visiting a Jewish burial ground.) Or it might be the rule which allows orthodox rabbis to attend church services in chapels and cathedrals, but never to set foot in a Reform or Liberal synagogue. I am thinking of these examples, but Jacob can rest assured: there will be plenty more in his own time.

He will encounter those for whom Jewishness is only ever a matter of the past, a set of memories to be preserved, ideally under museum glass. For them, when nostalgia clashes with vitality, nostalgia must always win. Or he will meet their cousins, those whose batteries are powered only by a negative charge. They are the Jews obsessed with the Holocaust, which they regard as a holy event whose story of Jewish death dwarfs the entire history of Jewish life. These are the people whose interest is seized only by existential threats, ranging from Israel's mortal foes to its media critics to the phenomenon of intermarriage. They will fight hard to keep the enemies from the gate, but ask them what exactly they are guarding and they will struggle to answer.

Jacob will encounter piles of rules that few people understand and many cannot accept. In an orthodox synagogue, he will see women and men seated separately, women denied the rights of participation they would take for granted in all other aspects of their lives. They will be caged behind a partition, their hair covered – lest they be a temptation to the men. Rules that would be ridiculed if advocated by the Taliban, Jacob will find indulged by the Jews.

He might come to know the pain caused by orthodox Judaism's bizarre rules on the admission of newcomers. While most nations are desperate for growth, the Jews have developed the collective equivalent of an eating disorder – apparently striving to become ever smaller. For while others count in, Judaism counts out. If a Jewish man marries a non-Jewish woman, neither she nor their children will count automatically as Jews. The only way in is for her to convert to Judaism. Ruth, great-grandmother of King David and therefore, according to Jewish teaching, the ancestor of the future Messiah, was an early example. She was a Moabite who became a Jew by making a simple and beautiful declaration: 'Where you go, I will go; where you dwell, I will dwell; your people shall be my people and your God my God.'

But what was good enough for Ruth is not, apparently, good enough today, at least not according to the orthodox authorities who alone can promise a convert universal acceptance among the Jews of the world. Now would-be Jews must submit to an elaborate, lengthy and demanding process, one that often ends up in rejection. There is a heavy emotional cost, paid by the thousands of couples whose love is deemed a threat rather than a joy. But there is a collective price too. Not only are Jews losing out, imposing on ourselves a demographic contraction with each mixed marriage, but we are also tolerating a damaging anomaly. For, as we have seen, the Jews are no longer just a religion; they are something looser and wider. So much larger is Jewishness than mere religion that a person born a Jew can be a Jewish atheist with barely a contradiction. Yet this same definition does not extend to new-comers. The only way they can join this people, this culture, is by walking through a turnstile marked faith. That remains true whatever the denomination – orthodox, Reform or Liberal – but it makes no sense. The Jews need an admissions process, akin to naturalization or citizenship, which reflects the Jews as they actually are today. Such a move would allow the Jewish people to welcome in those who fall in love with Jews, rather than shun them and their children. It would see our numbers rise and our rulebook fit the people we have become. And it would prevent a lot of heartache.

Such a move would require a completion of the Zionist revol-ution, the movement that, over the course of half a century, shook the Jewish world by fundamentally altering the Jews' sense of themselves. It declared that the Jews were not merely adherents of a faith but a nation, and that they should start living like one, in a land of their own. That aim has been realized, but the wider goal has not. For if the Jews are a nation, then surely they should be like other nations, fully sovereign over their own affairs. In most countries, that means full-blooded democracy with the people in charge. The Jews may call themselves a nation, but in crucial areas of day-to-day life they have not completed the transition from pre-modern religious sect. Marriages, divorce and the whole battery of so-called status issues are still in the hands of un-elected rabbis rather than the people themselves. That is not how nations, as opposed to religions, organize themselves. Establishing a Jewish state was an enormous step forward, but the Zionist revolution will not be complete until the Jews are fully sovereign over their own lives. And that means democracy triumphing over theocracy.

It will seem an impossible task. Jews have led movements that have changed the world, but they have never quite managed to overhaul their own tired institutions and practices. There is much stubbornness to overcome – not for nothing does the Bible describe us as a 'stiff-necked people'.

Jacob will come face to face with all this. He might shake his fist at the Mathildas who look obsessively inward, always concerned for their fellow Jews and forgetting the rest of humanity. Or he might be enraged by the do-gooding Rosas, so busy rescuing mankind they overlook their own. Whichever way he goes, there are bound to be days when he sighs with despair for his people.

He may even wonder whether he should stick with it or give up. After all, it exacts a price – whether it be association with a people whose history has been pained and who have no shortage of present-day enemies, or the pressures of continuity, the obligation to stay 'in', marry 'in' and have Jewish children. These are substantial burdens. If he has no religious faith he may find them especially hard to bear. One day he might ask a simple question: 'If Jewishness is simply a cultural inheritance, what is there to hold me to it? In the absence of a divine duty to honour Judaism, why should I feel obliged, required, to carry on being Jewish?'

Now I have a better idea what answer I would give. I would tell him that inclusion in a culture, especially an ancient one like the

Jews', bestows a sense of constancy, even security, in a rapidly changing and often distressing world. I believe Jewishness did that for my mother, even though much of the distress was coming from her own, Jewish family. In all the chaos that enveloped and nearly submerged her, one thing never wobbled. She may have lived in different places, with different parents, in a world turned upside down. But she was always a Jew.

And I would say that Jewishness is worth embracing because it has the potential to give something valuable to the world: a universal mission to make human life better. Who could refuse the opportunity to take part in such an adventure? I would point out too that the latticework of Jewish civilization – the music, the stories, the tastes, the memories – has grown over the millennia into something intricate, rich and very beautiful. Access to this treasure is not to be passed up lightly. And I would say that the Jews' experience has given them – given us – a unique insight into the human condition itself. We are old in the world; we have witnessed much; we have glimpsed both the best and the worst in human conduct and we are left with a kind of wisdom.

Jacob might vary the question. 'If I am under no divine obligation to stay Jewish, then who says that of all the cultures in the world I should stick with this one rather than any other? Why shouldn't I shop around, see what's out there and join whichever is best?' He could say that and, in theory, he would have a point. But only in theory. He might as well ask, 'Why should I not join a different family? There are surely better ones around. Since I do not believe that God demands certain actions from me, and therefore I am a free agent, why should I not look around for parents and siblings that suit me better?'

Such a thought is absurd. I am in my family because it is mine. And I am Jewish, even when I hear no heavenly command, because it is mine. It is where I was born and where I belong.

So what do I want to give Jacob? I want him to have what Nat craved all his life: the right to be both. I want him to have a life full of choices, without ever having to choose between two parts of himself. I want him to see that he can be 'Jewish and', never to feel that he has to be 'Jewish or'.

I would like him to have a heart like the great-great-uncle he never knew, Mick Mindel – a heart that yearns for justice and sees the humanity in every person, even those who look and sound different. I would like him to see that to be a Jew is to be a human being, one whose history and experience qualify, and oblige, him to take part in the struggle for a better world. I hope that he will see Jewishness as a way to understand the wondrously varied, complex peoples of the world, not to shy away from them. He would then realize that since the days of Abraham, Isaac and Jacob, Jewishness was meant as a way in, not a way out. I would like Jacob to learn from me what Mick learned from his father: that history happens not in books but right in front of you, and that every one of us needs to pay attention.

I would like him to hear the stories of my mother, his grandmother. I hope he hears them not as tales of woe and hardship but as lessons in resilience and human strength. I hope he sees that if Jews have a knack for survival it is not because they are saints but because they are people. I hope he sees that he can be a strong, proud Jew even if faith deserts him and even if it never visits him at all. And I wish for Jacob the same wish I uttered when he was just eight days old and I entered him into the covenant of Abraham: 'May this young child grow into manhood as a blessing to his family, the family of Israel and the family of mankind.' May he belong to all three.

I do not believe any of these ideas are for Jews alone. I believe they apply to plenty of communities and nations, some of them small minorities, like the Jews of the diaspora, some of them large societies coping with a new, diverse future. I believe these are stories the Jews can tell the world after our long, strange odyssey on the planet. The founder of the House of Israel was Jacob and I believe these are among Jacob's gifts to the world.

Less grandly, I hope that Jacob may find in here what I did not have that day at school when we were told to draw a family tree.

Sometimes I look at my mother or I remember Yiddi or I chat with Mick's widow, Sylvia, and I feel their world slipping away. I have memories of it: I sat in Yiddi's flat in the East End, hearing the voices of the Jewish past. But Jacob will never hear that music himself.

Perhaps through these pages he will come to know the people who went before him. For here they are. I now understand that even the dead can live again so long as we tell their stories. And every family has stories.

Jacob, we are more than the products of our families and our pasts. They account for much of us but not the whole. We are not blank pages, but nor are we yet filled up with words. It is up to us to choose, up to us to write our own stories. Jacob, this is my gift to you. And the chance to know my own family, my own people – that is your gift to me.

A Note on Sources

This book is the fruit of many years of reading and argument, which makes it tricky to single out sources of information and inspiration. Even so, what follows is a guide to the books or documents that I found indispensable on this journey – and which, I hope, may also serve as a trigger for further reading.

Part One: Beginnings

The circumcision ceremony is set out in countless prayer books; I used the *Authorized Daily Prayer Book of the United Hebrew Congregations*, more commonly known as the *Singer's* (London, Eyre and Spottiswoode, 1950) and *Forms of Prayer for Jewish Worship, Volume 1 – Daily Sabbath and Occasional Prayers* (London, Reform Synagogues of Great Britain, 1977). On identity itself, Derek Parfit's *Reasons and Persons* (Oxford, OUP, 1984) offers a philosophical overview, while Amin Maalouf's *In the Name of Identity* (New York, Arcade, 2001) is a concise gem. *In the Blood* by Steve Jones (London, HarperCollins, 1996) proved a fascinating primer on 'God, genes and destiny'. There are a thousand books on the immigrant experience, but W.G. Sebald's *The Emigrants* (London, Harvill, 1996) is especially haunting. For narrative approaches to identity, the right place to start is Alastair MacIntyre's *After Virtue* (London, Duckworth, 1981).

Part Two: Wanderings

Nat's story was easily the most well documented of the three. The history of Dunilovich comes from a Yiddish book, *Khurban Glubok*

(Buenos Aires, 1956), kindly translated for me by Norman Carp-Gordon. I was able to gain a glimpse into Nat's education thanks to *The Jews of Hackney Downs School* by Gerry Black, published in *The Jewish Year Book for 2001* (London, Vallentine Mitchell, 2001), and *Talmud Torah Ivrit Be-Ivrit: Fifty Years of its Existence 1901 to 1951* (London, Talmud Torah Ivrit Be-Ivrit, 1951).

Nat's naturalization papers and war files were waiting to be found at the Public Records Office or PRO (the former in HO 144/1146/209731, the latter in WO 339/86194). Further information was generously supplied by the Royal Logistic Corps Museum at Deepcut, Surrey, in the form of the *Royal Army Service Corps Quarterly* for October 1920 and January 1921, which included a detailed account of the Camel Transport Corps and Egyptian Expeditionary Force, 1915–19.

The online archive of the *Palestine Post*, which gazetted the key milestones in Nat's career, was a great help, along with the personal correspondence he maintained with his friend Sam Epstein. Many of the words I have attributed to Nat are either directly quoted or adapted from those letters, which I saw for the period from 1916 to 1936, or from later ones to Nat's daughter, Aviva, spanning the 1940s and 1950s. The perspective of his wife, Miriam or Marjorie, was provided by interviews with her children but also by her own unpublished memoir, authored in collaboration with her family.

Nat's work in the Department of Immigration is well preserved in the Israel State Archives or ISA in Jerusalem. His handwritten account of his 1921 mission to Trieste sits in מ-11 1170/5 (IMM 3/3). *Palestine Immigration Policy under Sir Herbert Samuel* by M. Mossek (London, Frank Cass, 1978) helped flesh out the wider picture, as did David H. Shpiro's *Aliyah by Any Means* (Tel Aviv, Am Oved, 1994), a history of illegal Jewish immigration into Palestine from 1918 to 1937, along with Albert Hyamson's *Palestine Under the Mandate 1920–1948* (London, Methuen, 1950). Golda Meir's passage to Palestine is recalled in her memoir, *My Life* (Jerusalem, Steimatzky's, 1975).

For the incident in Hebron which became a turning point in Nat's life, I relied on the detailed account in Tom Segev's *One Palestine Complete* (New York, Metropolitan, 2000) but also on the original report of the *Palestine Commission on the Disturbances of August, 1929* (London, HMSO, 1930) as well as the Zionist Organization's own cables on the topic (contained in PRO file CO 733/A5/2). I came across the 1933 application on behalf of a German Jewish would-be immigrant in ISA file מ-11/1215/45 (PERS/1/1). The details of Nat's fateful mission to Basle were in the PRO file FO 371/23246.

The dilemmas of British-Jewish officials in the Mandate administration are beautifully set out in Bernard Wasserstein's *The British in Palestine* (Oxford, Blackwell, 1978). I drew especially on his account of the case of Norman Bentwich, supplemented by PRO file CO 733/A5/3. Max Nurock made his remark about Nat's inability to shed what he described as his East End Jewish accent in a 1969 interview with Wasserstein, a transcript of which is stored in the Oral History Division of the Institute of Contemporary Jewry at the Hebrew University of Jerusalem. The document containing London's misgivings about Nurock himself is stored in the PRO as CO 733/317/10. Isaiah Berlin's comparison of the Jews of Palestine to the Jewish boys in an English public school similarly came from a 1970 exchange with Wasserstein. Edwin Samuel's *A Lifetime in Jerusalem* (London, Vallentine Mitchell, 1970) shed light on similar terrain.

Nat's 1943 trip to Tehran and his clash with Avraham Zilberberg is recounted with verve in the latter's autobiography, whose Hebrew title translates as *Mission for the People and the State* (Tel Aviv, Author's Press, 1995).

Mick Mindel's life began in the Rothschild Buildings and Jerry White's wonderful book of that name (London, Routledge, 1980) took me right there. The trade union movement that would win his devotion is meticulously analysed in *Uniting the Tailors* by Anne J. Kershen (London, Frank Cass, 1995), while the colour and texture of the *schmutter* trade is brought alive by Kershen's pamphlet 'Off the Peg' (London, London Museum of Jewish Life, 1988). *The Jewish East End* by Aumie and Michael Shapiro (London, Springboard, 1996) powerfully evokes through photographs the world Mick (and my mother) inhabited. Arnold Wesker's delightful autobiography, *As Much as I Dare* (London, Century, 1994), recalls the Mick who romanced the author's aunt, Sara. The records of the United Ladies' Tailors' Trade Union, now kept in the Hackney Archives, were packed with gold: they included the minutes of union executive meetings, including those chaired by Mick. Several of the political statements I have attributed to him appear verbatim there.

The tensions of the Jewish left are caught well in Henry Srebrnik's *London Jews and British Communism 1935–1945* (London, Vallentine Mitchell, 1995), while Phil Piratin's *Our Flag Stays Red* (London, Thames, 1948) conveys the fervour of the age. I found much relevant wisdom in 'Jews and Socialism: The End of a Beautiful Friendship?' published in the *Jewish Quarterly*, Vol. 35, No. 2, 1988, and in *The Red and the Blue: Essays in Socialist Zionism*, edited by Sam Jacobs and others (London, Poale Zion, 1984).

My mother's story barely exists on paper, but I was very grateful for *Shefford*, a memoir of the country village that took in a Jewish school, by the former headmistress, Judith Grunfeld (London, Soncino Press, 1980). Information on religious life in the Jewish East End came from *A Documentary History of Jewish Immigrants in Britain 1840–1920* (Leicester, Leicester University Press, 1994).

Part Three: Reckonings

So many books informed this section that I shall confine myself to those that made a direct contribution. *The Jew in the Modern World*, edited by Paul Mendes-Flohr and Jehuda Reinharz (New York, OUP, 1980), is a stunning work, collecting the documents that make up modern Jewish history in a single volume. Many of the voices quoted in this part of the book, from Sigmund Freud to Rosa

Luxemburg, can be heard there. *The Zionist Idea*, edited by Arthur Hertzberg (New York, Atheneum, 1969), does a similarly definitive job for Jewish nationalism. From Herzl to Pinsker, Hertzberg is the source.

The letter from German-Jewish ex-servicemen pledging allegiance to Adolf Hitler appears in *Documents of the Holocaust*, edited by Yitzhak Arad and others (Jerusalem, Yad Vashem, 1981). The group photograph of Nat and his fellow British soldiers was lovingly reproduced in *The British Jewry Book of Honour* (London, Caxton, 1922). Amos Elon's *The Pity of It All* (London, Allen Lane, 2003) is a consummate history of German Jewry, charting with great poignancy their attempts to swim in the mainstream.

Nothing Sacred by Douglas Rushkoff (New York, Crown, 2003) is an inspiring polemic on the progressive possibilities inherent in Judaism. I strongly commend it. Robert Wistrich's *Revolutionary Jews from Marx to Trotsky* (London, Harrap, 1976) served as a useful reality check for those likely to have a rose-coloured view of Jews' red legacy. Isaac Deutscher's *The Non-Jewish Jew* (Oxford, OUP, 1968) was essential reading in the same area. Unhappily, there are too many books on anti-Semitism to mention, but the unique view of George Steiner quoted can be found in *The Portage to San Cristobal of A. H.* (London, Faber, 1981).

On Israel, Amos Oz's *In the Land of Israel* (London, Chatto & Windus, 1983) still grips me each time I pick it up. It was a formative influence. Philip Roth's *The Counterlife* is equally unassailable. For the Yiddish song by Leo Fuld I am indebted to Brian Klug, who cited it in 'A Time to Speak Out' in the *Jewish Quarterly*, Vol. 49, No. 4 (188), Winter 2002/3. Those interested in the long history of the *Guardian's* relationship with Israel will enjoy *Disenchantment* by Daphna Baram (London, Guardian Books, 2004).

To those others whose words or thoughts sank so deep into the soil I can no longer recall their origins, I apologize. Jewish tradition demands acknowledgement of the sources of one's ideas, and I offer my grateful thanks.

Glossary

aliyah	(lit. ascent) emigration to Israel
balabusta	Yiddish for housewife
bar mitzvah	ceremony to mark a Jewish boy's passage to adulthood at the age of thirteen
beshert	destined
bimah	platform in synagogue from which the Torah is read
booba	Yiddish for grandmother
brit	covenant
brit milah	circumcision ceremony
chalutz	pioneer
chametz	leavened bread
Chanukah	festival of lights that commemorates the Maccabees' revolt and the rededication of the Temple in Jerusalem in 165 BC
chazan	cantor
cheder	religion classes
chutzpah	cheek
cohen	member of priestly caste
dayan	judge in a religious court
dreidel	four-sided spinning top with a letter on each side, used in games during Chanukah
droshkey	horse-drawn buggy
edel	Yiddish for noble, hence ladylike

Eretz Yisrael	the land of Israel (sometimes pronounced Eretz Yisroel, especially by orthodox Ashkenazim)
fellah	(lit. tiller of the soil) Egyptian peasant
gevalt	exclamation of surprise or incredulity
golus	Yiddish for exile
goyim	Gentiles
goyische	Gentile (adj.)
Habonim	(lit. the Builders) Jewish youth movement
hacham	wise man
halacha	religious law
HaShem	(lit. the Name) one way of referring to God
Hassid	type of ultra-orthodox Jew
.Ivrit	the Hebrew language
kaddish	prayer for the dead
kashrut	dietary laws
ketuba	marriage contract
Ketubot	a tractate, or section, of the Babylonian Talmud
kibbutz	communal farm
kibbutznik	a member of a kibbutz
kneidlach	matzah balls (dumplings) for soup
Kratzmach	Yiddish for Christmas
kugel	pudding made from potatoes and other vegetables
kvatter, kvatterin	godfather and godmother at circumcision
kvutza	group, especially socialist commune
labneh	a strained yoghurt cheese
latkes	fried cakes of potato and onion
lokshen	noodles

mechayer	physical treat
menorah	candelabrum used at Chanukah with nine holders
mensch	person, especially a good person or person of substance
Midrash	rabbinic commentary on biblical texts
mikve	ritual bath
minyan	the ten-person quorum necessary for communal prayer
mitzvah	commandment
mohel	circumciser
moshav	cooperative community with more independence for its members than the collective kibbutz
Moshiach	the Messiah
nachas	Yiddish for joy or blessings; pride, especially from one's children and grandchildren
nebuch	loser, a hopeless case
Ostjuden	Eastern European Jews
Pesach	Passover
platzels	bread rolls
Purim	festival that celebrates the escape of the Jews of Persia from the plots of Haman in the fifth century BC, as recorded in the Book of Esther
rachmones	kindness, mercy
rebbe	Yiddish for rabbi, particularly the leader of a Hassidic sect
rosh	head
Rosh Hashanah	New Year (lit. head of the year)
sandak	man who holds baby during circumcision
schlep	drag or trek

schmutter	rag, hence rag trade
seder	the combined service and meal held at Pesach
sefer torah	Torah scrolls
shabbes	Ashkenazi pronunciation of Shabbat, the Sabbath
shadchan	matchmaker
shammas	beadle of a synagogue
Shavuot	festival of the first fruits that also celebrates the giving of the Ten Commandments at Mount Sinai
shikse	non-Jewish girl (*shiksele*, little *shikse*)
shiva	(lit. seven) the period of mourning, which traditionally lasts seven days
shtarker	Yiddish for tough
shteibl	small house of prayer
shtetl	town or village
shul	Yiddish for synagogue
shvitz	sweat
siddur	prayer book
sidra	Torah portion
simcha	celebration
sukkah	tabernacle or booth
Sukkot	harvest festival of booths
Talmud	a collection of the oral tradition that interprets the Torah
tefillin	phylacteries, small leather boxes worn on the arm and head by religious Jews during prayer
tehillim	psalms
tikkun olam	repairing the world
Torah	the five books of Moses, the first five books of the Old Testament
toranut	chores
treif	food that is not kosher
tzedakah	(lit. justice) charity, therefore also the injunction to give to charity

tzitzit	fringed undergarment worn by religious boys and men
yeshiva	talmudic academy
yeshiva bocher	someone who studies at a *yeshiva* (from Hebrew *bachur*, lit. boy)
yiddishkeit	Jewishness, a sense of things Jewish
Yishuv	the Jewish community in Palestine
yock	slang for non-Jew, highly pejorative
Yom Kippur	Day of Atonement
yontuf	Yiddish for religious festival (from Hebrew *yom tov*, lit. good day)
zaida	Yiddish for grandfather

Read more from

CAMPO SANTO
W. G. SEBALD

Translated by Anthea Bell

'A writer whose explorations of time and memory make him arguably the closest author modern European letters has to rival Borges' *Sunday Times*

At the heart of *Campo Santo* are four lyrical and meditative essays from a great, still incomplete work that W. G. Sebald was planning, centring on the island of Corsica. To read this marvellous book is to step into what one critic has called 'the quirky treasure-house of Sebald's mind'. It is a moving memorial to an author who has been described by the *TLS* as 'the most significant European writer to have emerged in the last decade'.

THE STORY OF A LIFE
AHARON APPELFELD

Translated by Aloma Halter

'Sometimes I felt that it wasn't I who was in the war but someone else, someone very close to me, and that he's going to tell me what exactly occurred, for I don't remember what happened or how it happened'

Seen through the eyes of a boy living through the Holocaust, and told by a man who survived it, *The Story of a Life* looks at the act of remembrance and illuminates both the fallibility and power of memory. This is an extraordinarily profound memoir and a starkly personal exploration of lost childhood, the weight of silence and beginning again.